A CENTURY OF *Irish Drama*

Drama and Performance Studies
Timothy Wiles, general editor

Nora M. Alter.
Vietnam Protest Theatre: The Television War on Stage

Karin Barber, John Collins, and Alain Ricard.
West African Popular Theatre

Johannes Birringer.
Theatre, Theory, Postmodernism

Katherine H. Burkman and John L. Kundert-Gibbs, editors.
Pinter at Sixty

Elinor Fuchs.
The Death of Character: Perspectives on Theater after Modernism

David Graver.
Drama for a New South Africa

Ejner J. Jensen.
Shakespeare and the Ends of Comedy

David McCandless.
Gender and Performance in Shakespeare's Problem Comedies

Jeffrey D. Mason.
Melodrama and the Myth of America

Robert E. Rinehart.
Players All: Performances in Contemporary Sport

Eugène van Erven.
The Playful Revolution: Theatre and Liberation in Asia

CONTENTS

Part IV
CONTEMPORARY THEATRE COMPANIES AND REVIVALS

Part V
IRISH HISTORY ON THE CONTEMPORARY STAGE

FOREWORD
On Attending "One Hundred Years of Irish Drama"

SHIVAUN O'CASEY

What was a conference with the title "Nationalism and a National Theatre: 100 Years of Irish Drama" going to be like? I had only appeared (a quick in and out) at two other conferences, both of which concerned Irish Studies. This conference, by contrast, dealt with Irish theatre on its own — something unusual, I was told by those who knew about these things. I had been a theatre practitioner for most of my life and was slightly nervous at the thought of talking to knowledgeable academics. I knew I had to give a talk (a kind of dramatized chat) about my father, Sean O'Casey, and after the talk show, I was to show a sixteen-minute videotape about Sean, including shots of the family, Sean's past interviews, and my mother talking about him — actually, a promotional tape for a documentary I am in the process of making with Albert Maysles.

To my delight, I was met at the Indianapolis airport by two young and charming students, Art and Elaine, who drove me to Bloomington and to a lovely inn, which was situated near the university in a peaceful, tree-shaded town — a town with brooks running through it, green grass, and porches with swinging chairs and rocking chairs. At the conference I met a great mix of energetic and interesting people, and I was glad to notice that a lot of them were young. During the three days I was there, I listened to most of the papers (missing those near my talk, as I was too nervous to concentrate) and was fascinated by the variety of topics discussed, all connected to Irish drama. I was glad Sean was there among them all, alongside his old friends Lady Gregory, G. B. Shaw, and W. B. Yeats — and his younger acquaintances (by phone), Brendan Behan and Sam Beckett; there with Oscar Wilde, John Millington Synge, Lennox Robinson; and there with such younger ones, too, as Brian Friel, Tom Murphy, Frank McGuinness, Stewart Parker, Sebastian Barry, Marina Carr, Christina Reid, Martin McDonagh, and Patricia Burke Brogan. Also the companies: Barabas, Passion Machine, Field Day, and Charabanc. Sadly, I arrived too late to hear Christopher Fitz-Simon's lecture, "Before the Abbey — Can There Have Been Such a Time?", a survey of turn-of-the-century drama that initiated the symposium. After the days' lectures we were able to attend three excellent performances, in the evening, of Micheál MacLiammóir's *The Importance of Being Oscar*, Patricia Brogan's *Eclipsed*, and Frank McGuinness's *Someone Who'll Watch over Me*. Each night of the symposium, I flopped into the big bed to digest all we had heard and talked about.

I hope many similar conferences will take place under the trees of Bloomington, and under the care and great spirit of Professor Stephen Watt.

June 1999

ACKNOWLEDGMENTS

We wish to express our gratitude, first and foremost, to the National Endowment for the Humanities (NEH), which generously supported the symposium, "Nationalism and a National Theatre: 100 Years of Irish Drama," from which these essays were selected. Without the support of the NEH, neither the meeting held at Indiana University (Bloomington) at the end of May 1999 nor this volume would have been possible. Additional support came from Kenneth R. R. Gros Louis, Chancellor of the Bloomington campus; George Walker, Vice-President for Research at Indiana University; Morton Lowengrub, Dean of the College of Arts and Sciences; and from the departments of English and Theatre and Drama. We thank, in particular, Kenneth Johnston, Judith Anderson, and Leon Brauner from these departments; and we thank Janet Brady James, Jennifer Gentry, and Tawana Green from Indiana University Conferences for their invaluable organization of the myriad details associated with this event. In addition, we want to thank the Waldron Arts Center in Bloomington for their production assistance with the plays staged for this meeting.

In addition to the papers and lectures presented during the four days of the meeting, talented directors and actors provided terrific productions of three Irish plays. Our thanks to Terry Hartnett, to Charlotte Headrick and the Department of Theatre and Dance from Western Kentucky University, and to Philip Johnston of Belfast and the University of Illinois at Urbana–Champaign for their outstanding productions. And to Bill Kerwin, Ellen McCallum, Will Murphy, Eileen O'Halloran, Seamus Reilly, Laurie Schmeling, Tom Shea, Janet Sorensen, Albert Wertheim, Timothy Wiles, and Christopher Wixson for their participation in and support of the symposium. We also want to recognize Art Bilodeau, Matt Brim, Colleen Hynds, John Paul Kanwit, and Sheila McDermott for their assistance; Erika Dowell of the Fine Arts Library at Indiana; and the Ulster Museum and the National Museums and Galleries of Northern Ireland for their generosity.

Our most sincere gratitude goes to the fine scholars who wrote papers for the meeting but whose work could not be included here, in some cases so that the work of younger colleagues at the beginning of their careers might find an audience. These generous and talented colleagues include Susan Bazargan, Scott Boltwood, Christopher Fitz-Simon, Michael Patrick Gillespie, Claudia Harris, Mitchell Harris, Charlotte Headrick, Philip Johnston, Brandon Kershner, Craig Owens, Gary Richardson, and Sanford Sternlicht.

And, finally, we must recognize three people without whose encouragement none of this would have been possible: Michael Bigelow Dixon of the Actors Theatre of Louisville and those two wonderful spirits at the NEH: Margot Backas and Alice Hudgins. Thank you.

INTRODUCTION
Re-thinking the Abbey and the Concept of a National Theatre
EILEEN MORGAN

> The Abbey [. . .] suffered the fate of many institu-
> tions that are too successful for their own good.
> [. . .] The theatre had thrived as a counter-cultural
> force, in opposition to a dominant British ethos.
> After 1922, it became the mainstream, the official
> national theatre of an increasingly conservative
> Catholic state.
> — Fintan O'Toole, "Shadows over Ireland" 17

> Perhaps by redefining the National Theatre as an
> abstract, federal entity, encompassing vibrant re-
> gional companies who might play parts of that
> canon, the Abbey could be freed to move in that
> direction. In this way the idea of a national theatre
> could be defended and updated.
> — Declan Kiberd, *Inventing Ireland* 653

Neither the Abbey Theatre nor the dramatic movements that preceded
it — the Irish Literary Theatre (1899–1901), the Irish National Dramatic
Company (1902–1903), and the Irish National Theatre Society (1903–
1904)[1] — have wanted for commemoration. Homages of various types have
been paid to the "national theatre" since the Abbey's establishment in 1904,
often but not always by those affiliated with it. The following backward
glances, for example, testify to the theatre's achievement: Lady Gregory's
"autobiographical chapter" *Our Irish Theatre* (1913); Yeats's Nobel Prize
acceptance speech, "The Irish Dramatic Movement" (1923); actress Máire
Nic Shiubhlaigh's memoir *The Splendid Years* (1955); Walter Macken's play
Recall the Years (1966), which christened the renovated Abbey after the fire
of 1951; and Hugh Hunt's history, commissioned to mark the Abbey's
seventy-fifth anniversary, *The Abbey: Ireland's National Theatre, 1904–1979*
(1979). To this list countless other tributes could be added, including less
conventional ones like that paid in Beckett's *Murphy* (1938) when the title
character requests that his remains be flushed down an Abbey toilet during a performance. The novelty of the essays gathered here is not, thus,
that they were written for a conference celebrating the theatre movement's centennial, "Nationalism and a National Theatre: 100 Years of Irish
Drama," which was held at Indiana University in Bloomington, Indiana
(26–30 May 1999). Rather, the novelty of these essays lies in their contribu-

tion to a re-valuation of Irish theatre spurred by the recent success of the "third wave" of twentieth-century Irish theatre.[2]

This introduction serves three primary purposes. First, it describes some of the events and conversations that made "Nationalism and a National Theatre" so memorable and productive, in order to salute the participants — especially the directors and actors who brought Irish theatre to Bloomington stages and the scholars whose essays do not appear in this collection as a result of space constraints — and to reconstruct the immediate context for the contributors' re-readings of Irish theatre. Second, it re-examines the changing status of the Abbey as the center of dramatic production in Ireland. Knowledge of this cultural history — of the national theatre's decline after its initial heyday and the corresponding development of other, less institutionalized dramatic organizations — underpins the contributors' commitment to recognizing the diversity of Irish theatre throughout the twentieth century. The contributors' efforts to recuperate a heterogeneous early theatre (rather than a predominantly nationalist one) and to acknowledge alternative theatre companies and traditions are motivated, in other words, by their shared desire to demythologize the national theatre and to recognize that, at least as a concept, it has outlived its privilege.[3] Finally, this introduction sketches the specific concerns that unify each section of this volume.

"Nationalism and a National Theatre: One Hundred Years of Irish Drama": The Conference

Overwhelmed by the prospect of learning American place names during a geography lesson, Stephen Dedalus (in James Joyce's *A Portrait of the Artist as a Young Man*) instead reviews the coordinates of his own existence, which he has inscribed in a notebook:

> Stephen Dedalus
> Class of Elements
> Clongowes Wood College
> Sallins
> County Kildare
> Ireland
> Europe
> The World
> The Universe. (15–16)

To this experience of cognitive dissonance involving the United States we could no doubt attribute multiple meanings. At the very least, however, Stephen's gesture confirms the gratification of mapping the relations among individuals, institutions of learning, and imagined communities of various sorts.

I invoke this familiar moment from Irish fiction because academic conferences rely on a cartographic logic similar to that of Stephen, a logic that is most visible in the obligatory name badges yoking individuals to institutions. Yet a graphic representation of the web of relations structuring "Nationalism and a National Theatre" would more likely resemble an air-traffic controller's diagram than it would Stephen's solar-system model, given the diverse affiliations and addresses of the participants (Hawaii, Utah, New York, Dublin, and many places in between). At the center of this diagram would be the daily gathering place for seminars, the Oak Room of Indiana University's Memorial Union, an appropriately named venue for reflection on the past 100 years of Irish theatre.

Harder to map would be the temporal and symbolic coordinates or overdeterminations. The conference dates were chosen because the Irish Literary Theatre's first performance was staged in May 1899 and because many academic institutions are in recess by late May. Less consciously planned was the conference's proximity to Memorial Day, a holiday that foregrounds issues of memory, nation, and service — especially military service — and prompts patriotic displays. One such display was President Clinton's proclamation at Arlington Cemetery: "Again and again, America has been tested in the twentieth century, coming through it all, down to the present day, with even greater blessings of liberty and prosperity" ("Clinton Praises Nation's Veterans"). The subtext of his remark, NATO's intervention in the Kosovo crisis, which many Americans regarded with skepticism, was also one of the conference's subtexts; that is, the crisis indirectly validated the conference's critical enterprise. But perhaps we need not look so far as Yugoslavia for a reminder of the continued need for analyses of national culture, history, and identities; as Laura E. Lyons suggests in her essay on early twentieth-century Ulster Theatre, the struggle to maintain a lasting peace in Northern Ireland is evidence enough. In addition to carrying unmistakable political implications, President Clinton's remark crystallized the impulse to take stock of national achievement before the year 2000 arrived. This "millennial urge," to borrow the phrase that Scott T. Cummings coins to characterize a tendency in Sebastian Barry's plays, was prevalent at the conference, as was a kind of "professional urge" to emphasize interaction between established scholars such as Michael Patrick Gillespie, R. B. Kershner, Christopher Murray, Judith Roof, and Sanford Sternlicht, and Irish studies scholars who are just beginning their careers.

Christopher Fitz-Simon, theatre historian, playwright, and Literary Manager of the Abbey, inaugurated the re-examination of Irish theatre with his provocative keynote address, "Before the Abbey — Can There Have Been Such a Time?" His tongue-in-cheek title anticipated his argument that theatre in nineteenth-century Ireland was not nearly so limited as the founders of the Irish Literary Theatre suggested when they proposed to produce plays that were antithetical to the commercial, staid, and often anti-Irish London theatre. In fact, according to Fitz-Simon, Irish theatre before the Abbey was a smorgasbord of different traditions, not to mention a mixture of "high" and "low" cultural forms. Irish melodramas by Dion Boucicault and J. W. Whitbread ran in Dublin concurrently with plays by Shakespeare and Molière. Through such incontrovertible facts, Fitz-Simon unsettled the mythological foundation on which Ireland's national theatre was built. Equally compelling, though, was his use of anecdotal evidence to bring to life the social stratification and consequent plurality of audiences and preferences in nineteenth-century Ireland.

The first of three dramatic productions offered at night — as diversion from the day's presentations and discussions — similarly exposed the social contradictions of late nineteenth-century Ireland, appropriately by drama-tizing excerpts from the life and writings of the period's most astute satirist, Oscar Wilde. Philip Johnston, of Belfast and the University of Illinois, performed the first act of Mícheál MacLiammóir's celebrated one-person play *The Importance of Being Oscar* (1963) in Indiana University's most inti-mate theatre space, the "T300." A finer tribute to Wilde's legendary wit and panache could not have been made. Trained in ballet, Johnston's grace-fulness was matched only by his agility at mastering the many voices of Wilde, including his Dorian Gray, Lady Windermere, and the French-speaking Salomé. In a famous remark,Yeats linked the start of the "Irish dramatic movement" to the void left by Parnell's demise in 1891.[4] Mac-Liammóir's homage to Wilde, as performed by Johnston, underscored what a devastating loss Wilde's premature death was for Irish culture. It is left for us to speculate, as Fitz-Simon suggested in his lecture, about the influence that Wilde might have exerted on the national theatre's develop-ment had he lived to see — and contribute plays to — the Abbey.

Whereas Johnston's performance enacted Wilde's life and works prior to his 1895 imprisonment for "gross indecency," the two other productions put on during the conference centered on twentieth-century captivity expe-riences. Written by Patricia Burke Brogan, directed by Charlotte Headrick of Oregon State University, staged at the Waldron Arts Center in down-town Bloomington, and performed by members of the Western Kentucky University Department of Theater and Dance, *Eclipsed* (1991) portrays the lives of young women who were literally shunned in the Ireland of the 1950s and 1960s because they became pregnant out of wedlock, in some cases as a result of rape. The play's title connects the reprehensible treatment they received — they were forced to work in the Magdalene laundries, kept from both the children they bore and the light of day, and generally treated as sinners who were beyond repentance — to the moral absolutism of their keepers, nuns whose hearts and sexualities had also been "eclipsed." In the 1990s the Republic has revisited this national trauma repeatedly, including during a segment of the American television newsmagazine *60 Minutes*, as Charlotte Headrick noted in her discussion of the play; this play has been revisited so often in part for the catharsis it produces and in part because it exemplifies a past to which southerners never want to return. That is to say, the abuse of unwed mothers has come to symbolize the nation's former slavish compliance with Catholic ideologies. *Eclipsed* underscores, through its frame — a daughter searching for traces of the mother she never knew — how thoroughly "hidden from history" the women of the Magdalene laundries had been. But its larger merit lies in its emphasis on the imagination and on the solidarity needed to survive such an ordeal. For the confined young women, acting out fantasies is the only way of sustaining hope and connecting to the world outside the laundry–prison, as exemplified by one woman's imagined affair with Elvis, a fantasy nurtured by the other women, who even go so far as to orchestrate a mock wedding between this woman and the "King."

In Frank McGuinness's *Someone Who'll Watch over Me* (1992), directed by Terrence Hartnett of Indiana University's English Department and acted by three Bloomington residents, fantasies of American and British popular culture similarly served as the survival mechanism for three men imprisoned in Lebanon. Although inspired by Brian Keenan's *An Evil Cradling* (1992), a first-hand account of Western hostages' experiences in Beirut, McGuinness's play contains troubling ambiguities. The reasons why the three men have been captured are not specified; references are made to oil, but no coherent motivation is established for their abduction. The play consequently ascribes an unspecified violence to the Arab "terrorists," who remain figments of the audience's imagination — McGuinness does not humanize the captors by presenting them. His primary concern is the psychological and, occasionally, sexually charged interaction of the three men who represent, respectively, the United States, Northern Ireland, and England. But nationality, the source of early tension between the Northern Irishman and the Englishman, does not develop into a full-fledged conflict. Instead, the play focuses on the claustrophobia and range of emotions experienced by the captives, which Hartnett's production ably conveyed. Chained to the ground of the sparse set in the Rose Firebay theatre of the Waldron Arts Center, the actors' movements and dialogue revealed whether they were succumbing to despair or combating it through escapist fantasies.

"Under a Colored Cap," a reading of and reflection on Sean O'Casey's works by his daughter Shivaun O'Casey was the last of the conference's special events. Drawing on her own theatre background, Shivaun effectively read excerpts from her father's plays, rendering the urban, working-class accents of his characters. Her reminiscences tempered the received image of O'Casey as contentious and bitter over the reception of his work by other writers, notably, W. B. Yeats, and by Catholic clergymen — an image that earlier in the day had been examined by Christopher Murray in a compelling paper on *The Drums of Father Ned*. O'Casey's plays lampooned his nationalist contemporaries and their efforts to secure Irish independence in a manner that, according to Shakir Mustafa in "Saying 'No' to Politics: Sean O'Casey's Dublin Trilogy," anticipated contemporary historical revisionism. Consequently, O'Casey has figured prominently in recent cultural debates, although no consensus has been reached regarding his achievement and place in the Irish canon. For example, during one such debate recently conducted at Boston College, Philip O'Leary characterized O'Casey "as a really minor writer who is fading fast" (qtd. in "Irish Studies at Boston College," n.p.). Shivaun's interpretation of her father's career, however, encouraged the opposite and more accurate impression: At the very least, Sean O'Casey's contribution to the national theatre in the 1920s is not likely to be forgotten.

It is, of course, impossible to render the spontaneous flow of ideas during the conference's less formal meetings, such as the opening reception at Indiana University's inspiring art museum; Christopher Fitz-Simon's slide show of Ireland's lesser known theatres, actors, and playwrights; or even the coffee breaks, for that matter. Nor is it possible to reconstruct the seven seminars, the titles of which I list here so as to acknowledge that the five-chapter book revises the original program: 1) "Yeats and Lady Gregory," 2) "Ructions and Identities," 3) "O'Casey, Robinson: Tenements and Big Houses," 4) "Beckett and Behan," 5) "Contemporary Irish Drama," 6) "Women's Writing," and 7) "Acting Companies and Northern Voices." A sense of the conference's spirit and achievement can, however, be conveyed through a brief review of the energetic conversations that took place during three seminars.

The first seminar, "Yeats and Lady Gregory," re-interpreted aspects of either the Abbey's early objectives or its founders' plays, typically by scrutinizing specific theatre practices or events, though Susan Bazargan turned to postmodern theory in "'We Merely Play With Images': Figura and Simulacrum in W. B. Yeats's *The Player Queen.*" The panelists' arguments collectively suggested that the received understanding of the early national theatre has been highly circumscribed; the Abbey and its founders' plays were, the panelists insisted, much more complex and contradictory than most scholars have recognized. Audience members asked about the ostensible discrepancy between the Abbey's international touring and its directors' commitment to creating a national theatre, which led to a related series of questions about the Abbey's urban location and repertoire of peasant plays. What emerged from the discussion was an understanding of the need for scholars both to re-examine the theatre's trafficking between the national and the international, the urban and the rural, the cosmopolitan and the parochial, and to reconsider the limitations of such categories for understanding Irish theatre history.

Debate during the fifth seminar, "Contemporary Irish Drama," reframed these vital questions by focusing on plays comprising the second and third waves of Irish theatre. Scott Boltwood's analysis of Brian Friel's "excavation of Irish spirituality" inspired a fascinating conversation about the tension between the pre-Christian and Catholic rituals and beliefs in *Dancing at Lughnasa* (1990). Similarly, José Lanters's analysis of Martin McDonagh's plays, including his Aran Island trilogy, and James Hurt's reflections on Frank McGuinness's *Someone Who'll Watch over Me* provoked discussion about the role of American popular culture in recent Irish drama. Its ubiquitousness seemed to some audience members to be yet another example of U.S. cultural imperialism. Others countered that Irish playwrights used American pop strategically as a means of connecting the concerns of particular Irish regions (the "local") to the international. For some audience members and panelists, Irish playwrights' "borrowing" was a form of cross-pollination with a long history; as Luke Gibbons recently summarized, Irish culture has always been porous ("Technologies of Desire"). The session concluded after one panelist pointed out that contemporary Irish drama does not reference American texts exclusively. McDonagh's work, for example, dialogically engages other foreign forms, notably Australian soap operas.

The next seminar, "Women's Writing," reflected on the contemporary conditions for Irish women's dramatic production in relation to papers on Patricia Burke Brogan, Marina Carr, Christina Reid, and the Belfast-based collective the Charabanc Theatre Company. The discussion period raised the crucial issue of institutional support for developing playwrights and identified the gender bias that is evident in the reception of Irish women's productions, which the panelists stressed has hindered many writers' careers. Dublin residents in the audience pointed out that the niche marketing used to promote women's productions often unnecessarily pigeonholed their work and deterred certain potential theatregoers. Another round of debate ensued when Christopher Fitz-Simon contrasted the development of Carr and Reid. There was literally never a lull in the conversation during this seminar nor in any of the others. The interests of the participants covered considerable range, yet there were also recurring concerns rooted in the particular conditions for Irish dramatic production today. Most of all, the conference fostered a sense of shared purpose and an excitement about the task at hand, re-reading and re-contextualizing twentieth-century Irish theatre, which also infuse the following collection of essays.

The End of the National Theatre As We Know It: The Collection

In the course of 100 years of Irish theatre, a cycle of sorts has been completed: Whereas a century ago a small coterie struggled to establish a national theatre and to foster an indigenous dramatic tradition, in the 1990s, critics and playwrights alike have rejected the very idea of a national theatre, along with the notion of a continuous dramatic tradition, as a totaliz-

ing and simplified concept.[5] Their language, as my phrasing has attempted
to imitate, betrays their debt to recent efforts to nuance the nationalist
narrative of Irish political history and, more generally, reflects the skepticism that has been building in Ireland for decades toward cultural institutions and constructs that posit a unified version of nation or nationality.
There is, though, a more pragmatic reason why contemporary critics and
dramatists have discredited the idea of a national theatre and tradition: the
simple fact that Ireland's official national theatre, the Abbey, while still a
prominent Dublin cultural institution, ceased by the 1960s to serve as the
hub of dramatic production. In fact, the major playwrights who emerged
during that decade — Brian Friel, Hugh Leonard, and Tom Murphy — built
their reputations through plays that premiered in London and New York
(Fitz-Simon 184, 192; O'Toole, "Today" 132).[6] That their successors — the
twenty-, thirty-, and forty-something playwrights who have commanded
international attention in the 1990s — have even more consciously bypassed
the Abbey in favor of international or regional theatres has confirmed that
the practice was not simply a reflex of an alienated generation but rather an
expression of a more pervasive weariness of national theatre per se.

This weariness was (and is) a sign of the times. Declan Kiberd rightly
correlates the 1960s generation's preoccupation with the concerns of their
native regions to the larger cultural shift begun during that pivotal decade:
"It was as if the old nationalist narrative was beginning to break down, and
'Ireland' once again became a problematic notion, as its people renewed
their interest in its constituent parts" (*Inventing Ireland* 496). But a more
specific explanation for this generation's aversion to the national theatre
can be found in the Abbey's degraded image at mid-century. As Fintan
O'Toole suggests in the passage cited as my first epigraph — and as Christopher Murray outlines later in this volume — the Abbey gradually lost its
experimental edge after independence, becoming "mainstream" in an "increasingly conservative Catholic state" ("Shadows over Ireland" 17). There
is no particular mystery to how this happened: The theatre was like many
other oppositional cultural formations whose nationalism, though suspect at moments, could nevertheless be made to serve the new state. Co-
optation was practically inevitable for another reason: When Yeats and
Lady Gregory accepted state funding in 1925, the Abbey was nearly bankrupt (Hunt 134–135). "Co-optation," though, may be too strong a word to
describe the state's relationship to the theatre. The repressive climate created by both state and church after independence certainly narrowed the
Abbey's expressive horizons. However, Yeats skillfully warded off government interference, at times by threatening to close down the theatre. After
one particularly repugnant censorship attempt in the mid-1930s, Yeats
took the matter to the top: He met with Eamon de Valera and helped to
formulate the kind of verbal clause that de Valera was known for — a disclaimer that simultaneously protected the government from liability and

criticism and preserved the Abbey's autonomy (Hunt 146–147). The Abbey's decline, therefore, should not simply be chalked up to its becoming an apparatus of the state.

Rather, according to drama critics in the first half of this century, the theatre's undoing was that it became "dominant" with middle-class Dubliners. Since the Abbey's vicissitudes have been carefully chronicled by theatre historians, my own brief backward glance focuses primarily on the mournful discourse that dogged the theatre — drama critics' newspaper laments over the deterioration of standards at the Abbey. These laments reveal that from its first decades, and increasingly after World War II, critics persistently tried to shame the national theatre into reform. Their damaging reviews not only sharply contrast the optimism of recent drama criticism, including this collection, which views the national theatre's decline as liberating, but they also suggest why the Abbey was so vulnerable to appropriation in the first place: Popularity was perceived as inimical to artistic achievement. That is to say, in the imaginations of those with the power to direct the theatre's development, only two choices existed: The Abbey could remain the preserve of an elite and produce avant-garde drama, or it could become a people's theatre and pander to a population whose exposure to drama heretofore was limited to repertories of commercial and nationalist plays, with some few revivals of Shakespeare, Sheridan, and the like thrown in for good measure. Financial necessity had by the 1920s already dictated the decision; to the deep chagrin of its founders, the Abbey had become a people's theatre "whose economic existence depended on a diet of popular comedies" (Hunt 135).[7]

If, then, the national theatre has been routinely feted since its establishment, it has also been continuously disparaged. Indeed, within a decade of its founding, drama critics began to pronounce the theatre moribund (Hunt 84). In the 1913 article "The Abbey Theatre: Is It on the Decline?," for example, Brinsley MacNamara declared: "The Abbey is exhausted. [. . .] A new inspiration is needed, an idea of a national theatre, retaining all that was best in the decaying form, and developing organically from that form [. . .]" (120). His suggestion for reform anticipated Declan Kiberd's similar prescription in *Inventing Ireland*, reproduced as my second epigraph, by more than eighty years, during which time critiques of the Abbey have varied little. Almost without fail drama critics have identified popularity with the masses as the mark of the theatre's ruin, often in language rivaling the elitism of Joyce's famous 1901 charge that the Irish Literary Theatre had yielded to "the rabblement" (69). Even the writer George Russell (AE), whose progressive social initiatives included organizing agricultural cooperatives, subscribed to this view, declaring in a 1925 article that "nothing can be worse for an intellectual movement than a chorus of approval. Universal approbation means that the people have come to be on its own level, and it is not ahead of them, and therefore it has ceased to belong to the aristocracy of intellect and character" ("Coming of Age of the Abbey" 139).

The Abbey unquestionably became more commercial and reached its artistic nadir under the nearly thirty-year tenure of Ernest Blythe, managing director from 1941 to 1967. Hugh Hunt and Tomás MacAnna have defended Blythe by insisting that dire financial conditions drove his policy of extending the runs of popular productions (Hunt 166–167; MacAnna, "Ernest Blythe and the Abbey" 171), primarily kitchen comedies and well-made plays that lacked all capacity to analyze Irish society (Brown 244). MacAnna also credited Blythe for procuring a new building for the Abbey's companion theatre, the Peacock, in addition to the "new Abbey" after the original theatre was destroyed by fire (171).[8] In stark contrast, Blythe's detractors perceived his Abbey as a betrayal of the high ideals of the theatre's founders, particularly those of Yeats, whose death in 1939 they retrospectively considered the theatre's own expiration date. Among these were the poet Valentin Iremonger and UCD lecturer Roger McHugh, who, in a 1947 incident analyzed further by Christopher Murray in Part III of this volume, rose before the final curtain of a lackluster revival of O'Casey's *The Plough and the Stars*, denounced Blythe as incompetent, and blamed him for destroying Yeats's glorious theatre. Immediately afterwards, established writers publicly called for Blythe's resignation, and the *Irish Times* jumped into the fray by supporting Iremonger and McHugh's gesture (Hunt 173; MacAnna, "Ernest Blythe and the Abbey" 168–169). By 1962, writers for the paper would go so far as to insist that the Abbey no longer deserved the title of "national theatre" (Hunt 181).

Such attacks made Blythe "the most abused man in Ireland" for three decades, as Hunt claims (166). Critics held him responsible for the national theatre's compromised state, yet their explanations had not fundamentally changed since MacNamara's 1913 assessment. The theatre's degeneration, in other words, was still measured in terms of its popularity. Donagh McDonagh's 1949 article "The Death-Watch Beetle" exemplified this tendency: "Ah, it is a poor thing when a great institution comes to the end of its days, and when those who saw it in its might mourn its decay and popularity. The Abbey in the days of its greatness was empty of the populace, but now, in its old age, 'with flattering tongue it speeds the parting guest'" (185). The populace in Paul Vincent Carroll's 1952 article "Can the Abbey Theatre Be Restored?" was less flatteringly referred to as "the loud-mouthed many" which threatened to hinder the "minority of genius," who, because they had staged a handful of "masterpieces," should control "the artistic destiny of the race" (189).

The rhetorical excesses of such critiques were no doubt partly intended for journalistic effect. Theatre historians in subsequent decades have insisted that such anti-Abbey discourse exaggerated the extent of the theatre's decline. Hunt, for example, tempers criticism of the theatre through the following mixed metaphors: "In the eyes of many of its former friends, the Abbey had sold its birthright for a mess of potage. The picture was not, however, as grey as has been painted" (183). Whatever the actual state of the theatre, its image had been thoroughly tarnished by mid-century. Thus, paradoxically, given their intentions, drama critics' laments helped put the proverbial nail in the Abbey's coffin. This is not to deny that the theatre had degenerated during the so-called de Valera years but instead to emphasize the power of critical discourse to shape images and to control explanations of cultural institutions.

Pursuing this line of argument one step further, it seems reasonable to suggest that critics' laments also propelled Irish theatre outside the Abbey.[9] Their descriptions of the national theatre's torpor at the very least confirmed the need for new initiatives. Phillip L. Marcus corroborates the idea of such compensatory efforts in observing that "the Gate Theatre, [. . .] the Lyric Theatre and other groups in the 1930s and later, helped to make some amends for a certain staleness in what the Abbey Theatre had to offer" (27).[10] Similarly, in *The Irish Theatre* (1983), Christopher Fitz-Simon reviews in detail the various organizations that arose in response to the Abbey's "wilting" (184), including the Dublin Theatre Festival (organized in 1957), which sponsored most of the major plays of the 1960s, and the various "fringe" or independent theatres, beginning with the short-lived but influential Pike Theatre Club (founded in 1953).[11] Of course, the Abbey itself must be credited for boosting interest in drama throughout Ireland (Ó hAodha 137); to conclude otherwise would be to deny both the range of its influence and perhaps its most enduring legacy.[12] Nevertheless, to different extents, these various enterprises were conceived as responses to the national theatre's stagnation.

Policy changes by one of Blythe's successors, Artistic Director Joe Dowling, renewed hope that the Abbey, or, rather, its companion the Peacock, would itself play a prominent role in the revitalization of Irish theatre. In the late 1970s, the Peacock did in fact become a forum for socially oriented plays by young playwrights, whose contributions to Irish theatre in the past three decades have been considerable, notably Bernard Farrell, Frank McGuinness, and Graham Reid. But as O'Toole claims, the Peacock was a "reluctant" alternative to the Abbey, one which produced significant plays but was far too cautious to regenerate Irish theatre in a broader sense ("Today" 135–136). For O'Toole, proof that contemporary Irish dramatists remain "the orphans of the Irish literary renaissance," whose famous forebears left them an institution but none of the systems needed to ensure its continued vitality, comes from the fact that contemporary playwrights have often had to create the conditions for staging their own work ("Today" 133). Brian Friel, for example, formed the Derry-based Field Day Theatre Company in 1980, along with actor Stephen Rea, because he felt that Ireland lacked a company capable of producing plays which explored political divisions within the island, including, of course, his own plays (O'Toole, "Today" 134).

The formation of such alternatives to the Abbey, especially those located outside Dublin, has greatly expanded dramatists' choices of venues within Ireland. Critics, therefore, were shortsighted in fixating on the Abbey and clinging to the idea of a centralized national theatre. As Kiberd underscores, when the long-awaited "revitalization [of Irish theatre] came, it would come from the provinces" in the form of writers, actors, and "regional companies which seemed to thrive in proportion to the waning of the Abbey" (*Inventing Ireland* 496). The youngest generation of Irish playwrights has clearly reaped the benefits of the surge in regional theatres. Indeed, if their achievement in the 1990s stems in part from the richness of their material (the contradictions resulting from the socioeconomic changes in Ireland since the late 1950s), it also results from the boom in regional theatres, which have enabled many writers to develop their plays and skills.

As a consequence of the third wave's success, critics no longer bemoan the national theatre's decline. Rather, many now celebrate the possibilities of a decentralized Irish theatre and a peripatetic tradition,[13] and insist that the revivalist notion of a national theatre never adequately expressed the plurality of twentieth-century Irish theatre. Among contemporary drama critics, Fintan O'Toole has most effectively popularized this optimistic view. For him, the shift away from the Abbey and the exuberance of regional companies—notably the Druid in Galway, the Bickerstaff in Kilkenny, the Red Kettle in Waterford, the Galloglass in Clonmel, the Corcadorca in Cork, and the Field Day in Derry—have exponentially increased the possibilities for dramatic production in Ireland ("Recent Theatre" 23).[14] (Young playwrights have also successfully exported work that was originally produced by regional companies, and their internationalism has been a source of great pride in Ireland.) Indeed, more than simply multiplying the number of venues and companies, these changes have made "room for a whole range of new voices, new styles and new concerns" ("Recent Theatre" 23).

The contributors to this collection share O'Toole's sense of the new opportunities for Irish drama that have resulted from the decentralization of Irish theatre. While only a few explicitly rehearse the narrative of the Abbey's decline, it is in many ways the foundation and impetus for most of their re-readings of Irish theatre. The remainder of this introduction summarizes the purpose and content of each chapter and offers a few final reflections. The collection as a whole, as I have tried to suggest, responds to the shift in the past three decades in the relations of Irish dramatic production, which has been thrown into relief by the recent success of the third wave. The collection also mounts a related argument about the need to recognize the heterogeneity of Irish theatre over the past 100 years, as the very brief outline below suggests.

Part I, "Challenging the Received View of Early Twentieth-Century Irish Theatre," attempts to broaden the dominant interpretation of early twentieth-century Irish theatre. John P. Harrington's "The Founding Years and the Irish National Theatre That Was Not," for example, demonstrates how "internationalism and denial of it were fundamental to the national theatre project." Rather than eclipsed tendencies within the national theatre, Nelson Ó Ceallaigh Ritschel's "The Alternative Aesthetic: The Theatre of Ireland's Urban Plays" and Laura E. Lyons's "Of Orangemen and Green Theatres: The Ulster Literary Theatre's Regional Nationalism" direct much-needed attention to theatre companies that developed in opposition to the Abbey's aesthetics and politics.

Returning to the Abbey, specifically to disputes over Abbey productions, part II, "Theorizing and Historicizing Theatre Controversies," offers new ways of decoding both theatre skirmishes and critical interpretations of them. Lucy McDiarmid revisits the political determination of Lady Gregory and Bernard Shaw in "The Abbey and the Theatrics of Controversy, 1909–1915," revealing how theatre controversies function as both discursive sites and alternative theatre. Controversies can also, however, mask or misrepresent cultural anxieties, as Susan Cannon Harris demonstrates in "More Than a Morbid, Unhealthy Mind: Public Health and the *Playboy* Riots," an analysis of the influence of British medical discourse and advertising on nationalist responses to Synge's play. And controversies can also be reactivated for ideological purposes, according to Shakir Mustafa's "Saying 'No' to Politics: Sean O'Casey's Dublin Trilogy," which considers how the revisionist debates of the past three decades reframe the 1920s dispute over O'Casey's Dublin plays.

The later O'Casey forms the bridge between Mustafa's essay and part III, "Reconstructing Drama during the 'Fatal Fifties'," which finds more experimentalism and cultural significance in mid-century drama than most critics have heretofore recognized (the moniker is MacLiammóir's; Murray, "Introduction: The Stifled Voice" 10). In "O'Casey's *The Drums of Father Ned* in Context," Christopher Murray suggests that the 1958 play about a Tóstal (festival of music and arts) signaled Irish culture's — and more specifically, the Abbey Theatre's — transition from the "old, conservative, pastoral world of de Valera" to "the new, pragmatic, progressive world of Seán Lemass and T. K. Whitaker." Stephen Watt's "Love and Death: A Reconsideration of Behan and Genet" situates Brendan Behan's preoccupations with death and sexuality in relation to both postwar European avant-garde theatre and investigations into sexuality, such as the Wolfenden Report and George Bataille's *L'Erotisme*. Acknowledging the limits of national context for readings of mid-century Irish drama is also

Judith Roof's project; her "Playing Outside with Samuel Beckett" analyzes the theory of theatre advanced through Beckett's use of props, more specifically, technological apparatuses such as tape recorders, which, like national identifications, help structure memory and desire.

Part IV, "Contemporary Theatre Projects and Revivals," considers recent efforts to revive, adapt, or subvert earlier drama and to explore issues of contemporary importance to local audiences. Mary Trotter's "Translating Women into Irish Theatre History" and Carla J. McDonough's " 'I've Never Been Just Me': Re-thinking Women's Positions in the Plays of Christina Reid" examine Marina Carr's and Christina Reid's attempts to represent Irish women's experiences by adapting male-centered dramatic forms, specifically the patrilineal family play in Trotter's analysis and masculinist political narratives of Northern Ireland in McDonough's essay. In "Neither Here nor There: The Liminal Position of Teresa Deevy and Her Female Characters," Christie Fox places the recent interest in Deevy's plays in relation to both earlier critical neglect of her work and her characters' precarious positions in 1930s Ireland. José Lanters examines Tom Murphy's and Martin McDonagh's debts to J. M. Synge in "Playwrights of the Western World: Synge, Murphy, McDonagh"; Lanters also examines the manner in which these playwrights subvert the conventional "Western" play to express the anxieties of their age. Returning to the urban theatre scene, Lauren Onkey's "The Passion Machine Theatre Company's Everyday Life" reflects on the company's history and commitment to staging plays about Dublin experiences.

Taken in toto, the four essays in part V, "Irish History on the Contemporary Stage," investigate the various dramatic forms that contemporary Irish writers have employed to represent an all-too-troubled history to their audiences. The problem of historical representation is, of course, as old as Aeschylus's *The Persians* and Shakespeare's *Henriad;* and, not surprisingly, playwrights of the ingenuity of Brian Friel, Frank McGuinness, Stewart Parker, and Sebastian Barry have devised various solutions to the problem. In "The Book at the Center of the Stage: Friel's *Making History* and *The Field Day Anthology of Irish Writing*," Kathleen Hohenleitner compares two overlapping Field Day projects, observing in both a rejection of traditional visions of national identity in representing Irish history. For McGuinness, as James Hurt argues in "Frank McGuinness and the Ruins of Irish History," history is not so much a tragedy, a model of historical action frequently employed on the Classical and Early Modern stages, but rather a Benjaminian *trauerspiel* or "play of mourning." And in Marilynn Richtarik's and Scott Cummings's respective essays on Parker and Barry, history is inevitably connected to local memory: Parker, whose *oeuvre* deals directly with Belfast, explores Northern history from the 1798 rising through the building of the ill-fated *Titanic* to the more contemporary "Troubles," whereas Barry filters Irish history through senility and at times a foggy memory, at moments revealing an impulse, or "millennial urge," that is shared by such non-Irish dramatists as Tony Kushner. Hence, in their own ways, the four contributors to this section return Irish drama to its century-long dialogue with a larger international community, through which it has attempted to communicate Irish history to audiences around the world, at times by employing dramatic forms or "impulses" that have been refined elsewhere.

Initially perceived as being at cross-purposes with the early Irish theatre's nationalist commitments, such internationalism is now touted as a sign of the confidence and the broad appeal of contemporary Irish writing. This introduction has focused on national cultural history, specifically the backlash against the Abbey, as a means of explaining Irish playwrights' gravitation toward foreign and regional theatres since the 1960s and, hence, the decentralization of Irish theatre. A fuller explanation of the shifts in Irish dramatic production results, of course, from reading the contributors' analyses, many of which examine either international contexts and influences or regional initiatives, and all of which encourage further reflection on the Irish theatre since the formation of the Irish Literary Society a century ago.

NOTES

1. In naming the Irish National Dramatic Company among the precursor organizations, I follow Hugh Hunt's precedent. Many historians of the Abbey gloss over this organization, which was established by Frank and Willie (W. G.) Fay, the brothers who coached the original Abbey players, because its relationship to the Irish National Theatre Society (INTS) is not entirely understood. Hunt records that a Black-and-Tan raid on the Fay Family's house resulted in the destruction of letters that would explain the emergence of the INTS (37). I am also distinguishing here between the INTS and the Irish National Theatre Society, Ltd., the private company established in 1904 as the governing board of the Abbey Theatre, which, though restructured in 1972, nevertheless still exists (Hunt 242).

2. Fintan O'Toole uses this metaphor to distinguish the plays of Ireland's youngest playwrights — Sebastian Barry, Marina Carr, Martin McDonagh, Frank McGuinness, and Conor McPherson, to name only the most celebrated — from the previous generation of dramatists, which includes Brian Friel, Hugh Leonard, and Tom Murphy ("Shadows over Ireland" 17). However, the metaphor was operative long before O'Toole's use of it. Hunt's reference to "the new wave of Abbey playwrights" (204) in the late 1960s, who first made their reputations overseas, links the metaphor to the internationalism of playwrights whose plays, like waves, rolled into England and the United States.

3. By this statement I do not mean to imply that the Abbey has no contemporary purpose, but rather I mean to underscore the perceived obsolescence of the theatre model advanced a century ago, when articulating a unified national image and unified cultural traditions made sense. At all costs I seek to avoid the danger of taking the Abbey for granted, which Christopher Murray warns against in *Twentieth-Century Irish Drama: Mirror Up to Nation* (245).

4. Delivered during his Nobel Prize acceptance speech, Yeats's exact remark was as follows: "The modern literature of Ireland, and indeed all that stir of thought which prepared for the Anglo-Irish war, began when Parnell fell from power in 1891" ("The Irish Dramatic Movement" 186). Most historians cite 1890 as the year that Parnell fell from power; in December 1889, Parnell was named as co-respondent in the O'Shea divorce case, and the Irish Party split shortly afterwards.

5. Ironically, this rejection also came from within the Abbey itself during Garry Hynes's tenure as artistic director (1990–1993). As Murray explains, "Hynes [. . .] served during her term of office to challenge the whole idea of a national theatre in Ireland today" (245). In stark contrast, her successor Patrick Mason has attempted to defend the century-old concept and restore the Abbey's dominant role in dramatic production (245).

6. These playwrights did not, however, categorically reject the Abbey. In fact, Friel's very first play, *The Enemy Within* (1962), was produced at the Abbey (Welch, *Oxford Companion* 204), and two of Hugh Leonard's early plays debuted at the Abbey (Fitz-Simon 184). Murphy submitted plays in 1960 and 1961 — respectively, *A Whistle in the Dark* and *The Fooleen* (later renamed *A Crucial Week in the Life of a Grocer's Assistant*); their rejection by Ernest Blythe drove Murphy to emigrate to London (Welch 384). As José Lanters notes in her essay in this volume, with the exception of only a few plays, most of Murphy's subsequent work has premiered at the Abbey. Friel and Leonard have less consistently developed their plays at the national theatre.

7. In fact, in the fall of 1919, Yeats published "A People's Theatre: A Letter to Lady Gregory" in the *Irish Statesman*, in which he aired his frustrations with the Abbey's popularity: "Yet we did not set out to create this sort of theatre, and its success has been to me a discouragement and a defeat" (qtd. in Bentley 331). The letter also expresses his hope of founding a theatre for Ireland's elite: "I want to create for myself an unpopular theatre and an audience like a secret society where admission is by favour and never to many" (qtd. in Bentley 335).

8. With the help of government funds, the Peacock, named for its blue uphol-stered chairs and blue walls, was opened in 1928 as an experimental arm of the Abbey. This early ambition was dashed, however, by the need to rent the theatre to other companies (Hunt 137).

9. Of course, many other factors contributed to the proliferation of Abbey alternatives. Murray identifies two such factors, for example, in describing the de-centralization of Irish theatre as "part of a general change in relationship between Dublin and the rest of the country," and he notes that "for the first time the Arts Council was obliged to recognise the claims of good artistic work in areas remote from Dublin" (*Twentieth-Century Irish Drama*, 239).

10. The Dublin Gate Theatre Studio, later simply the Gate Theatre, was founded in 1928 by Hilton Edwards and Mícheál MacLiammóir in order to stage world drama and experimental productions; from its inception, therefore, it served to supplement the Abbey's offerings. For more on the Gate's history, consult Peter Luke, ed., *Enter Certain Players: Edwards, Mac Liammóir and the Gate, 1928–1978,* and John Cowell, *No Profit but the Name: The Longfords and the Gate Theatre.*

The Lyric Theatre of which Marcus writes should not be confused with the still-operative Lyric Theatre in Belfast. The former, the Lyric Theatre Company (1944–1951), was started in Dublin by Austin Clarke and Roibeárd Ó Faracháin as a "theatrical offshoot" of the Dublin Verse Speaking Society after Clarke's verse plays were rejected by the Abbey directorate; the company's plays appeared biannually at the Abbey (Welch 321). The Lyric Players Theatre, founded in Belfast in 1951 by Mary and Pearse O'Malley, was inspired by its Dublin namesake and was similarly committed to the performance of verse plays, especially those written by Yeats and

Austin Clarke. In 1968 this company acquired a building of its own; three decades later it is still going strong (Welch 321). For more details of its history, see Sam Hanna Bell's *The Theatre in Ulster.*

11. Fitz-Simon's survey of initiatives designed to compensate for the Abbey's lethargy occurs in chapter 18, "Conservatives and Shape-Changers: After 1950" (184–201).

12. See Terence Brown's *Ireland: A Social and Cultural History, 1922–Present* for first-hand testimony of the Abbey's influence on amateur theatre companies throughout rural Ireland (138).

13. Murray, for example, abandons the notion of a linear dramatic tradition and suggests instead that "Irish drama oscillates always between tradition and innovation" (224).

14. To this list Murray adds Meridian in Cork, Island in Limerick, Yew Tree in Ballina, and Red Raincoat in Sligo (*Twentieth-Century Irish Drama* 238–239). O'Toole and Murray also both note the number of new Dublin companies that have further decentralized Irish theatre, including the Passion Machine (see Lauren Onkey's essay in this volume), Rough Magic, Wet Paint, and Pigsback (Murray 239; O'Toole "Recent Theatre" 23).

Part I

———•———

CHALLENGING THE
RECEIVED VIEW OF
EARLY-TWENTIETH-CENTURY
IRISH THEATRE

—1—

The Founding Years and the
Irish National Theatre That Was Not

JOHN P. HARRINGTON

During one of his early ventures into theatre — the production of *The Land of Heart's Desire* in 1894 — W. B. Yeats wrote to the old Fenian John O'Leary that "The whole venture will be history any way for it is the first contest between the old commercial school of theatrical folk & the new artistic school" (qtd. in Foster, *W. B. Yeats* 142). In addition to a contest between new and old schools, that formative instance in modern Irish drama marked a complicated conjunction of Douglas Hyde's *Love Songs of Connacht*, Florence Farr, "the Bedford Park circuit" (Foster, *W. B. Yeats* 137), Villiers de l'Isle-Adam's *Axel*, Yeats's first visit to the Continent, his competition with Shaw, a broken engagement with Mallarmé, and a full range of the kinds of insinuating factors that both make history and make history more than a series of literary texts, dramatic or otherwise. Now, the whole venture *is* history, "any way," on the centenary of the birth of the Irish Literary Theatre, at the Antient Concert Rooms, in Dublin on 8 May 1899, with Yeats's *The Countess Cathleen*. That opening night was another entanglement of insinuating factors that have been interpreted differently at different times: sometimes, as per Yeats, they were viewed as representing the confrontation of commercial and artistic theatre, and at other times during the intervening 100 years, these factors were interpreted to represent different constructions of cultural nationalism.

The performance of 8 May 1899 certainly represented a break with contemporary theatrical practices, especially in Dublin. It led directly to the series of companies and corporations that continue to the present day: the Irish National Theatre Society, the Abbey Theatre, and the National

Theatre Society of Ireland. The accomplishments of modern Irish drama during its century of existence are certainly quite formidable. The phrase "Irish drama," much more than "German drama" or "American drama," suggests a fairly specific and homogeneous kind of theatre. In this century, Ireland's four Nobelists have been principally dramatists (Shaw and Beckett), notably dramatist (Yeats), and occasionally dramatist (Heaney). But the work of the first two of those Nobel dramatists is not consonant with the common image of Irish drama if that image consists of Catholic and ruralist plays, and those two (Shaw and Beckett) wrote, respectively, from London and Paris. Now, on the centenary, the work of one new playwright *is* consonant with the image, but Martin McDonagh's "Aran Trilogy" is in development at the National Theatre in London rather than the one in Dublin. In short, the outcome, 100 years after initial plans for a modern Irish drama were formulated, does not resemble the founding intentions, in part because of subsequent developments in Irish theatre, but also because Irish drama was never homogeneous to begin with.

The prospectus underlying the opening of the Irish Literary Theatre has become familiar, especially through Lady Gregory's account in *Our Irish Theatre*. Now, though, it is worth re-examining with a full century's worth of hindsight and with regard to one particular unforeseen outcome that I would like to emphasize. Gregory misremembered the date (1897, not 1898) when a plan for the Irish Literary Theatre was committed to paper at Coole Park. One impetus was the possibility that Edward Martyn's plays *The Heather Field* and *Maeve* would be produced in Germany before Ireland. Gregory remembered composing the project's definition on the Remington typewriter given her by Enid, Lady Layard, Ambassadress at Constantinople and Madrid. Roy Foster has examined a preliminary draft written out by Yeats "with many excisions and afterthoughts." Among the excisions was Yeats's complaint that "dramatic journalism has had full possession of the English stage for a century" (qtd. in Foster, *W. B. Yeats* 184). The clarified version produced on the Remington — a version that was also devoid of names and titles and financial sums — has those resonant phrases that begin: "We propose to have performed in Dublin in the Spring of every year certain Celtic and Irish plays, which whatever their degree of excellence will be written with a high ambition, and so to build up a Celtic and Irish school of dramatic literature" (Gregory 8). Lady Gregory later observed that "I myself never quite understood the meaning of the 'Celtic Movement,' which we were said to belong to." After that opening declaration, the prospectus proceeds thus by means of the rhetoric of difference and definition by negation: "that freedom to experiment which is not found in theatres of England"; "show that Ireland is not the home of buffoonery and of easy sentiment"; "confident of the support of all Irish people, who are weary of misrepresentation" (Gregory 8–9).

In retrospect, the rhetoric scarcely disguises the degree to which the plan was less a fully formed assertion of independence than a reaction against contemporary culture. The reaction was quite specifically aimed against English culture. While, as phrased here, the Irish Literary Theatre chose to represent itself as a fully formed and wholly autonomous "Celtic and Irish school," in practice the project would continue to reveal the culture and consciousness elided from the statement — all those insinuating influences represented by Germany, Constantinople, Madrid, and farther abroad. The continuing presence of those influences is especially evident in the history of the national theatre movement as theatrical activity — the great texts along with the history of companies, theatrical buildings, legal documents, comparable movements, and the cultural context of performance. In these "activities" one sees that one reason for the discrepancy between the Irish national drama as imagined in 1899 and as fact in 2000 is that Irish drama is international, and indeed was so from its origins, although the national theatre's founders often insisted it was strictly national.

As written by Yeats and as improved by Lady Gregory, the prospectus certainly is remarkable for its ambitions, many of which have been pointed out before and many of which have been largely realized. One is the ambition to replace "low" culture with "high" culture, to address "the deeper thoughts and emotions of Ireland." Twenty-five years ago Robert Hogan and James Kilroy documented popular theatrical fare in Dublin at about the time of the opening of the Irish Literary Theatre in 1899. The shows running included a long list of touring musical reviews and melodramas with titles such as *The Belle of New York*, *The Skirt Dancer*, *A Greek Slave*, and *The Squatter's Daughter*. "Irish Drama" was represented by Boucicault, whose productions opened in New York or London. The more exotic entertainments included Sardou's *Tosca*, an American production called *Our Irish Visitors*, which was visiting Dublin, and Coquelin's productions of Rostand and Molière (Hogan and Kilroy 11–13). On examination a century later, this list and the longer rolls of theatrical activity in Dublin at the turn of the century seem "low" in artistic ambition by later standards, but they are nevertheless impressive in their degree of internationalism in a city that at the time was often described as a provincial stop for touring companies from the London stage. The useful reminder, not provided in the Yeats–Gregory prospectus, is that Yeats and Gregory's agenda of local priorities, of works produced in Dublin for an Irish audience, was not formulated solely to fill a theatrical or even an artistic vacuum but rather as a direct response to a fairly cosmopolitan theatrical scene. The formulation for a national theatre was thus both reactionary and insular, though the founders and other participants in the project were quite cosmopolitan in their personal histories and theatrical experience.

Similarly elided from the prospectus as written was the ambition to link a remote past ("ancient idealism") to a future ("to build up a Celtic and Irish school of dramatic literature"), without reference to an exploitable present.

There were, of course, important Irish theatrical traditions and influences more varied than those of Boucicault. The obvious names that were written out of its context by the project were Congreve, Farquhar, the Sheridans, Goldsmith, and more — both stage playwrights and stage performers — in whose time there was less urgency in making a distinction between England and Ireland than there was in 1899. Frank Fay, whose falling out with the national theatre project is described within this volume by Nelson Ó Ceallaigh Ritschel, was a useful witness to the continuing presence of these names in Dublin theatre at the time of the Irish Literary Theatre. At the turn of the last century he was writing a series of articles (for the *United Irishman*) on Boucicault, on the Irish historical melodramas of J. W. Whitbread, and on frequent revivals of Sheridan and Goldsmith. Once distinction and separation became the priority of cultural nationalism, these figures were found wanting by Fay and others. Whitbread's offense to Fay was opening *The Irishman* in London rather than Dublin, and Sheridan's that his work performed in Dublin required "the traditional method of playing Sheridan on the English stage" (Frank Fay, *Towards a National Theatre* 46). Even Boucicault could have offered some exemplary instances, however erroneous. In 1874, after his great success in *The Shaughraun*, Boucicault declared, in language very like that of Yeats and Gregory, that "it is Irish character as misrepresented by English dramatists that I convict as libel" ("Shaughraun" 5). But Fay and others found that all figures were guilty of affiliations with London or New York, a charge which Yeats, Gregory, and even Fay could scarcely defend themselves against. And so, in the period of cultural revival, the internationalists of the Irish stage were disqualified from both the past and the present of the "Irish school." A continuing characteristic of the Irish national drama would be this tension between the fact of cosmopolitan influence and the ambition for singularity that was intrinsically local.

The internationalism of the proto-native theatre is nowhere better represented than in the entire first volume of *Beltaine*, which was printed (in London) for the opening performances of the Irish Literary Theatre in Dublin. It included a prologue for the Irish play:

> Come, then, and keep with us an Irish feast,
> Wherein the Lord of Light and Song is priest;
> Now, at this opening of the gentle may,
> Watch warring passions at the storm and play;
> Wrought with the flaming ecstasy of art,
> Sprung from the dreams of an Irish heart. (*Beltaine* 1: 5)

The prologue on the Irish heart was written by and performed on the first night by the English poet Lionel Johnson. The first sentence of the text of the journal, by the "Editor of 'Beltaine'" (Yeats), read, "Norway has a great and successful school of contemporary drama, which grew out of a national literary movement very similar to what is now going on in Ireland" (*Beltaine* 1: 6). Yeats's citations (with varying degrees of approval) for allied projects continued through the roll call of Spain, Germany, Théâtre-Libre (Paris), The Independent Theatre (London), Ibsen, Maeterlinck, Hauptmann, and José Echegaray. *Beltaine* also prepared audiences for the Irish Literary The-atre by reprinting an essay by C. H. Herford on "The Scandinavian Dra-matists," especially the early Ibsen. All this provided context for *The Count-ess Cathleen*, which was performed by an English cast with an English director and incidental music ("Suite on Irish Airs") by a German composer ("Herr Bast"). Many issues surrounded the opening of this production. They included issues of elitism: Arthur Griffith, conspicuously absent from the list of benefactors, called it Yeats's "attempt to produce a really high-class Anglo-Irish" (qtd. in Foster, *W. B. Yeats* 206). Famously, there was a campaign to call the play's nationalism into question, a campaign spear-headed by Frank Hugh O'Donnell, the "Mad Rogue" whom Yeats accused in his *Memoirs* of being an agent of the Boer Republic. However, intrinsic to these issues and increasingly conspicuous in the later course of modern Irish drama was this conflict between the international and cosmopolitan nature of the theatrical event and the counterinsistence that the project was profoundly Irish and Celtic.

The Irish Literary Theatre and *Beltaine* continued through two more annual productions and two numbers of the journal. The second program, performed in February 1900 at the Gaiety Theatre, included George Moore's *The Bending of the Bough*, Alice Milligan's *The Last Feast of the Fianna*, and Martyn's *Maeve*. Moore brought the expertise of a member of the board of the Independent Theatre in London as well as impeccable credentials as author of scandalous "naturalistic" English novels derived from French sources. The entire second program was rehearsed in Lon-don. *Beltaine* advertised the fact that in the past year, Martyn's *Heather Field* had been produced in London; translated into German; performed in Ber-lin, Vienna, and Dresden; and planned for American productions. Milli-gan's play was a counterbalance toward the indigenous. Her program an-notation on the play explained that "if it was to be produced before a company of Kerry peasants, a single note would not be needed," though she did allow that in her story, "what happened reminds us of a similar incident in Shakespeare's *Richard III*" (*Beltaine*: 2; 18, 20). The Irish–English ten-sion of the endeavor was the unnamed theme of the ostensibly separatist issue. The "Editor" inveighed that *The Bending of the Bough* should not offend any "but those persons and parties who would put private or English interests before Irish interests" (4); Martyn contributed an anti-English diatribe ("England, then, being rank garden that she is . . ." [12]); and Moore repeated his well-known 'scepter passing to Ireland' trope by la-menting how London Theatre has "necessarily declined to the level of a mere amusement" (9). Conflicts between insular assertion and broader

debts continued in the third and final production (and journal) in October
1901 (also at the Gaiety Theatre) of the Moore–Yeats collaboration *Diar-
mud and Grania*, along with Douglas Hyde's *Casadh an tSúgáin*. The former
was staged by the Frank Benson Company, with music by Elgar, and the
latter by others coached by William Fay. This final production of the Irish
Literary Theatre brought forth, among other responses, James Joyce's
broadsheet "The Day of the Rabblement," which, among louder declama-
tions, expressed disappointment that "the official organ of the movement
spoke of producing European masterpieces, but the matter went no further.
Such a project was absolutely necessary" (70).

The Fays were well aware of pleas, like that of Joyce, for international
works. Frank Fay wrote in 1901 that "James A. Joyce," with his "rather
superior attitude," "will see that the Irish Literary Theatre still hopes to do
that" (F. Fay, *Towards a National Theatre* 79). But the next evolution of the
national theatre would *not* do that. W. G. Fay's Irish National Dramatic
Company produced *Deirdre* (by George Russell) and *Kathleen ni Houlihan*
(credited solely to Yeats and not to Lady Gregory) at St. Teresa's Total
Abstinence Association in April 1902. The casts were Irish, including both
Fays in different plays, the scenery was designed by Russell, and the cos-
tumes were by members of the Inghinidhe na hÉireann company. This was
a considerable transformation of the work of the brothers Fay, which had
previously taken form in the Ormond Dramatic Society, or in "Mr. W. G.
Fay's Celebrated Variety Co.," or in "Mr. W. G. Fay's Comedy Combination" (Gerald Fay 32, 33). These productions certainly satisfied Frank Fay's
demands for Irish actors in Irish plays, although he continued to define "the
greatest actors" in reference to "a Duse, or a Coquelin, or a Réjane" (F. Fay,
Towards a National Theatre 75). The company was formally legalized in the
fall of 1902 as the Irish National Dramatic Society, with Yeats as president.
With the help of Cumann na nGaedheal, it completed an additional program of Irish plays with Irish actors at the Antient Concert Rooms. On the
front page of the *United Irishman* the result was hailed as "a powerful agent
in the building up of a nation" (qtd. in Foster, *W. B. Yeats* 279), and the
project certainly seems to serve as a fulfillment of the Yeats–Lady Gregory
prospectus "to build up a Celtic and Irish school of dramatic literature." It
did not address pleas for "European masterpieces" or Fay's insistence that
such be on the agenda for the national theatre.

It is not hard to understand the Irish National Dramatic Society's
desire, just after the turn of the last century, for a means to demonstrate
difference and distinction from a pervasive and institutionalized culture.
Their effort, after all, was little more than to claim a niche in Dublin's lively
performance activity. However, the program for insularity did hold inherent risks, and within the performing arts, the parallel history of art music in
Ireland's formative period of cultural nationalism demonstrates some of
those risks. Ireland was justifiably famous for its musical history, which, like

theatre, to that date included European imports — perhaps most famously the premiere of Handel's *Messiah* (in Dublin) — and contributions by Irish composers and performers to European forms, notably ballad opera. Like dramatic theatre in the eighteenth century, Irish music in the nineteenth century included many composers who worked outside of Ireland and whose work was addressed to audiences external to Ireland. The best known examples are the pianist John Field and the opera composers Michael Balfe and William Vincent Wallace. Music enjoyed its own antiquarian revival even before Thomas Moore's *Irish Melodies* became fashionably popular early in the nineteenth century. The gap between an external heritage in art music and the discoveries of an indigenous one in what was called "traditional" music presented musical Dublin with as clear a dichotomy of imperatives as that faced later by the national theatre.

One result of revivalist impulse meeting performance requirements was O'Brien Butler's Irish-language opera *Muirgheis*, which was first performed in the same year as the formation of the Irish National Dramatic Company. Like the Fay company, the *Muirgheis* production drew support from Irish-language and cultural nationalist organizations. However, while the intention was generally applauded, the result was generally deplored. By virtually universal opinion, the linear quality of Irish traditional music was incompatible with the harmonic requirements of operatic form. In *Irish Musical Studies*, Joseph Ryan parses the problem as follows: "The principal and predictable problem faced by those ambitious to fashion a distinctive music founded on a folk idiom was that the very constitutions of the tradition, with its linear character and small structure, left it unsuited as the basis of extended composition; folksong is simply not the stuff of extended composition" (110). The ambition continued, inspired, perhaps, by the success in Dublin of folk drama. Interesting examples include Robert O'Dwyer's opera *Eithne* (1910), the keyboard compositions of Arnold Bax, or the orchestral compositions, including *Irish Symphony*, of Charles Villiers Stanford. Shaw, as always, is eminently quotable on Stanford and the conflict between internal and external imperatives. "The Irish Symphony, composed by an Irishman, is a record of fearful conflict between the Aboriginal Celt and the Professor," Shaw wrote in 1893. "The Professor succumbed to the shillelagh of his double" (*Great Composers* 344, 345). Eventually Stanford and the other composers found better inspiration elsewhere, and music in Ireland succeeded only when the obligation to internal and indigenous imperatives lessened. According to Ryan, "it took decades of autonomy to instill the communal confidence necessary for Irish composers to present to audiences at home and abroad original works created free of the shadow of parochial expectation" (114). That is, free from the shadow of parochial expectation that knew its opposite and so frequently took reactionary form, as in Stanford's "double."

The Yeats–Gregory prospectus for an Irish Literary Theatre proclaimed complete confidence in distinction derived wholly from internal inspiration and resources. But the tension between internal and external imperatives became more apparent as the national theatre project evolved, and the question of parochial or cosmopolitan expectations and criteria for success quickly became central to the project. When the Irish National Dramatic Company was reorganized in 1903 as The Irish National Theatre Society, its purpose was stated as follows: "to continue on a more permanent basis the work of the Irish Literary Theatre" (Kavanagh 36); but this goal could not maintain the simplicity of the original intentions to perform in Ireland plays from Ireland and for Ireland. The company's greatest new asset, John Millington Synge, was perceived as a prodigal from France, hence artistically impure. Later his role became more complicated, but in 1903, Synge was perceived as an outside agitator: "The play has an Irish name," Arthur Griffith wrote about *In the Shadow of the Glen*, "but [it] is no more Irish than the *Decameron*" (Kavanagh 41).

Nor was the audience of the Irish National Theatre Society exclusively that local, uncorrupted, and imaginative audience hypothesized by Yeats and Gregory only six years before. In May 1903, the company made its first weekend tour for performances of plays by Synge, Yeats, Gregory, and others at the Queen's Gate Hall in South Kensington, where, as would regularly happen over the next century, the performances received a generally more respectful and positive reception abroad than at home. In the same summer, Yeats's plays were performed in New York, and John Quinn, an American benefactor of the Irish National Theatre Society, was preparing a transatlantic audience for the poet and the company. At the same time, while the company was becoming international, there was considerable counterpressure toward cultural insularity. That summer (1903), Arthur Griffith founded *Sinn Féin* (Ourselves Alone), and by October Maud Gonne was pleading in the *United Irishman* for "freedom from the insidious and destructive tyranny of foreign influence" (qtd. in Foster, *W. B. Yeats* 299). Among the competing tensions at this point one can note the Irish National Theatre's disinclination to perform foreign masterpieces for Irish audiences and an inclination instead to perform Irish works for foreign audiences.

In 1904 the question of priorities and first obligations for a national theatre was being argued by Gonne and Griffith in the *United Irishman* and by Yeats in *Samhain*, the publication of the Irish National Dramatic Society that replaced *Beltaine*. Yeats's essay "First Principles" addressed this problem directly, although it is not usually cited in this context, or if it is, it is only cited as a testimony to Yeats's "leisured class" aspirations and fealty to his English benefactor (Frazier 105). Allowing for the personal context and for the additional complication of the developing argument over bylaws for the company, Yeats surely deserves credit for some genuine resistance, in "First Principles," to what Joseph Ryan called "the shadow of parochial expectations." He addressed the issue head-on:

> I have not asked my fellow-workers what they mean by the words National
> literature, but though I have no great love for definitions, I would define it
> in some such way as this: it is the work of writers who are molded by
> influences that are molding their country, and who write out of so deep a
> life that they are accepted there in the end. (*Explorations* 156)

Yeats did not deny the earlier imagination of Irish authenticity in "passing"
emblems of identity: "It is sometimes necessary to follow in practical matters some definition which one knows to have but a passing use. We, for
instance, have always confined ourselves to play upon Irish subjects, as if no
others could be National literature." Then, referring to Goldsmith, Sheridan, and Burke, Yeats presciently warned against a more reductive, parochial project: "If our organizations were satisfied to interpret a writer to his
own countrymen merely because he was of Irish birth, the organizations
would become a kind of trade union for the helping of Irishmen to catch the
ear of London publishers and managers" (*Explorations* 159). Such a trade
union, one could add, would not represent communal confidence so much
as communal defensiveness.

Some form of organization was necessary, of course, and in 1904, in
pursuit of the building that would become the Abbey Theatre, Yeats composed a memorandum for attorneys in which he sought the required license
for a theatre under English and Irish patent laws. Among the company's
past accomplishments he listed "discovering and training into articulate-
ness J. M. Synge, who I believe to be a great writer, the beginning it may be
of a European figure" (qtd. in Foster, *W. B. Yeats* 322). By summer, the
terms of the patent were circulated before legalization. Joseph Holloway,
who would design the Abbey Theatre in Mechanics Hall, recorded his
version of these terms in his diary on 20 August: "The patent shall empower
the patentee to exhibit plays in the Irish and English languages, written by
Irish writers on Irish subjects, or such dramatic works of foreign authors as
would tend to interest the public in the higher works of dramatic art" (42).
The final patent was issued on 22 December 1904, with Yeats's English
benefactor Annie E. F. Horniman listed as "memorialist" and Lady Gregory as patentee, because she alone of the three had an Irish address. The
memorialist guaranteed the lease on the building on Abbey Street, and the
patentee bore liability for scandalous or blasphemous offenses.

The key licensing passage of the patent was a better approximation of
Yeats's ideals in "First Principles" than the limitations paraphrased by Holloway, which were tilted a bit toward what he, and the larger local audience
of which he was a part, would have liked. In the patent, license is granted to
perform: "Interludes, Tragedies, Comedies, Plays in the Irish or English
language written by Irish writers or on Irish subjects and such dramatic
works of foreign authors as would tend to educate and interest the Irish
public in the higher works of dramatic art as may be selected by the Irish

National Theatre Society" (Kavanagh 216). The patent is a legal document rather than an institutional statement of artistic principles. Much of its legal apparatus is devoted to protecting the commercial interests of the other Dublin theatres: the Theatre Royal, the Gaiety Theatre, and the Queen's Theatre are all named in the document. But it is nevertheless striking that the patent allowed that Irish subjects might be treated by playwrights not of Irish birth ("written by Irish writers or on Irish subjects"), while Holloway's version did not ("written by Irish writers on Irish subjects"). Both versions allow for that distinct breed, "foreign authors," but the patent version is much closer than Holloway's to Yeats's conception in "First Principles," that Irish birth of authors was only a passing emblem and that "Irish subjects" might not be the only subjects of a national literature. The patent, in its chatty fashion, even suggested that on off nights the Irish National Theatre Society might, without exceeding its limits, offer its theatre to the Elizabethan Stage Society. The patent has been described before as being significant because of restrictions on politics or profitability, but it is even more remarkable for the breadth of its conception of a national theatre as a project much more extensive than the "trade union" for Irish literature that Yeats warned against. The conception of the patent is distinctly international and cosmopolitan, although one could not infer that from the national theatre that followed.

Holloway's version of the Abbey patent is worth quoting because it indicates what he, a member of the audience, thought was crucial to the enterprise of a national theatre for Ireland, and that was "Irish writers on Irish subjects." It is also worth recalling that such a mission is more singular than ordinary in national theatre projects. Yeats and colleagues took significant inspiration from Ole Bull and the foundation of a Norwegian National Theatre in Bergen in 1849. Norway offered a useful parallel to Ireland because it had endured cultural and linguistic colonization from Denmark and Sweden. But Ole Bull's project included no exclusivist statement of mission. Its opening performance, along with "native" dancing and music, included a performance of Mozart's Jupiter Symphony; later, that national theatre's principal asset, Ibsen, abandoned history and folk culture plays, severing his ties to the theatre project. Many national theatres were founded in the late nineteenth century in eastern Europe, including the National Theatre in Belgrade, which today boasts, in dauntless English, to Web browsers that "During the 129 years long history of the National Theatre in Belgrade almost all great European artists have had great performances on its stage and so a number of foreign companies."

At the time of the creation of the Irish National Theatre Society, most other comparable endeavors were directed, at least in word, more toward prestige and public access to the arts than toward the project in Dublin. The closest example from the same time was the long campaign to form the English National Theatre. In 1904 that project had taken the form of

Scheme and Estimates for a National Theatre by Harley Granville-Barker, William Archer, and others. Their plan was to provide England with a subsidized theatre as a model for "any of the great cities of Europe" because of its financial policies: "we regard economy . . . as the indispensable means to an artistic end." Their prospective repertory included Yeats's *The Countess Cathleen*. A second version of their plan in 1907 explicitly opened the repertory of playwrights. Barker's preface stated: "I should unhesitatingly . . . advocate the inclusion in our repertory list of every author whom we so carefully excluded four [*sic*] years ago: Ibsen, Hauptmann, d'Annunzio, Shaw and the rest" (Kennedy 192). By contrast, the Irish National Theatre cannot be said to have chosen *théâtre d'art*, for it had forsaken foreign masterpieces, nor *théâtre populaire*, because it was by patent both non-commercial and selective. Instead, and despite its fundamentally international inspirations, it was singular for the exclusively local conception of itself, and its subsequent history can be read in terms of the shifting tensions between "Irish writers" and "foreign authors."

What the Irish National Theatre Society did produce in the first two seasons was the well-known, narrow vein of works by the familiar names. Five playwrights constitute the whole of the first two seasons: Yeats, Gregory, Synge, Padraic Colum, and William Boyle. In the years immediately following, two kinds of exceptions formed the sole diversifications of the repertory. The first was appropriation of "foreign authors" for transformation into Abbey style. The best example is Molière, whose *The Doctor in Spite of Himself* was "translated" by Lady Gregory into Kiltartan and produced at the Abbey in Spring 1906. Terence De Vere White has described the need for the experiment and its failure: "Until the Gate was established there was no opportunity to see international theatre in Dublin. Lady Gregory had Kiltartanised Molière for the Abbey. I have read but never saw the result on stage. Nobody has ever asked for its disinterment" (Luke 28). The second kind of exception was, remarkably enough, production of a foreign masterpiece based on its own merits. Maeterlinck's *The Intern* was performed at the Abbey in Spring 1907, but nothing similar was attempted again until Hauptmann and Strindberg were staged in 1913. Immediately after that, the national theatre of international masterpieces was the national theatre that was not. Of the several avenues opened to the National Theatre Society by its patent, the focus on "Irish writers on Irish subjects" prevailed to the exclusion of all others.

A related endeavor was the Abbey Theatre Series of Plays, which began publication in 1905. The marketplace of publishing encouraged development of an even narrower and thus more distinctive product, and so the first fifteen volumes published through 1911 added to the past roll of five Abbey names only those of Lennox Robinson, T. C. Murray, and St. John Ervine. Marketplace incentives also narrowed the touring repertory, and the consistent success of the company on tour seemed to confirm the wisdom of

this evolving identity. Curiously omitted from most logs of Abbey productions, the tours were a fundamental part of the company's existence: the second season of 1905–1906 included three separate trips to English, Welsh,
and Scottish stages. Oddly, this put the National Theatre of Ireland in the
position of consorting with foreigners and misrepresenting its country,
rather in the fashion of those earlier playwrights whom Yeats and Gregory
had excused from the tradition.

There are many superb statements from this period of the benefits of
an Irish identity articulating itself on its own terms, and the ideal of Ireland's national theatre was a noble one. Sean O'Faoláin provided a very
evocative expression in defense of the parochial identity in his memoir *An
Irish Journey*. Like the National Theatre Society, O'Faoláin was nearly the
same age as the century, and in retrospect he described the heady sensation
of seemingly discovering a youthful identity in an upstart culture:

> Nobody who has not had this sensation of suddenly "belonging" some-
> where—of finding the lap of the lost mother—can understand what a
> release the discovery of Gaelic Ireland meant to modern Ireland. I know
> that not for years and years did I get free of this heavenly bond of an
> ancient, lyrical, permanent, continuous, immemorial self, symbolized by
> the lonely mountains, the virginal lakes, the traditional language, the sim-
> ple, certain, uncomplex modes of life, that world of the lost childhood of
> my race where I, too, became for a while eternally young. (136)

O'Faoláin testifies to some of the passion inherent in the effort to articulate
a local agenda, and that effort was not without intellect or art. There were
extreme isolationists, like D. P. Moran, whose *The Philosophy of Irish Ireland*
came out a year after the Abbey opened, but one can cite many others, like
Maud Gonne, who objected to the tyranny of foreign influences without
calling for absolute abolition of them. And one can cite the many alternatives to the national theatre in the theatrical life of Dublin, including many,
like the Dublin Drama League in 1919 or the first season of the Gate
Theatre in the Abbey's Peacock space in 1928, which to a large extent owed
their existence and degrees of success to the Abbey's self-imposed limitations and creation of anti-Abbey opportunities. However, O'Faoláin, of
course, did grow up, and his personal project evolved into an ardent critique, from within Dublin, of reactionary parochialism. Maude Gonne, also
Maude Gonne Millevoye, was herself part of the foreign influence on Ireland. And anti-Abbey companies lacked the subsidies of the Irish National
Theatre Society. Hence the choice to pursue in a national theatre an internal aesthetic despite the fact of international practice was of consequence
and was in complicity with other cultural developments more to the liking
of the D. P. Morans of the period. With reference to that other performing
art, music, Harry White has bluntly described the consequence with these

words: "Irish cultural history produced and then rejected the literary revival in favor of a Catholic-nationalist synthesis" (*The Keeper's Recital* 96).

The defining moments for the Irish national theatre came long before the period when the disadvantages of the Abbey's artistic isolationism and exclusivism were apparent enough to inspire a counter-revival, and these moments fundamentally concerned internationalism or reaction against it. In December 1906, in the midst of the second Abbey season, Yeats was dictating another memorandum to Lady Gregory on the future of the Irish National Theatre Society. Its future, he thought, could not rely "indefinitely on peasant drama." Instead, its future required "foreign masterpieces," including foreign companies and actors, and so the project, "if it is to do the work of a National Theatre [must] be prepared to perform[,] even if others can perform them better[,] representative plays of all great schools" (qtd. in Foster, *W. B. Yeats* 354). A week later Yeats told a meeting of the National Literary Society that "the end . . . would be creation of a theatre in Dublin like the municipal theatres in Germany where all plays could be produced" (qtd. in Holloway 79). By 1911, when the National Theatre Society patent was renewed, the defining language on its educational mission instead retracted to "furtherance in Ireland of Irish dramatic art" (qtd. in Kavanagh 201).

Thus, there is a key contradiction in the founding years of the Irish National Theatre Society between goals and practices: on the one hand, furtherance in Ireland of Irish dramatic art, and on the other, the first American tour, also in 1911, as well as the opening, in 1912, of two plays, T. C. Murray's *Maurice Hart* and Lady Gregory's *The Bogey Man*, in London at the Court Theatre. Irish writers and Irish subjects prevailed, but often for foreign audiences, and playing to foreign audiences narrowed the sense of Irish subjects that the theatre could communicate. The interest of this contradiction is not a revelation of hypocrisy or mendacity. Rather, the interest is that in the founding years of modern Irish drama, especially when viewed through theatrical practice rather than theatrical works — and especially from the perspective obtained a century later — internationalism and denial of it were fundamental to the national theatre project. In practice the Irish national theatre is not, as the late Robert Hogan suggested some time ago, when its history was shorter, "basically an ingrown and an inward-looking movement" (Luke 14). From the day when Yeats and Lady Gregory set down their prospectus, Irish national theatre seemed ingrown but was in fact a maze of international debts and ambitions.

From the perspective gained a century later, charting whether and how those debts and ambitions are or are not acknowledged helps us understand modern Irish drama in more inclusive ways than have prevailed, and other essays in this volume similarly seek to appreciate the contradictions and complexity of Irish dramatic tradition. The general trend certainly was toward artistic parochialism, even after post–World War I intellectual movements turned to internationalism and even after the creation of the Irish Free State afforded some opportunity for what Joseph Ryan called "communal confidence." But more attention to the contrary pressure will help characterize the Irish national theatre: for example, by reference to those Abbey Theatre rejections: Shaw's *John Bull's Other Island*, Joyce's *Exiles*, and O'Casey's *The Silver Tassie*. A narrative including the international context would bring into the foreground of the history of Irish drama instances such as a symposium at the Gate Theatre in 1932 on the question "Should Theatre be International?" In this context, Ernest Blythe's later administration of the national theatre would appear in relation to Irish public policies, such as neutrality in World War II. Analysis on themes of internationalism rather than of nationalism would also help account for the Irish playwrights of the 1960s and their "revolutionary" response, as Christopher Murray has described it, to the "hemorrhage of emigration" (*Twentieth-Century Irish Drama* 165) or to the distinctions between the "Abbey" and the "non-Abbey" works of Brian Friel, Tom Murphy, and others. Analysis along these lines would also require an account of the internationalization of the Field Day Company in the 1980s and the Druid Theatre Company in the 1990s.

Such a narrative, finally, would lead to the contemporary moment of Martin McDonagh and colleagues. The original Yeats–Gregory prospectus had the effect of writing Boucicault and Sheridan out of the history of the Irish national theatre for their cosmopolitan impurities, but in the winter of 1998–1999, the Abbey produced *The Rivals* between revival and re-revival of *The Colleen Bawn*. The Dublin Theatre Festival has evolved, like the Wexford Opera Festival, by offering an international repertory. At the end of the century, the Royal Court Theatre in London launched new Irish work and playwrights such as Conor McPherson, Sebastian Barry, Billy Roche, and Tom Mac Intyre, all of whom are presumably contributing to Ireland's national dramatic literature. None of this prophesies the obsolescence of that well-known genre of "Irish drama" or the administrative structure of the Irish National Theatre Society. The national theatre that *was not* was the one that could successfully occlude its international context, and the national theatre that is *now* is the one that embraces it. That revelation of history — "the whole venture will be history any way," as Yeats wrote at its outset — gives Irish drama a more complicated and considerably more provocative tradition than was imagined a century ago.

—2—

The Alternative Aesthetic:
The Theatre of Ireland's Urban Plays

NELSON Ó CEALLAIGH RITSCHEL

In March 1909, W. B. Yeats attended productions at the Abbey's rival, the
Theatre of Ireland, which, on this occasion, was playing in Dublin's Ro-
tunda Hall. This rival theatre was formed in 1906 after Yeats profession-
alized the Irish National Theatre Society with payments for its actors.
Fearing that payments from an English sponsor, namely Annie Horniman,
might interfere with the Theatre's nationalist goals, some of the Abbey's
actors left the company. The most significant was Máire Nic Shiubhlaigh,
who had triumphed as the first Nora in Synge's *In the Shadow of the Glen*.
However, there may have been more to this secession. Once these actors
left the Abbey, they soon joined forces with Edward Martyn, who since
1902 had been a vocal opponent of the rural-based dramas that Yeats offered and who had himself been experimenting with what might be called
an alternative aesthetic. In 1907 the Theatre of Ireland was joined by Fred
and Jack Morrow, recent defectors from the company discussed in the next
essay by Laura E. Lyons, the Ulster Literary Theatre, where they had
specifically staged and designed non-rural plays like Lewis Purcell's *The
Reformers*.[1] By 1909, when Yeats attended the Theatre of Ireland, not only
was the company established, but so was the urban aesthetic.

While at the rival Theatre, Yeats spoke to a man sitting beside him.
Recognizing Yeats, this gentleman reported that he too had been to the
Abbey and had specifically enjoyed plays like W. F. Casey's non-rural *The
Suburban Groove*, which the Abbey had revived two days earlier. Casey's first
Abbey play, *The Man Who Missed the Tide*, premiered in 1908, and, accord-
ing to Máire Nic Shiubhlaigh, "is worth [. . .] mention [. . .] because it was

the first piece given in the Abbey Theatre which had a Dublin setting [. . .]. For the first time Dubliners were able to see themselves on the [Abbey] stage, and they took happily to the idea" (93). The audience member next to Yeats added that he disliked the Abbey's rural plays, primarily because of their dependency on Irish history and/or mythology. Pressed by Yeats, the gentleman explained that he did not understand such works and—more importantly—that knowledge of Irish history and mythology was "dying out amongst" the peasantry (*The Death of Synge* 505). Thus, ironically, Yeats was facing a growing preference for the urban aesthetic—an aesthetic that he had made possible. This alternative aesthetic is the subject of this essay.

When *Kathleen Ni Houlihan* premiered in April 1902 with the Fay actors, Yeats knew that he, with Lady Gregory, had created not only a truly native Irish theatre but also a distinctly Irish theatrical aesthetic to serve an Irish cultural and political agenda. But Yeats's Ireland, based on a rural ideal, was not necessarily shared by all nationalists—even in 1902. Besides, most of the Dubliners who participated in the Irish theatre movement between 1902 and 1916 had little direct experience with rural Ireland. Obviously, Lady Gregory, with her Coole Park estate, was in the extreme minority, but few could have afforded to explore Aran, Galway, Mayo, and Kerry, as did Synge, and even less enjoyed a Connemara cottage, such as Pearse's in Rosmuc, or benefited, as did Yeats, from either childhood summers on the Sligo coast or Gregory's direct rurally minded influence and assistance. Indeed, the experiences of the majority of the Irish theatre movement's participants were almost completely confined to Dublin, Belfast, or Cork.

One such Dubliner was Frederick Ryan, who, within months of *Kathleen Ni Houlihan*'s premiere, challenged Yeats's rural aesthetic with his only play, *The Laying of the Foundations*. It premiered in October as part of the Irish National Theatre Society's 1902 Samhain presentations—when the Society was still utilizing close to a democratic process for play selection and desperately needed new scripts. The play is set in Dublin, with act II transpiring specifically in Michael O'Loskin's office. Michael is the son of a wealthy publican, who, unbeknownst to Michael, arranged with his business partner, City Alderman Farrelly, to have Michael appointed city architect.[2] Essentially, the position's duties involve the overseeing of city construction projects and inspection of existing buildings. Because this was a patronage appointment, Michael learns that his father and Farrelly expect him to look the other way regarding their projects. Michael relates that during an inspection he discovered that Farrelly's construction firm is building a new city asylum with a concrete foundation of only four feet, while the approved plans call for an eight-foot foundation. The audience further learns that Michael is planning to condemn tenement houses that Farrelly owns with Michael's father.

The young city architect discovers that his father is Farrelly's partner in the tenement houses, which are described as being "unfit for beasts" (Frederick Ryan 25). Michael meets with a labor leader named Nolan, who is most likely based on a young James Connolly, who reveals that Farrelly's construction company is the worst employer in the city, yet it receives lucrative city contracts — like the asylum — because of Farrelly's position as city alderman. Also, the iron to be used in the asylum project is from Farrelly's own iron foundry, where workers' wages are being cut and where workers' jobs are threatened by foreign labor. Thus informed, Michael confronts his father about Farrelly, labeling him "a swindler, a corrupter, a liar. One who uses his public position to rob the city he is supposed to guard" (Ryan 33). Michael is further outraged by Farrelly's attempt to bribe him. The play climaxes when Michael tells Farrelly that he will remain as city architect and fight Farrelly's corruption. Michael defiantly proclaims: "I do not compromise. I do not sell myself." Farrelly replies, "Then let it be war!" The play closes on Michael's words: "The city of the future demands it. It can be nothing else but war" (Ryan 37).

Ryan, following Yeats's example with *Kathleen Ni Houlihan*'s character Michael Gillane, presents an ideal nationalist image/hero, the noble Celt in the form of Michael O'Loskin. At personal and professional risk, O'Loskin gallantly takes up the fight against the selfish greed of Farrelly and his own parents, a greed which threatens the lives of many Dubliners. The intended nationalist inspiration of Michael's stand was not lost on Arthur Griffith's radical paper, *The United Irishman*, which noted: "That is enough; we want no more. He has taken his line, he will compromise nothing. If he succeed in defeating his adversaries, well; if he fail, if he be defeated, disgraced, dismissed, well also; for we know that he will go down fighting, with [. . .] his soul unconquered" (Seumar 1). At the time of *Kathleen Ni Houlihan*'s premiere, Yeats described his play's theme as follows: "the perpetual struggle of the cause of Ireland . . . against private hopes and dreams" ("Mr. Yeats' New Play" 5). In that vein, Ryan's O'Loskin makes the same choice as Yeats's Michael Gillane — of putting his duty to public Ireland before his personal concerns. Yet O'Loskin does it without a rural environment and without inspiration from a mythological icon like Kathleen Ni Houlihan; the noble Celt has been removed to Ryan's Dublin. Perhaps sensing the play's departure from Yeats's rural allegory, contemporary critic Stephen Gwynn described the significance of the premiere of *The Laying of the Foundations* as "a new force let loose in Ireland" (qtd. in Welch, *Oxford Companion* 504).

It is well known that Yeats, Gregory, Synge, and Fitzmaurice used a language (prose, or in Yeats's case, verse) based on Irish Gaelic to help create the environments of their rurally based plays. They would have argued that such a stage language, complete with Gaelic idioms, also worked to dignify the Irish image. However, not all of Yeats's fellow Dublin nationalists believed in the validity or relevance of this rural dialogue. Edward

Martyn, for example, who had personal ties to County Galway, believed "that nobody in Ireland ever spoke like" the characters of Gregory and Synge (qtd. in Courtney 101). In fact, in 1911 Frederick Ryan publicly argued that the Abbey's rural plays, with their affected language, had "little or no relation to the life of the country as a whole" (qtd. in Hogan, Burnham, and Poteet 145). For Ryan, such plays were too remote; he felt that plays of the Irish Theatre Movement needed to speak more directly to Dublin nationalists. Toward this end, Ryan and the dramatists who followed his example attempted to create a dramatic setting that reflected their urban existences, including everyday Dublin language.

Michael O'Loskin's last line, however awkwardly phrased, demonstrates this aspiration: "The city of the future demands it. It can be nothing else but war." Common English would probably use fewer words, like "the future demands it. Let it be war." Actually, this was the original phrasing that Ryan wrote, but according to Frank Fay's surviving prompt book for the play's premiere, the line was altered to the above phrasing (F. Fay's *The Laying of the Foundations* Prompt book 45). Perhaps the change indicates an effort to instill in the line, although it is spoken in English, a hint of Irish. This same type of dialogue is found in Joyce's *Dubliners*. In "The Dead," for instance, when Miss Ivors asks Gabriel, "And why do you go to France and Belgium [. . .] instead of visiting your own land?" (189), Joyce's dialogue is close to common English but retains some of the wordiness of native Irish. Declan Kiberd, on occasion, has noted that even "Swift, who was probably tended by an Irish-speaking nursemaid, noted with interest the spread of Gaelic [. . .] phrases" and syntax patterns into his English-dominated Dublin ("Irish Literature and Irish History" 297). The everyday Dublin dialogue of Ryan's day, which was Joyce's day as well, was close to English English but bore some Irish influence. The point, however, is not necessarily that Ryan and his fellow urban aesthetic playwrights consciously wrote an English dialogue with a slight Irish influence but rather that these writers used their own everyday urban language, which was bound to be influenced by native Irish and heavily influenced by the British presence in the main urban areas since the days of the Pale. The speech familiar to urban nationalists was, thus, an integral part of the urban aesthetic, an alternative way to portray dignity in the Irish image. Ryan's O'Loskin becomes the ideal courageous and unselfish nationalist hero in part through his use of everyday Dublin language.

Early disenchantment with the emerging rural orientation that Yeats was trying to force onto the Irish National Theatre Society may have been represented by the Players' Club, formed by Edward Martyn and George Moore in 1903. Their first productions, staged by Moore, included a revival of Martyn's *The Heather Field* and Ibsen's *A Doll House*. A number of National Theatre Society actors appeared in these productions, prompting Yeats to note, "I daresay this company may attract away a few of our actors.

[...] [And] neither Martyn nor Moore would ever have been satisfied with our methods" (*The Collected Letters of W. B. Yeats* 390). We can surmise that Martyn's dissatisfaction was flavored by a desire for an Irish drama that was not based on a perception of rural Ireland, as evident by his later involvement with the Theatre of Ireland (1906–1912) and the Irish Theatre Company (1914–1920). Both of these theatres staged many urban plays (but none of Ibsen's works). Moore's 1903 dissatisfaction with Yeats's rural inclination was more likely a sole result of his desire for an Ibsen-based drama in Ireland (Martyn too was influenced by Ibsen, but not to the same extent). Yet while Moore's Ibsen-minded work in the Irish Literary Theatre (1899–1901), namely his input into Martyn's *The Heather Field*, his revision of Martyn's *The Tale of the Town* into *The Bending of the Bough*, and his collaboration with Yeats on *Diarmuid and Grania*, may have offered some precedent for a drama that was not rurally based, the urban aesthetic dramatists ultimately owed more to Yeats. This is seen in the urban play's consistent effort to present self-sacrificing characters like Ryan's Michael O'Loskin, essentially the same "type" as *Kathleen Ni Houlihan*'s Michael Gillane — or, for that matter, as *The Countess Cathleen*'s title character. There was no room in early Irish theatre's urban or rural aesthetic plays for Ibsen-type characters suffering with personal dilemmas. It was a theatre that primarily attempted to offer an elevated Irish model rather than to portray people as they were.

Perhaps the most accomplished urban aesthetic play of the Irish Theatre Movement was Seumas O'Kelly's *The Shuiler's Child*, produced in 1909 by the Theatre of Ireland (this theatre's highest artistic achievement). At first glance one might erroneously conclude that this play is a rural one. After all, one of the play's characters, Andy O'Hea, is listed as a farmer, and there is a reference in the text to his having some fields. However, the O'Hea family lives in the County Galway town of Kilbeg, and their neighbor Sarah Finnessy lives close enough to be able to drop in frequently and can view activities in the O'Hea's home, where the play is set, from her own kitchen. This is an urban phenomenon rather than a rural one, considering the characteristic isolation of rural Ireland. Characters Tim O'Holloran and Cecilia Cecilia are officers representing parts of the municipal government.

The play's premise is that characters Nannie and Andy O'Hea have recently adopted an abandoned child from the local workhouse; the child is named Phil. Moll Woods, the "Shuiler" and the boy's mother, arrives at the O'Hea's home. She travels door-to-door singing songs, hoping to receive handouts. She is surprised to see Phil, thinking he was still in the workhouse. Afraid that Moll wants Phil back, Nannie tries to befriend the visitor. Moll explains that she had married a "wild" man who squandered "the little place my father left me" (O'Kelly 12). With no money or home, she and her child entered the workhouse, where the authorities humiliated her by placing her with prostitutes. Found to be insubordinate, she was sent briefly to prison. The government inspector, Cecilia Cecilia, appears with the purpose of inspecting the living conditions of the boarded child. She takes personal offense to Nannie's every effort to argue that her home is good for Phil. Cecilia proclaims that the child would be better off with the people "up on the hills. . . . He wants plenty of bracing air" (O'Kelly 16). The shuiler joins in, arguing that such a life for her son would be cruel. The inspector finds Nannie to have a violent disposition and feels the natural mother's presence to be inappropriate. Moll attacks the inspector, obviously sealing the report.

Act II opens on the following day. It is explained that Moll has returned to the workhouse, demanded the return of her son, and then left with him. Nannie grows distraught, asking what kind of life Phil will have on the road.

> Wandering in wind and rain, maybe in the cold of winter with no roof to his head. What heart will Moll Woods have for him when she brings him to strange places? . . . What regard will rough wild people have for him? (O'Kelly 35)

The shuiler returns with Phil, saying that she knew the inspector would recommend Phil to the mountain people; therefore, she returned to the workhouse to reclaim her child. After this, she was free to give him legally to the O'Heas, knowing that they will provide a better home. When all seems fine, the Royal Irish Constabulary arrive outside with a warrant for Moll's arrest. The workhouse master swore evidence against Moll for abandoning Phil the first time, which comes into effect now that she no longer has the child. Allowing Phil to remain with the O'Heas, the shuiler exits to be arrested — having sacrificed everything for her son.

One might still be tempted to think of *The Shuiler's Child* as a rural aesthetic play. After all, a shuiler (from the Irish) means a wanderer. Moll is first seen living on the road, going from door to door, singing ballads for food. One might conclude that she is following Antoine Raftery's rural bardic tradition of the early nineteenth century, like the tramp in Synge's *In the Shadow of the Glen*. But there are significant differences. Upon initially hearing Moll singing a ballad offstage as she approaches the house, Nannie replies, "That poor creature has not much heart for a song" (O'Kelly 10). Obviously, such could never have been said of Raftery by the rural aesthetic supporters, nor can it be said of Synge's tramp. The latter is full of heart and commitment when he tells Nora of the wonderful life to be experienced under the Irish sky, beautifully painting images of the landscape with his words. Nora agrees to go with him, replying, "you've a fine bit of talk" (*In the Shadow of the Glen* 43). In short, life on the road, close to the land, is celebrated and honored by Synge's tramp. Not so in *The Shuiler's Child*. In act I, Nannie says, "The roads are the last place that would suit the like of

Phil. A body would be in constant dread to have him going from one place to another" (O'Kelly 12). Moll concurs:

> There is many a thing for a woman to be in dread of on the roads. I met a dark man on a bog road in Sligo once. The way he looked at me took the breath out of my body. I passed houses that day where there was good food, for the dread of him was upon me till I came to a town. (O'Kelly 12)

Clearly Moll's account is not the idealized life that Synge's tramp describes to Nora, one in which she will "be hearing the herons crying out over the black lakes, and [. . .] the grouse and owls with them, and the larks and the big thrushes when the days are warm" (*In the Shadow of the Glen* 43).

Perhaps revealing O'Kelly's subtle touch and sense of humor, it is in rural Sligo that Moll recalls the terror of being on the road. Sligo is where Yeats spent his childhood summers and first came to appreciate the rural west. Some of his earliest rural-inspired poetry, such as "The Lake Isle of Innisfree," is set in Sligo. Significantly, Moll says she kept moving until she came to a town after seeing the frightening, mysterious man in Sligo. It is an urban sensibility, not a rurally inspired one, that has her seeking shelter in a town rather than in the rural landscape. This is the opposite of the situation in *In the Shadow of the Glen*, in which the Connacht tramp leads Nora to her salvation in an idealized rural Ireland. And interestingly, the shuiler describes the strange man she encountered in Sligo as "dark," the same description that contemporaries of Yeats have used for him (Nic Shiubhlaigh 15). This passage, then, is most likely a jab at both Yeats and his rural aesthetic — his Sligo connection was well known.

In *The Shuiler's Child*, it is extremely clear that Moll has taken to the road because she has no choice. She repeatedly speaks of losing her pride and hope among the prostitutes in the workhouse and then in prison. Quite distraught, she tells Andy O'Hea that no one would take her in, that "I have nothing before me but the long roads" (O'Kelly 39). Life on the road is her only course. By contrast, in *In the Shadow of the Glen*, there is no sense that the tramp has taken to the roads because he has no choice. He is far from being distraught over such a life; to him, life under the open sky represents spiritual freedom. To Moll, it represents spiritual imprisonment. She asks, "What is there before a woman that got gaol but the roads of Ireland?" (O'Kelly 12). O'Kelly's portrayal of the shuiler reflects the Irish urban view that those wandering on Ireland's rural roads are fallen people, not the idealized folk of the rural aesthetic. In his criticism of *In the Shadow of the Glen*, Arthur Griffith proclaimed (in *The United Irishman*) that the Irish woman in a loveless marriage "lives in bitterness — sometimes she dies of a broken heart — but she does not go away with the Tramp" ("All Ireland" 1). This urban perspective that Irish wanderers are fallen rather than non-colonized free spirits is in the tradition of Jonathan Swift's "A Modest Proposal" (1729). In this early urban nationalist satirical pamphlet, Swift speaks of the "beggars who crowd these *Streets*, the roads" of rural Ireland (Swift 389, emphasis in original). His target is the government, which he sees as responsible for turning so many of the native Irish into destitute beggars and thieves. The point is that the urbanist, Dublin Swift saw the Irish who had taken to the country roads as a fallen people. In this light, he would have viewed a wandering bard like Raftery — icon to Yeats, Gregory, and Synge — as a degraded beggar.

This preference for the urban or urbanized over the rural is found throughout O'Kelly's play. It is the threat of the inspector to remove Phil and place him with the extremely rural mountain people that leads Moll to re-enter the workhouse to reclaim Phil and eventually give him to the O'Heas. When she first hears of this threat, she replies that being with such people would be tantamount to living "among goats and half-starved people" (O'Kelly 16). Later she says, "To send a child like him up to mountainy people! You might as well put a young linnet in the nest of an eagle" (O'Kelly 38). This view of rural people is greatly removed from the idealized Celt of the rural plays. Moll gives Phil to the town O'Heas rather than keeping him herself on the roads of Connacht or giving him to the mountain folk. Again, this decision is uncharacteristic of the rural aesthetic.

Moll's decision to secure a comfortable home for Phil makes her a model of self-sacrifice in the vein of Ryan's Michael O'Loskin or Yeats's Michael Gillane. It is the representative of the British government that seeks to remove Phil from the O'Heas and place him among dangerous mountain dwellers. This is the same government whose administrators had placed Moll with prostitutes in the workhouse and who later imprisoned her, leading her to alcoholism. It is the same vindictive, unjust, and petty government that tries to destroy her at play's end by prosecuting her for originally leaving Phil in the workhouse, even after she has placed the child in a loving home. Moll's own sense of being persecuted by the English is evident when she asks the inspector, "Did you ever hear of the wild hare being hunted and lost to her young?" (O'Kelly 17). O'Kelly presents a woman who is standing and acting against British interference in Ireland, and considering the context of Irish theatre prior to 1916, the shuiler becomes symbolic of nationalist womanhood (its plight under English rule) as she gives herself to save her son, who symbolizes Ireland's future.

Like all plays of the Irish Theatre Movement of 1899–1916, *The Shuiler's Child* relies on language to create a realistic Irish environment. In his introduction to the 1971 De Paul University edition of the play (based solely on the 1909 Maunsel edition), George Brandon Saul writes that the play's "dialogue is [. . .] Irish without, for the most part, any yielding to 'Kiltartan' extravagance" (3). In other words, the language is Irish in character but is decidedly not the heightened stage language of the rural aesthetic, as exemplified in Gregory's plays. When Synge's tramp in *In the Shadow of the Glen* first calls on the Burke house, he says "Good evening to you, lady of the house" (34). Upon first calling on the O'Hea house, the shuiler of O'Kelly's play says only, "Something for the poor singer" (10). Granted, the two characters are quite different — one troubled, the other possessing a great freedom — but the examples from each demonstrate the abundance of words in a rural play and the urban economy of O'Kelly's. Throughout Synge's play, the tramp constantly addresses Nora as "lady of the house." He works the phrase into almost every speech, exhibiting the overuse of, and emphasis on, nouns as found in Irish-Gaelic speech.

By contrast, the characters in O'Kelly's play rarely address those to whom they are speaking by constantly repeating either their name or an identifying phrase. However, when Nannie speaks of O'Halloran to another when the former is not present, she calls him by his full name, Tim O'Halloran. This supports Saul's statement that the play's language, although not Kiltartan, is Irish in character. At one point the shuiler states, "I might well say I have hardly a boot on my foot, but I'd sooner walk the roads of Ireland barefoot than try their workhouse again" (O'Kelly 13). Rural prose might phrase this as, "Might well I say, Mrs. O'Hea, that I have hardly a boot on my foot, but I'd sooner myself be walking the long and the crooked roads of Ireland than try their workhouse again." Eight words are added, including one noun and one pronoun. Common English would be far more efficient: "Although I have hardly a boot, I'd sooner walk Ireland barefoot than return to their workhouse." Thus, like Ryan in *The Laying of the Foundations*, O'Kelly uses a stage language that is more economical than the prose of the rural plays, yet wordier than idiomatic English.

Turning again to Joyce's *Dubliners*, this time to "Araby," we see what was characteristic Dublin vernacular at roughly the time of the play's premiere. In one moment a character speaks the following: "The people are in bed and after their first sleep now" (33). The line, like O'Kelly's language in his play, is more economical than Synge's or Gregory's prose, yet it is wordy when compared to standard English. The latter might say, "People are in bed trying to sleep." The same can be found in the Dublin short story "Hunger" (1918), by James Stephens, who was in the original cast of *The Shuiler's Child*. The protagonist says to her husband, "And send us what you can spare. Send something this week if you can" (110). Common English would certainly at least eliminate the first sentence. Again, my inference is that the language used by O'Kelly — and Joyce and Stephens — reflects English influence while retaining some influence from the Irish, and also resides somewhere between conventional English and the rural aesthetic's prose. Being closer to English than Synge's prose, the language of Ryan's and O'Kelly's urban plays appropriately displays the strong influence that the British had on Dublin speech. Such language helped create an Irish atmosphere, with which urban aesthetic supporters were familiar.

The Shuiler's Child's use of an Irish urban language and its exceedingly strong urban sensibilities identify this play as an urban aesthetic work.

Indeed, after *The Laying of the Foundations*, it is perhaps the earliest extant play expressing such strong urban sensibilities. And in many ways it is actually more urbanized than Ryan's play, because it casts suspicion upon the Irish wanderers. O'Kelly's portrayal of life on the open road as being frightening and unromantic, along with his portrayal of rural people as being rough, half-starved mountain dwellers, encouraged some urban nationalists to envision a modern Ireland that would be more urban than rural. For these urban nationalists, the rural Ireland that Yeats, Synge, and their followers celebrated was too removed from their experiences. In effect, they were challenging the rural sentiment expressed by Synge in March 1907, when he argued that for the present, Irish drama needed to be based on the rural, not the urban — "You cannot gather grapes off chimney pots" ("Historical or Peasant Drama" 149).

Máire Nic Shiubhlaigh, who portrayed Moll in the premiere, recorded that *The Shuiler's Child* was "one of the most memorable Irish plays produced in Dublin during these years [. . .] and definitely placed O'Kelly in the front ranks of the younger Irish dramatists" (Nic Shiubhlaigh 97–98). The paper *Sinn Féin* felt that the premiere brought "a feeling of enthusiasm about the Society [Theatre of Ireland], a sense of adventure and token of that devotion to ideal aims, which springs from unjaded vitality" (K, "Theatre of Ireland" 1). Another *Sinn Féin* article, authored by the nationalist poet Susan Mitchell, chastised Yeats as "a fool" for letting Nic Shiubhlaigh leave the Abbey (1). Indeed, the play had become a vehicle for Nic Shiubhlaigh, who excelled in plays of both aesthetics, being strongly associated with roles from each. Some of *The Shuiler's Child*'s other original cast members are also worth noting; in addition to the above-mentioned James Stephens, Constance Markievicz played the government inspector.

The Theatre of Ireland revived *The Shuiler's Child* months later, in November 1909, demonstrating its success with its audience. Following a litany of error-filled productions, O'Kelly's play was the Theatre's first quality presentation. Susan Mitchell commented that "they are getting into the stride now," and "Mise," also in *Sinn Féin*, added, the Theatre "has produced its best play, and produced it well" (Mise 1; Mitchell 1). Perhaps this was due to Fred Morrow's work with the company, but was there a correlation between this "stride" and the Theatre's finally staging an effective urban aesthetic play? Earlier bills contained revivals of some rural plays, such as Douglas Hyde's *Casadh an tSúgáin* and AE's (George Russell's) *Deirdre*. Clearly O'Kelly was the first playwright totally of the company's own, and their success with *The Shuiler's Child* might suggest that both the company's sensibilities and talents were aligned with the urban aesthetic. Interestingly, the Theatre of Ireland did not produce political plays of an agit-prop nature, which one might have expected if its split from the Abbey is understood to originate solely in politics. Instead, the Theatre's plays were, like the Abbey's, political in that they pursued cultural nationalism. The secession had more to do with the way nationalism, or the new Ireland, was to be represented — in other words, it was a question of aesthetics.

The urban aesthetic continued to dominate the Theatre of Ireland until the enterprise faded in 1912. In its wake came the Irish Theatre Company, organized in 1914 by Thomas MacDonagh, Joseph Plunkett, and Edward Martyn. Because Martyn still adamantly believed that the Abbey's rural plays could only be "partially representative of Ireland" (qtd. in Feeney, *Drama in Hardwicke Street* 33), this theatre offered significant urban plays, like MacDonagh's *Pagans* (in 1915). *Pagans*'s subtitle, "A Modern Play in Two Conversations," proves appropriate. The action is set in the sitting room of Frances and John Fitzmaurice's Dublin home on "a spring day a year or two ago," or in other words, during 1913 or 1914 (MacDonagh 30). The play starts out as an exploration of marriage and romantic relationships. Not coincidentally, the day is also the fifth anniversary of Frances and John's wedding, which is also the third anniversary of their separation and of John's departure from Dublin. Frances continues to lament the state of her marriage and is visited by an artist, Helen Noble, who returned from Paris the evening before. The day is also the fifth anniversary of Helen's self-exile from Dublin. She left on the day of the Fitzmaurice wedding, as she too had been in love with John. While in Paris, she ran into John twice at the Louvre as he stared at the *Victory of Samothrace*. On both occasions she thought she was undetected. The last incident had occurred three days prior and had prompted her to flee Paris.

During their discussion, Helen expresses her belief that marriage should be "the free interplay of like-minded persons" (Feeney, "Introduction" 10). She believes that individuals in a marriage should be only themselves, hence the need for similar people. Frances, on the other hand, maintains that "the individuality must make concessions to the corporate state of marriage" (Feeney, "Introduction" 10). She feels that opposites can attract and that one should make sacrifices and change one's ways for a romantic partner. Since John is a writer who is more at home in literary circles, he was out of place among Frances's upper middle-class socialite world. Helen believes he would have been more compatible in her artistic environment. The conversation gives both women an opportunity to discuss why they lost John, who left Frances to find himself.

John returns in the second part of the play, and is ushered into the room moments after Helen exits. Frances is excited, given that this is their anniversary. However, his return has less to do with the anniversary than with his coincidental sighting of Helen studying the *Victory* sculpture, followed by her fleeing the museum. Realizing that he had hurt Helen by marrying Frances, he felt compelled to return to Dublin. John and Frances seem reconciled when a friend of Frances calls at the door. Exiting to meet with her, John is left alone with the maid, Sarah, with whom he has a friendly atypical master–servant conversation.[3] Frances returns and realizes from this conversation and from her friend's visit that John does not fit into her world. She tells him so. He in turn reveals that he is giving up mere writing: "I shall do better than write," he says. He informs her that he is embracing "the great opportunity" to lead the fight to free Ireland (MacDonagh 53).

In his biography of MacDonagh, Johann Norstedt writes of this play that its "ending on the national note is the play's fault—it has not been anticipated in any way, and it negates any dramatic effect Frances' attainment of knowledge might have had" (130). Although not necessarily condemning the play, William Feeney notes that MacDonagh has provided little foreshadowing for this ending ("Introduction" 10). Such reactions demonstrate an ignorance or a lack of consideration of the contemporary conditions of reception. In *Drama in Hardwicke Street*, Feeney accurately states that the play's two main women are symbols: Helen symbolizes Dublin's artistic life and Frances, Dublin's conventional high society (*Drama in Hardwicke Street* 85). Yet in the context of the Irish Theatre Movement of 1899–1916, specifically about 1915, Feeney's observations can be taken further: the two women represent two types of private, individual life. Seeing that neither woman (neither society life nor the artistic life) helped him to fulfill his identity, John ultimately devotes himself to the public life of nationalist Ireland—just as Yeats's Michael Gillane does in *Kathleen Ni Houlihan*. Given the context in which the play was written and performed, John Fitzmaurice's decision could not possibly have been unexpected by its initial audience—an audience that frequently included members of the Theatre who were dressed in their nationalist Volunteer uniforms.[4] Feeney points out that for most of the play, MacDonagh seems to be drawing on an Ibsenite convention of "having unwomanly women and unmanly men" (*Drama in Hardwicke Street* 85). The idea of an unmanly man standing up and finally demonstrating his "manhood" at the play's resolution is consistent with the Irish Theatre Movement's universal theme of a dormant Irish manhood, or Irish spirit (as in *The Shuiler's Child*), awakening into a nationalist role model. The Irish reviewer Michael Crevequer recalled, six years after seeing *Pagans*'s premiere, that as a young man, having exited the Theatre

into the lamplit April evening we felt impelled to run down the crowded length of O'Connell Street talking as we ran, dodging round the pedestrians and meeting again to continue our conversation, and finally reaching our rooms in a fever to prolong till morning the festive ecstasy Pagans had aroused among our half-formulated theories on a thousand subjects. (Qtd. in Feeney, *Drama in Hardwicke Street* 86–87)

This play clearly spoke to its urban audience. Characteristically, Fitzmaurice makes his choice in reaction to the circumstances of his life. The setting is Dublin rather than rural Connacht, and the language is not the poetic prose of the rural aesthetic. *Pagans* also assaults the non-political or apathetic worlds of 1915 Dublin. MacDonagh's biographer, Norstedt, believes that Frances's character grows in the play, but again, given the context, where does she go? She retreats back into her trite little socialite world, while the new Ireland is being born around her. Fitzmaurice tells her late in the play, "You will not know yourself in the Ireland that we shall make here" (MacDonagh 53).

Again, the play's language is consistent with other urban plays, retaining some (slight) influence of Irish Gaelic, therefore placing it between the rural prose and common English. A quick example is John's line, "Sooner than you think Frances, [British constitutional] politics will be dropped here, and something better will take their place" (MacDonagh 53). The Irish influence can be recognized in the inclusion of "Frances" and "here" as well as in the general wordiness of the sentence. The use of the other person's name in the intimate conversations of the play is almost constant. However, one might counter that this relatively realistic language and some Ibsenite conventions make *Pagans* (and the urban plays) merely a realistic work, distinguishing it from the symbolist-type plays of the rural aesthetic. Fuel for such an argument could be found in MacDonagh's description of the set, which reads like a realistic portrayal of a bourgeois sitting room: "an armchair, with a cushion, a chair, a small table . . ." (30). However, the set for the premiere, which was staged by Thomas MacDonagh, was hardly realistic:

> On the stage, blue curtains in great austere folds made a semicircle broken somewhat by the tall black stem of a pedestal bearing a tiny white cast of the Victory from the Louvre. Against this background John and Frances Fitzmaurice and Helen Noble moved in their modern clothes, as calmly as the abstractions in a morality play. (Qtd. in Feeney, *Drama in Hardwicke Street* 86)

Seemingly, MacDonagh viewed the production in symbolist or perhaps even in allegorical terms. And modern critics' likening of the text to Ibsen notwithstanding, one audience member remarked that the characters "lacked personality"; [. . .] it was a philosophical statement" (qtd. in Feeney, *Drama in Hardwicke Street* 86). The three characters, as Feeney comes close to suggesting, are types representing Dublin conventionality, Dublin's 'art for art's sake' life, and awakened nationalism. Like other plays of the urban and rural aesthetics, this play develops character types and a political–cultural agenda in order to create allegorical models for a new Ireland.

While the Irish Theatre Company never seriously rivaled the National

Theatre Society, its primary reliance on urban plays may have reflected the continued or growing preference of some Dublin theatregoers for the alternative aesthetic. With Synge's last illness and subsequent death in 1909, the national theatre lost not only an ally in the rural aesthetic but also the aesthetic's genius. Into the void left at the Abbey came playwrights of the urban aesthetic. One can argue that by 1911, the urban aesthetic was actually gaining a strong foothold at Yeats's theatre. This perhaps explains why George Fitzmaurice, who might have developed into nearly as fine a playwright of the rural dramas as Synge, was essentially discarded by the Abbey prior to 1914. Maybe it was simply that the majority of the playwrights who were then coming to the theatre lacked the connection to the rural west. Or perhaps it had to do with the audience's general preference for the urban plays. In 1910 Horniman withdrew her subsidy from the Abbey, forcing Yeats and Gregory to be mindful of their audiences. Or maybe the Abbey's move toward the urban was tied to the growing political tensions in Dublin, which might suggest that plays drawn from Connacht and from its mythology were too far removed from the nearly erupting Dublin.

Demonstration of the prevalence of urban plays at the Abbey can be seen in examples like St. John Ervine's Belfast-set *Mixed Marriage* (1911) and Lennox Robinson's 1912 *Patriots*. In the latter, for instance, the protagonist James Nugent, an ardent nationalist, elects to turn to Dublin, not rural Ireland, to re-ignite a nationalist movement. He announces at play's end, "To Dublin. I'm going to Dublin to open my campaign in Dublin" (Robinson 59). Another often-overlooked Abbey urban play, one which returned to Frederick Ryan's theme of municipal corruption, is Edward McNulty's *The Lord Mayor*.

Premiering in 1914, *The Lord Mayor* is set in contemporary Dublin and centers on Mr. O'Brien, who begins the play as a bankrupt ironmonger. His financial hardship was largely caused by his ambitious wife, who urged him to become part of the municipal government of Dublin (the Dublin Corporation). His position in the Corporation stretched O'Brien's means and led to his financial ruin; all of this transpires before the play begins. The first act is set in Gaffney's office, where the O'Briens and their creditors are to meet to work out a settlement. The manipulating Gaffney is O'Brien's solicitor. As the creditors wish for fifteen shillings on the pound and O'Brien can only pay two, Gaffney introduces a scheme to earn the creditors twenty shillings and to increase their business opportunities. His plan is to have O'Brien elected lord mayor of Dublin. The meek O'Brien seems hardly fit for the position, but his speeches will be written by Gaffney's clerk, Kelly, and his campaign issue will be his refusal, as lord mayor, to welcome the English king to Dublin on the upcoming royal tour. Such a promise, Gaffney hopes, will gain the support of advanced nationalists, Home Rulers, and labor advocates who are unhappy with English rule. This is where the play starts to echo Ryan's in that a powerful profiteer or capitalist like Gaffney puts up "his man" for a city government position.

Act II, set in the upper room in the Mansion House, reveals that in addition to his expected profits, Gaffney expects O'Brien's daughter Moira to marry him. Moira, a strong nationalist, is horrified at the prospect and prefers the young Kelly. Nevertheless, Mrs. O'Brien tries to push Moira toward Gaffney, hoping for a financial fortune. Mrs. O'Brien has a private meeting with Major Butterfield of the English secret service attached to Dublin Castle. He easily persuades her to try to manipulate her husband, now the lord mayor, to go against his campaign promise and officially welcome and bow to the king. In return, Butterfield promises that O'Brien will be made a baronet and will be offered the position of insurance commissioner when the mayoral term ends.

Act III opens with the arrival of a deputation that is waiting to see O'Brien about new public baths. The group is made up of O'Brien's former creditors, who are coming for their first big profit. They own a number of tenement houses in the city that they wish to sell at an inflated price under the guise that the city plans to tear them down and build public baths on the sites. Remembering how they tried to squeeze him, O'Brien tells the deputation, "I'm not going to help you sell out your rotten holdings at the expense of the taxpayers" (McNulty 42). Although a little daft or simple, O'Brien stands up to the slum landlords, as did Michael O'Loskin in *The Laying of the Foundations*. O'Brien is then confronted by Butterfield, who tries to convince him to welcome the king. O'Brien says he is worried about how Moira and Gaffney will react to such a change in stance. Gaffney enters and obviously has been promised compensation from the English, as he tells O'Brien to do as Butterfield instructs. He then reminds O'Brien that he saved him from bankruptcy, made him lord mayor, and now wants Moira as his wife. O'Brien refuses to force Moira into marriage and then refuses to receive the king. Gaffney threatens to destroy O'Brien for rebelling, but the meek O'Brien dramatically takes control:

> And when you tell the people that Jimmy O'Brien wouldn't receive the king, even to be made a baronet, we'll see who'll be in the mud. Do you see now? And, you know the way out. There's the door. [. . .] But for the future, I'll make my own speeches in my own way. I'll neither be run by clique or Castle. I'll be the [. . .] champion of the people's rights. I'll be the citizens' Lord Mayor. (McNulty 50)

The curtain falls as O'Brien throws Gaffney and Butterfield out.

The play is blatant in showing its urban concerns and colors. At its heart is its assault on the problem of corrupt city government, an inept man being made lord mayor to serve the capitalist swindler who manipulated the election; city government is seen serving materialistic individuals rather than either the city or its people. The play takes its place among other works in the Irish Theatre Movement by presenting O'Brien as the self-sacrificing hero who foils Gaffney's scheme. And, like Fred Ryan's O'Loskin, O'Brien reaches this state on his own, responding to his former creditors, Butterfield, Gaffney, and his daughter. No single person nor mythological transformative agency shapes O'Brien; his spirit awakens on its own, and he becomes "the citizens' Lord Mayor." These were interesting anti-capitalist words indeed, which were delivered in the premiere by the rising Abbey actor Sean Connolly, a captain in the Irish Citizen Army who would later be the first rebel killed during the Easter Rising.

Another telling sign of *The Lord Mayor*'s urban aesthetic is its language, as seen in a representative example (from act II) of O'Brien's speech: "I want to say that I'd like to act straight and fair with my fellow citizens; that, when I make a promise, I'd like to keep it; that I won't betray my country for the biggest bribe her enemies can offer" (McNulty 47). Again, we have not the poetic rural prose but a wordier speech than that of accepted English. The first phrase could be cut down to "I'll be fair with my fellow citizens." The *Irish Times* even noted the play's "smart dialogue" in its review of the premiere (qtd. in Hogan, Burnham, and Poteet 326). Perhaps this admiration was for a language that was Dublin-like. The language, the setting, and the issues of McNulty's play unmistakenly create a Dublin/urban atmosphere.

Interestingly, in the famous cartoon of Yeats rejecting O'Casey's *The Silver Tassie*, McNulty's *The Lord Mayor* is on the Abbey marquee in the background. The implication was that in 1928, Yeats was still more willing to tolerate an Irish play from before 1916, one which embraced the alternative aesthetic, over a play with little connection to Ireland — no matter how intriguing the latter might be. Yet regardless of their differences, in the end both the urban and rural aesthetics reached the same ideal image. This figure represented the awakened nationalist, the anti–stage Irishman defiantly standing against forces which literally or symbolically threatened public Ireland. This in turn allowed both aesthetics to portray the Movement's theme of public duty over private concerns — as established, perhaps most famously, in *Kathleen Ni Houlihan*.

In the essay that precedes this one, John P. Harrington investigates the national theatre's secret engagement with internationalism during its first decade. The urban aesthetic emerged during this same formative moment and represented the first challenge to, and alternative direction for, the Abbey. As such, it could be said to foreshadow or even set the precedent for the numerous changes and shifts in philosophies that Irish theatre would undergo in its first century. At the very least, the alternative (urban) aesthetic reminds us of the heterogeneity of early Irish theatre and of the experiments conducted in the name of cultural nationalism.

NOTES

1. Lewis Purcell was the pen name of David Parkhill. Fred Morrow was one of the Morrow brothers who worked with the Ulster Literary Theatre (ULT) in Belfast. Fred staged numerous ULT productions before joining the Theatre of Ireland in Dublin, where he staged Seumas O'Kelly's *The Shuiler's Child.*

2. *The Laying of the Foundations* was never published from Ryan's manuscript, but it does exist in part in the 1970 publication *Lost Plays of the Irish Renaissance*, which is based on Frank Fay's surviving prompt book for the premiere production. Fay's book, however, includes only act II (being a short two-act play). The 8 November 1902 *The United Irishman*, however, contains a detailed synopsis of the play, so that between that and act II, we can formulate a good idea of what was originally staged under its title in the fall of 1902.

3. This conversation may be a conscious reflection of MacDonagh's growing concern with Dublin's working class. He was one of the few nationalists, along with Pearse, Plunkett, and (perhaps surprisingly) Yeats, who publicly supported the workers during the 1913 Lock Out.

4. It was recorded that Irish Theatre Company playwright and member Eimar O'Duffy "went one night to the Irish Theatre dressed up in his Volunteer rigout . . . and became quite a hero on the occasion" (qtd. in Feeney, *Drama in Hardwicke Street* 69).

—3—

Of Orangemen and Green Theatres: The Ulster Literary Theatre's Regional Nationalism

LAURA E. LYONS

This Ulster has its own way of things . . .
—W. B. Reynolds, *Ulad* 1: 1

The Ulster Literary Theatre (ULT), which operated in Belfast from 1904 through the 1930s, has received relatively little critical attention in histories of Irish theatre or studies of Irish culture.[1] *The Field Day Anthology of Irish Writing*, for example, which began as a project to document Irish literary traditions and history on both sides of the border, contains only a passing mention of the ULT: "The company, amateur to the end, survived into the 1930s and developed in kitchen comedy and tragedy a regional variant of the Abbey's style, of which it was not invariably respectful" (Maxwell 564). Unfortunately, this characterization of the ULT both typifies the scant attention given to the ULT in surveys of Irish drama and trivializes the theatre's aesthetic and political project. For the ULT was not only dis-respectful of the Abbey's style, but it was also often openly critical of the Abbey's attempts to define and represent "Irishness," especially in terms of those Abbey plays that grounded Irish identity in either Celtic mythology or images of rural life in the West of Ireland.[2] Although the ULT did perform comedies set in northern kitchens and tragedies propelled to dra-matic ends by sectarianism, their repertoire also included a set of satiric plays by Gerald MacNamara that parody Irish history as viewed through the orange-colored glasses of a recurring character, the devoted Orange-man Andy Thompson. The character of Andy Thompson is enlisted both as a caricature of the dangerous parochialism of the Orange Orders and as an explicitly regional challenge to the regionalism that the Abbey was attempting to parlay into a national cultural consciousness. Through the plays of Gerald MacNamara, the ULT simultaneously positioned itself within the distinctive region of Ulster and sought to forward the nationalist cause.

In their day, MacNamara's plays were quite popular with Belfast audiences and never provoked the kinds of controversies experienced at the Abbey. Ironically, John Millington Synge's *Playboy of the Western World* and Sean O'Casey's *The Plough and the Stars* are now among the most canonical works of Irish drama, those that the Abbey can still count on to attract large audiences. Yet, as the essays by Susan Cannon Harris and Shakir Mustafa in section 2 of this volume elucidate, the original productions of these plays prompted virulent criticism of the Abbey's project and occasioned debates, riots, and long-standing controversies. By contrast, most of the ULT plays are now unknown; given the current political climate, especially the violent confrontations of the marching season, if MacNamara's plays were produced in Belfast today, they would likely meet with such strong opposition.[3] Even though the ULT plays, and particularly MacNamara's satires, were popular, their irreverent representations of Orange ideology ensured that they would never become "consensus dramas," the term Cheryl Herr uses to define the nationalist melodramas produced at the Queen's Royal Theatre in Dublin between 1890 and 1925 (Herr, *For the Land They Loved* 5).

Both Herr's and Stephen Watt's groundbreaking works on political melodrama have transformed our understanding of Irish theatre in the early part of the century. To extend their project of recovering Irish theatrical traditions outside of the Abbey, I believe that we need to look beyond Dublin for other, equally unrecognized, dramatic enterprises which engaged the problematic of representing the "Irish nation." Although largely neglected in the criticism of Irish drama, the ULT presents us with an important instance of an attempt, in the North, to use the theatre to foster both regional and national identity.

The relationship between "a region" and "the nation" is often conflicted, for there is never just one region. Any discussion of a given region necessarily assumes that other such units make up a larger territory. The ULT forwarded a form of what Kenneth Frampton, speaking of architecture, identified as "critical regionalism," that which "may find its governing inspiration in such things as the range and quality of the local light, or in a *tectonic* derived from a particular structural mode, or in the topography of a given site, but which is never aligned with simple-minded attempts to revive the hypothetical forms of a lost vernacular" (21).[4] In their dramatic and journalistic productions, members of the ULT promoted those aspects of Ulster culture that distinguished it from the other Irish provinces. But what differentiates this company's regional project from those that Frampton describes is its insistence that the region need not stand in opposition to the nation. The ULT's understanding of "regionalism" is critical in two senses:

its members recognized the critical differences among the four provinces of Ireland to be one of the nation's greatest strengths, and they were critical of those regional factors, particularly Orangeism, that prevented Ulster from playing its full role in the formation of a new nation. In other words, the ULT actively promoted a regional nationalism, a way of imagining the nation's strength and integrity in terms of its regional diversity, rather than a false homogeneity.

In this essay, I argue that by insisting on a critical tension between regional and national interests, the ULT performed a powerful, though often overlooked, critique of the cultural iconography promulgated by both the Abbey Theatre and the Orange Orders of the North. In Celtic mythology, representations of Irish peasantry, and Orange versions of history, the ULT found images that tried to fix, and so to limit, the ways in which theatrical production contributes to the formation of a national culture. Their plays insist that the North of Ireland, no less than the celebrated West of the Abbey, represents a crucial domain of the Irish cultural imaginary. In so doing, these dramas agitate against the naturalization of the national status of the Abbey Theatre and admonish scholars of Irish culture not to ignore the history of contestation that lies behind the consolidation of "national treasures" like the Abbey.

"Damn Yeats, We'll Write Our Own Plays"

As its name suggests, the ULT took much of its initial inspiration first from the Irish Literary Theatre, and like the Abbey, the ULT, founded by Bulmer Hobson and David Parkhill, consisted mainly of nationalist-minded Protestants of the middle and ascendancy classes (Flann Campbell 377).[5] In fact, Hobson and Parkhill had originally met with W. B. Yeats and others from the theatre in Dublin to propose that a branch of the Irish National Literary Theatre be established in Belfast. Yeats's refusal dramatically changed the course of Hobson and Parkhill's project. Years later, Hobson related the meeting to theatre historian Sam Hanna Bell: "Everybody was most cordial and helpful except for Yeats—haughty and aloof [. . .] we wanted to put on in Belfast Yeats'[s] *Cathleen ni Houlihan* and Cousins's *The Racing Lug*. Dudley Digges and Maire Quinn promised to come and act in our first production. But Yeats refused permission" (2). On the train back to Belfast, Hobson, annoyed by Yeats's attitude, proclaimed "Damn Yeats, we'll write our own plays" (1). Despite Hobson's outrage and his determination to create an independent theatre in Belfast, the ULT's beginnings were confounded by a desire to be like the Abbey and a contradictory need to define the ULT as different from the theatre from which it took its inspiration. Ironically, it was Yeats's own *Cathleen ni Houlihan* and James Cousins's *The Racing Lug* that the ULT first performed in 1904.[6] Later that year, this program was followed by a second production of Yeats's *Cathleen ni Houlihan* and George Russell's *Deirdre*.

According to both the reviews and the actors' accounts, these productions, while effectively performed, failed to spark any excitement in their northern audience, people generally unfamiliar with the figures of Celtic mythology. In fact, *Cathleen ni Houlihan* was met with yawns, as Gerald MacNamara recalled: "The Belfast public were not taken by *Cathleen ni Houlihan*. Ninety-nine percent of the population had never heard of the lady — and cared less; in fact someone in the audience said that the show was going 'rightly' till *she* came along" (S. Bell, *The Theatre in Ulster* 4). In Belfast, where people were largely unaware of attempts by those in the Abbey's circle either to collect and preserve Irish myths and folklore or to enlist them for political and artistic expression, the nationalist content of these plays was lost on the audience, and the audience mistook the performance for "a rather funny peasant play" (18).

The reception of these plays convinced those involved in the ULT that what worked in Dublin would not necessarily play in Belfast. As a result, this group set forth as one of its purposes the encouragement of a uniquely northern theatrical style. From the outset, then, the ULT's position with regard to the Abbey was vexed. On the one hand, they objected to Yeats's dismissal of their idea and set out to create their own style; on the other hand, they took as their model the very theatre that had rejected them. This mimicry is reflected even in the name, but more importantly in the content of its earliest productions and in its establishment of a literary journal, *Ulad*, an idea that followed Yeats's publication of the theatre journals *Beltaine*, *Samhain*, and *The Arrow*.

The first issue of *Ulad* serves as a political and artistic manifesto for the group's mission. In its editorial, W. B. Reynolds begins by delineating the geographical space that *Ulad* occupies:

> Ulad means Ulster. It is still often necessary to state as much; we intend to insist. Draw an imaginary line across Ireland from that great bight, Donegal Bay, in the West, to Carlingford, on the East, and draw it not too rigidly; north of that you have Ulster. This Ulster has its own way of things, which may be taken as the great contrast to the Munster way of things [. . .]. (1: 1)[7]

For Reynolds, the line, though imaginary, demarcates different experiences. "To insist" that Ulster be recognized as a province with its own identity was *not* to endorse a form of cultural separatism but rather to suggest that a nation is made up not only of similarities but also of regional differences. Bulmer Hobson's poem, "Ulad," which follows Reynolds's editorial, elaborates the point by assigning to each geographical region of the island an essential quality:

> In the north is the strength of the wind, of the whirlwind;
> In the south there are murmuring waters;
> The east has a caoine for its song;
> In the west is strengthless love. (1: 3)

In subsequent stanzas, Hobson develops these qualities, but it is the wind, and thus the north, that he ultimately upholds: "Water touched by the wind/The wind is your master, is strongest" (1: 3).

Where Hobson poetically compares the difference between the north and south to wind and water, Reynolds suggests that in the theatre, the divide exists along generic lines:

> We recognize from the outset that our art of drama will be different from that other Irish art of drama, which speaks from the stage of the Irish National Theatre in Dublin, where two men, W. B. Yeats and Douglas Hyde, have set a model in Anglo-Irish and Gaelic plays with a success that is surprising and exhilarating. Dreamer, mystic, symbolist, Gaelic poet and propagandist have all spoken on the Dublin stage, and a fairly defined local school has been inaugurated. We in Belfast wish to set up a school; but there will be a difference. At present we can only say that our talent is more satiric than poetic. (1: 2)

Recognizing that any theatre established at this time, and particularly one with nationalist intentions, would have to define itself in relation to the Abbey, Reynolds acknowledges both that theatre's accomplishments and the variety of its theatrical endeavors. But Reynolds also carefully contains the Abbey's importance by emphasizing its location in Dublin. For Reynolds the Abbey is, as he hopes the ULT will become, only "a fairly defined local school." Reynolds's description suggests that even a theatre with the range that the Abbey possesses cannot adequately account for the talent of the nation as a whole, especially where that theatre is isolated from other areas.

It is perhaps with this sense of isolation in mind that Reynolds discusses the imperative of creating such a theatre in Ulster. Not only is it important for *Ulad* "to cover the whole of Ulster local activity," but the magazine and the theatre must also provide a place for "the impressions of the younger men principally, of whom we have most to hope and most to fear" (1: 2). Without vehicles for expression, the best men in Ulster, Reynolds fears, will be drawn to foreign soil: "We have most to fear for the young men in that, if they do not find an outlet in Ulster, they will either go away, or gravitate upon the sloblands of American or English magazine work, which is purely commercial and has no pretension to literature whatever" (1: 2).[8] Despite his culturally and sexually exclusionary tone, Reynolds's caution was justified. Many playwrights who got their start with the ULT left to find greater success with the Abbey or on the stages of London and New York. One of the most regrettable losses in this regard was Whitford Kane, who left after helping the ULT attain bookings in England and directing its tour of the United States in 1912. Others who left included Rutherford Mayne, who became an official with the Land Commission following the formation of the Free State. The noted Ulster novelist Forest Reid departed for Oxford after contributing two pieces to *Ulad*.[9] In its own limited way, the ULT attempted to curb the flight from Belfast to the more cosmopolitan environs in England, a phenomenon similar to the "brain drain" many former colonial countries experience today.

Ulad's central concern was the relationship of center to periphery. Belfast's wealth, in the late nineteenth and early twentieth centuries, was made through industrialization, particularly in the shipbuilding and linen industries. Although industrial wealth often confers upon cities a metropolitan status, in the case of Belfast, the rewards of that wealth were not channeled into the cultural development of the city or region. Although cities like Belfast and "Londonderry" were centers within the province of Ulster, their relationship to Dublin, from which England's colony was then administered, was peripheral. Belfast might have been Ireland's industrial seat, but Dublin was its cultural capital. Like the money from the estates of absentee landlords, the profits made from Belfast's industries, many owned primarily by London businessmen, were often channeled back to England. Landowners and industrialists with holdings in the North generally did not invest their money in the cultural and intellectual development of the province. At the turn of the century, amusements from the English stage and music halls continued to be imported as the predominant entertainments for Belfast audiences long after such work had begun to lose its audience in Dublin.[10]

Throughout the four issues of its existence, *Ulad* attempted to describe the difference between Ulster and the rest of the country. A review of the ULT's productions of the Abbey's plays in its first issue uses the "creditable, but, at the same time, very bad" performances as an opportunity to discuss how the milieu of "Presbyterian crudeness and repression" in Ulster have stifled the "necessary forgetfulness and self-abandonment" that "mimickry and pantomime demand" (1: 7). Catholicism, with its emphasis on ritual and pageantry, contained a performative dimension that the ascetic sensibilities of Northern Protestantism, and especially Presbyterianism, rejected. In the following issue, a review of the ULT's first production of its own plays explains the doubly difficult task of establishing a theatre in Ulster along nationalist lines. J. W. Good complained that "In Dublin, the project for a national theatre was bound to find many supporters from the first. There the drama has always been a force, and new ideas, even in the darkest days of reaction, have been granted a free hearing" (Reynolds, *Ulad* 2: 4). By contrast, theatrical activity in Ulster "is not recognized but merely tolerated, and the idea that the stage may afford a medium for the expression of national sentiment, as vital and as sincere as a great poem or a great picture,

would be regarded by thousands as little short of blasphemy" (2: 4). Introducing the idea of a national theatre into a terrain that was openly hostile to
both the performance arts and Irish nationalism proved a difficult task. Indeed, as Good observed, "In Belfast to take thought for Ireland is the first
step towards proclaiming oneself a traitor to one's kith and kin" (2: 4).

Another *Ulad* writer, "Connla," concurred with Good's observations.[11]
While nationalist thought flourished in other parts, Ulster, with its "narrow
and barren creed, which excludes all native beauty in art and literature [. . .]
ignored it entirely" ("Literature and Politics" 17). In a subsequent article,
Connla explains that Ulster "has not yet sufficiently assimilated the rudi-
ments of *national* culture on which she must base the development of her
best *provincial* characteristics" ("The Theatre and the People" 13, emphasis
in original). Commenting further on the relationship of regionalism to
nationalism, Connla writes:

> To mould their plays from their experience of humanity as typified in the
> Ulster Irishman is indeed a worthy aim; better defined as an attempt to
> realise Ulster to the rest of Ireland than to set up a new "school" of
> dramatic art. [. . .] Let us labour patiently at our own material. If the
> product be really good, [. . .] our identity and our differences will be
> simultaneously manifest. ("The Theatre and the People" 14)

The need to create a regionally inflected form of nationalism, one that
could take account of the different circumstances under which any nationalist ideology would be received in Ulster, was often cast as a separatist
and "provincial" undertaking. In his second editorial, Reynolds refutes
such a position:

> We have not striven to erect a barrier between Ulster and the rest of
> Ireland: but we aim at building a citadel in Ulster for Irish thought and art
> achievements such as exists in Dublin. If the result is provincial rather than
> national it will not be our fault, but due to local influences over which we
> have no control, but which we shall not deliberately nourish and cultivate.
> That the work in Ulster will for some time be of a critical and destructive
> nature, as well as constructive and creative, no one who knows the condi-
> tions will deny. (2: 1)

Although Reynolds and most of the other writers in *Ulad* never directly
name the target of their critique, the subject matter of ULT's plays, as we
shall see, left no doubt. In discussing criticisms that the ULT is only interested in savaging "the qualities that have made for the success of the Northern province," Connla writes,

> It does not attack them but it does attack that caricature of them that is so
> complacently accepted as the real thing in Ulster to-day. All are good
> things in themselves; but when thrift verges on meanness, when tenacity

becomes obstinacy, and energy finds its only outlet in a frantic struggle for wealth, it is time for those who care for life and the beauty and graciousness of life to protest. ("The Theatre and the People" 14)

Both Reynolds and Connla believed that the ULT's project was not simply one of mimetic representation. They viewed the peripheral status of Ulster as a cultural and political problem that needed to be addressed by a didactic and reformist program. It would not be enough to remind audiences of the United Irishmen and of a time when the Protestant settlers identified themselves as Irish. The more difficult work would involve combating the "religious bigotry" that had largely supplanted this tradition of dissent.[12]

The Orangeman on Stage

In December 1907, the ULT performed a remarkable theatrical piece that addressed the sectarian problems in Ulster by satirizing the origins of the Orange Movement. *Suzanne of the Sovereigns: An Extravaganza,* by Lewis Purcell and Gerald MacNamara, was first publicly staged by the ULT at the Belfast Exhibition Hall.[13] Unscripted and improvised performances of the Battle of the Boyne had been an amusing part of the annual Christmas party given at the Morrow residence each year (Hobson 5). But when Mac-Namara and Purcell reworked a play, *Suzanne,* first devised by the Morrow brothers, for the same occasion in 1900, their contribution to the party so entertained the guests that they were encouraged to develop it into a curtain-raiser for the ULT.

The play takes as its subject the Siege of Derry — from April to August 1689, during which the Apprentice Boys held out against the Catholic pro-James forces until relief came from supporters of William of Orange — and the Battle of the Boyne, in which William of Orange personally intervened in July 1690 to defeat James II. These two events continue to be the most celebrated among loyalist Protestants in Ireland, who see themselves as a historically besieged minority whom William III defended against the native, Catholic Irish. William of Orange provides the name of those Protestant lodges that formally institutionalized, in the late eighteenth century, the ideology of Orangeism, which urged members "to support the King and his heirs as long as he or they support the Protestant Ascendancy" (qtd. in Foster, *Modern Ireland* 275). McHenry's synopsis of the play suggests the degree to which Purcell and MacNamara took liberties with the official history:

King William and King James each appear very eager to win the hand of the imaginary Suzanne of many charms and equally eager to avoid accepting responsibility for the unheard-of Ulster. They are supported, now and then, by generals who are quite willing to change their policies whenever the inducement of a sandwich is offered, and they are finally scandalized by the report of the elopement of Suzanne with Van Tootil. (McHenry 17)

The theatre's management worried that such a representation of the famous battle might cause protests similar to those in Dublin over Synge's
The Playboy of the Western World. Hobson writes of the opening night: "[...]
when the curtain rose it was touch and go for a few minutes whether we
would have a riot started by indignant Orangemen but the play was so
absurd and history was portrayed in such a ridiculous guise that the laughter of most of the audience drowned the protests of objectors" (5). Similarly, Rutherford Mayne reports that "what might have been the cause of
first-class riots was turned by irresistible wit and humour into an uproarious
success" (qtd. in Sam Hanna Bell 30). Indeed, following the success of the
first night's performance, in which the action was staged in the center of the
Exhibition Hall, the stage space had to be pushed back farther and farther
into the hall to accommodate a growing audience. By the last performance
on New Year's Eve, the stage was placed against the far wall. *Suzanne and the
Sovereigns* was the first widely popular success of the ULT.

Beyond the obviously farcical nature of the play, it is difficult to understand why disturbances did not break out. Because *Suzanne and the Sovereigns* was first staged during the Christmas season, the audience might
have understood the performance within the generic terms and logic of the
Christmas pantomime, which treated historical material in an irreverent,
often fantastical manner. A reviewer of the 1910 production notes that
"[t]he only protest seems to have been occasioned by the programmes sold
at the January 1909 production. These were printed broadsheets with a
drawing by Joseph Campbell of King William astride a rockinghorse" (qtd.
in S. Bell 30).[14] In fact, the 1909 production was slightly expanded and a
musical accompaniment added. W. B. Reynolds provided an "Overture of
1690," which was based on songs like "The Boyne Water" and "The Boys
of Wexford," which were sung at Orange Order lodge meetings and parades. The play's success led to revivals during the Christmas season in
1910, 1914, and 1916. Whenever the theatre was having a difficult year,
they could rely on *Suzanne and the Sovereigns* to make money for them. In
fact, *Suzanne and the Sovereigns* was also responsible for establishing a connection between the ULT and the Belfast Opera House. During the 1909
run of the play, the famous British actor Edward Terry was playing to small
audiences at the Belfast Opera House. The manager soon found his audience in attendance at the ULT play, and offered his venue for a week's run
(McHenry 24).

The importance of representations of William III to Orange Orders in
the North helps to explain why it was a *visual* representation of the king that
elicited protests and not the content of the play. Jan Wyck's 1692 painting
of William III was the first known to depict the king in a heroic manner:
sword out and riding a white horse whose front legs are slightly raised
(Loftus 19–20). And it was this position that Campbell copied in his cartoon version of King Billy on his rocking horse. The character of the

portrait painter in the play, Van Tootil, is undoubtedly based on Wyck. By having their eponymous heroine fall in love not with the beloved Protestant king but with a man responsible for creating his image, Purcell and Mac-Namara satirize the reverence given in Ulster to any representation of William III. Power is placed in the ability to represent and immortalize the king as the singular icon of Protestant rule rather than in the historic deeds of the king himself. Purcell and MacNamara pillory the tendency in Protestant culture in the North to invest libidinal energies in representations — both symbolic and political — of the king. William III's image, of course, has graced parade banners, certificates, seals, and medals of the Orange Order since the organization's foundation. In fact, the first loyalist mural in Belfast, a rendering of the Battle of the Boyne, was painted in 1908, the year following the popular debut of *Suzanne and the Sovereigns* (Rolston, "When You are Fighting . . ." 120). Although William III is all but forgotten in other parts of Britain, in Northern Ireland, one in ten Protestants still belongs to the Orange Order, and reproductions of William III's image on domestic products surpass in sales both that of the Royals and of Ian Paisley (Loftus 14).[15]

Suzanne and the Sovereigns was the first of a series of satiric, fantastic, and political plays that MacNamara wrote for the ULT. Two of these plays — *Thompson in Tir-na-nOg* and *No Surrender* — directly address the political imagery and ideology of the contemporary Orangeman. First staged in 1912, *Thompson in Tir-na-nOg* concerns the predicament of Andy Thompson of Scarva, who, following the explosion of his gun during a Twelfth of July celebration, finds himself transported to Tir-na-nOg (land of "eternal youth"), where all those heroic figures who have fought for Éire live in eternal youth and peace.

Much of the play concerns the problem of defining Irish identity, especially for those in Ulster. Both Thompson and the ancient heroes of Irish legend who inhabit Tir-na-nOg — Angus, Finn, Cuchulain, Conan, Maev, and Grania — consider themselves "Irish," but the heroes are suspicious of this new man from Ulster, who not only is unable to speak a word of Irish but who also refuses to do so when placed under a spell. Another spell is cast, making it possible for the heroes to speak to Thompson in English. When Cuchulain introduces himself to the visitor — "I was of the Red Branch, foremost of the fighting men of Ulster" — Thompson mistakenly thinks he has met a fellow loyalist. On trial to authenticate his identity, Thompson fails to prove that he is a "true Irishman" because he knows none of the Irish heroic sagas.

When questioned by Cuchulain about Irish history, Thompson can only recall what he knows about the Battle of the Boyne from Orange banners, and he is embarrassed when he must admit that William III was neither Irish nor English but Dutch. The King of Tir-na-nOg continues the examination:

> *King.* Do you know aught of your country's history save that of this Battle
> of the Boyne?
> *Thompson.* I know that King Charles was beheaded.
> *King.* Was Charles an Irishman?
> *Thompson.* No.
> *King.* What more do you know?
> *Thompson.* I know that King Henry VIII was a "Roman" till he converted.
> *Cuchulain.* Of course he wasn't an Irishman.
> *Thompson.* He was not.
> *King.* What has all this got to do with Ireland? We want to hear of Irish
> history.
> *Thompson.* Shure they never teach you Irish history in the schools in Ire-
> land. (33–34)

Having failed his trial, Thompson is to be burned, and he is finally led off
the stage, shouting "No Surrender!"

MacNamara uses the trial to critique English colonial education in
Ireland. Andy Thompson's understanding of history concerns events in
England rather than those in Ireland. Even his knowledge of those events
that define his identity as an Orangeman, like the Battle of the Boyne, is
truncated and based more on pageantry and symbol than on historical facts.
Of the origins of Andy Thompson, Sam Hanna Bell writes: "Gerald Morrow, MacNamara's nephew, says that *Thompson* was originally written by
request for the Gaelic League. It was then in three acts. But they rejected it
because they said it held up the Gaelic heroes to ridicule. The author then
made it into a one-act and gave it to the Ulster Literary Theatre" (43). If
Gerald Morrow's account is right, it is ironic that the Gaelic League, which
sought to promote Irish culture, would reject this play, which satirizes
Orangeism and critiques the colonial practice of denying the importance of
Irish history and culture. On opening night, however, it was reports of
Orangemen with bolts and rivets in their pockets sitting in the audience
that most concerned the group. As with *Suzanne and the Sovereigns*, distur-
bances, though anticipated, never materialized.

MacNamara was extremely fond of poking fun at any group's reliance
on particular images and icons, and his play does satirize the centrality of
Celtic mythology in the Irish renaissance project. The inhabitants of Tir-
na-nOg, irritated by having to speak the "barbarous" English tongue, argue
with each other at the beginning of the play, mostly over the details of their
heroic deeds. For example, Cuchulain asks Queen Maev to confirm to the
others his brave holding of the ford against Ferdia at the Yellow Ford.

> *Queen.* Durst doubt the word of the warriors of our cycle, thou low-born
> third cyclarian.
> *Grania (to Queen).* Put no reproach upon my people. Our cycle is as good
> as thine. Our records of great deeds are not as numerous as thine, but
> ours are at least true. (13)

The heroes engage in a battle of intertextuality and dispute who can know which sections of the cycles given their own placement in the legends. If MacNamara locates in the Orange version of history a typically colonialist insistence on the importance of events in "the Mother Country," he is equally critical of attempts to establish a version of Irishness that would have Celtic mythology as its foundation. By staging a confrontation between icons of Ulster Unionism and Irish nationalism, MacNamara reveals that the claims of both are based on nostalgic versions of the past equally incapable of accommodating in the present the particular ways in which the other side identifies itself as "Irish."[16]

In 1909 MacNamara had already written a one-act play, *The Mist That Does Be on the Bog*, satirizing Synge and the use of peasant speech in *Playboy*. In the ULT play, which MacNamara called "a fog in one act," several actors make their way to the cottage of Michael and Bridget Quinn of Connemara to rehearse their parts in a peasant play and to perfect their dialects. When a tramp passes by their lodgings, the players decide to see if the tramp will recognize them as authentic peasants. In the end, the tramp reveals that he, presumably like Synge, is a "playwright from Dublin in search of local color." Throughout, the play stresses the artificial quality of the actors' representation of peasants, which, as Nelson Ó Ceallaigh Ritschel has shown in the preceding essay, the Theatre of Ireland also explicitly rejected. The peasants Bridget and Michael speak in MacNamara's version of Synge's overly poetic rendering of the western dialect.

> *Michael.* It's one thing to hear a motor horn when the sun do be shinin' in the canopy of the heavens and the young ewes do be dancin' in the corn—but it is another thing to hear the toot of the horn when the black clouds do be restin' on the top of the Slieve Girnin and the white mists do be comin' up from the bowels of the sea. (n.p.)

During their stay, the actors hope to replicate such speech, which is full of picturesque images:

> *Clarence.* And you think, kind ladies, that I have the gift of the bards upon me?
> *Cissie.* Sure it's as plain to be seen as the staff of a pike, for the beautiful words pour from your lips like a delft jug, and it full of buttermilk. (n.p.)

In this play, MacNamara stages both the linguistic and political dissonance between the peasants of the west and the actors and playwrights of the Dublin-based Abbey Theatre. Just as the actors' attempts to represent the dialect of the peasants ring false, so too their belief that they can locate in these peasants an "authentic" voice for Ireland appears if not exploitative then certainly naïve. For the very process of gathering material or subjects of ethnographic study has the capacity to change or to alter those materials. MacNamara intimates that Michael's excessively figurative language is the result of the presence of the playwright, who is now able to pass for an authentic tramp of the West. Fearing that their Ulster audience would not be familiar enough with Synge's work to understand the play, the ULT agreed to premiere it at the Abbey. There is some discrepancy over its reception. McHenry suggests that those in the Abbey seemed to take the play in good humor, but Sam Hanna Bell reminds us that thereafter, most of the ULT tours to Dublin were staged at the Gaiety Theatre (Sam Hanna Bell 41).

Whereas *Thompson in Tir-na-nOg* placed an Orangeman in a world beyond time in order to point out the thin basis for his beliefs, one of MacNamara's last satires for the Ulster Theatre used the future to point out the anachronistic quality of Orange ideology.[17] *No Surrender!*, first per-formed in 1926, takes place in 1990 on the eve of the three-hundredth anniversary of the Battle of the Boyne in a united and vice-free Ireland, where political conflict has been resolved among all groups except vege-tarians and carnivores. The setting is the Orange and Hibernian Museum of Antiquities in Belfast, an institution whose function is "to foster a sense of humor in Ulster," according to Miss Thompson, the assistant curator (n.p.). The museum is full of sashes, drums, and banners from the parades of the Orange Order and various unnamed Hibernian societies. As Miss Thompson explains to a visitor from East Africa, "These exhibits are placed here to illustrate to the present generation, the ridiculousness of the past" (n.p.).

In fact, much of the play revolves around Miss Thompson's 113-year-old grandfather, William Thompson, who is labeled exhibition "number one: The Last Orangeman!" William shouts "No Surrender!" at passing visitors and sings out verses from "The Boyne Water." This last Orange-man is the only thing preventing Professor McCrum, who acts as a spirit medium for Northern Ireland as well as a museum curator, from using his knowledge of "Buddhi-Astralagism" to call forth William III for the anni-versary celebration. McCrum's character and the discussion of Buddhi-Astralagism is clearly a send-up of the interest in theosophy and spiritual-ism in Yeats's circle.

A certain amount of plot summary will be necessary here. William III, it seems, has changed his stance and now refuses to appear until the last Orangeman has indeed surrendered. But a greater threat to the possibility that William III will appear comes from William Thompson's grandson, Andy Thompson, an Orangeman of a new generation, recently returned from the Island of Bambooza, where he has become a millionaire. Of her brother's political beliefs, Miss Thompson explains, "King William himself would look like a lemon beside my brother Andrew. [. . .] Orange? He is positively tangerine!" (n.p.).

Andy attempts to credential himself for the monarch, who appears briefly, with stories of his adventures upon leaving home with nothing but an orange sash and a book from the Order to guide him, but the monarch finds him both boring and dangerous. Having made his fortune in Bambooza, where he reformed the islanders — "ignorant and superstitious natives" — into subjects who are "All true blue," Andy has returned to Belfast to continue his missionary work at home (n.p.):

> *Andy.* Wait till I tell you. I have come back to rid out the scorpions and venomous serpents that infest this fair land of Ulster. I have come to cast them into outer darkness and to bring those who will into the fold — to bring them back to the paths of virtue. (n.p.)

King William is appalled to hear Andy cast his mission in terms of "civil and religious liberty." Oblivious to his hero's distaste for him, Andy continues his argument against the new Ireland, where "all creeds and classes are mixed up here and as thick as thieves," and promises to reform those in Ireland as he did those in Bambooza: "I'll let them know that there will be only one crown, one flag, one constitution and one faith — the true faith" (n.p.). A "negro boy" from Bambooza appears, playing a lambeg drum, as a testament to Andy's reformative powers, and King William asks to be sent back to Purgatory rather than risk being converted to Andy's obnoxious ideas.[18]

While the fantastic premise of the play remains foregrounded throughout, the encounter between Andy and William III allows MacNamara to make some of his most pointed critiques of Orangeism. Andy's speeches are full of the mixture of religious and political rhetoric common on the Twelfth of July. MacNamara suggests that the kind of zeal with which the Orange Order campaigned against Home Rule not only is bigoted, but is also underwritten by the same kind of supremacist mentality that drives colonialism in general. Andy wants to wrest back the privileges afforded the Orange Order in previous days, the kind of status he has secured for himself in Bambooza. But if Bambooza is to be the model for Ireland, then whose children will politely play the drum when called upon?

McHenry remarks that in the mid-1920s *No Surrender!* and a revival of *Suzanne and the Sovereigns* were not particularly well received compared to earlier productions of MacNamara's satires. She explains this unenthusiastic reception, in part, through the theatre's over-reliance on programs that included the standard favorites of their established audience. Those in attendance, she suggests, had grown weary of such plays. Sam Hanna Bell has called this period of the theatre (1920–1934) that of "slow but perceptible decay" (72). But there is another possible aspect to the change in attitude. From the time that the ULT began through the production of *Suzanne* in 1907, liberal attitudes were prevalent in Ulster, not just among those Protestants who explicitly identified themselves as nationalists but even within groups like the Orange Order. In 1902 Tom Sloan, an independent Unionist for South Belfast, was elected in a by-election when he ran on a populist platform. Sloan's advocacy of trade unions and old-age pensions as well as his attacks on Ulster Unionism resulted in his suspension from the Orange Order (Geoffrey Bell 75). In 1903 Sloan and Lindsay Crawford formed their own Independent Orange Order. The attendance at the Twelfth of July demonstration grew from 500 in 1903 to 2000 in 1904 (75). In the following year, the Independent Orange Order met at Magheramore in County Antrim and issued a manifesto that "called for compulsory land purchase, urged a revision of Irish finances and accused English Liberals and Tories of playing Protestants and Catholics off each other" (76). The Magheramore Manifesto states: "We consider it high time that the Irish Protestants consider their position as Irish citizens and their attitudes towards their Roman Catholic countrymen and that the latter should choose once and for all between nationality and sectarianism" (76). The Independent Orange Order stopped short of advocating Home Rule, a position Crawford was expelled for espousing in 1908. During a period when even those most closely aligned with Orangeism were critical of its sectarian orientation, plays like *Suzanne* were received without too much fuss. *Thompson in Tir-na-nOg* had its first showing at the height of the Home Rule campaign, but the concern that the players would be pelted with metal objects on opening night proved to be unfounded.

Between the premieres of *Thompson* and *No Surrender!*, partition had changed the political geography of Ireland, and the Free State had been established. Whereas in the first decade of the century, "the Protestant establishment could afford to ignore the Dungannon Clubs . . . [and] to turn up their Philistine noses at the pretensions of poets, playwrights, musicians and a handful of revolutionaries" (Flann Campbell 383), as Home Rule became a political possibility, dissent in Ulster would find less hospitable ground. A weakened economy contributed to a hardening of the lines drawn by the old Orange Order, which increasingly became a recruitment ground for private Unionist armies like the Ulster Volunteer Force (Farrell 19). Between 1918 and 1921, massive expulsions of Catholic and disloyal Protestant workers took place in the factories of Belfast (28). The Orange Order was also used to recruit the infamous B Specials, a heavily armed police force structured according to the occupations of the participants. Mill owners and landlords acted as commanders, and their workers and tenants filled in the ranks (29). During this period, the Orange Order gained its working-class base and "became an integral part of the state machine" (G. Bell 56). The Orange Order continues to attract many Protestant workers, Geoffrey Bell believes, because they "provide a social life, a meeting place, a club, where the Protestant worker can feel he is something special — the white man's club where none of Ulster's niggers darken the door. The Order adds a dash of colour to the otherwise drab life of the ordinary working man" (57).

In one sense, MacNamara created in these satires his own version of the stage Orangeman, an "Andy Thompson" rather than a "Paddy." This figure was precisely what groups like the Independent Orange Order had feared was developing in the mainstream Order. They could recognize "Andy" as a type, note the excesses of his ideas, and still laugh at him, precisely because he seemed to have no real power. Yet Orangeism still wielded a great deal of political influence, even though the traditional Orange mentality appeared to be breaking up during the years 1903 to 1908. As the privileges of membership became institutionalized and as private armies patrolled the streets, Orangeism became less of a joke. A bigoted "Andy Thompson" with an orange sash singing "The Battle of the Boyne" could evoke laughter. But the same "Andy Thompson" with a gun was no laughing matter. During the period in which the ULT operated, Orangeism appeared briefly to be undergoing a split that had the potential to move its politics in a more class-based and inclusive direction, until the ranks once again closed, and the leaders exploited sectarian sentiments to protect their own privileges. As the ground for their satires became increasingly hostile, the Ulster Theatre lost its standing, and by the early 1930s, the Ulster Theatre disbanded to allow its players and artistic staff to join the newly forming Group Theatre in Belfast.

Between the Region and the Nation

As I observed in the beginning of this essay, the few existing commentaries on the ULT stress the group's status as an "amateur" theatrical enterprise, emphasizing their inability to achieve the success of the Abbey. Although the satiric plays of MacNamara are occasionally given mention, they are oddly overshadowed by the ULT's early — and less popular — peasant plays, which are most often referred to as "County Down kitchen comedies" or "County Down peasant dramas." While it is true that the ULT excelled in this genre, the very categorization works to contain the group's contribution. The peasant plays produced at the Abbey are never simply called Connacht or Mayo peasant plays, even when critics may rightly suggest that the Abbey peasants were based on the rural people of that province and county. The formulaic "County Down kitchen comedies or dramas" not only ignores the explicitly nationalist agenda of the ULT, but further reinforces the idea that some counties either cannot or do not represent the nation.

In MacNamara's satiric plays, the ULT's stated mission was most fully realized. Reynolds writes of the northern theatre's prospects in the second issue of *Ulad*: "The Ulster Theatre may never produce an epoch-making play, or evolve a distinctive school of acting; but if it aids, even a little, in breaking down the barrier that has so long divided the North from the South, its work will not have been in vain" (2: 5). The goal of "breaking down the barrier" is one to which any number of contemporary Irish dramatists would most certainly aspire, though they may not be aware of their dramatic forerunners in the ULT.[19] When Reynolds drew the imaginary line that marked out Ulster in the first issue of *Ulad*, he was, in a sense, tracing a line that Yeats had inadvertently drawn by refusing to have a branch of the then Irish National Theatre Society established in Belfast. Although the ULT is often described as fundamentally a "provincial" theatre, that label reveals more about its location than its outlook. The recognition of regional differences within the nation was at the heart of the ULT's statement of purpose.

   The partition of Ireland in the 1920s was, thus, in some ways preceded by an unacknowledged cultural partition. Cut off from the cultural nationalist project in the South of Ireland, the ULT was increasingly critical of projects like the Abbey Theatre, which claimed to represent the nation but whose understanding of that nation too often excluded Irish people in the North. MacNamara's plays represent what the Abbey and other nationalists based in the South ignored at a great cost: the problems of the industrial North and its sectarian heritage. Writing about the emphasis on and meaning of the West for the Irish renaissance, Luke Gibbons argues that "the appeal of the west of Ireland for writers like Synge and Yeats lay precisely in the fact that it offered a refuge from such puritan ethos, from the suffocating moral atmosphere of Ireland dominated by the emergent bourgeoisie, both Catholic and Protestant" (*Transformations* 24). Gibbons goes on to explain that the emphasis in Yeats and Synge on lawlessness represents "a desire to return to the prelapsarian world of ascendancy Ireland, when the rule of law and the centralizing structures of a developing capitalist economy had still not brought about the landed gentry's fall from grace" (25). Such a vision could not accommodate the industrialization and sectarian history of the North. Andy Thompson, MacNamara's stage Orangeman, served as an uncomfortable reminder to the Abbey of a set of deeply ingrained regional practices and beliefs that did not lend themselves easily to a homogenized vision of Irish culture founded on another, ostensibly more "Irish," part of the country.

   But Andy Thompson's purpose was not merely to point out the shortcomings of the Abbey Theatre; the ULT and MacNamara also consciously satirized those beliefs and organizations in Ulster that they believed hindered the development of a national identity. Early on they recognized that such an undertaking necessarily would be "critical and destructive." The ULT reminds us, in this time when the people of Ireland once again must negotiate the relationship between the North and the South, that regional differences need not naturalize or reify division, but rather they must be understood as part of the difficult project of creating a flexible and non-exclusionary nation.[20] Those in the ULT believed that it was not enough for the people of Ulster to assert unreflectively their difference from the rest of Ireland, a practice that could only confirm ideas that those in the North were indeed "provincial." Thinking within a regionalist–nationalist frame-work afforded them a perspective to reevaluate those aspects of Ulster that stifled cultural creativity and thought, and they were deeply suspicious of those projects that held tradition and culture outside of the realm of cri-tique. Giving these plays more scholarly attention—instead of blithely passing over them by way of comparisons to the Abbey that find the Dublin theatre superior—might help us to understand better the range of ways in which theatre was used in Ireland early in this century to promote and cri-tique different forms of nationalism and to consider for the future the diffi-culties of, and possibilities for, creating a nationalism that neither ignores nor romanticizes regional and national identifications.

NOTES

1. Any study of the ULT will necessarily be indebted to three important sources: Margaret McHenry's 1931 dissertation, "The Ulster Theatre in Ireland"; Sam Hanna Bell's *The Theatre in Ulster*; and Hagal Mengal's *Sam Thompson and Modern Drama in Ulster.* McHenry had access to the personal files and manuscripts of some of the ULT's principal playwrights. Sadly, much of this material has been lost. Bell's book is the only Irish account. In its theatre collection, the Linen Hall Library in Belfast has a small archive of ULT plays and materials. I am indebted to Robert Bell, former curator of the Linen Hall Library's Political Collection, for introducing me to these materials, and to current curator Yvonne Murphy for subsequent assistance. I am also grateful to Nandi Bhatia, Purnima Bose, Cynthia Franklin, Andrea Feeser, and Beth Tobin for their readings of an earlier version of this essay.

2. For a discussion of the West in relation to the peasant plays of the Abbey, see Edward Hirsch's "The Imaginary Peasant."

3. Ulster Television produces an apparently popular northern sitcom that fea-tures a stereotypical and bigoted Orangeman who bears some resemblance to Mac-Namara's Andy Thompson. Nonetheless, I think that many in the North of Ireland would find stagings of MacNamara's plays, especially *No Surrender!*, difficult to watch.

4. Cheryl Herr usefully enlists Frampton's "critical regionalism" in her impor-tant book, *Critical Regionalism and Cultural Studies: From Ireland to the American Midwest.*

5. Lewis Purcell was the only longstanding member of the ULT to have an independent income. Unlike his colleagues in the ULT, Bulmer Hobson came from a Quaker background. Hobson is also credited with establishing (in 1905) the short-lived but significant Dungannon Clubs, named after a Northern town in which volunteers issued a document of religious freedoms in 1728. See Flann Campbell's *The Dissenting Voice: Protestant Democracy* for details on this organization, which brought together Protestants and Catholics throughout Ireland.

6. Maud Gonne granted permission for staging *Cathleen ni Houlihan*. She claimed that as Yeats wrote the play for her, she had the right to say who could perform it. Unlike Yeats, Gonne was excited by the possibility of a theatre in Belfast.

7. In 1904, when Reynolds wrote this editorial, the current partition of Ireland was not yet established. His description of Ulster as including the entirety of the

northern-most sections of the country stands in contrast to the border drawn in
1920, in anticipation of independence, a "line," to pick up on Reynold's language in
this passage, drawn more rigidly over the last twenty years.

8. The emphasis on young men is Reynolds's. Although the writer Alice Milli-
gan contributed an article for the magazine and Rutherford Mayne's sister, Helen
Waddell, had one of her plays produced, the ULT tended to be male-dominated.
McHenry notes that even in these women's works, women tended to be peripheral
characters, used more for set decoration than as elements of the drama (68).

9. Reid's contributions are noteworthy insofar as they are the only pieces that
do not address Ulster explicitly. They include a review of a painting exhibition in
Dublin and a short story called "Pan's Pupil."

10. For commentaries on the deleterious effects of the commercial theatre on
Dublin audiences, see Edward Martyn, "A Comparison between Irish and English
Audiences" (*Beltaine* 2 [1900]: 12–13), and George Moore, "Is the Theatre a Place
of Amusement?" (*Beltaine* 2 [1900]: 7–9).

11. McHenry claims that Connla was James Connolly. Mengel, however, dis-
agrees. He asserts that given that Connolly was in the United States during this
time, the more likely writer is James Cousins, who wrote a short story with a
character named "Connla."

12. Many of the ULT's peasant dramas and tragedies were set within this
history of radical Protestant dissent or addressed growing sectarianism in a more
serious manner than the plays discussed in this essay. I would particularly call attention to Lewis Purcell's *The Enthusiast* (*Ulad* 3 [1905]: 29–35) and Rutherford
Mayne's plays *The Troth* (1909) and *The Turn of the Road* (1909).

13. Mengel, the most recent commentator on the ULT, reports that several
scarcely legible copies of *Suzanne and the Sovereigns* are in the Linen Hall Library in
Belfast. Unfortunately, these copies have either been misplaced or lost. McHenry's
manuscript does, however, include a comprehensive plot summary and extensive
quotations from the play. Only three of MacNamara's eight plays are easily available: *Thompson Tir-na-nOg* (the only play to be published), *No Surrender!*, and *The
Mist That Does Be on the Bog*. The latter two are in working typescript at the Linen
Hall Library in Belfast.

14. Bell reports that for "subsequent productions a drawing of martial trophies
was substituted" (31). McHenry was able to obtain and reproduce the program
with Campbell's cartoon version of King Billy, which is included in copies of her
dissertation.

15. For a comprehensive account of the historic and contemporary commem-
orative practices of the Orange Order and other Protestant groups in Ulster, see
Neil Jarman, *Material Conflicts: Parades and Visual Displays in Northern Ireland*.

16. Ironically, the Ulster Defense Association, a paramilitary group, has begun
to reclaim their connections to Irish mythology. Starting in 1993, UDA murals on
the Newtownards Road in Belfast have featured Cuchulain as the "ancient defender
of Ulster against Irish attack over 2000 years ago." See Una Murphy, "UDA Mobilises CuChulainn," and Bill Rolston, *Drawing Support 2*.

17. In 1915, the ULT dropped "literary from its name to become the Ulster
Theatre," and was sometimes referred to as the "Ulster Players."

18. Unfortunately, I have not found an account that discusses who played the
"negro boy" or how. Given that race tends to go unmarked (and often unremarked)
until more than one race is represented, it is worth considering how race constitutes
an important element of this play's spectacle.

19. See, for example, the essays in this volume by Mary Trotter and Marilynn
Richtarik.

20. In the context of the North, Bill Rolston reminds us that cultural projects

that attempt to reconcile the two traditions without acknowledging their different histories of privilege create a "chimera of symmetry" ("Culture as a Battlefield" 32). As Rolston demonstrates, cultural funding and policy, when guided by the goal of such symmetry, can, in fact, be used to depoliticize cultural movements and to roll back those hard-won cultural programs and developments within minority communities. This practice he aptly terms "multiculturalism as counterinsurgency" (32).

Part II

THEORIZING AND HISTORICIZING THEATRE CONTROVERSIES

—4—

The Abbey and the Theatrics of Controversy, 1909–1915

Lucy McDiarmid

The history of the early Abbey Theatre offers a good means of understanding the way controversies, like theatre itself, transform the belligerent into the ludic. Three successive controversies in particular constitute a little sequence of causes and effects: the controversy over Bernard Shaw's play *The Shewing-Up of Blanco Posnet*, which was banned in England for blasphemy and obscenity but which was performed in Ireland in 1909; the controversy over the Philadelphia performance of John Millington Synge's *The Playboy of the Western World* in January 1912; and the 1915 debate over whether Shaw's *O'Flaherty VC* should be produced at the Abbey. Controversies, as these examples show, are not a means of resolution but rather a sign of its absence, functioning as a conduit of strong feeling.

Controversies create a field for disputation where almost anything is allowable, and almost any word or action can be read in the context of public antagonisms. A tactical genius like Lady Gregory could stake out a position with whatever materials came her way — a cup of tea, for instance, or a potato. On 20 August 1909, Lady Gregory was meeting at the Viceregal Lodge with the viceroy of Ireland, Lord Aberdeen, and he was pressuring her, in his polite, dithering way, to withdraw *Blanco Posnet* from production by the Abbey. He happened to offer Lady Gregory (and Yeats) some tea: she felt, she wrote, "a consuming desire for that tea after the dust of the railway journey all across Ireland," but she didn't accept it. Making note of what occurred during the meeting, Lady Gregory refers to "the kindly offers of a cup of tea," the "consuming desire" for it, and then "our heroic refusal, lest its acceptance should in any way, even if it did not weaken our resolve, compromise our principles" (Gregory 93). Of sacrifices made in the name of Irish cultural autonomy, this one may not rank very high, but Lady Gregory was conscious of the meaning she would be able to give it. Four years later, the heroic refusal would be recorded in her book *Our Irish Theatre.* The point of the sacrifice was to publicize it.

The potato was originally someone else's gesture. It was thrown at the Abbey actress Eithne Magee as she played the part of Pegeen Mike in *Playboy* in New York on 27 November 1911. According to newspaper accounts of the evening, Lady Gregory gave interviews backstage "drinking tea and holding in one hand the potato that had struck Miss McGee" [*sic*] ("Riot" 2). Lady Gregory held the potato not because she wanted to throw it at someone else but because she wanted to transform the angry gesture into a playful pose. It was always her way, as a controversialist, to underreact, to remain calm and amused, and to make her antagonists seem like hysterical fools. Holding the potato, like refusing to drink tea, was a piece of improvisation that signaled both superiority and invulnerability. Lady Gregory had control of the potato, and she also had self-control—she did not throw it at anyone. Throwing vegetables or eggs is, of course, a traditional gesture of repudiation and insult, but it doesn't happen every day. The license of controversy is one of the unwritten rules of the genre.

Although neither drinking the tea nor holding the potato was hostile, both gestures were agonistic, part of a larger and complex system of antagonisms. The term "system" suggests the way in which any of a number of gestures or moves—a letter to the editor, a flung potato, a hiss, a riot, a satirical poem—can all be related to one another. Controversies come in groups, and it is also useful to think of "systems" of controversies, especially when they are related historically. Abbey controversies form such a system. The argument I want to make requires you to shift your focus a bit. Instead of seeing the plays in the foreground, the controversies in the background—instead of seeing the plays as primary and the controversies as secondary—you need to see them all in the same plane, all as equally important; you need to see the plays and the controversies both as forms of expressive behavior, both as forms of theatre. Controversies, like plays, require scripting, casting, directing, and timing; they also require imagination in their planning and daring in their execution. They require publicity, advertisement, and a genius for visibility. And so if you can shift your perspective and see the controversies not as an afterthought or as secondary but rather as equal in significance and in theatricality to the plays, then you can understand my argument—that the controversies constitute a tradition themselves, that they have a history, and that they refer back to other controversies more than they refer to the plays. The modern Irish controversy is a genre with its own traditions and customs and allusions. To say that controversies form a genre, or type, of expression, and that as a sequence they form traditions, implies that controversies are intertextual:

they refer to one another, they copy forms and styles and modes of expression. By that I mean something as simple as throwing vegetables to express disapproval or heckling or coughing excessively so that the actors can't be heard. All of these are actions copied from previous controversies, a theatrics of protest handed down because controversies are modeled on, and are the model for, other controversies.

The *Blanco Posnet* controversy (1909) marks the convergence of two traditions of controversy: Irish and English. The English tradition involved the continuing debate about stage censorship, a long-running controversy that became more important in the late nineteenth century.[1] The relevant law, dating from 1737, required submission of plays to the Lord Chamberlain (an officer of the Royal Household) two weeks before the first performance. The Lord Chamberlain had the power to deny licenses without giving any reason and to issue fines if he was not obeyed. The plays were actually read by a man called "the examiner of plays"; in 1909, this was one George Alexander Redford. Shaw was involved in debates, symposia, and letter-writing campaigns about censorship throughout his career; he was an interested observer in 1892, when the House of Commons Select Committee on Theatres and Places of Entertainment held hearings but did not ultimately recommend any changes in the law relating to theatrical censorship. And in 1894 *Mrs. Warren's Profession,* Shaw's serious and provocative play about a prostitute, was denied a license. So when, in the spring of 1909, the Joint Select Committee of the House of Lords and the House of Commons on the Stage Plays/Censorship was announced, Shaw wrote two plays as a challenge. In other words, the debate about censorship itself inspired these plays. One of those, *The Shewing-Up of Blanco Posnet,* Shaw pointedly titled "a sermon in crude melodrama" (Shaw 169). *Blanco Posnet* is an American morality play, set in the Wild West, about a horse thief who gives his stolen horse to the mother of a dying child. The child dies anyway, and that death causes Blanco, the horse thief, to undergo a religious conversion. A benign and charitable sheriff presides over the whole scene, and the play ends when the entire community happily adjourns to the local saloon.

Why would anyone want to censor such sentimentality? The play was a tease, taunting the censor with high-minded banality and a very few naughty passages. Here, for example, is the passage in which the "bad" brother Blanco tells his "good" brother, Elder Daniels, what it feels like to be "shewn up" by God:

> *Blanco.* . . . He hasnt finished with you yet. He always has a trick up His sleeve —
> *Elder Daniels.* Oh, is that the way to speak of the ruler of universe — the great and almighty God?
> *Blanco.* He's a sly one. He's a mean one. He lies low for you. He plays cat

and mouse with you. He lets you run loose until you think youre shut
of Him; and then, when you least expect it, He's got you.
Elder Daniels. Speak more respectful Blanco — more reverent. (Shaw 254)

Shaw essentially put pointers into the text to draw the examiner's attention
to the blasphemy. In case the examiner was too dense to notice it, Shaw has
Elder Daniels say, "Speak more respectful . . ." The other passage that was
intended to awaken the attentions of the examiner occurs when Blanco says
of the local whore, "I accuse the fair Euphemia of immoral relations with
every man in this town . . ." (263). By contemporary standards, this "obscenity" is not even noticeable, and even by 1909 standards, it was pretty
mild, but the point was to include a few, just a few, offensive phrases necessary to provoke the examiner, in a story that is otherwise pious and nonsub-
versive. In other words, the whole play was driven by the idea of controversy, by 170 years of debate about censorship. The play was duly denied its
license, as Shaw had hoped, while it was already in rehearsal in May 1909.[2]

But there was a funny loophole in that 1737 law: the examiner's writ did
not run in Ireland. So Ireland, as Shaw had long anticipated, might offer a
site from which to defy the Lord Chamberlain. There, *Blanco Posnet* would
find its place in a sequence of Abbey controversies. From the first play
produced by the Irish Literary Theatre in 1899, Yeats's *Countess Cathleen*,
through Synge's *In the Shadow of the Glen* (1903), and especially his *The
Playboy of the Western World* (1907), Abbey plays had tended to irritate certain types of people, especially strong nationalists, because of their seemingly cavalier attitude toward female virtue, toward Irish masculinity, and
toward Catholicism.[3] In 1909, the *Playboy* riots were relatively recent and
the Abbey was still suffering from the accusation that the play had insulted
Irish country people of both genders.

So when in June 1909 Shaw offered the Abbey directors *Blanco Posnet*
for performance in Dublin, they grabbed it at once because it was a great
opportunity. An Irish performance of the play would be perfect all-around,
contributing to the two separate controversy traditions: Shaw could defy
the English censor by having the play produced, and the Abbey could
advertise itself to the world as defying the authority of English law and
thereby win back its nationalist supporters. The construction of the *Blanco
Posnet* controversy as an answer to the *Playboy* controversy is emphasized in
Lady Gregory's book, *Our Irish Theatre*, because chapter 4 is entitled "The
Fight over 'The Playboy'" and chapter 6 is entitled "The Fight with the
Castle."

The 'mentality' of the controversy, as Lady Gregory designed it, was
very much like that of her plays *The Rising of the Moon* and *Gaol Gate*. The
whole event was given the coloration of mid-nineteenth–century Irish
nationalism — militant, populist, unambiguous. When the play was in rehearsal in early August, Lady Gregory wrote to Shaw, "One of the Belfast

papers in its notice that Blanco was to be performed put as a heading 'Probably interference of the Lord Lieutenant' but that is too good to be true — we could raise a great cry of injustice to an ill treated son of Erin if this were done" (Laurence and Grene 12–13). And Shaw wrote back, catching her tone, "If the Lord Lieutenant would only forbid an Irish play, without reading it, . . . at the command of an official of the King's household in London, then the green flag would indeed wave over Abbey St" (Laurence and Grene 18–19). Gregory constructed the event by recasting a type of Young-Ireland discourse with a touch of Fenian intensity: "great cry of injustice to an ill treated son of Erin" is a deliberately theatrical use of patriotic rhetoric, as is Shaw's talk about the green flag waving over Abbey Street. They are talking in quotation marks, as Lady Gregory was when she wrote of her "heroic refusal" of the viceroy's tea. Later in the controversy, Shaw wrote Lady Gregory: "If we can only fix the suppression of the play on the King, then 'if the colour we must wear be England's cruel red,' we perish gloriously" (Laurence and Grene 36). In short, even in private correspondence, Shaw and Lady Gregory used a discourse designed to associate their opposition to Dublin Castle with popular nationalism. In her letters to Shaw and in her visits to Dublin Castle — in all these private occasions — Lady Gregory spoke as if she were the leader of a popular uprising and as if every word were being broadcast to her followers. Of course, every word was published in her accounts of the event, so all the private visits were on the record — her record.

It is important to realize that no one knew whether or not the viceroy had the power to suppress a play in Ireland based on the objection of the Lord Chamberlain in England. The viceroy didn't know himself.[4] The final clause of the Abbey Theatre's patent vested power in him to declare that patent null and void, but the patent would have to be violated in performance before a play could be stopped. In fact, the Abbey's existence was at risk in this episode, because Aberdeen *might* have found that the patent was violated. This is classic controversy territory: the problem arises in an area that hasn't been legislated, an interstitial area that no one has ever thought about.

The Castle tried to negotiate with the Abbey and avoid a showdown: they didn't want to find out how little power they had. In Lady Gregory's meetings with the undersecretary, Sir James Dougherty, and with Lord Aberdeen, the viceroy (Lord Leftenant), on 12, 13, 14, and 20 August 1909, Lady Gregory used the Young Ireland discourse again in a sardonic manner, as if to remind the Castle authorities that in threatening the Abbey Theatre they were playing the role of nasty colonial rulers. The first visit came after the Castle got in touch with the Abbey solicitors, and the others followed thereafter. (Yeats, as the other Abbey director, was with Lady Gregory on several, but not all, of these visits. In her journal, most of the good lines that Lady Gregory quotes are her own.) Gregory's rhetoric

constructed the Castle's position as well as the Abbey's. Her very first words
to the undersecretary in her very first visit are notable. He said, "Well."
And she said, "Are you going to cut off our heads?" Although her metaphor
appears to grant political superiority to the Castle, it is clear from her
flippant tone that she thinks this use of power silly. In fact, Sir James's
response was a rebuke: "This is a very serious business" (Laurence and
Grene 15). At the end of her fourth meeting with Sir James, Lady Gregory
flaunted a misquotation from Parnell: "who shall set bounds to the march
of a Nation?" (Laurence and Grene 34).

This rebellious tone surprised the gentlemen in the Castle, because it
wasn't what they were expecting from Lady Gregory. Lacking any vision of
how to reconstruct the controversy or how to get rid of it, they fell back on
manners and what they hoped would be common class assumptions. Holding up the newspaper with the announcements of *Blanco Posnet*, Sir James
said in bewilderment, "You defy us, you advertise it under our very nose, at
the time everyone is making a fight with the Censor," and then later, "Oh,
Lady Gregory, appeal to your own common sense." While Lady Gregory,
ever mindful of public relations, was positioning herself to "raise a great cry
of injustice" and make a "heroic sacrifice," Lord Aberdeen was trying to
find common ground and show how close, in fact, their positions really
were. He said to her, "You must not think I am a sour faced Puritan. I am
very interested in the drama. In fact at Oxford it was often said that that
would be my line. My Grandfather also, though considered so strict, went
so far as to take part in plays under a pseudonym. So you see I have a great
deal of sympathy with you" (Laurence and Grene 32). Lord Aberdeen
implied that it was only a bureaucratic accident that obliged him to prevent
the performance of *Blanco Posnet*, "because of the courtesies of officials
toward one another; and I as the King's representative cannot go against the
King" (Laurence and Grene 33). Sir James also tried to show his sympathy
by distancing himself from the examiner of plays. Lady Gregory cited one
of Redford's sillier objections to *Blanco Posnet* and said to Sir James, "How
can we think much of the opinion of a man like that?," and Sir James
replied, "I believe he was a Bank Manager" (17). All these sophisticated
titled people, who loved theatre, enjoyed Shaw, and were not themselves
bothered by fake blasphemy and obscenity, were held in thrall by George
Alexander Redford (the censor), who, like the good bureaucrat he was,
blue-pencilled the offensive passages in the play. It was really he who made
possible the redemption of the Abbey's nationalist reputation.

Of course, the whole point of producing the play was to be threatened
in public: that was why Lady Gregory had written to Shaw that viceregal
interference would be "too good to be true." Throughout the negotiations,
the viceroy had been unable to explain which clause in the Abbey patent was
being violated: the patent required the plays to be Irish, and he made the

case that a play written by a Londoner about an American horse thief wasn't Irish. He argued that the blasphemous and obscene language might instigate a riot, which was forbidden by the patent. He kept trying to find a reason. Finally, after all the conversations, which led nowhere, the Castle issued a press release that was published in the evening papers. It said that "His Excellency . . . has arrived at the conclusion that in its original form the play is not in accordance with the conditions and restrictions contained in the Patent as granted by the Crown"; the statement also mentioned "the serious consequences which the production of the play . . . might entail" (Laurence and Grene 40–41). This vaguely worded threat was a threat nevertheless, and it gave the Abbey directors just what they wanted, an opportunity to issue a defiant press release in response. Here is what the Abbey directors claimed in their press release:

> If our Patent is in danger it is because the English censorship is being extended to Ireland, or because the Lord Leftenant is about to revive a right not exercised for 150 years, to forbid at his pleasure any play produced in any Dublin theatre, all these theatres holding their Patent from him. We are not concerned with the question of English censorship, but we are very certain that the conditions of the two countries are different, and that we must not by accepting the English censor's ruling, give away anything of the liberty of the Irish theatre of the future. (Gregory 218)

The nature of the play itself was so clearly a secondary issue to everyone that the Abbey waited until the next day's papers to defend it as "a high and weighty argument upon the working of the Spirit of God in man's heart" (Laurence and Grene 43). But everyone knew that the play was not blasphemous or obscene; Irish cultural autonomy was the issue, not theology or morality.

The art of this controversy, the deliberate construction of the controversy to resemble an act of nineteenth-century nationalist resistance, is clear when you look at some of the 'unrebellious' facts that made the 'resistance' successful. The opening-night audience was a very stylish crowd. The first performance (25 August) took place in the middle of Horse Show week, and all the commotion about the play made it the 'place to be' on opening night. In fact, Lady Lyttelton, the wife of the commander-in-chief of British forces in Ireland, was there with a large party.[5] (Two days later the Lytteltons gave a dance attended by Lord and Lady Aberdeen, so no important friendships were ruined ["Vice-regal Court"].) Dublin's richest unionist, Lord Iveagh, was at opening night with a party of six. In his diary, Joseph Holloway observed the presence of "all artistic, literary and social Dublin": John McCormack, George Russell, William Orpen, Frank Sheehy Skeffington, Mrs. Shaw, Robert Gregory (Laurence and Grene 48). James Joyce was also there, reviewing the play for a Trieste newspaper. Lily Yeats, who attended both the dress rehearsal and the opening performance with her brother Jack and his wife Cottie, noted the presence of Lord Dunsany (Lily Yeats).

These, then, were the people, titled folk and the artistic elite, who made the green flag wave over Abbey Street, who took part in the "march of a Nation," who helped Lady Gregory make her stand against the viceroy. Her nationalist construction of the event continued backstage, where she taught the actresses the ballad "The Lower Castle Yard," a song about a radical nationalist of the 1850s whose political poems get him in trouble with Dublin Castle. And in Lady Gregory's account in *Our Irish Theatre*, the audience's applause is interpreted as a gesture in the controversy:

> The play began, and till near the end it was received in perfect silence.
> Perhaps the audience were waiting for the wicked bits to begin. Then, at
> the end, there was a tremendous burst of cheering, and we knew we had
> won. Some stranger outside asked, what was going on in the Theatre.
> "They are defying the Lord Lieutenant" was the answer; and when the
> crowd heard the cheering, they took it up and it went far out through the
> streets. (Gregory 96)

Lily Yeats also describes "a big buzzing crowd of onlookers" and then says the play "went with great go all through & got a great reception — the English Press men made a bolt for the door where the post-office had messengers waiting to take the telegrams" (Yeats). The passage from Lady Gregory presents the controversy itself as theatre and indicates how the crowd in the streets, those people who hadn't even seen the play, participated vicariously in defying the Lord Lieutenant. When they start cheering, the defiance shifted from the stage to the streets. The applause of the stylish audience was transformed into the seditious cheers of the crowd outside, and it was not the end of the play but rather the Abbey's triumph in the controversy that was being cheered.

The controversy around *Blanco Posnet*, then, became part of the lengthening sequence of Abbey controversies and contributed to the style, atmosphere, and assumptions of later controversies. The American tour of the Abbey (1911–1912) was dominated by the history of Abbey controversies. The Abbey brought *Blanco Posnet*, as well as *Playboy*, to America as well, but the excitement was all generated by *Playboy*.[6] The local protests that greeted performances of *Playboy* and a few of the other plays were less responses to the plays themselves than to Dublin protests and protests in other American cities: Boston responded to Dublin, Providence responded to Boston, New York responded to all the previous cities, and Philadelphia to Dublin, New York, etc.. Each separate controversy was inspired not by what was happening on the stage but by the dynamics of the whole sequence. Actually, by this time, Dublin audiences were not interrupting productions of *Playboy*: it could be acted there without incident. However, *The Gaelic*

American, the newspaper run by the New York Fenian John Devoy, kept up a barrage of angry, sarcastic attacks on the Abbey players in news items, features, and editorials throughout the six months of their American tour. More space was devoted to *Playboy*, Yeats, Lady Gregory and company than to John Redmond and the third Home Rule Bill. "A Great Work of Dirty Art," *The Gaelic American* proclaimed on its front page ("Paints the Playboy in Glowing Colors"). The week before, *The Gaelic American's* editorial had noted of *Playboy* that "The whole setting is barbarous, bizarre, and untrue to life, and so grossly libellous that if the writer was sane he must have been a malignant creature" ("Stamp Out the Atrocious Libel"). As the players moved from city to city, Irish-American societies had time to plan their protests: Philadelphia would have felt shamed if the Abbey players had been able to perform there uninterrupted. An Irish-American in Pittsburgh wrote to a friend in Philadelphia after the protest there, "Tell them the boys here are all proud of them" (O'Loughlin).

Not all Irish-Americans were throwing potatoes at the actors: then, as now, Irish-America was not a monolithic social group but rather a cluster of subcultures—the AOH, the Gaelic League, urbane political figures—whose members did not necessarily think alike. In fact, members of the Boston Gaelic League visited Lady Gregory to tell her that they supported the Abbey players (Gregory 100). William Leahy, the representative of the mayor of Boston, enjoyed all the plays and said "They are most artistic, wonderfully acted, and to my mind absolutely inoffensive to the patriotic Irishman" (Gregory 102). In New York, Chief Magistrate McAdoo, who attended a performance of *Playboy* on behalf of the mayor, said he had seen many more objectionable plays in New York and that he didn't think the theatre's license should be suspended (Gregory 114).

The Irish-Americans who protested against *Playboy* and a few of the other plays that the Abbey brought to America did not necessarily aspire to assimilation with Anglo-Saxon Protestant American social customs but rather to the control of culture exercised by that dominant class. Thus, they played, in this controversy, the rebel role that Lady Gregory and Shaw had played in 1909, when the Abbey had welcomed the opportunity to assert its independence from the cultural authority of a decrepit and silly royal bureaucracy. In America, the Abbey directors were identified as Irish landlords: as *The Gaelic American* said of Lady Gregory and *Playboy*, "a woman with a foreign title was patroness of the vile thing" ("Philadelphia Spanks 'The Playboy' "). As Lady Gregory traveled with the players from city to city, she was welcomed and entertained by, and generally identified with, the American upper-class Protestant establishment. These were the people who controlled culture in America in 1912: people like Isabella Stewart Gardiner of Boston, famous now for the museum that used to be her house; the people who sent their children to Vassar, Bryn Mawr, and the University of Pennsylvania, where Lady Gregory lectured; and the lawyer Henry

LaBarre Jayne and his wife, with whom Gregory stayed in Philadelphia. Through the Jaynes, Lady Gregory met the members of the elite American Philosophical Society, and then they all went off to "a ball at the Assembly rooms" (Gregory 118).

High culture, linked with high society, was in the control of wealthy Protestants, and from the point of view of the Irish-American Joseph McGarrity, the Jaynes, Wisters, Rodmans, Biddles, Warburtons, and other members of Philadelphia "society" played the role that Dublin Castle had played in 1909—as agents of a moribund institution exercising its powers to determine what was allowed on the stage. McGarrity, a businessman born in County Tyrone in 1874, was the genius behind the Philadelphia controversy. Because in 1912 he was selling liquor, Lady Gregory refers to him as a "publican," but he also edited a newspaper and conducted many business ventures (Laurence and Grene 71). He later became wealthy and left his enormous collection of Irish books and manuscripts to Villanova University. It was his cultural aspirations that (I believe) gave energy to his involvement in this protest: this is the most Philistine moment in the life of a great bibliophile.

Lady Gregory and her allies had created the expressive field that was the *Blanco Posnet* controversy through public relations strategies: through press releases, behind-the-scenes politicking, and published accounts of their victory. What McGarrity and his lads did was different: they had to expand the field in which the Abbey's plays existed so that it included themselves. They created an alternative theatre, distracting the audience drawn by the original play using their own performance. As is clear from the notes of the Irish-American Club in Philadelphia (for 14 January 1912), the Philadelphia Irish first expanded the field in which *Playboy* existed by writing their own script. The minute book records the debate about what precisely these men (only men were involved) should do. The question was one of stagecraft and strategy.

> Brother McGinn gave it as his opinion that the wisest course would be to place the men in sections all over the house, and keep up a disturbance through the Acts to the end. Brother Crossin dissented from Course stating that he believed in union and that the opposition when made should come unanimously from all parts of the house. [. . .] Brother Harry Carney was for an entire program of "passive resistance" by which he meant hissing and other signs of disapproval at all objectionable parts . . . Brother H. Carney stated that it was advisable that twenty men witness the Play on Monday evening. Brother McLaughlin agreed with Brother Carney's report and the recommendations contained therein "viz" to protest vigorously by hissing at all objectionable items. The recommendations of the Committee were unanimously adopted. (*Minute Book of the Irish American Club, Philadelphia*)

By speaking during the play, they would challenge the authority of the producers and attract the notice of the audience. By offering a counter-play, they would draw attention to the issue of who controls culture — by controlling it, however briefly and intermittently, themselves.

Performances of *Playboy* were disrupted on two nights, 15 and 16 January. Here is an account of the first night from the *Philadelphia Ledger*:

The presentation of J. M. Synge's comedy *Playboy of the Western World* caused an immense disturbance last night at the Adelphi theatre. [. . .] The play had proceeded only about 10 minutes when a man, said to be Joseph McLaughlin, national vice-president of the AOH, rose from his place in the centre of the house and called out, "I protest against this play. It is a shame. Why don't you present Irish character as it really is?" The audience, which was one of the most fashionable which has assembled this season, had been rather expecting, not to say hoping, that something of the sort would occur. Everyone turned round and those in the balcony and gallery rushed forward to see as much as they could of what was taking place. [. . .] Meantime, the man who had started the trouble was approached hastily by several policemen [. . .] they at first merely tried to quiet the disturbers — there was quite a group of them by this time — but, failing in this, the trouble makers were promptly ejected from the playhouse. The fashionable audience applauded loudly, and many a sedate personage could be heard calling, "Put them all out! Let the play go on! This is an outrage!" [. . .] The noise had become so great in all parts of the house by this time that the actors had to give up in despair, and, although the curtain was not lowered, they stood about the stage in rather bored attitudes. [. . .] During the first series of disturbances 30 persons were put out and two men were taken to City Hall under arrest, charged with assault and battery and inciting to riot. [. . .] This first outbreak was immensely exciting, but members of the fashionable set who were present [. . .] were rather amused at it all. [. . .] Indeed, it developed that one well-known matron had laid a wager with her husband that there would be trouble, he declaring that such a thing could not occur in Philadelphia. [. . .] When seeming quiet had been restored, there was yet another outburst, this time started by a man in the first row of the balcony, who said, "As one born and bred in Ireland, I protest." Realizing his possible fate, he was content with this and stalked out. It was evident, however, that a sort of cabal existed for the interruption of the play. [. . .] Another man downstairs who had presumably arranged his protest in the oratorical measures of a Patrick Henry cried out, "From time immemoriam" [*sic*]. That was all he could say, for a big policeman promptly took him in hand. [. . .] Those who went ostensibly to show their disapproval did not by any means wait for those passages in the play which in other cities have been the occasion of difficulties. The beginning of troublous times came much

> sooner here, and many of the subsequent lines, to which objection has
> been taken, were left unchallenged. [. . .] (Abbey Company United States
> Tour, 1911–1912)

The reporter makes it clear that this controversy was caused by a previous
controversy, not by any of the offensive lines in the play: they don't even
wait for the "bad" parts. Actors and audience have changed places, because
the "bored" actors on stage give up and watch the drama taking place on the
other side. In addition, an Irish-American controversy has replaced an Irish
one, because the warring parties are the "fashionable" set and the members
of the Irish-American club, with McGarrity and McLaughlin determined
to confront the consumers of this anti-Irish high culture—the Wisters,
Rodmans, Biddles, and so forth. You can see the license of controversy in
action here: the society types are yelling back at the Irish-Americans, but
then, as the reporter says, they were hoping for some excitement anyway.
The ludic and the antagonistic are mixed, and the reporter clearly enjoyed
the greatly expanded expressive field.

The Gaelic American actually made a similar point when its reporter
wrote of the two nights of protest, "If there was a genuine dramatist among
the Abbey Theatre crowd, he would find in these scenes and incidents
better material for a good play than he could discover . . . in the shebeen
houses and the dunghills [. . .]" ("Real Comedy Off the Stage" 4). By the
end of that week, the expressive field of the controversy had been expanded
even more: it now included the Magistrate's Court and the Court of Quar-
ter Sessions in Philadelphia and an extended cast of lawyers and judges.
Joseph McGarrity earned the accolades of *The Gaelic American* for getting
the Abbey players arrested, something that happened in no other American
city. Only the year before, in preparation for a visit by Sarah Bernhardt in
La Samaritaine, the Pennsylvania State Legislature had passed a bill forbid-
ding "any dramatic, theatrical, operatic, or vaudeville exhibition . . . or
moving pictures, of a lascivious, sacrilegious, obscene, indecent or immoral
nature or character"; violation was punishable by fine, imprisonment, or
both ("Pennsylvania Air Bad for 'Playboy' "). The night of 17 January, the
players were "technically arrested" in the theatre (they were never actually
locked behind bars), and the morning of 19 January, witnesses about the
moral character of the play were examined before a magistrate and then
before Judge Carr. The courtroom testimony, like the protest, made excellent "alternative theatre." So Lady Gregory seemed to think as she wrote to
her son Robert:

> At three o'clock we went to the court, a large one this time, and the Judge
> had a nice face. He had been to my lecture here the first time I came and is
> a friend of the Jaynes. He didn't know anything of the play, and had to be
> told the whole story as it went on, just like old Wall [the magistrate who
> tried the *Playboy* rioters] in Dublin at our first riot, so before the case was
> over audience and officials were in a broad grin. Mr McGarrity the liquor

dealer got a different hearing this time, was asked some pertinent questions instead of being simply encouraged, as by Magistrate Carey. [. . .]
The dramatic event was the arrival of [John] Quinn while a priest [Father
P. J. McGarrity, John McGarrity's brother] was being examined. We had
got leave from the Judge for him to cross-examine, and the priest had to
confess that the people of Ireland do use the name of God at other times
than in blessing or thanking those who have been kind to them [. . .] as he
had at first asserted upon oath. Also when he based his attack on indecency
on the "poacher's love" spoken of by Christie he was made to admit that a
few sentences earlier marriage had been spoken of "in a fortnight's time
when the banns will be called." Whether this made it more or less moral
he was not asked to say. He called the play libidinous. The players beamed
and the audience enjoyed themselves, and then when the Director of
Public Safety was called and said he and his wife had enjoyed the play very
much and seen nothing to shock anybody, the enemy had received as
Quinn said "a body blow. . . ." It was a little disappointment that the Judge
did not give his verdict there and then, that we might have cabled home.
(Laurence and Grene 73)

The *Blanco Posnet* controversy was a famous victory for the Abbey, but the
Philadelphia *Playboy* episode was claimed as a victory by both sides. Judge
Carr (on 23 January) simply discharged the players and made no comment
whatsoever about the case. Lady Gregory was by then in Pittsburgh with
the company, and she "made a little speech" from the stage of Carnegie
Hall there (Gregory 128). *The Gaelic American's* boldface headlines read,
"PENNSYLVANIA AIR BAD FOR 'PLAYBOY'" and then "McGarrity
to Carry Case to Superior Court." Lady Gregory could claim that the
Abbey had won: those arrested were never found guilty, and the *Playboy* was
performed without interruption in Indianapolis and Chicago during the
following week. McGarrity, however, had created a serious obstacle for the
Abbey and had caused Lady Gregory some anxious moments.

In the debate over the proposed Abbey production of Shaw's *O'Flaherty
V.C.*, the controversy was suppressed as well as the play itself. I suggested at
the beginning that instead of seeing the plays as primary and the controversies as secondary, you need to see them all in the same plane, all as equally
important, all as forms of expressive behavior. In this case, as in the case of
Blanco Posnet, the composition of the play was controversy-driven. The
inspiration for *O'Flaherty V.C.* was actually the tradition of Abbey controversies. Writing a deliberately provocative play, Shaw wrote competitively
against Synge, hoping for riots in the theatre. The play's subject is an
Irishman home on leave from the Great War, and Shaw wrote to Lady
Gregory, "The picture of the Irish character will make the Playboy seem a
patriotic rhapsody by comparison." Expecting the actor Arthur Sinclair to
play the lead, Shaw wrote, "Sinclair must be prepared for brickbats" (Laurence and Grene 95). The play was set at Coole, and Shaw wrote Lady

Gregory, "The scene is quite simply before the porch of your house" (Laurence and Grene 94). Following is Shaw's summary of the plot: "The idea is that O'Flaherty's experience in the trenches has induced in him a terrible realism and an unbearable candor. He sees Ireland as it is, his mother as she is, his sweetheart as she is; and he goes back to the dreaded trenches joyfully for the sake of peace and quietness" (Laurence and Grene 95). No doubt to ensure a good healthy riot, the script included insults aimed at many categories of people: landlords, women, Irish nationalists, and English patriots.

Shaw also anticipated a replay of the *Blanco Posnet* controversy: in the same letter he said of the play, "At worst, it will be a barricade for the theatre to die gloriously on" (*Collected Letters* 95). In a letter to Yeats, Shaw wrote, "It is by no means sure that it will be licensed in England; and a few preliminary trials in Dublin might do no harm" (*Collected Letters* 104). Shaw's happy vision was of the completely offensive play, offensive to audiences and to civil and military authorities, and he envisioned commotion everywhere: audiences rioting, Dublin Castle issuing threats, and Lady Gregory calm, smiling, and defiant throughout it all. Purporting nonetheless to believe that his play might be construed as part of the war effort — a patriotic gesture — Shaw subtitled it "A Recruiting Pamphlet" and wrote Yeats: "It is written so as to appeal very strongly to that love of adventure and desire to see the wider world and escape from the cramping parochialism of Irish life which is more helpful to recruiting than all the silly placards about Belgium and the like . . ." (*Collected Letters* 110). After the first performance was announced, however, in November 1915, Dublin Castle intervened in the person of undersecretary Sir Matthew Nathan, suggesting that the play be postponed. While all this was transpiring, Lady Gregory was in America again with the Abbey players, and Yeats wrote her that when he told Shaw they wouldn't fight the issue, "Shaw, I thought, was disappointed. He said, if Lady Gregory was in London, she would fight it, but added afterwards, that he didn't really want us to but thought you would do it out of love of mischief. I told him that was a misunderstanding of your character . . ." (*Collected Letters* 106).

Sir Matthew Nathan's letters make clear that it was precisely the license of controversy that Dublin Castle didn't want. In 1915 recruitment in Ireland was not doing very well, and the last thing the civil and military authorities wanted was a riot in a theatre about that cause. Politely Nathan suggested that it would be better for all parties involved if the play were withdrawn: " . . . the representation of this play at the present moment would result in demonstrations which could do no good either to the Abbey Theatre or to the cause that at any rate a large section of Irishmen have made their own." Outside of Dublin rumors that the play had been suppressed under the Defence of the Realm Act and a few newspaper interviews with Shaw, there was no public controversy. The first performance of the play actually took place at the Western Front in 1917, with Robert Loraine (Robert Gregory's commanding officer) in the title role; Robert

Gregory played O'Flaherty's mother. On the actual field of battle, it was beyond controversy.

Because it is the custom to consider controversies of limited importance, most people would consider all these things quite petty — all this 'fuss and bother' about not drinking tea, throwing potatoes, issuing press releases, and winning little victories that are soon forgotten by everyone (until they are rediscovered by scholars). I could come up with a whole series of dismissive phrases — tempest in a teapot, much ado about nothing, blowing off steam — that assume the insignificance of most controversies. But as the dismissive metaphors themselves imply, controversies are large forces in a small site. The great drama of social revolution that historians see in wars, or political demonstrations, or in voting patterns, in the Magna Carta or *Brown v. The Board of Education of Topeka* — that drama I see in controversies, which are micro-units of social change. They show as if in miniature, in polite visits to an imperial official or rude shouts in a Philadelphia theatre, the gradual shifts of power which gather force for decades before historians accept their reality. Although controversies don't generally cause change, they make it visible, in the theatre, on the other side of the stage.[7]

NOTES

1. For an account of English stage censorship by one of the last English censors, see Johnston's *The Lord Chamberlain's Blue Pencil.*

2. For more commentary and analysis on this and other aspects of the *Blanco Posnet* controversy, see McDiarmid's "Augusta Gregory, Bernard Shaw, and the Shewing-Up of Dublin Castle."

3. See Frazier's *Behind the Scenes: Yeats, Horniman, and the Struggle for the Abbey Theatre* for an analysis of these and other early Abbey controversies.

4. See McDiarmid, note 15, 41–42.

5. So Shaw wrote Gilbert Murray after the opening performance: Lady Lyttelton "brought her whole flock to the play with military honors" (Shaw, *Collected Letters* 865).

6. See John Harrington's *The Irish Play on the New York Stage* for a detailed commentary on the Abbey's November 1911 production of *Playboy* in New York.

7. I would like to thank my hosts on the occasions when this paper was read: Sheila O'Donnellan of the Lady Gregory Autumn Gathering (Gort, County Galway); Christina Hunt Mahony of the Irish Studies Center (Catholic University of America); and Stephen Watt, Indiana University. I am grateful to Mary Helen Thuente for presenting this paper for me at the symposium entitled "Nationalism and a National Theatre: One Hundred Years of Irish Drama," Indiana University, May 1999. The National Library of Ireland has generously granted permission to quote from unpublished work in the Manuscript Collection; and PMLA has given permission to use parts of an earlier version of this essay. Permission to quote from unpublished letters by Lily Yeats has been given by A. P. Watt on behalf of Anne Yeats and Michael B. Yeats.

More Than a Morbid, Unhealthy Mind: Public Health and the Playboy Riots

SUSAN CANNON HARRIS

We both need Home Rule . . . but the first home
rule we need is Health in the Home.
— Mrs. A. S. Hunter, "Health and Nationality"
(*Sinn Féin*, 5 January 1907: 1)

I should begin by explaining what public health has to do with the *Playboy* riots, since the connection is not intuitively obvious. By "public health" I mean the complex of ideas and practices generated by the British medical establishment during the first decade of this century in order to safeguard the strength, vitality, and purity of the British race. Public health sought not only to control contagious disease but also to eradicate hereditary disease by promoting "healthy" breeding practices. My argument is that this concern with protecting the individual body from noxious germs or protecting the body politic from irresponsible reproductive behavior was one of the factors that shaped nationalist responses to Synge's play and that by investigating the public health connection we can better understand how the nationalist community's objections to Synge's play came to be expressed primarily as objections to Synge's representations of Irish women.

As it happens, 1907, the year of the premiere of Synge's *The Playboy of the Western World*, is also the year that the Eugenics Education Society was founded in England. The Society's foundation marked the establishment of eugenics as a cornerstone of British medicine. But even if the British medical community was formally embracing eugenics at the same time that Synge's play was being protested, it does not necessarily follow that either Synge or his critics were aware of, or cared about, this trend in medical theory and practice. However, a look through Arthur Griffith's nationalist newspaper *Sinn Féin* indicates that Synge's opponents were aware of — and concerned about — the public health movement in England. In the weeks leading up to the *Playboy* riots, one of the 'hot' topics in *Sinn Féin* was compulsory vaccination, a public health initiative which was read by many of Griffith's contributors as an assault on the Irish race. While sharing the sense of panic about physical health and racial purity that motivated the advocates of social hygiene, Griffith and his contributors identified imperial science, when practiced in Ireland, as a vector of disease and degeneration rather than as a prophylactic.

But even the fact that these Irish nationalists were concerned about current trends in British medicine does not prove that these things are relevant to *Playboy;* and for that we have to go to the work itself. As I will argue, Synge's audiences protested in part because they were profoundly disturbed by the fact that so many of the Irish bodies he put on stage were diseased, decrepit, or dead. Synge's play was dangerous because it mobilized the discourse of infection, filth, and degeneracy promoted by eugenicists in England — a vocabulary that both the play's defenders and its detractors recognized.

While early twentieth-century nationalist readings of *Playboy* tend (to put it mildly) toward the reductive, they are reductive in part because they respond to what they see as Synge's reductionism — his insistence on a materialist point of view in which the body usurps the place of the soul and people are reduced to the sum of their pathologies. If trivial details like the word "shift" take on exaggerated importance during the *Playboy* controversy, it is partly because *Playboy* seems to its critics to dispense with allegory and symbol and instead define the spiritual and cultural purity, to which the "Irish Ireland" segment of the cultural nationalist movement was so attached, in the most narrow and concrete terms possible — returning it from the realm of song, story, and myth to that of the corporeal body. And though anti-*Playboy* hysteria focused on the female body, it is my contention that this outcry masks deeper anxieties fomented by the public health movement — anxieties which referred to the health and purity of the *male* body.

In arguing that these issues informed the public reaction to *Playboy*, I am not trying to suggest that the objections voiced more explicitly were not real or that *Playboy*'s detractors were making a conscious effort to disguise the "true" source of their discontent. In fact, these more obscure anxieties have everything to do with one of the main problems that these protestors repeatedly raised — the fact that Synge is claiming to produce a representational, mimetic portrait of Irish life while at the same time he is manifestly doing something else. What I *am* arguing is that the question of accuracy becomes as important as it does in part because Synge's treatment of the human body seems to these audience members to coincide with constructions of the Irish as a degenerating race. To admit that his portrait was accurate would be to agree that the story that British medicine has been

telling about Ireland and the Irish is correct. And that is an admission that
Griffith realizes Irish nationalists cannot afford to make.

Blood Is Life: Pestilence and Pollution in the Dublin Press

Playboy's critics are consistent in citing a few key offenses of the play:
1) Synge's insinuation that Irish women find parricide sexually exciting;
2) his use of "coarse" language; 3) his implication that Irish people are
violent and lawless; and 4) his misrepresentation of Irish language and Irish
peasant life. They are also consistent in their expressions of revulsion and
horror. Griffith's review brands Synge a "moral degenerate" ("The Abbey
Theatre" 2); Holloway speaks of his "morbid and unhealthy mind" (81);
Máire Nic Shiubhlaigh recalls the performance as emphasizing the "nasti-
ness" of the characters (Berrow 76); Pearse calls *Playboy* a "revolt against
sane and sweet ideals" (qtd. in Kiberd, *Synge and the Irish Language* 252); the
Freeman's Journal characterizes it as "sordid, squalid and repulsive" (qtd. in
Kiely 164). This universal condemnation of *Playboy* as disgusting and vile is
bewildering to most modern readers, who find it difficult to understand
why *Playboy* should be considered "filthy." This bewilderment is not entirely due to the fact that standards of sexual decency have changed. The
kind of sexual license supposedly evident in Synge's choice of language had
become associated with disease through the eugenist movement's rhetoric
of degeneration, which had already claimed words like "morbid," "degenerate," and "squalid."[1] Without that context, it is hard to see why Synge's
play was condemned in these terms or why his "morbid" approach to plot
and characterization should have become a specifically nationalist problem.

The public health movement that supported eugenist medicine began
with panic over the male body. Fears of racial degeneration first became
news in Britain as a result of the problems the British Army encountered
when it tried to recruit for the Boer War.[2] Once it became public knowledge that recruits had to be disqualified for failing to meet physical fitness
requirements, the fear that the British race was in decline led to increased
government support for eugenist medicine, whose premises and tactics
seemed to promise a return to racial fitness and, by implication, the right
and the ability to conquer and control other races. Starting from the premise that heredity determined physical, moral, and intellectual fitness, eugenist medicine stressed the need to control reproductive practices so that the
fit procreated and the unfit did not.[3]

This emphasis on heredity complemented the doctrine of differential
fertility, a new variation on Malthusian themes, which posited that the poor
were inherently more fertile than the rich. Since poverty and debility were
held to be virtually synonymous, the result of this "fertility gap" would be
racial deterioration, as the ranks of the "defective" swelled while those of
the fit dwindled.[4] At the same time, technological advances made it possible

to identify microorganisms, a development which "created a widespread sense of psychological unease about the sinister invisible undercurrents of modern urban living" (J. Harris 55).[5] Linked to "fears about degeneracy and physical deterioration," germ paranoia spawned an "Edwardian obsession with 'cleanliness'" (J. Harris 55), one that focused not only on physical hygiene — public sanitation, disease control, and vaccination — but also on "racial hygiene" (J. Harris 236), which involved cleaning up the British gene pool by discouraging diseased or "defective" individuals from reproducing.

The obsession with heredity meant that sexuality became not only a moral problem but also a physical liability: misdirected sexual energy led to pathogenic unions, which produced unfit children and accelerated racial deterioration. Private sexual practices became a matter of public health; fear of degeneration through irresponsible breeding attached itself to microbe-related paranoia and emerged as a crusade against venereal disease, which Armstrong suggests was "invented" (18) for the purpose of allowing greater control over the British working class. As this 1909 report indicates, venereal disease became the cause and symptom of debility among the underclass: "I am convinced that the greater majority of children born in the poorest districts (slum) are tainted with syphilis [. . .]. They are mostly feeble in body and mind, possess no inhibitory power, and readily give way to the vices by which they are surrounded. It is from this class that paupers and criminals are made" (qtd. in Mazumdar 32). Venereal disease serves as the link between moral and physical decay while simultaneously identifying both forms of degeneration with the marginalized underclass.

Thus, in Edwardian Britain, "'purity' and 'pollution' [. . .] were no mere anthropological abstractions" (J. Harris 55); they were part of the framework of modern medicine, which sought to ensure racial purity through the elimination of pathological agents. Whether these agents were microbes or the people who were presumed to carry them, the British government believed it had a compelling interest in attacking them. Accepting the premise that, as George Newman put it in his pamphlet *The Health of the State*, "the physical health and fitness of the people is the primary asset of the British Empire" (qtd. in J. Harris 60), the state threw its weight behind a program of public health measures that, while ostensibly designed to control the spread of disease, also attempted to regulate sexual practices and to reconstruct the individual bodies of its subjects. And, as José Harris suggests, "latent fears about the global eclipse of higher races by lower ones" (J. Harris 235) translated the classist bias of eugenist medicine into a racist one that identified colonized populations as unfit and therefore legitimate targets for intervention.

As both the mainstream and nationalist presses demonstrate, Ireland was as firmly in the grip of anti-germ paranoia and as concerned about infection and degeneration as England was. The difference between the mainstream presentation of disease, as illustrated in the *Dublin Evening Mail* and the *Irish Times*, and the nationalist approach taken by *Sinn Féin* lies in an awareness on the nationalist side of the imperialist uses of both the rhetoric of disease and public health policies. But Griffith does accept the principles of eugenics, as illustrated by his attempt to turn the rhetoric of disease against the British—and this requires him to accept the eugenist view of sexuality as a vector of racial degeneration and thus to see *Playboy* as an attack on the health of the Irish race.

Concurrent with the rise of Synge as the Abbey's major dramatist, the *Dublin Evening Mail* began devoting more attention to medical issues. Five days before the premiere of *In the Shadow of the Glen*, the *Mail* ran an article entitled "Microbes and their Doings: The Curious Tricks They Play," which introduced its readers to Edwardian germ paranoia. With subheadings like "Places Where They Lurk" and "The Hostile Microbe Everywhere," this article is typical of the paper's sensationalist attitude toward infectious disease. It also shows that paranoia about germs is translating into more general anxiety about the permeability of the body's boundaries: "The hostile microbe is in fact everywhere—within and without us, seeking, we might say, what it may devour. All the natural cavities of the body—the nose, the mouth, and the digestive tube—having exterior openings are seeded with microbes brought from without by air or food, and afterwards multiplied" ("Microbes"). Since the vagina does not appear on this list of dangerous orifices, the passage appears to refer to a male body, which, even without this most dangerous port of entry, is porous, vulnerable, and susceptible to foreign invasion.

The *Mail*'s advertisers capitalized on this paranoia, incorporating the vocabulary of purity and corruption into their copy. Ads for patent medicines or other health products focused on the need to cleanse the bloodstream of unwanted pollutants. For instance, in 1905, Veno's Seaweed Tonic positioned itself as a cure for "blood and skin diseases" and declaimed, "BLOOD IS LIFE. LET IT BE PURE." The smaller print elaborates: "If your blood is pure your skin will be clear and healthy-looking; the direct cause of skin eruption is found in the blood. Purify the blood and you purify and clear the skin" ("Veno's Seaweed Tonic"). If the good people at Veno's claimed that corruption worked from the inside out, the copywriters at Zam-Buk Skin Rub were certain that it worked from the outside in:

> A tiny pimple on the face is usually attended to, because of the disfigurement it causes; but if the same kind of trouble manifests itself on back or chest, it is too often neglected—with dire results. Taking root in the unnoticed little sore, skin disease gets a firm hold on the tissue, and increasing irritation eventually compels attention to what may be by this time a mass of eruptions, a discharging ulcer that will eat deep into the flesh, or an obstinate poisoned wound. ("Zam-Buk Skin Rub")

Although the text claims that "men and women" alike suffer from the heartbreak of skin disease, the graphic shows a man standing in front of a mirror searching anxiously for lesions or blemishes. Thus, the integrity of the male body is clearly at stake here. That body's surface becomes the symptom and the cause of corruption at the heart; through the porous skin, the hostile microbe seeps into the bloodstream and poisons the well.

Nor did the hostile microbe present the only potential for corruption. Almost anything that entered the body could become a pollutant, at least according to the makers of Dr. Butler's Tonic Digestive Pills, who warned prospective clients that "FOOD IS POISON!": "If [food is] not digested, fermentation and decomposition are set up in the Stomach and Intestine. Poisonous gases and effete products get into the blood, vitiating the whole system" ("Dr. Butler's"). Once the connection between superficial and internal pollution is established, it becomes necessary to attack corruption invasively, even if the only evidence of pollution is a skin infection. These advertisements use their audience's fear of foreign substances to convince them to consume their medicine, playing on their paranoia about infiltration and pollution to get them to allow patent medicines to infiltrate and pollute them.

This tactic repeats in the commercial realm what is happening in the medical profession, which promotes and manipulates fear of infection in an effort to justify public health measures. The *Mail's* medical correspondent shows how this logic works:

> An infant a few months old, born of healthy parents, is found to have a mass of internal cancer. A woman, struck on the breast, has the disease at that very point where she was struck. A sore on the lip, fretted for years with a clay pipe, becomes malignant. A group of cottages round a village-green seems to be haunted by the disease. What theory will cover all these cases? ("The Study of Cancer")

The author doesn't know, but he is sure of one thing: " . . . we must not dream of trying, for the present, to get away from the surgeon." The cancer patient who "must not dream of trying" to avoid the surgeon's knife stands for his society, which must not dream of resisting the medical establishment's regulation of its habits and behaviors.

What emerges from the pages of the *Mail*, then, is the idea that the body — this time the male body as much as the female one — is endangered as never before, beset and besieged by invisible agents bent on corrupting it. If one eludes the "hostile microbe" at home, one runs the risk of infection during the "Deadly Tram Rides," against which the *Mail* warns its readers in January 1907 in an article that suggests that tuberculosis, rheumatism, sciatica, and neuralgia fester in the trams' "Dangerous Cushions." While the *Mail's* use of the language of invasion, pollution, and corruption was unselfconscious, in the hands of writers with a more highly developed nationalist sensibility, this sense of being threatened by foreign pathogens became a description of imperial power over the Irish subject — a power exercised by the medical establishment both literally (through projects like vaccination) and metaphorically (through the rhetoric of degeneracy). In this context, the meaning of sacrifice shifts, and blood becomes a symbol not simply of the purity of the martyr's intention but rather of the purity of his body — a purity which is constantly jeopardized. This sense of embattlement led to increased vigilance over the body's borders and, inevitably, increased attention to sexuality. Venereal disease, once it corrupted the individual, would poison the lifeblood of the race, passing defects down through the generations. Sex was now a weapon that could be used against the Irish.

Our Bodies, Our Selves: Sinn Féin *and Imperial Science*

While the *Dublin Evening Mail*'s coverage of public health efforts was generally supportive of the medical establishment's efforts to control disease, the contributors and correspondents published in *Sinn Féin* (the 1907 reincarnation of *The United Irishman*, still under Griffith's direction) took a very different approach. Their resistance to British public health measures bespeaks an understanding of the coercive power of imperial medicine, yet it also indicates a fundamental acceptance of the principles of eugenist science. As a result, outrage which might have been used to challenge a classist and racist medical establishment's attempts to "breed out" genetic liabilities was instead marshaled in defense of Irish racial purity against a playwright whose work appeared to attack it.

During the weeks leading up to *Playboy*'s premiere — January and early February 1907 — compulsory vaccination was under debate in *Sinn Féin*, with opinion running overwhelmingly against this measure. All of these arguments rested on the same premise — that vaccination polluted the bloodstream without conferring any health benefit and that by compelling the Irish to submit to it, the British government was trying to weaken the Irish race. The fact that there was a "conscientious objector" clause in effect for England and Wales but not for Scotland and Ireland supported this view of vaccination as a coercive tool, one designed more for Britain's subjected Celtic populations than for use at home.

It is easy enough to look back now and see the vaccination controversy as an example of groundless paranoia, and indeed I do not mean to suggest that by taking the anti-vaccination argument seriously that compulsory vaccination really was a diabolical plot. Nor am I implying that vaccination is somehow an evil thing simply because it has been associated with repressive public health measures.[6] But just as eighteenth-century distrust of Jenner's cowpox vaccine makes sense, considering how dangerous and ineffective most forms of eighteenth-century medical treatment were, uneasiness about compulsory vaccination makes sense in the context of Irish history.

Hunter's language is unambiguous: vaccination is nothing more than "compulsory rottenness" inflicted on a helpless population with the express purpose of "polluting the pure Irish blood" (1). Hunter conflates economic health and the integrity of the home with the purity of the body itself:

> But, seeing you advocate the boycotting of all foreign commodities, you may as well boycott this "pure rottenness" from the English pharmacopaeia — with your fine climate, and with the inheritance of health still due from clean living progenitors, you could easily get quit of the English "rottenness" by living on your own home-grown products and educating your people on the advantages of cleanly [. . .] and healthy homes.

In this strain of nationalist discourse, the individual body becomes the body politic; as it does in imperialist discourse, the body's borders, moreover, stand for the nation's borders. Violating the body's borders violates national sovereignty, and protecting that sovereignty becomes synonymous with policing the body's boundaries.

The dire effects of this "rottenness" are laid out in more graphic detail by F. O hUaithne, who describes the process by which the vaccine was produced:

> The fluid is taken in a vessel, "purified," skin, hair, scabs, etc. removed, and after various processes glycerine is added, and "pure calf-lymph" is ready for distribution to the dispensary doctors, who will impregnate the blood of our children — the children we are rebuilding a nation for. [. . .] We can never hope for a virile, healthy race, when the life stream is so early polluted with an animal excrescence.

The equation of health with virility indicates that from the nationalist perspective, the target of this plot is the body of the male patriot. The Empire's attack on the male body is presented in terms of a physical health risk, whereas its effect on the female body is depicted in moral terms. Hunter encapsulates the distinction when she charges that vaccination will "suck out the virility from our men and the morality of our women."

As in British medical discourse, the link between moral and physical decay in the anti-vaccination argument is venereal disease, specifically syphilis:

> [M]any experts regard vaccination and syphilis as identical. [. . .] The Army is vaccinated and re-vaccinated subject to the caprice of the Medical Department, and it seems plain they receive successive doses in an attenuated form of the above dread affliction. May not this be the cause of the early loss of the teeth, a syphilitic symptom, in those countries where cowpox, or "calf-lymph," is so extensively used? (O hUaithne)

O hUaithne's logic shows how unerringly panic about the permeability of the body returns to the question of sexual continence. However ridiculous it seems to equate smallpox vaccination with syphilis, eugenist science's rhetoric of pollution and degeneration rendered this analogy plausible. Both syphilis and this smallpox vaccine are acquired through a breach of the body's boundaries. Both are conceived of as pollutants that taint the Irish bloodstream. Both are believed to corrupt the body into which they are introduced. Both are "foreign-imported diseases"; vaccination is brought to Ireland by the British public health system, and syphilis is brought in by the British Army. As a result of this analogy, the moral rot associated with syphilis attaches to the physical debility associated with vaccination, and just as refusal to be vaccinated preserves the subject against both infectious and venereal diseases, chastity becomes a prophylactic against not only sin but also sickness — a barrier against syphilis and against the more insidious germs entering the Irish bloodstream via the British doctor's needle.

Hunter's formulation indicates that while this anxiety about the purity of the body is focused on the *male* patriot whose body is exposed to disease and corruption, the fear of moral contagion into which it translates is more easily projected onto the *female* patriot's body. W. E. Fay's "A Note on National Games," for instance, which appeared in *Sinn Féin* during the vaccination controversy, argues that the rehabilitation of the physical body should be one of nationalism's prime objectives. It is clear, however, that Irish men and Irish women will be engaging in different sports:

> If there is one fact more than another which the study of physiology and psychology has emphasised, it is the intimate and inseparable connection that exists (in this life) between soul and body. The Greeks saw this connection clearly, and sent their women to look upon beautiful statues before child-birth, in order that their children might be beautiful. (W. E. Fay, "A Note on National Games")

While the male patriot keeps himself fighting trim with rugby and hurling, the female patriot does her part by producing beautiful children. The corruption or decay of her body is important not so much in and of itself but because it will be transmitted to her children. According to eugenist theory, it is in the mother's body that disease becomes degeneration — that syphilis engenders birth defects, that promiscuity produces blind, palsied, or insane children, that moral turpitude translates into racial deterioration. For the mother, health becomes almost exclusively a matter of sexual purity; her duty is to protect the race by protecting herself from venereal disease. The anxiety with which male nationalists contemplate the infiltration and pollution of their own bodies is displaced onto the Irish woman and emerges as concern over her ability to protect her body from corruption by refusing sexual contact and by thus refusing to accelerate racial deterioration.

The vaccination controversy, then, shows that Griffith's coterie not only identified disease itself as an imperial weapon used to destroy the strength and purity of the Irish race, but also conflated imperial medicine and the diseases that medicine attempts to control. At the same time, Griffith shows in "The Immorality of the British Army" that he knows that the *discourse* of disease can be an equally powerful weapon, one he hopes to turn against its imperial wielder. Citing the fact that Patrick Lagan has been prosecuted for circulating statistics about venereal disease in the British Army, Griffith suggests that the accusation of disease is dangerous enough to prompt the British authorities to make it "a new crime" ("Immorality"). He then charges that the British Army has the highest per capita rate of venereal disease among European armies; he cites this fact to prove that "the British army is the most immoral army in civilisation" and is therefore unfit to enforce the dictates of an empire that justifies itself in terms of its civilizing mission ("Immorality").

Griffith thus accepts the equation of disease with "personal immorality" ("Immorality"). Although the British Army is perhaps too tempting a target to pass up, seizing the moral high ground is a costly maneuver. Griffith allows imperial medicine to define the terms of the conflict; any suggestion that the eugenist model of degeneracy might be flawed is foreclosed, and the only question remaining is whether it is the British or the Irish who are more unfit. Under these conditions, the charge of degeneracy that Griffith sees Synge making in *Playboy* becomes almost as dangerous as the threat of actual disease and debility represented by the doctor's needle.

"A Fine Husband This": Playboy *as Eugenist Parable*

It is not surprising, therefore, that Griffith should be suspicious of a play whose central premise is "the fighting of the women of the West for the hand of a parricide because he is a parricide" ("The Abbey Theatre"). That Irish women should fight over anyone at all is, of course, bad enough. But the fact that they are competing for the attentions of a murderer is especially problematic, because it suggests not simply that Irish women share the amorality that supposedly accompanies sexual incontinence, but also that this kind of violence is itself a hygienic practice. The competition further implies that the ideal of patriotic sacrifice central to Irish nationalism is itself merely a "gallous story" that disguises some 'dirty' facts about Irish physical and moral debility.

This is the attitude clearly taken by P.M.E.K., the author of "A Plea for the Playboy," the only pro-Synge article published in *Sinn Féin*. Arguing that the play's detractors are, so to speak, protesting too much, he claims the riots prove Synge's point, which is that "we have really no saintliness, no morals whatsoever." P.M.E.K. assumes that this lack of "morals" is both the cause and symptom of an epidemic of physical debility which marks the Irish as a deteriorating race:

> [Pegeen's community] is a village [. . .] nay, a handful of men and women,
> a fragment of a once strong and healthy race of which the existing male
> representatives are Shawn Keogh, a poor craven, weak in body and brain,
> and Philly O'Cullen; Jimmy Jarrell and Michael James, none of them
> much better. (P.M.E.K.)

This degeneracy could be cured by exactly what Griffith and company are most horrified by — the Irish woman's sexual attraction to an Irish murderer: "A fine husband this, for a spirited girl, but better than none, thinks she, and is ready to put up with him till Christy Mahon arrives, strong, well-favoured, and courageous; has he not laid his father low with a lick of a spade, and Pegeen exalts him to a hero" (P.M.E.K.). Her attraction to Christy is described as "a healthy girl's admiration for a strong man" (P.M.E.K.), that strength having (supposedly) been demonstrated by Christy's willingness and ability to murder his father. Thus, a complicated plot is boiled down to a story about the survival of the fittest, and *Playboy* becomes a cautionary tale about the importance of eugenics: Pegeen recognizes the right breeding partner but is unable to fly in the face of public disapproval and therefore rejects him for one of the weaklings in the village, which is "the whole tragedy of the play" (P.M.E.K.).

P.M.E.K. echoes the argument put forward a week earlier in the *Irish Times*, an article by P. D. Kenny, who wrote under the pseudonym "Pat" (Holloway 277). Kenny seems to have been even more forcibly struck by the play's eugenist moral. He describes Pegeen's dilemma in strikingly Darwinian terms:

> Why is "Pegeen" prepared to marry [Shaun]? "God made him; therefore,
> let him pass for a man," and in all his unfitness, he is the fittest available!
> Why? Because the fit ones have fled. He remains because of his cowardice
> and idiocy in a region where fear is the first of the virtues, and where the
> survival of the unfittest is the established law of life. (Kenny)

Christy, on the other hand, is "a real, live man," superior to poor Shaun, who is too craven and weak-minded "even to kill his father" (Kenny). Pegeen chooses Christy "instinctively and immediately," as her hormones acclaim the arrival of a suitable mate.

The eugenist reading of *Playboy* was thus reproduced on both sides of the political divide — in the nationalist *Sinn Féin* and in the conservative *Irish Times*. It is also endorsed by Synge in a letter to the editor of the *Irish Times* (31 January 1907). Synge does express a hope that other reviewers may find more in the play, but he appears to see Kenny's reading as legitimate rather than reductive or wrong-minded. And indeed, there is support for Kenny's reading of *Playboy*; enough to indicate that Synge was aware of, and playing with, the connections being made in medical discourse between disease, degeneracy, and sexual immorality.

Pegeen, teasing Shawn about his papal dispensation, describes her community as stocked with what eugenist science would call "defectives": "If I was him I wouldn't bother with this place where you'll meet none but Red Linahan, has a squint in his eye, and Patcheen is lame in his heel, or the mad Mulrannies were driven from California and they lost in their wits. We're a queer lot [. . .]" (*Plays and Poems* 177). There has evidently been a falling-off, since Pegeen sighs for the heroes of yore: "Where now will you meet the like of Daneen Sullivan knocked the eye from a peeler, or Marcus Quin, God rest him, got six months for maiming ewes [. . .]?" (177). And when Michael James gives his blessing to Pegeen and Christy, he justifies it in eugenist terms:

> It's many would be in dread to bring your like into their house for to end them, maybe, with a sudden end; but I'm a decent man of Ireland, and I liefer face the grave untimely and I seeing a score of grandsons growing up gallant little swearers by the name of God, than go peopling my bedside with puny weeds the like of what you'd breed, I'm thinking, out of Shaneen Keogh. (222)

Michael James, like the rest of Pegeen's fellow villagers, sees Christy's parricide as proof of his virility, assuming that Christy's physical strength and the "savagery" of his anger make him worthy to be numbered among the 'dead and gone' local heroes. The fact that Christy wins the games and excels in the sports in act III supports the villagers' assumption that violence and virility go hand in hand, and a lad "with the great savagery to destroy his da" (201) is exactly the lad a "spirited girl" like Pegeen should select as her mate.

However, the repeated use of the word "savagery" offers a different answer to the question Stephen Tifft poses when he wonders why "the notion of rising up in violent retribution against a tyrannical father" should "seem outrageous to nationalists who themselves paid lip-service, at least, to the Fenian revolutionaries of former days" (315). Tifft, along with other modern commentators, reads Christy's rebellion as an allegory of national struggle.[7] H.S.D., while reviewing the play for the *Dublin Evening Mail*, also suggests that "it is an allegory, and the parricide represents some kind of nation-killer." He adds, however, that "if it is an allegory it is too obscure for me." If H.S.D. cannot appreciate the parallel between parricide and nation killing, the context in which Synge constructed that allegory can help explain why.

The title of the review by H.S.D., "A Dramatic Freak," indicates that in this climate, a parricide is seen not as an allegory for nationalist violence but rather as the expression of some moral, mental, or biological defect—an atavistic "savagery" that healthy humans should have outgrown. Thus, if Michael James and Pegeen see Christy's supposed violent tendencies as proof of a healthy and laudable virility, these tendencies can also be read to

be indicative of insanity or hereditary degeneracy. These conflicting interpretations illustrate the double bind in which eugenist medicine puts any
population that British medicine can classify as degenerate. On the one
hand, that population becomes an enfeebled race which desperately needs
an infusion of health and virility; on the other, the violence that indicates
this virility becomes proof that this race is insufficiently evolved or defective. *Playboy* seems to put the Irish in this very vulnerable position by reading Christy's imaginary violence both as eugenic and dysgenic — something
that produces Christy's physical prowess but that is also linked to disease.

Playboy connects violence and insanity through the character of Old
Mahon, Christy's father. Christy's description of him stresses his irrational
fits of anger, his alcoholism, and his violent outbursts: "[. . .] and he after
drinking for weeks, rising up in the red dawn, or before it maybe, and going
out into the yard as naked as an ash-tree in the moon of May, and shying
clods against the visage of the stars till he'd put the fear of death into the
banbhs and the screeching sows" (188). Mahon has more than once been
"locked in the asylums for battering peelers" (189), which suggests that the
authorities read his violence as mania. Mahon admits to having been studied as a psychiatric case: "there I was one time, screeching in a straightened
waistcoat, with seven doctors writing out my sayings in a printed book"
(216). The kind of "savagery" Christy has presumably demonstrated is
associated in Mahon with congenital mental illness. The fact that insanity
was often attributed to a family history of syphilis makes the insult worse —
Mahon and Christy could be read as evidence of moral decline as well as
intellectual and physical deterioration.

Later commentators are free to read Christy's story as an Oedipal
allegory, but for contemporary nationalists, the equation of parricidal and
revolutionary violence was dangerous, and Synge seems to be insisting on it
in act I. The great men of yore that Pegeen cites as evidence of her village's
degeneracy are perpetrators of patriotic violence: Daneen Sullivan attacked
a British policeman, Marcus Quin engaged in agrarian violence.[8] When the
men try to guess what Christy has done, they assume that if it is not theft or
rape it must be political. "Maybe the land was grabbed from him, and he did
what any decent man would do." "Maybe he went fighting for the Boers,
the like of the man beyond, was judged to be hanged, quartered, and
drawn" (182). Once they learn the story, the men decide that Christy's
parricide qualifies him as a defender of the Irish home: "The peelers is
fearing him, and if you'd that lad in the house there isn't one of them would
come smelling around" (184). The assimilation of Christy's presumed parricide into the category of patriotic violence brings with it both sexual
connotations — his implied virility, potency, and eugenic fitness — and the
implication of insanity or feeble-mindedness, casting these other acts in a
clinical light.

This comparison between parricide and revolutionary violence can only be threatening to nationalists. Either it suggests that nationalism and insanity are the same thing or it suggests that when *Cathleen ni Houlihan's* audiences applauded Michael's decision to take up arms for Ireland they were applauding not his patriotic fervor but the physical prowess of which the play makes it a signifier. *Playboy* thus appears to literalize what is symbolic in *Cathleen*, and it suggests that the male patriot will rejuvenate Cathleen not by shedding his blood on the battlefield but by impregnating Irish women, begetting children whose genetic material will represent an improvement over the current degraded stock and who will achieve the physical health and moral purity that is clearly an impossible goal for the citizens of Pegeen's village.

By turning the sacrificial narrative into a story about racial redemption through better breeding, this eugenist reading implies that in Synge's Ireland, degeneration is already far advanced—that the Irish have already been polluted by "foreign-borne diseases"—and that the Irish body is already weakened, etiolated, and corrupt. Kenny makes the implication explicit in his peroration on the significance of Shawn's character:

> We see in [Shawn] how the Irish race die out in Ireland, filling the lunatic asylums more full from a declining population, and selecting for continuance in the future the human specimens most calculated to bring the race lower and lower. "Shaneen" shows us why Ireland dies while the races around us prosper faster and faster.

To read Pegeen's attraction to Christy as laudable rather than reprehensible is to accept Kenny's assessment of her alternatives. Pegeen's choice is offensive to Griffith for the same reason that it strikes Kenny as natural and right: she recognizes the murderer as a "real live man" because his local competition is so woefully unfit.

The kind of sexual prudery Synge's critics exhibit is thus related to more troubling anxieties about the health of the Irish race—a connection made clearer by the fact that it is not until after Old Mahon makes his appearance that the audience begins to find the play offensive enough to protest.[9] Like Pegeen and the villagers, Synge's audiences revolt when confronted with the evidence that Christy's story of violence represses the decrepit male body that Christy's virility should have destroyed. In act II, Old Mahon walks into Pegeen's tavern and shows Widow Quin "his head in a mass of bandages and plaster" (205). Padraic Colum's account of the first production cites that entrance as the real catalyst for the initial protest: "That scene was too representational. There stood a man with a horribly bloodied bandage upon his head, making a figure that took the whole thing out of the atmosphere of high comedy" (qtd. in Berrow 76).

Colum's suggestion that it was actually the body of the father—and more specifically, his graphically depicted wounds—that the audience could not stand to watch suggests that the outcry over Synge's alleged slander on Irish womanhood masks an unspoken resistance to *Playboy's* message about the state of Irish manhood. When Mahon, the primary link between violence and insanity, appears on stage wounded, bloody, and infirm, he becomes living proof of Irish vulnerability to corruption. His body has been suborned from within by drink and disease and breached from without by Christy's attack. His is a body under siege, and worse, a body that has lost the battle and so must be banished and replaced by Christy's in order to stop the deterioration of the Irish race. Instead of banishing it, however, Synge drags this corpse out of the void into which it is supposed to disappear and flaunts before his audience the decrepit, polluted body that Christy's violence should have destroyed.

What *Playboy's* detractors are perhaps reacting to when they castigate Pegeen and the women of her village for loving a parricide, then, is not their sexual incontinence but their complicity in this eugenist narrative — their recognition of Christy as their righteous partner not in spite of but *because* of his supposed destruction of this corrupted Irish body and the shedding of this tainted Irish blood. And if the play is described as "calumny gone raving mad" (qtd. in Kiely 167), the choice of insanity as a metaphor is perhaps not coincidental. In *Playboy*, a treasured nationalist doctrine has been transformed into a doctor's prescription, a cure for the mental and physical weakness that afflicts these Irish peasants. Depicting the Irish as already in decline and in need of genetic redemption makes the play, as its critics charge, "insulting" in the extreme; moreover, as Griffith and the anti-vaccinists believe, under a colonial regime, this particular insult leads to injury.

The anti-vaccinist contributors to *Sinn Féin* believed that the presence or threat of disease and infection in a subject population already served as a rationale for the British government's deployment of invasive procedures; the threat of contagious disease, for instance, became an excuse for injecting "rottenness" into the Irish bloodstream. Similarly, congenital disease, as a marker of racial unfitness, could be used to justify the extirpation of a particular population. Griffith's attack on *Playboy* shows how the insinuation of degeneracy translates into an argument for extinction:

> The author [. . .] declares in the programme that "the central incident of the Playboy" — that is the fighting of the women of the West for the hand of a parricide because he is a parricide — "was suggested by an actual occurrence in the West." This is a definite statement, and if the author can sustain it, we shall regret that so vile a race should be permitted to exist. ("The Abbey Theatre")

Even in Griffith's rhetoric, poor racial hygiene is grounds for extermination. From the anti-vaccinist perspective, a play that suggests that the Irish are in decline also offers them up as a target for imperial intervention. Even

Kenny, while endorsing the eugenist tenets that he believes the play illustrates, responds to this message with intense discomfort:

> The merciless accuracy of [Synge's] revelation is more than we can bear. Our eyes tremble at it. The words chosen are, like the things they express, direct and dreadful, by themselves intolerable to conventional taste . . . It is as if we looked in a mirror for the first time, and found ourselves hideous. We fear to face the thing. We shrink at the word for it. We scream.

In other words, Kenny admits that the play represents Ireland as the monster England believes it to be. Kenny accepts Synge's play because he believes the portrait is accurate, yet even he sees this depiction of "Irish life" as terrifying and dangerous.

Synge's attack on the purity, and thus the fitness, of the Irish body — through his dramatization of Old Mahon, through his suggestion that Irish women may be unwilling or unable to control their sexual urges, through his mockery of the sacrificial paradigm — coincides both with public anxiety about vulnerability to disease and with the nationalist concern over boundaries and the bloodstream that emerges as one of its variants. His attack also coincides with real efforts on the part of England to manipulate the behavior and makeup of the Irish race. If compulsory vaccination was not the nefarious plot that Hunter and O hUaithne took it for, the institutionalization of the insane, warehousing of the sick, and promotion of "racial hygiene" justified the general Irish apprehension about the anti-vaccination campaign. And it is for this reason that both Griffith and P.M.E.K. read *Playboy* the same way — as a parable about the relative unfitness of the Irish, one which proposes violence as a possible course of treatment.

A Gallous Story: Playboy *and the Power of Lying*

But if we examine the interpretations offered by Griffith, Kenny, and P.M.E.K., we can see some of the contradictions and elisions that mark both eugenist doctrine and the *Playboy* controversy. P.M.E.K., in proposing Christy as Pegeen's naturally selected husband, overlooks two major problems. One is that according to the laws of heredity, Mahon's defects would have to be passed down to Christy, which would make him an unlikely solution to the problem of degeneration. The other is that Christy has not actually *done* the deed that supposedly proves his fitness and virility. What turns Christy from a "dribbling idiot" into a "likely man" is not parricide but a story *about* parricide. If, as I am hardly the first person to argue, *Playboy* is about the power of language to affect reality,[10] then perhaps instead of validating eugenist medical practice, *Playboy* critiques the power of eugenist *discourse* and the dangerous relationship between it and reality.

After all, Old Mahon's insanity is created by context — by the authori-

ties who lock him up or the doctors who write down his ravings. The
Widow Quin's plot to convince everyone that Old Mahon is mad is perhaps
a commentary on the power of diagnosis. What convinces Mahon to accept
Quin's diagnosis is Christy's transformation:

> *Widow Quin.* You seen that you're mad. [. . .] Aren't you after saying that
> your son's a fool, and how would they be cheering a true idiot born?
> *Mahon* (*getting distressed*). It's maybe out of reason that that man's himself.
> *Cheering again.* There's none surely will go cheering him. Oh, I'm
> raving with a madness that would fright the world! *He sits down with
> his hand to his head.* Here was one time I seen ten scarlet divils letting
> on they'd cork my spirit in a gallon can; and one time I seen rats as big
> as badgers sucking the lifeblood from the butt of my lug; but I never
> till this day confused that dribbling idiot with a likely man. (215)

Mahon assumes he is mad because he accepts Quin's implication that if his
son is "a true idiot born" that this kind of transformation would have to be
impossible. In the eugenist worldview, a "dribbling idiot" dribbles because
of congenital defects. Rather than challenge the basic premise of eugenist
science—that heredity determines fitness—Mahon, with Quin's help, explains away this contradictory evidence by diagnosing himself as insane.

One thing medical discourse can do, then, is silence opposition by
pathologizing it. As Christy's transformation implies, it can also alter the
subject to fit the diagnosis. When Widow Quin finds Christy, she mentions
that he looks "fitter to be saying [his] catechism than slaying [his] da," but
by telling his story to the village girls, Christy starts becoming the hero that
they want him to be. By assuming that violence equals virility, the village
girls create not only the athletic prowess he displays in the sports but also
the implied sexual prowess that Griffith sees as the basis for their attraction
to him. By accepting P.M.E.K.'s reading of Christy as a eugenic hero who
will redeem the Irish race first through violence and then through sex, the
village girls work the magic that unsettles Mahon and turns Christy into the
Playboy of the Western World.

The plot of *Playboy* thus points out a contradiction in imperial science
that reveals it for the lie that it is. Christy becomes the incarnation of fitness
and virility only through a process of construction that ought to be impossible. Similarly, Old Mahon provides evidence of racial deterioration only
because he has been manipulated by Christy's descriptions, the "seven doctors" who restrain and study him, and the Widow Quin's duplicity. The
congenital debility of which Old Mahon is supposed to be the symbol is
constructed and imposed on him right in front of the viewing audience. All
the evidence for the eugenist reading advanced by Kenny and P.M.E.K. is
created by that first lie—the "gallous story" that sets in motion a process of
transformation through description, a process that is precisely what eugenics argues can never happen. What *Playboy* proves is that the power of

eugenics is built on a lie — and that eugenist science is valuable to its believers *as* a lie, as a tool that creates the reality it pretends to describe.

Realizing the power of that lie appears to liberate Christy and Mahon from it, although Pegeen and the villagers remain in its grasp. As Christy discovers to his grief in act III, the villagers' admiration for him bears little relationship to his deeds; when he attacks his father for real, the villagers merely reverse his diagnosis: "He's going mad! . . . Run from the idiot!" (225). But for Christy, realizing the gap between the story and the deed teaches him that what matters is not physical reality but who has the power to describe it. Christy refuses to abandon the role of hero–martyr, claiming it through language even as he is tied up and dragged out: "Then let the lot of you be wary, for if I've to face the gallows, I'll have a gay march down, I tell you, and shed the blood of some of you before I die" (227). When Mahon reappears, Christy corrects his earlier mistake by using language to enact the transformation that violence could not: "Go on now and I'll see you from this day stewing my oatmeal and washing my spuds, for I'm master of all fights from now" (229). Mahon appears to understand and appreciate what Christy is doing: "Glory be to God! I am crazy again" (229). He has once again witnessed Christy's impossible transformation from dribbling idiot into powerful man, but this time he embraces this "madness" as preferable to the perspective of the "sane" villagers, who refuse to believe that Christy could be the hero they made him.

One or Two Words Only: Authenticity and the Aran Islands

Playboy can thus easily be read as anti-imperialist — a critique demonstrating, among other things, the damaging effects of imperial discourse on the Irish subjects to which it is applied, suggesting that although the nationalist story about patriotic violence may be a lie, it is a lie that undermines imperial power. Nevertheless, the evidence shows that the play was read by both supporters and detractors as being complicit in that discourse, specifically as an attempt to transform the trope of sacrificial redemption into a diagnosis of degeneration and depravity. *Playboy* became an attack on the purity of the Irish body, a manifestation of disease in Synge's own mind and body or a deliberate attempt to poison Irish culture the way the medical establishment attempted to poison the Irish bloodstream. Why were Griffith and P.M.E.K. unable to see the story and the lie for what they were or unable to read the play as subverting materialism with the power of language?

An anecdote Yeats tells after the fact may help answer that question. Discussing the protests that broke out at the premiere, Yeats recounts Synge's response: "As I stood there watching [. . .] Synge came and stood beside me, and said, 'A young doctor has just told me that he can hardly keep himself from jumping on to a seat, and pointing out in that howling mob those whom he is treating for venereal disease' " (*Essays and Introduc-*

tions 312). Synge's point is that the protestors are hypocritical because their own behavior proves that Irish men, at least, are having sex out of wedlock. But for evidence, Synge turns to imperial science — the "young doctor" whose diagnosis brands these nationalist rioters as degenerates. And as eugenist science used venereal disease to link poverty, dirt, disease, and sex, and thus to keep subject populations subjected by constructing them as unfit for anything else, Yeats tells this anecdote to denigrate the "howling mob" and to argue that the riots were simply "that defence of virtue by those who have but little" (312). Here we see both Synge and Yeats, when under attack from nationalists, turning to medicine for authority — making the statement that imperial science *does* tell the truth about the Irish.

The howling mob could neither hear Synge's young doctor nor read Yeats's apologia. But Synge's appeal to medical authority had a more blatant parallel in Yeats's decision to call in the police. Synge's gratitude toward the doctor whose diagnosis helped discredit *Playboy*'s critics reflected the Abbey coterie's acceptance of some forms of imperial authority — a phenomenon of which Synge's audiences would have been aware. After the riots, a reporter from the *Dublin Evening Mail* asked Synge whether he intended the play as a realistic representation of Irish life, to which Synge replied no, "rather emphatically." Synge's critics can perhaps be forgiven for reading this denial as disingenuous. The preface to the play, which was printed in the program, made a very different statement:

> On the stage one must have reality, and one must have joy; and that is why the intellectual modern drama has failed, and people have grown sick of the false joy of the musical comedy, that has been given them in place of the rich joy found only in what is superb and wild in reality. In a good play every speech should be as fully flavoured as a nut or apple, and such speeches cannot be written by any one who works among people who have shut their lips on poetry. (*Plays and Poems* 174–175)

Despite an ambivalence about the permanence or materiality of "reality" evident in almost all of his plays, Synge claimed to have represented "reality" on stage. Since he identified this reality so closely with the "fully flavoured" speech he wanted to reproduce, he substantiated this claim with his anthropological work: "In writing 'The Playboy of the Western World' [. . .] I have used one or two words only that I have not heard among the country people of Ireland, or spoken in my own nursery before I could read the newspapers" (174). Anticipating, perhaps, the complaints of his audience, he justified the plot the same way: "Anyone who has lived in real intimacy with the Irish peasantry will know that the wildest sayings and ideas in this play are tame indeed, compared with the fancies one may hear in any little hillside cabin in Geesala, or Carraroe, or Dingle Bay" (174).

Synge, by numbering himself among "those of us who know the people," constructs himself as an authority, arrogating to himself the right to tell the truth, to represent the Irish not only to the rest of the world but also to themselves. Although his purpose is clearly not simply mimetic, Synge does ground his entire philosophy of drama, as expressed in this preface, on the idea that because he has lived with the Aran Islanders, he now has access to a "reality" that is denied to others. And as *The Aran Islands* demonstrates, for all his "morbid" sensibilities, he is just as interested as Griffith in finding in the heartland the purity that has disappeared from the outlying world.

Although his book documents the influence of Europe on Aran Island culture, there is one last place where Synge finds unsullied and unadulterated Irishness: the body. Not only is he struck by the "strange beauty of the women" of the islands he observes, but with an eye trained by eugenist science he also registers the health and vigor of the men:

> The absence of the heavy boot of Europe has preserved to these people the agile walk of the wild animal, while the general simplicity of their lives has given them many other points of physical perfection. Their way of life has never been acted on by anything much more artificial than the nests and burrows of the creatures that live round them, and they seem, in a certain sense, to approach more nearly to the finer types of our aristocracies — who are bred artificially to a natural ideal — than to the labourer or the citizen, as the wild horse resembles the thoroughbred rather than the hack or cart-horse. Tribes of the same natural development are, perhaps, frequent in half-civilized countries, but here a touch of the refinement of old societies is blended, with singular effect, among the qualities of the wild animal. (*The Aran Islands* 48)

Here, then, are the Irish bodies that W. E. Fay, Griffith, O hUaithne, and A. S. Hunter are looking for — the unconstrained, uninfected, unpolluted bodies that readers of the *Dublin Evening Mail* can never hope to maintain. But Synge defines this health in terms of the class system supported by eugenics, identifying fitness with "aristocracies" and unfitness with "the labourer." The gift of "physical perfection" comes at the price of language that associates the Aran Islander with "wild animal[s]," that identifies civilization with degeneration but equates the "natural ideal" with primitivism, that bestows health and virility with one hand and takes it away with the other.

The dangers of this approach become clearer when Synge tells the story that gave him the idea for *Playboy*.[11] The story is the stuff of which nationalist legends might be made. A man who kills his father in a fit of anger flees to a neighboring town. He is hidden for weeks from the state authorities, who attempt to bribe a community which proves "incorruptible." This story of Irish resistance to British authority becomes, in *The Aran Islands*, proof of the "tribal" nature of these islanders:

> This impulse to protect the criminal [. . .] seems partly due to the association between justice and the hated English jurisdiction, but more directly to the primitive feeling of these people, who are never criminals yet always capable of crime, that a man will not do wrong unless he is under the influence of a passion which is as irresponsible as a storm on the sea. (96–97)

In other words, what looks like nationalism is "primitive feeling." For these people, violence is not rational nor strategic but rather the result of an "irresponsible" passion.

However hysterical the anti-*Playboy* voices became, then, they were right about one thing: Synge's project is, in a sense, reductive. Translating "the association between justice and the hated English jurisdiction" into a putative "primitive feeling," Synge subordinates history and politics to a universalizing, essentialist vision of Irish culture, and instead of an act of resistance to British authority, the acceptance and concealment of a parricide become the expression of tribal feeling, a primal recognition of the irresistible strength of passion. Synge uses, moreover, the language and paradigms of imperial science to accomplish this reduction — or, as Griffith would call it, dissection.

At the same time, *Playboy* is much more complex than Griffith or P.M.E.K. realizes, much more complex than Synge's own preface gives it credit for being. What disappears from the nationalist critique is the statement *Playboy* makes about the constitutive power of discourse — the relationship between what is perceived as "reality" and the language that represents it. In the birth of *Playboy* from this story of impulsive violence and "incorruptible" community loyalty, we see the struggle in Synge's own mind between his desire to retain his idealizing view of the Aran Islanders and his awareness of the discourse of disease and degeneracy that was already fastening onto the Irish body.

Although modern commentators now agree that Synge suffered from Hodgkin's disease, during Synge's life and for many decades after his death his chronic ill health was attributed to tuberculosis, one of the contagious diseases that the *Dublin Evening Mail* warned its readers against. As a man forever denied the health with which virility had become synonymous, accused of both representing and fomenting the decline of the Irish body, Synge experienced the power of medicine at the most intimate level. Between 1897 and his death in 1909 he was operated on several times for the removal of swollen glands. Gogarty claimed to have diagnosed Synge just from looking at him when they met on a train in 1907 and speculated that Synge probably never knew what he was really dying of because "it was not a general practice at that time for a physician to tell a patient that he was not going to recover" (qtd. in Greene and Stephens 17). Synge has to have been aware of the limitations of medical science, not only of its inability to cure his disease but also of its power to alter his own identity and others' perceptions of him and his work.

Given that many of Synge's later critics explained his "morbidity" in terms of his illness, it is hard not to read the ad hominem attacks against Synge by his contemporaries—the accusations of degeneracy, morbidity, unhealthiness—as having some reference to his physical condition, which was deteriorating during the production of *Playboy*.[12] In Christy—the slight, shy, physically weak hero who constructs out of words alone the virility and health that biology has apparently denied him—Synge both accepts and resists eugenist conceptions of disease and the body. He seems to accept perhaps the diagnosis but not the prognosis—the presence of disease, but not its inevitable outcome. If biological purity remains a lost cause, there is still the chance of redemption through reconstruction—not just through the shedding of blood but also through the telling of lies. Disease may have breached the borders, invaded the body, but as long as Christy's command of language makes him "master of all fights," imperial science will not have the last word.

NOTES

1. "Morbid variation from an original type" was officially incorporated by Morel into the definition of "degeneration" in 1857 (Soloway 38); the belief that this genetic degeneration would ultimately destroy the human population was one of the tenets of eugenist science. The eugenist association of disease and genetic "defects" with urban poverty meant that "squalid" had pathological as well as sociological connotations.

2. On the effect of Boer War hysteria on the public health movement, see Hopkins 245–247; Soloway 13, 38–41.

3. For a basic overview of the eugenist movement and its theoretical premises, see Pauline Mazumdar's *Eugenics, Human Genetics, and Human Failings: The Eugenics Society, Its Sources and Its Critics in Britain* (London: Routledge, 1992).

4. On the doctrine of differential fertility, see Mazumdar 35–38.

5. The "Harris" cited here is Jose Harris, author of *Private Lives, Public Spirit: A Social History of Britain, 1870–1914.*

6. If I were to imply this, however, I would not be alone. Chris Carter, producer of *The X-Files*, recently revived vaccination paranoia with a plot suggesting that the federal government used smallpox vaccines to identify and keep tabs on Americans. Carter's use of this motif both references this country's colonial history—the smallpox subplot appears first in the episode "Anasazi," which is set on a Navajo reservation and which is obscurely related to the fate of the now-lost Anasazi tribe—and forms part of a "colonization" story line in which an alien race uses human collaborators to prepare the ground for its colonization of Earth.

7. Greene and Stephens endorse this reading in *J. M. Synge: 1871–1909*; Kiberd incorporates it into his treatment of Christy as a parodic Cuchulain (*Synge* 113–114); Kiely reads *Playboy* as an allegory about the rise and fall of the Irish nationalist leader Charles Stewart Parnell (177–179).

8. Here I am reading Quin's penchant for "maiming ewes" as part of the agrarian campaigns of the nineteenth century, in which tenants vandalized property and livestock in retaliation for evictions. I am thus contradicting Declan Kiberd's reading of this passage, which treats Quin's ewe-maiming as simply an expression of the cruelty Synge commented on in *The Aran Islands*. However, given that Quin was jailed for this offense, I feel justified in reading it as a political act.

9. The word "shift" occurs twice before the third act, which is when the initial rioting began.

10. Weldon Thornton treated this theme thoroughly in *J. M. Synge and the Western Mind*. However, numerous other scholars have produced alternative interpretations. For instance, Bretherton argues that the community creates him through their interactions with him (128–129); James F. Kilroy reads the play as an allegory of the poet's growth (119).

11. The fact that Synge's protestors identified James Lynchehaun as the source for Christy is another illustration of the connections they were making between violence, sexual misconduct, and insanity. Lynchehaun was concealed from the police by village girls after committing a crime, but his crime was not parricide — he attacked a woman he was sexually obsessed with, maiming but not killing her. The bizarre details of the case were familiar to readers of the Irish press. In Lynchehaun, violence is connected both to sexual incontinence and mental instability, and the protestors' insistence that Christy was Lynchehaun's fictional equivalent indicates that they read Christy's violence the same way (Greene and Stephens 260).

12. Greene's "J. M. Synge: A Reappraisal" credits Masefield with starting this trend. Although Greene challenges the view of Synge as a chronically weak and sickly invalid, he feels bound to accept the agreement on Synge's "morbidity," attributing it not to Synge's own illness but rather to a hereditary tendency toward gloom and seriousness in Synge's family (17–18).

—6—

Saying "No" to Politics: Sean O'Casey's Dublin Trilogy

Shakir Mustafa

> I wish to God it was all over. The country is gone mad.
> — Seumas Shields in *The Shadow of a Gunman*

> Here is something rotten, desolate, and to be destroyed by the sense of decent men and by the workers' red resentment! Sean closed his eyes, and saw a better sight.
> — Sean O'Casey, *Inishfallen, Fare Thee Well*

The second epigraph comes from a suggestive episode in one of Sean O'Casey's autobiographical volumes, in which he describes taking part in serving a meal to children at a Dublin school (*Autobiographies II*: 67). The hunger and general backwardness he sees at that school are depressing, and his response as a committed worker is that such misery should not continue. No sensible person would argue against this. What I find open to argument, however, is the kind of remedy O'Casey seems to suggest: Looking past this misery to a better world. Such escapism is even more conspicuous in his Dublin trilogy, *The Shadow of a Gunman*, *Juno and the Paycock*, and *The Plough and the Stars*, in which O'Casey offers a vision of Ireland's turbulent history that sidesteps meaningful engagement with that history and presents instead a blueprint for escaping its conflicts. Politics, especially nationalist politics, often disrupts the lives of his plays' characters. For some of them politics is an activity through which they evade overpowering social, economic, or domestic pressures. But the exit out of their dilemmas that politics offers O'Casey's characters proves tragically illusory. These characters, moreover, are rarely given opportunities to be aware of the destructive impact of politics on their lives, and thus, they continue to be helplessly drawn into it.

O'Casey's representation of nationalist politics is especially problematic because those of his characters who fail to say "no" to its allure do so
out of pretensions, fears, or cowardice, and so Irish nationalism is relayed to
audiences and readers through vulnerable vantage points. O'Casey's male
characters, in particular, show nationalist discourse as a web of futile proc-
lamations and gestures more destructive than these characters would ever
suspect. Consequently, this essay argues that O'Casey's refusal in the trilogy
to engage the political experiences of his characters is evident in his presentation of politics as a threat to domestic space; in his iconoclastic representations of past events, especially the Easter Rising; and in his insistence that
the only possible outcome of political activity is indiscriminate violence. By
presenting nationalists as pretenders destructive to self and others, O'Casey
does not allow them to make their case adequately or persuasively, and
he thus denies Irish nationalism a narrative sequence. Nationalist politics
becomes a peripheral activity in his plays, since it fails to contribute positively to the lives of his characters. As an incoherent, destructive, and irrelevant narrative, nationalism in the Dublin trilogy lacks justification and
legitimacy.

Among Ireland's major literary figures, O'Casey has enjoyed the un-
flattering distinction of receiving polarized critical and ideological recep-
tions.[1] The polarization that his work has generated, however, suggests its
significant potential in terms of understanding Irish politics and culture,
particularly during the revolutionary era. Critics and historians who frown
upon nationalism have generally applauded his plays and have sought in
them confirmations of their own political views. For many of O'Casey's
admirers, his theatre self-consciously sought to demythologize Irish nationalism, and hence, to describe it as "revisionist" would be justified.[2]
Pro-revisionist and anti-nationalist critics have also attempted to defend
O'Casey against those who criticized his representations of Irish nationalists, and the debate has sometimes taken polemical turns. David Krause, for
instance, claims that "Ulster republicans have consistently urged their Nationalist dogs to defile his work" ("Paradox of Ideological Formalism" 518).
It is disconcerting, to say the least, to equate criticism with defilement or to
see unsympathetic critics as belonging to a non-human species.

Conversely, some of O'Casey's disgruntled critics have argued that his
work confirms many of the colonial stereotypes of the Irish and that the
British, rather than the Irish, were his primary audience. Accusations like
these had surfaced during the "whirlwind" that the *Plough* aroused in its
first week on the Abbey stage. O'Casey qualified the specific accusation but
did not deny it categorically in his debate with Hanna Sheehy-Skeffington
over the *Plough*'s representation of the Easter Rising: "It has been said I
have been writing for England. I am not writing for England. I am writing
for England as well as for Ireland" (*Letters I:* 180). More recently, Ann Blake
has claimed that English audiences will favorably respond to O'Casey's

plays because "the savagery in the ironic attack of an Irishman on his own countrymen offers an elevated version of the effect of an 'Irish joke'" (76). The critical waters, obviously, have already been muddied with conflicting interests and ideologies. The rest of this essay will examine the Dublin trilogy against the ramifications of polarized interpretations to illustrate O'Casey's deepening estrangement from Irish nationalism.

The Shadow of a Gunman

After a period of frustrated dramatic efforts, *The Shadow of a Gunman* was accepted by the Abbey directors and opened on 12 April 1923. The single most important outside event governing its action is the Anglo-Irish War, which had ended only a few months earlier when the play premiered. Building on the fresh memories of the conflict, O'Casey presents a tenement community that has been tragically touched by the War. It is a little baffling, however, to hear O'Casey describe the subject of his drama in a letter to Abbey Director Lennox Robinson as "the difficulties of a poet who is in continual conflict with the disturbances of a tenement house, and is built on the frame of Shelley's phrase: 'Ah me, alas, pain, pain ever, forever'" (*Letters I:* 105). Although the War is not quite reduced to merely a nuisance that distracts a poet, O'Casey's description is unwittingly revealing. The Anglo-Irish conflict remains confined to the background, and we are only allowed glimpses of those participating in it. The play instead foregrounds illusions of involvement in this conflict when the tenement residents believe Donal Davoren, an aspiring poet, to be a guerrilla fighter "on the run." The prestige Davoren enjoys would seem to confer a similar respect on the nationalist anticolonial struggle, yet O'Casey emphasizes the residents' attraction to the image, not the cause. Davoren, then, easily exploits their misperception and plays the role of a gunman's shadow to enjoy Minnie Powell's attention, without regard for the danger he introduces into the lives of the other residents.

Davoren's problematic position actually hinges on sharing a room in the tenement with a peddler, Seumas Shields. IRA fighters and fugitives were known in that period to reside with others to help dodge the authorities. O'Casey skillfully manipulates this detail and creates a persuasive situation that dramatizes the political issues relevant to the current conflict when he makes Shields a repenting republican who is preoccupied with the way the War has thwarted his business. Shields is, however, still a nationalist, he says, although he has seen enough of Kathleen ní Houlihan to turn against nationalism and, indeed, against political commitment of any kind:

> I'm a Nationalist meself, right enough — a Nationalist right enough, but
> all the same — I'm a Nationalist right enough; I believe in the freedom of
> Ireland, an' that England has no right to be here, but I draw the line when

I hear the gunmen blowin' about dyin' for the people, when it's the people
that are dyin' for the gunmen! (*Three Plays* 111)

The line Shields draws indicates his unwillingness to embrace nationalism
when it becomes a sacrificial trap for civilians. But Shields is too elusive a
character to be taken at face value. Indeed, in him O'Casey creates a master
of evasion. He is "splendidly slippery," as John O'Riordan describes him,
and he is the precursor of *Juno*'s Captain Boyle and the *Plough*'s Fluther
Good (30). Although he is a self-proclaimed nationalist, his derogatory
references to the Irish as backward and unfit for self-rule and to the Irish
nationalist tradition represented by Kathleen ní Houlihan (80–84, 88, 109–
111, 119, 120, 125) are frequent enough to make the play's foundation,
rather than Shelley's phrase, his refrain: "Oh, Kathleen ní Houlihan, your
way's a thorny way."[3] Shields' claims to be a nationalist do not in and
of themselves legitimate his anti-nationalist comments, especially since
O'Casey also presents him as a coward who lets Minnie take the bombs to
her room and who loses his composure during the Tans' raid on the tenement. But his discourse is deliberately empowered by the dramatic irony
implied in the above speech: Civilians do die for gunmen, as we see in the
case of Minnie's tragic end.[4] His discourse is further empowered by the
mere fact that Shields keeps in front of the play's audience an image of a
ravishing Kathleen ("she's a ragin' divil now," 110), who has dragged the
country into the present violence.

O'Casey empowers the anti-nationalist discourse to the degree that it
becomes the drama's master discourse. Krause considers Shields to be the
play's central character, the one who delivers its message that "life is more
sacred than *patriotic* slogans; that human realities are more meaningful than
fanatical abstractions" (*Sean O'Casey: The Man and His Work* 68, emphasis
added). In this reading, Irish nationalism eventually becomes slogan-ridden
and life-threatening. Krause here merely points out the logical conclusion
the play develops in Shields' discourse as well as in the course of its action:
Needless death results from nationalist illusions of heroism. It is not surprising that Krause consolidates the play's message by providing polariza-
tions of his own: "life"/"slogans" and "realities"/"abstractions." Other
critics have noted that the play exposes "violence as destructive" of the
tenement community (McLoughlin 346) or that "ordinary people's lives
are invaded by violence and terrorism" (Murray, *Twentieth-Century Irish
Drama* 101) without identifying responsibility for them. In the absence of
an adequate historical context, violence does seem pointless, but such representation clearly falls short of providing an understanding of political
violence per se since it does not engage it on its own terms but rather on
those of the dramatist.[5] If O'Casey is dismissive of nationalist resistance,
should his critics duplicate his attitude? Murray's vague reference to "terrorism" may further discredit anticolonial struggle by relating it to the

most abhorrent term in the contemporary Western political lexicon. Representations such as Krause's and Murray's imply a rejection of the nationalist contestation of colonial rule due to its violent nature and thus suppress the issue of whether this violence had legitimacy.

Critics and students of O'Casey often interpret pacifist signals in his plays as the playwright's demythologization of Irish nationalism. Maurice Harmon, for instance, argues that the work of O'Casey and others, such as Denis Johnston and Sean O'Faoláin, was a reaction against "the romantic nationalism that had flowered in the 1919–21 period" (45). Interestingly, Harmon draws support for this argument from O'Casey's *Gunman*. The playwright, he says, subverts the period's "militant nationalism" by undermining violence and the figure of the gunman (46). But this conclusion has been thrust upon us by Shields himself, who says no to guns despite his belief in Ireland's freedom and Britain's unlawful presence. What I find ironic is that demythologizing, which surely implies scrutiny and serious questioning, is equated in the *Gunman* with the kind of impulsive line-drawing Shields performs.

Another equally problematic treatment of Irish nationalism in the play is O'Casey's indirect approach to nationalism; his ridicule, that is to say, is not of the movement but of a shabby pretense at nationalism. A cowardly nationalist who rationalizes abandoning nationalism and a gunman's shadow can at best be shadowy nationalists. The only nationalist who pays with his own life for what he believes in, Maguire, "blows in" for a few seconds to deliver a *coded* message about catching "butterflies" (83, 84) and then disappears. Obviously, O'Casey does not allow him to make a significant visual and emotional impression on us, which further inhibits us from feeling the impact of his death in an ambush later that day. Bernice Schrank is right in noting that Maguire "never explains his patriotic motivation, so his own death seems unnecessarily meaningless" (" 'You Needn't Say No More' " 78). His verbal failure hinders our understanding of and sympathy with his political action; on the other hand, the bag of bombs he leaves with Shields threatens the whole tenement house and eventually leads to another meaningless death. Admittedly, the play's final point may be the "contradictions between appearance and reality," as Kosok observes (16), but as an audience, what we see is only appearances, and hence, the presumed contrast between the two never materializes. Such is the case with the other character that has any pretensions to being a nationalist, Minnie Powell, a hero-worshiper who dies for a gunman's shadow. In Hayden White's terminology, neither Maguire nor Powell is given an opportunity to "speak" themselves "as a story" (2). White convincingly argues that writers extend the form of a story or deny it as a way of granting or withholding meaning. The denial of narrativity to nationalists in the play is consequently tantamount to a denial of meaning and legitimacy. The nationalists, nearly speechless or mesmerized, are virtually absent, and their ideology is appropriated and relayed to us through questionable agents. No wonder, then, that what otherwise could be narrativized as the Irish "War of Independence" becomes in the *Gunman* a senseless conflict engulfing innocent civilians.

In *Inishfallen, Fare Thee Well,* O'Casey describes the Anglo-Irish War as "another tussle between Saxon and Gael" (*Autobiographies II:* 33) and irreverently notes that "Christian Protestant England and Christian Catholic Ireland were banging away at each other for God, for King, and Country" (34). Critics and commentators who see in the *Gunman* a pacifist tendency have not misread the play's message but rather O'Casey's politics. The distance from which he views the conflict between the British and the Irish ensures that his play remains a partial engagement of the event. Pacifism in that period, as Greaves reminds us, "was not part of the situation in Ireland" (113). To partially engage an explosive situation is to commit to an imaginary middle between two extremes. What Ronald Ayling says in his commentary on the play's two songs (the nationalist song sung by Tommy Owens and the Unionist song sung by Adolphus Grigson) can be extended to the Anglo-Irish confrontation as well: "[A] plague on both kinds of extreme chauvinism" (84). But to plague the two extremes comes close to imparting a blanket rejection of contesting colonial rule. It is also a curiously one-sided view of the colonial encounter that flattens historical events by assigning responsibility for their development to one partner. Shields performs such a leveling when he declares, "I wish to God it was all over. The *country* is gone mad" (110, emphasis added). The "country," as later exchanges with Davoren clarify, exclusively refers to Irish nationalists.

Juno and the Paycock

The Irish Civil War is the backdrop for O'Casey's second successful play. A fresh round of violence erupted a few months after the Anglo-Irish War was brought to an end on 6 December 1921 (with the signing of the Treaty with Britain, which effectively liberated all but the six counties comprising the present Ulster region). A faction of the republican movement (the Die-hards or Irregulars) was not satisfied with the deal and opted for a militant course of action to bring about independence for the whole island. When *Juno* premiered on 3 March 1924, some pockets of the Die-hards were still resisting the Free State, although nearly a year before they had been decisively defeated. The Civil War had split the Irish nationalist movement, and the rupture further exposed the movement's retrograde aspects. In *Juno,* O'Casey turns to those new soft spots and explores their impacts on two tenement families.

At the center of the drama is Juno, a female Job who is in continuous negotiations with two crippled men: her husband, "Captain" Boyle, and her son, Johnny. The Captain, often drunk, is reluctant to work and claims the pains in his legs are crippling, and Johnny has lost an arm and a leg to recent conflicts in Ireland: the 1916 Rising and the ongoing Civil War. Johnny becomes rather agitated whenever he hears talk of violence. For much of the play's duration, no reasons are given for his anxiety, but the figure of a crippled and terrified IRA man soon becomes a significant component of the play's representation of nationalist ideology. Obviously, all the likes of Johnny and Boyle can really produce is idle talk, or what Raymond Williams describes as "endless, bibulous, blathering talk" (15). The Captain's failure to gain his household's respect is expressed through open parodies of Irish nationalism: "Today, Joxer, there's goin' to be issued a proclamation be me, establishin' an independent Republic, an' Juno'll have to take an oath of allegiance" (*Three Plays* 24). The play's audience at the time would recognize the Captain's proclamation as an irreverent reference to the 1916 Proclamation of Independence. The oath of allegiance refers to the British demand that officers of the Irish Free State swear allegiance to the crown. Boyle also presents his fellow drunkard and parasite, Joxer, as "an oul' front-top neighbor, that never despaired, even in the darkest days of Ireland's sorra," which Joxer parrots with: "Nil desperandum, Captain, nil desperandum" (41). These parodies mock the sentiments associated with republicanism, not just its rhetoric, and by association with the figures who enact them; rather, their ultimate purpose is ridicule of the movement itself.

Johnny's blather in particular turns doubly idle when it is debunked by a more effective counter-discourse provided by Juno:

> *Mrs Boyle.* None can deny he done his bit for Irelan', if that's goin' to do him any good.
>
> *Johnny (boastfully).* I'd do it agen, ma, I'd do it agen; for a principle's a principle.
>
> *Mrs Boyle.* Ah, you lost your best principle, me boy, when you lost your arm; them's the only sort o' principle that's any good to a workin' man.
>
> *Johnny.* Ireland only half free'll never be at peace while she has a son left to pull a trigger. (27)

His "Ireland only half free'll never be at peace" is a rephrasing of a Sinn Féin Civil War slogan, but it will soon turn out to be even more of an empty slogan when we realize Johnny has betrayed a fellow fighter. Thus, Johnny's discourse is mere rhetoric because his bragging will soon be revealed as a cover-up for his betrayal. O'Casey leaves Johnny's motives for informing on a comrade vague and consequently further alienates him; moreover, Johnny's moral and verbal inadequacy prevent our identification with him. Jack Mitchell has remarked that Johnny's principles are the "abstract" principles of republicanism: "[A] sacred, finished, total reality, needing no thought and demanding preservation, not change" (100–101). Mitchell is right, I think, because O'Casey's portrayal of Johnny voids republicanism of any sustaining vigor and thus denies narrative sequence to the movement.

An informer undermined by his own ineptitude and his mother's empowered counter-discourse cannot be but an abstraction. Robert Hogan's discussion of Johnny's function in the play is relevant here. He shows that his
implication in Tancred's ambush and his own death have no connection to
the play's plot of the illusive inheritance. Johnny's tragic end is one of the
devices O'Casey uses to turn the play into a tragedy (37–41).

By making him a vulnerable target, O'Casey facilitates deconstructing
whatever political and ideological positions Johnny stands for, and he does
this through Juno. Ayling has claimed that O'Casey narrates history from
the viewpoint of "the ordinary people" (78, 83). Juno thus assumes the
heroic function of representing hard realism in the face of the destructive
legacy of nationalist idealism. Her response to the tailor Needle Nugent's
appeal that the tenement residents show more "respect for the Irish people's
National regard for the dead" has been frequently quoted in support of her
identification with life: "Maybe, Needle Nugent, it's nearly time we had a
little less respect for the dead an' a little more regard for the livin' " (49). It is
Juno who works and provides for the family, and by virtue of that fact, it is
she who subverts the traditional value system represented in part by cripples
like Johnny and Captain Boyle. When she ridicules Johnny's appeal to principles, for instance, she makes "principles" look hollow and worthless, despite the fact that by losing an arm and a leg, Johnny did stand for those principles.[6] But Johnny has lost the power to narrativize himself or his cause (i.e.,
republicanism or nationalism), since what he stands for is denied meaning
and legitimacy. Hence, republican discourse becomes impotent rhetoric
that has nonetheless created a mad reality of bloodshed and betrayal.

More so than the other two Dublin plays, *Juno* shows the impact of a
writer's views on a work's characters and conflicts. The problem here is not
so much with expressing personal views as with forcing them on Juno.
Stanley Weintraub has pointed out that O'Casey could not refrain from
expressing his views through his characters. In part, this is due to his misunderstanding of Shavian dialogue and his subsequent reduction of it into a
mere vehicle for the playwright's agenda. Juno, Weintraub says, "is reading
an O'Casey editorial, however eloquent" (213), and he is right. O'Casey
himself had commended Shaw for showing him the real Ireland. Shaw's
Ireland, he wrote in *Drums under the Windows*, is plain and rough, unlike the
"lady" surrounded by dancing peasants, which Yeats presents (*Autobiographies I:* 559). It is revealing that O'Casey saw the difference between Shaw
and Yeats as one of "fac[ing] the facts" versus "the dreadful dreaming"
(560).[7] And, indeed, these are the very terms several of O'Casey's critics use
as well (as do revisionist historians in describing the type of demythologizing that their writings intend to achieve).[8] This kind of binary conceptualization, as expressed in the opposition of reality and dream, clearly empowers a perceived reality and hence reinforces the narrativity O'Casey
extends to the side he favors.

The play's celebration of the realism for which Juno stands is actually a blatant rejection of all types of political commitment. On this point there is considerable consensus. Even a critic like B. L. Smith, who defines O'Casey's vision as "satiric," produces an interpretation of *Juno* that runs along these lines. The play, he assumes, is about survival, which he sees in "heavy reliance on the bedrock of Juno's human love and sense of responsibility, and by not becoming involved. [. . .] The rank and file tenement dwellers [. . .] have no political or nationalistic commitments" (38). Smith is right in maintaining that satirists offer alternatives to what they satirize (4–5), but he does not interrogate what O'Casey offers as the alternative in *Juno*. To represent nationalist politics and commitment as nothing more than tenement calamities and then reject this politics is a refusal to engage nationalism as an ideological and historical phenomenon. O'Casey commits the fallacy Aijaz Ahmad describes when he points out that critics who debunk nationalism

> [N]o longer distinguish, in any foregrounded way, between the progressive and retrograde forms of nationalism with reference to particular histories, nor do they examine the even more vexed question of how progressive and retrograde elements may be (and often are) combined within particular nationalist trajectories; what gets debunked, rather, is nationalism *as such*. (38, emphasis in original)

The anti-nationalist atmosphere that revisionist writers and historians have helped to create has thwarted recognition of nationalism as a significant tradition in Ireland. O'Casey's insistence that nationalism is synonymous with its retrograde elements has contributed to this atmosphere. The result is usually the presentation of Irish nationalism as detrimental to progress and modernity and the call for an unscrupulous dismantling of its heritage.

The Plough and the Stars

O'Casey's ultimate confrontation with contemporary nationalists came with a bang. If the *Gunman* and *Juno* made them fidget, the *Plough* forced the nationalists out of their chairs and into verbal and physical protest. The play's hot spot now was the 1916 Easter Rising, which was at the time slowly passing into canonization as the formative event of the Irish Free State's founding. Public interest in the event and in its interpretations and representations then and now have made the Rising not just an historical happening but also a cultural phenomenon. This may explain why assessments of the Rising have produced their own share of controversy. Revisionist historians have generally made the event a prime target of their deconstruction of the nationalist narrative of liberation and independence. At the core of revisionist historiography's evaluation is the assumption that the Rising was more of a literary or romantic gesture than a meaningful military rebellion. "An enactment on stage" (Garvin, *The Evolution of Irish National-ist Politics* 112), "a dramatic pageant" (Fitzpatrick 101) — with these assess-ments a significant number of historians and critics with revisionist sympa-thies agree: F. X. Martin, Francis Shaw, William Irwin Thompson, Sean Cronin, Roy Foster, George Boyce, F. S. L. Lyons, and Conor Cruise O'Brien. Revisionists also tend to see the event as "emblematic" and "irra-tional" — in Foster's terms, as lacking practical planning and execution and as having had no chance for success. Perhaps most importantly, revisionists have popularized the assumptions that the Rising inscribed the politics of bloodshed and violence in Irish history and that its tradition has endured in today's Ulster. The Rising presented "young Irish nationalists with a pro-gram for the future," Martin claims (59).[9] In brief, revisionists believe that the Rising has achieved a status close to sacredness because of the early nationalist histories and that the time has come for more objective assess-ment. They also believe the event was not legitimate or representative of the Irish majority, and hence, they relegate it to the domains of the idiosyn-cratic and the irrational.

Responses to revisionist evaluations have attempted to correct or tone down some of the excesses apparent in critiques of the Rising. F. S. L. Lyons, for instance, rebuts Shaw's article on the event and its leader, Patrick Pearse ("The Shadow of the Past"), and Tom Garvin has recently at-tempted a better contextualization of the rebellion in his analysis of the period's political atmosphere. Colonial rule in Ireland and the absence of the consensual politics it entailed, Garvin acknowledges, created the condi-tions for violent protest: "[T]he British caused 1916, the War of Indepen-dence and the Civil War by their self-indulgent misrule over a long period" ("The Rising and Irish Democracy" 24).[10] Another historian sympathetic to revisionist contentions, George Boyce, departs from the general con-sensus that the uprising was a failure or that its leaders had a sectarian (i.e., Catholic) agenda (*Nationalism in Ireland* 309–311). Boyce also criticizes the lack of appropriate contextualization for the event in revisionist historiogra-phy when he says it is impossible to separate the Rising from the "rediscov-ery of ancient, Gaelic, free and equal Ireland, inspired by the Revival move-ments of the turn of the century, and spread through a range of nationalist publications, organizations, and clubs" ("1916" 171). Boyce's reference to the nationalist narrative of continuity with the Gaelic past indicates that isolation of the event is intended to deny it the legitimacy derived from collective endeavor and imagining.[11]

In the *Plough*, O'Casey once again directs his attention to a tenement community and looks at history and nationalist politics as they affected the residents' lives. More than either the *Gunman* or *Juno*, the play's external action shapes the residents' destiny, especially that of the Clitheroes. Ignor-ing his wife's appeals, Jack Clitheroe decides to join a nationalist parade. What we see in relation to that parade is the figure of the shadowy speaker who is heard mobilizing the public. When the Rising takes place a few months later, Nora Clitheroe tries to save her husband by persuading him to stay away, but she fails: He is killed during Easter Week, and she loses their premature baby. Meanwhile, the tenement dwellers, who have been indifferent to the Rising, join the looters who take advantage of battered shops.

To illustrate O'Casey's unsympathetic dramatization of the rebellion, I will begin by considering two passages from the play's final act. In the first, Captain Brennan reports Jack's death to the tenement residents:

> *Bessie (with partly repressed vehemence).* Ay, you left him! You twined his Rosary beads round his fingers, an' then you run like a hare to get out o' danger!
>
> *Capt. Brennan.* I took me chance as well as him. . . . He took it like a man. His last whisper was to 'Tell Nora to be brave; that I'm ready to meet my God, an' that I'm proud to die for Ireland.' An' when our General heard it he said that 'Commandant Clitheroe's end was a gleam of glory.' Mrs. Clitheroe's grief will be a joy when she realizes that she has had a hero for a husband.
>
> *Bessie.* If you only seen her, you'd know to th' differ. (204, ellipsis in original)

Earlier, Brennan says that Jack was shot in the arm and chest, that their building collapsed, and that they had to abandon it along with their dying comrade. The heroism celebrated in the passage is thus preceded with what would eventually undermine it, since those who survived dishonored themselves by leaving behind a wounded fellow fighter. Bessie is quick to point that out, and she makes it the central issue of her litany. Jack's heroism and the General's eloquent words are dismissed as mere madness and rhetoric through Bessie's common-sense responses. Bessie's two speeches effectively bracket the heroic leftovers of Brennan's words and thus circumscribe their circulation.

The second passage provides an even sharper reaction to death and loss:

> *Nora (thoughtfully).* There is something I want to remember, an' I can't. *(With agony)* I can't, I can't, I can't! My head, my head! *(Suddenly breaking from Bessie, and running over to the men, and gripping Fluther by the shoulders)* Where is it? Where's my baby? Tell me where you've put it, where've you hidden it? My baby, my baby; I want my baby! My head, my poor head. . . . Oh, I can't tell what is wrong with me. *(Screaming)* Give him to me, give me my husband.
>
> *Bessie.* Blessin' o' God on us, isn't this pitiful!
>
> *Nora (struggling with Bessie).* I won't go away for you; I won't. Not till you give me back my husband. *(Screaming)* Murderers, that's what yous are; murderers, murderers! (205, ellipsis in original; emphasis added)

Despite the pathos of Nora's speech, death here becomes an overwhelming reality. Mad or not, Nora is still able to condemn the rebels as murderers. The ambiguous referent in "[g]ive him to me, give me my husband" could mean baby and/or husband, and this statement delivers in a painful nutshell the message of a domestic sphere caught up in the unpredictable courses of violence. The manner in which O'Casey contextualizes the two accounts again raises the issue of narrativity. Bessie's disparaging response to Brennan's leaving Jack in a burning building and her doubts that Nora will be overjoyed to hear about his heroic death are meant to prevent the nationalist narrative from achieving coherence. They represent this narrative in terms of defeat and cowardice, and suggest that its relevance to the tenement could be seen only in the collateral damage it brings. The counternarrative, which ridicules heroism and celebrates domesticity, is empowered and allowed to circulate. Its legitimacy, indeed, is established when Jack, broken and retreating, tells Nora: "My Nora, my little, beautiful Nora; I wish to God I'd never left you" (194). This counter-narrative has already been foregrounded at the end of the previous act with sights of frightened rebels (196–197), with accusations that rebels fled the fighting (195), and with Bessie's shouts of joy at the retreating fighters (194–196).

An economy of circulation such as this is the play's dominant mode of representing the nationalist project. We see it in another scene when the wounded Lieutenant Langon demonstrates through cries of pain the ultimate consequences of sacrificial tendencies. Langon occupies the stage for a considerable time (193–197), serving apparently to subvert the speaker's rhetoric of "the red wine of the battlefields" (164). The nationalist narrative is undermined in this scene from a number of angles: the rebels' irresponsible urge to shoot the "slum lice" looting the shops; Nora's futile and sentimental attempts to hold on to Jack; the feelings of guilt, shame, and fear that shove the fighters toward an inevitable doom; and Bessie's spiteful jeers at the broken rebels. In these pathologies of total disarray, the nationalist narrative deconstructs itself. This dissolution takes a particular direction when we compare Langon's ordeal to a single British casualty reported in act 4. Private Taylor, we are told, "got 'it roight through the chest, 'e did; an 'ole in front of 'im as 'ow you could put your fist through, and 'arf 'is back blown awoy! Dum-dum bullets they're using" (213). This brief but graphic description of the fatal injury does not suggest the kind of subservience to a morbid rhetoric that Langon's agony implies. Rather, the loss is due to the rebels' violation of the rules of the game. The allegations that the rebels used dum-dum bullets had been found groundless by an official British inquiry, and thus, denial of narrative sequence is complicated by distortions. On the other hand, Private Taylor is given the status of being "one of hour men" (212), and his membership in such a camaraderie makes his death meaningful and legitimate.

O'Casey also employs other strategies to discredit the nationalist narrative. The speaker in act 2, for instance, is clearly identifiable with the Rising's leader, Patrick Pearse. O'Casey keeps him offstage but carefully dramatizes the inflammatory impact of his words on some of the play's characters.[12] O'Casey uses quotations from Pearse's speeches and writings, but his rendering of these further undercuts the figure. W. A. Armstrong compares the Pearse quotations in the play with their original contexts and concludes that the dramatist utilizes the select passages to depict his speaker in "more dogmatic, aphoristic, and oracular" ways (236). This deformed Pearse is a natural product of the deformed nationalist ideology one finds in the *Plough*. Indeed, his image comes close to the oversimplified version of the Rising's leader common in revisionist readings. J. J. Lee relates such derogatory representations to their producers' failure to find the man behind the famous "quotable quotes" ("In Search of Patrick Pearse" 126). It is an oversimplification, Lee states, to equate Pearse with such passages: "His actions cannot simply be read off from sentiments expressed in either his political or his creative writings" (128). Lee also rebuts the typical image of Pearse as a master of blood-sacrifice ceremonies when he documents his concerns with supplying the rebels with sufficient arms, his "revulsion against violence," and his attempt to save lives when he gave the surrender orders (127–134). Nevertheless, the play inscribes an image of the speaker that many critics have been circulating for years: He is obsessed with death, Bernice Schrank says ("Anatomizing an Insurrection" 217); and Nicholas Grene notes the dramatist's "brilliantly malicious selection of the more sanguinary passages" from Pearse to create "a grotesque and terrifying parody of Pearse's Messianic rhetoric" ("Distancing Drama" 48–49). That such selective strategy does justice neither to Pearse nor Irish nationalism does not typically become part of the critical inquiry. Also, to assume that the Rising in the *Plough* has been subverted by "romantic impulses," such as "primitive bloodlust" (Schrank, "Dressing Up" 7), rather than by O'Casey's refusal to narrativize and contextualize the event, is to betray an ambivalent attitude toward representation itself. This ambivalence is characteristic of revisionists who concentrate on the effects of such representations but who rarely question their intentions. Kiberd has even suggested that to show Pearse as a sacrificial "dealer in the deaths of others" accords with the revisionist image of gunmen as "Catholic bigots" (*Inventing Ireland* 227). Again, certain revisionist analyses of Irish history and culture serve to facilitate uncritical condemnation of nationalist politics.

O'Casey's denial of narrativity to Irish nationalism confronts us in other forms in the *Plough*. The kind of contrast O'Casey establishes between "hearts o' stone" and "hearts o' flesh" in *Juno*, for example, and between gunmen and civilians in the *Gunman* reappears in a more subtle manner in the *Plough*'s polarization of the domains of domesticity and politics. Some critics have already noted this contrast: Seamus Deane sees it in terms of the "separation between private and public value" (*Celtic Re-*

vivals 112); George J. Watson in terms of tragic politics versus domestic affection (277); and Shaun Richards in terms of the public space's "threat" to the "domestic world" (34). The domestic space unfolds in act 1 at the home of a newly married couple: Nora is working hard on turning the couple's plain residence into a paradise of sorts, and Jack is singing to that little, red-lipped wife. Then comes the dreaded knock at the door and the intrusive weight of politics. Songs in melodramatic love scenes, as Stephen Watt has argued, are a popular theatre tradition that has generally celebrated nationalist sentiments (143–176). Its subversive use in O'Casey's drama, Watt explains, is part of the playwright's drive to deconstruct the "dominant ideologies of Irish society, religion and nationalism" (149). But the nationalism that O'Casey demythologizes in the *Plough* is a sham, since we have already been told that Jack's ties with the Citizen Army are bred by his desire to be "conspishuous" (140), his envy of Captain Brennan (151, 153), and his vanity (158). Kiberd has noted the play's failure to "render the full pressure of the nationalist appeal" (*Inventing Ireland* 228), and nowhere better does this failure register than in Jack Clitheroe. The martyr praised by the General as a hero is only someone who makes a fetish of a uniform. Jack is by no means an anomalous example, and that is why he becomes, to some of O'Casey's critics, a representative of "the *patriotic* infatuation with fancy uniforms" (Schrank, "Dressing Up" 11, emphasis added). O'Casey's refusal to present a nationalist with complex motivation is part of his act of denying the Rising narrativity. Conversely, the domestic space is allowed narrative sequence in the love scene and in Nora's courageous, though futile, endeavor to wrest her husband from politics.

O'Casey's most severe critique of Irish nationalism in the *Plough* comes in the public house scene in act 2. Nationalists were outraged to see the flag associated with Irish nationalism, the tricolor, brought to the pub.[13] O'Casey further juxtaposes the Pearse quotations and the public house discourse, particularly the prostitute's jeering remarks that the nationalists' "holy mood" is hurting her business (161). Rebels also appear there to drink and seal their allegiance to Mother Ireland. In defending his iconoclastic scene, O'Casey argues that he had seen the tricolor in worse places (*Letters I:* 169).[14] Obviously, the nationalist objection is based on selective representation that denies the nationalist symbol any particular status. The tricolor, Peter Alter states, has become for the Irish a symbol of an historical era: "The symbols of revolutionary nationalism gained popularity as the majority of the Irish people identified with the political aims of the Easter revolutionaries" (15). For the nationalists, the flag carried the weight of memory, and therefore, it called for a rhetoric of commemoration, not desecration.

It is illuminating to view O'Casey's treatment of the flags in the light of Pierre Nora's arguments about memory and national symbols. Nora notes that a nation's symbols become "sites" of memory to preserve past values and traditions that a nation deems worth keeping. Hence, he likens iconoclasm to "running a knife between the tree of memory and the bark of history" (10). Memory sites embody collective consciousness of the past and the present as constructed narratives, and consequently, an individual's endeavor to deconstruct these narratives is bound to provoke a group reaction. O'Casey is practically substituting the pub as a memory site for the more privileged site of the General Post Office. Public houses, as Watt remarks, "were frequently connected in the public imagination with the worst variety of Stage Irishmen" (168). In this sense, Irish nationalist sentiments are linked in the *Plough* to a trajectory of abominable stereotypical representations of the Irish. On the other hand, the linkage may suggest just a "pseudo-nationalism," deliberately conceived and staged as such to facilitate its "demythologizing." That may explain why the linkage is effective enough for anti-nationalists, who often note its consequences but not its subversive agenda. Thompson, for instance, notes that O'Casey's "irony is ferocious, but artistically, it is an irony that works by suggestive juxtapositions" (217). The focus in Thompson's statement falls on how ironic juxtapositions work rather than on what is being juxtaposed.

Nationalists, of course, took a different position in regard to these juxtapositions. In her debate with the playwright, Hanna Sheehy-Skeffington unequivocally asserted that her objections are based on nationalist grounds (*Letters I:* 167), and O'Casey responded by claiming demystification as his intention: Shaking the "tinsel of sham [. . .] from the body of truth" (169). This polarization of truth and sham is at the base of the revisionist rationale for assaulting whatever is deemed nationalist mythology on the grounds that such mythology is false. Responding to this artificial binary, Sheehy-Skeffington's objections to the play revolved around matters of representation. She emphasized, for instance, that the Rising's image was too negative and one-sided, because cowardice, pretensions, and looting could not fairly represent that event. She did not take kindly, moreover, to the quotations from Pearse, which she claimed were "spoken in almost his very accents" (*Letters I:* 172), nor did she find the play's characters representative enough: "Nora Clitheroe is no more 'typical of Irish womanhood' than her futile, snivelling husband is of Irish manhood" (173). O'Casey defended his characterizations by appealing to his interest in men and women in a universal sense (*Letters I:* 175). He depicted, he said, the fear that he knew some rebels had and explained why the British, by comparison, were more positively represented: "Isn't it natural that [the Tommies] should have been a little steadier than the Irish fighters?" (*Letters I:* 175). What Sheehy-Skeffington actually pointed out was O'Casey's denial of narrative sequence to the Rising. To depict the event and the rebels through exceptions is, in effect, to misrepresent them, as O'Casey has also done in *Gunman* and *Juno*. Similarly, to defend unfurling the tricolor in a pub by saying that one had seen it painted on a lavatory may amount to a self-serving reduction of the terms of representation.

It is unlikely O'Casey missed Sheehy-Skeffington's point about negative representation, but he did not take her critique seriously enough to develop a careful reply to her concerns. In his very first response, O'Casey dismisses the critique as worthy only of "the charity of our silence," because his opponent sings "on a high note wildly beyond the range of her political voice" (*Letters I:* 171).[15] The sexist gesture of extending the charity of silence to Sheehy-Skeffington is comparable to O'Casey's reaction to women's protests against his dramatization of the Rising. "The Republican women shouted with loud voices," he wrote, "against the representation of fear in the eyes of the fighters" (169). As Laura E. Lyons remarks, the claim that women protested because the image of the rebels was less than heroic "oversimplifies the concerns of these women" (102). Lyons has also demonstrated that women's participation in the Rising was largely motivated by their drive toward gender equality (101–140). For them, the rebellion was "an inaugural event" (116), and they kept agitating to realize its promises in regard to both national and gender issues. It is curious that O'Casey's critics who find in his plays positive images of women do not pay sufficient attention to sexist attitudes in his representation of Nora and in his debate with Sheehy-Skeffington.[16]

The sexist attitude O'Casey reveals during his debate with Sheehy-Skeffington illuminates another problematic association in his work between nationalist commitment and women's bodies. In the *Plough*, for instance, Jack's involvement in nationalist politics correlates with his lack of interest in his wife (Schrank "Anatomizing an Insurrection" 218; Thompson 219). What is even more revealing, however, is O'Casey's portrayal of his own estrangement from Irish nationalism in similar terms. Under the title "A Terrible Beauty Is Borneo," he records his impressions of the Irish Civil War in a parody of Yeats's line, "a terrible beauty is born." The Ireland he sees has been transformed into an "old hag": "Turn your back on it all, Sean, a vic o! Turn your back on the green and the gold, on the old hag that once had the walk of a queen" (*Autobiographies II:* 125). The old hag reappears later when he finds himself sharing a table with Maud Gonne, the staunch nationalist who came to support Sheehy-Skeffington in her debate with O'Casey:

> Sean saw, not her who was beautiful, and had the walk of a queen, but the poor old woman, whose voice was querulous, from whom came many words that were bitter, and but few kind. [. . .] She, too, was changed, changed utterly, for no ring of glory now surrounded that crinkled, querulous face. Shadows now were all its marking, shadows where the flesh had sagged. (*Autobiographies II:* 152)

Gonne becomes one with Ireland, nationalism, and what is physically unattractive in women. His description of the demystified Ireland of the revolutionary era, "the terrible beauty was beginning to lose her good looks" (*Autobiographies II:* 72), seems to have a literal meaning as well as a metaphoric one. The old hag undergoes a further metamorphosis during the *Plough* riots at the Abbey: "He saw now that the one who had the walk of a queen could be a bitch at times" (*Autobiographies II:* 150).

Commenting on the Dublin plays, Tomás MacAnna, a former Abbey director, declares that O'Casey creates a tenement world touched and changed by indifferent violence and that he "takes no sides. He writes as he sees. He stands aside, he does not get involved" ("Nationalism from the Abbey Stage" 98). Undoubtedly, many will find this assessment unfair to O'Casey, for he gets involved, and he definitely takes sides. O'Casey's dramatic juxtapositions, as we have seen in the public house scene, for instance, are not uncommitted commentaries; rather, they offer a deliberate critique of Irish nationalism. But O'Casey's representation of nationalist politics is in fact uninvolved, since he does not persuasively engage his characters' political experiences and commitments. Seamus Deane has described O'Casey's politics as "a form of shadow-boxing" (*Celtic Revivals* 109), an apt analogy that reveals the detrimental distance between engaging politics to show its importance and impact on communities, and refusing such engagement. To say "no" to politics in that period is to refuse to recognize that Irish nationalism provided a community under colonial hegemony with a viable form of collective resistance. Undermining nationalist politics while ostensibly championing the domestic sphere also overlooks the negative impact of colonial domination on this sphere and, rather perversely, faults nationalism instead.

Admittedly, histories and ideologies have always been the subject of scrutiny and revision, but demythologizing the past should not mean disowning it. Nor should it mean wholesale rejection of politics. In the *Gunman*, one of the auxiliaries responds to Seumas Shields' claim that "no one in the house has any connection with politics": "We're a little bit too ikey now to be kidded with that sort of talk" (123). On this matter I agree with the auxiliary. The British soldier has realized from experience that it would be difficult to stay away from political involvement during a major confrontation such as the Anglo-Irish War. Like Shields, O'Casey chooses denial over investigation of what makes politics such a dynamic force in Irish society. Like his gesture in the school meal episode, he closes his eyes and sees better sights. The problem is that for better or worse, politics will still be around when he opens his eyes. The dichotomous vision of the Dublin trilogy, which privileges humanity over political activity, produces a false opposition merely to denigrate politics. Michael Kenneally has pointed out a suggestive pattern in O'Casey's autobiographical writings, one which I think illuminates the politics of the Dublin trilogy. According to Kenneally, O'Casey uses reveries and fantasies to juxtapose "fanciful passages with more realistic accounts of experience" to heighten the "discrepancy between the world as it is and as O'Casey believes it might be"

(140, 142). If this reverie world is "idealistic," then the *Plough* riots have shown that even idealism could be found wanting.

NOTES

1. Those who have defended his politics have found in his plays a vision of Irish history and society that counters the nationalist narrative and that offers as an alternative pacifism or universalism. David Krause, for example, has been arguing along these lines for over three decades, presenting the Dublin plays as early studies in pacifism in the face of the violent rhetoric and deeds of Irish nationalism. Krause also interprets what he calls "the desecration of Ireland's household gods" in O'Casey's Dublin plays as a deliberate act of substituting for the presumed values of Irish nationalism higher human values, such as domestic commitments ("Sean O'Casey and the Higher Nationalism"). Occasionally, those who defend O'Casey's politics do so on the grounds that no particular ideological commitment or position in any of his plays is identical with the dramatist's own positions or commitments. In *O'Casey the Dramatist*, for instance, Heinz Kosok claims that O'Casey's plays are "objective" in the sense that their author "dramatically juxtaposes various views without identifying with any of them" (24). Other critics have approached O'Casey's ironic distance as being indicative of his political naiveté. For example, C. Desmond Greaves insists that O'Casey's political consciousness has been considerably shaped and troubled by the fact that "he was not 'out' in 1916." His negative rendering of the 1916 Rising in the *Plough* as well as in his *Autobiographies*, according to Greaves, was motivated by self-justification (11). A more negative evaluation of O'Casey's politics is that of Seamus Deane. O'Casey, he says, does not "develop a critique of Irish history or politics, even though he makes gestures in that direction" (*Celtic Revivals* 108). Further, these gestures sentimentalize or rationalize politics rather than explore it in any meaningful manner (114). George J. Watson also expresses reservations concerning what he believes to be an oversimplification of Irish nationalism in the Dublin plays. Of particular relevance to my approach is Watson's argument that O'Casey's faulty politics arises from presenting Irish nationalism as destructive *and* irrelevant at the same time (280).

2. Christopher Murray's characterization of the *Plough* as "demythologizing" and "revisionist" (*Twentieth-Century Irish Drama* 94) would readily fit the other two Dublin plays.

3. O'Casey's biographer, Garry O'Connor, mentions that Michael Mullen, on whom Shields is based, "did not take kindly to seeing himself portrayed as a pedlar of second-rate cutlery and a cynical commentator on the new nationalism" (136).

4. Krause finds Shields' position convincing and identifies it with the play's ultimate message. According to him, the reason behind O'Casey's move away from nationalist politics is "fanatical nationalism and the terror of indiscriminate bloodshed [which] began to destroy the people it was supposed to save" (67).

5. According to Garry O'Connor, O'Casey's sympathies during the Irish Civil War were with the Irregulars, the extreme wing of the IRA (147–148). He was probably working on the *Gunman* toward the end of that period. If this is the case, it would be difficult to explain the quick change in his political allegiance. It is also well known that he was a supporter of guerrilla tactics when he was with the Irish Citizen Army.

6. Joseph Holloway records in his diaries a conversation he had with O'Casey,

during which the dramatist tells him that he, like Bernard Shaw, wants to express his views through his characters (227).

7. O'Casey says he "gave up" nationalism after reading Shaw's *John Bull's Other Island*. According to Robert Lowery, this happened in 1912 (2). But if the assumption and date are accurate, one wonders why O'Casey would publish newspaper articles in 1913 defending nationalism against the demythologizing critique of Euchan (*Letters I:* 13–25).

8. Some of the critics who identify the dichotomy of illusions and reality as central in O'Casey's *Juno* are Krause (*Sean O'Casey: The Man and His Work*); John O'Riordan; B. L. Smith; and Murray (*Twentieth-Century Irish Drama* 103). Revisionist historians' formulations of the dichotomy are best represented in Theo Moody's "Irish History and Irish Mythology."

9. Maurice Goldring states that "history plays a part in the present violence [in Northern Ireland] because any social movement looks to the past for models" (139). This is a good example of the anti-nationalist atmosphere popularized by revisionism, to which I referred earlier in this essay.

10. George Boyce casts some doubts on Garvin's motives in modifying his views when he claims Garvin's "irreverent style" and the criticism it drew might be the reason behind such change ("Past and Present" 226).

11. Stronger critiques have come from several contributors to *Revising the Rising*, the Field Day volume on the controversy around the seventy-fifth anniversary of the Rising. Declan Kiberd, for instance, warns against "communal amnesia" ("The Elephant" 5) and revisionist reinterpretations when they amount to a "process whereby the history of a colonized people is taken from them" (11). Other contributors examine the presumed connection between the Rising and the current conflict in the North. Michael Laffan, for example, asserts that "to mention Pearse and the Provos [IRA] in the same breath does not lead inexorably to convicting the Easter rebels of terrorist atrocities" (113). Others challenge revisionist assumptions that the motive behind the uprising was blood sacrifice. J. J. Lee, for instance, rejects the exclusive identification of the rhetoric of blood sacrifice with Irish nationalist politics and concludes that in comparison to his contemporaries, Pearse "was close to the mainstream" ("In Search of Patrick Pearse" 132).

12. I discussed this aspect of the scene in "Damning Uphill and Down Dale" (10–11).

13. Holloway mentions that the night before rioting started at the Abbey, the actor playing the role of Lieutenant Langon, Arther Shields, "unfurled his tricolor, as he came in, in a defiant manner. He usually is out for cheap notoriety" (253).

14. O'Casey mentions this in his debate with Hanna Sheehy-Skeffington, which I will discuss in some detail later.

15. O'Casey's line between literature and politics is symptomatic of the political vision his drama presents, which essentially privileges life and the living over political commitment. This division is also held dear by anti-nationalist and revisionist critics. David Krause, for instance, praises Edna Longley's championing of the segregation between poetry and politics ("The Paradox of Ideological Formalism" 516).

16. Murray has recently described women's hostile reactions to the play as "ironic," since "O'Casey's analysis of the Rising is actually in favor of women" (*Twentieth-Century Irish Drama* 99). Such a position somewhat simplifies the play's politics, because it identifies feminism with anti-nationalism and depicts nationalism as an exclusively male ideology.

Part III

RECONSTRUCTING DRAMA

DURING THE "FATAL FIFTIES"

—7—

O'Casey's The Drums of Father Ned *in Context*

CHRISTOPHER MURRAY

If the subject is Irish drama at mid-century, it may seem questionable to focus on O'Casey. After all, he left the place in 1926. It might be thought that his successors, among them Denis Johnston, Paul Vincent Carroll, Michael J. Molloy, Louis D'Alton, Walter Macken, and Brendan Behan, should make up the list of worthy candidates for an exploration of mid-century Irish drama. Brendan Behan, at any rate, may be exempted, since his work will be examined by Stephen Watt in another essay within this volume. For good measure, Samuel Beckett, whose *Waiting for Godot* chronologically fits into our period of study, also wins a chapter in this section. Are these sufficient compensations for the omission of the other playwrights just mentioned? Is the centering of O'Casey in this chapter defensible? Clearly not, if the purpose were to provide a survey.

What I have in mind here, however, is something different. I am not claiming that *The Drums of Father Ned* is a neglected masterpiece, the outstanding play of the period. I am not even necessarily saying that it is among O'Casey's best plays, although I have no hesitation in putting it forward as one of his most interesting in terms of theme and form. It is its context which lends to this play its strongest claim for attention. It is one of those rare cultural productions which provides a signpost or marks a point of transition in a writer's work or a theatre's history. This does not necessarily coincide with the highest artistic achievement: *When We Dead Awaken* is hardly Ibsen's greatest achievement, but it is the play which sums up many of his themes and preoccupations, while — to change direction — Osborne's *Look Back in Anger* will always hold its place in the history of

English drama in spite of its artistic flaws because it ushered in a new era of post-war realism. O'Casey's *The Drums of Father Ned* is a landmark of just such a kind. It situates itself within Irish cultural history at a strategic, revelatory point, just as the old, conservative, pastoral world of de Valera is about to yield to the new, pragmatic, progressive world of Seán Lemass and T. K. Whitaker in 1958. And so it challenges, by its insertion into the debate on censorship, the traditional attitudes and values which had choked freedom of expression in the arts in Ireland since the foundation of the state. Further, although this point is mainly biographical, *The Drums of Father Ned* brought the older O'Casey into confrontation with a figurehead of Irish Catholic authoritarianism, who, as it were, fatally provided a terminus for O'Casey's extended battle to expose repression. This was John Charles McQuaid (1895–1973), archbishop of Dublin from 1940 to 1972. It was as if this figure was conjured up by O'Casey in proof of all he had been saying since the 1930s. And the black genie destroyed him.

So much for melodramatics. As for detailed history of the drama at mid-century, I refer the reader to the relevant chapters of my *Twentieth-Century Irish Drama* in modest excuse for my unwillingness to enter into the subject in any depth here. Rather, what I hope to suggest is that O'Casey's *The Drums of Father Ned*, once placed in context, may be read metonymically as a more effective critique of the dominant culture than most of the Irish plays staged at the Abbey in the decades before its reopening in 1966. In summarizing the plays staged during the period from 1951 to 1966, a recent historian of the Irish "National Theatre in Exile" at the Queen's says: "The dramas and revivals staged during the sixteen-year span were often selected for their prospects of winning a wider popular audience by means of long runs, even if the choices lacked artistic values" (O'Neill 12). Even the best of the playwrights available felt the pressure to present contrived plots and happy endings. Such work cannot also confront monoliths of church and state. Rather, as the Abbey managing director of the time (a figure as powerful in other ways as McQuaid) put it, the role of the playwright was to present certain controversial issues, "sources of misunderstanding and division," which "may well be combed out on the stage and rendered innocuous by thorough ventilation there" (Blythe n.p.). The Abbey as sanitized clearinghouse of "innocuous" ideas is frighteningly defined here.

When the Abbey Theatre burned down on 18 July 1951, it was already in a "parlous" state. Eric Bentley, then but a sprightly young director, reported — as sympathetic outsider on his rather amazing sabbatical at the Abbey in 1950 — that the place was caught in a time warp and to all appearances was dead (308). Bentley's testimony might pass for the mere casting of a cold eye by a sophisticated American who happened to be passing by were it not for the highly publicized fact that in 1947 there had been something of a public protest in the Abbey. It happened during an interval in a production of O'Casey's *The Plough and the Stars:* two young men, the poet Valentine Iremonger and a UCD lecturer and playwright, Roger McHugh, stood up and declaimed against the travesty of O'Casey's work that they had witnessed on the Abbey stage; then they walked out in protest. There followed much controversy in the newspapers, most of the commentary siding with the protesters and deploring the collapse of artistic standards at the Abbey under the management of Ernest Blythe. Actors, actresses, writers, directors — indeed, all members of the profession — took the opportunity to speak out on what came to be known as "the Abbey Incident." Some actors, however, spoke *sotto voce*, writing in confidence to Roger McHugh about their long-held disaffection with the Abbey but begging him not to disclose their names upon any account.[1] Such was the temper of the times. Fear of authority, and especially fear of challenging those who could damage an artist in her or his profession, led many to cheer on from the sidelines those brave few who dared to criticize cows sacred or allegorical. Blythe's way of dealing with criticism was notoriously phlegmatic: a shrug, a public disclaimer of any problem, and a swift but silent manner of dealing with any opposition. Roger McHugh was turned away at the Abbey box office when he next came to buy a ticket, and he remained a stranger to the Abbey until after Blythe resigned as managing director in 1967. McHugh's and Iremonger's view of the Abbey's disgraceful state, however, was entirely vindicated in 1950 by the publication of Peter Kavanagh's *The Story of the Abbey Theatre: From its Origins in 1899 to the Present*, which saw Blythe's ten years as manager as a betrayal of Yeats's idea of a theatre and which roundly declared the Abbey to be "dead" (184).

Yet a point which Eric Bentley makes in the same essay referred to above suggests that it is dangerous to confuse the theatre with the drama:

> One looks in vain through the external history of the Abbey Theatre for the full explanation that we are seeking of the mark the theater has made in the world. We come closest to it, as far as the external facts go, in the conception of a *national* theater. . . . But the real glory of the Abbey lies precisely where the simplest student would place it — namely, in the drama, and specifically in the plays of its three most famous writers: Synge, O'Casey, and Yeats. . . . It is the way in which they embody the idea that the manifestoes of Martyn and Yeats championed: the idea of a national theater. It is the way in which they embody the national movement, the way they *are* Ireland. (315)

Bentley goes on to argue that "love of Ireland" is what provided these three playwrights with "the initial impulse" to write drama. "Love leads to concern, and concern to criticism. They are pitiless critics of all that does not deserve their pity. O'Casey is the directest critic and the most simply effective playwright . He is less of a special case than the other two, more of a model national dramatist: he straightforwardly criticized and amused the nation at the same time" (318). Bentley's analysis, made so many years ago, in 1951, still stands up. What it means, in relation to the "Abbey Incident," is that there came a time when Ireland's greatest drama no longer mattered to those in charge of the theatre, when, indeed, those in charge were happier with mediocrity and transformed even masterpieces into innocuous entertainments (Hogan, *After the Irish Renaissance* 8–19).

I turn now to look at O'Casey's later work in the context of this rather dreary picture of the state of the Irish theatre. Following the Abbey's rejection of *The Silver Tassie* in 1928, O'Casey made his home in England and never again submitted a play for production by the Abbey. Yet from his vantage point in Devon, O'Casey clearly perceived, and in his later work accurately registered, the lapses and flaws in Irish culture and society, of which the Abbey Theatre was but the symbol. In recent years, Irish cultural historians (Brown, Lee, Keogh) have clarified the hegemonic nature of Irish Catholicism in the years following Eamon de Valera's introduction of a new Irish Constitution in 1937. As J. H. Whyte has pointed out, "in a mainly Catholic country, the Catholic hierarchy has a weapon which no other interest group possesses: its authority over men's consciences" (368). Censorship became the metonymic agent of postcolonial conformity. All culture was screened not just through topical Eliotic ideas of a Christian society but also through the narrower meshes of those same nets which Joyce saw closing around Stephen Dedalus a generation earlier and which now, in the war years and after, allowed only suitably striped artistic minnows to swim by them. When Sean O'Faolain, Ireland's answer to Raymond Williams as cultural theorist, invited O'Casey to respond in *The Bell* to an article which saw censorship as a positive good for society, he got this provocative response, which he bravely published: "To me, it doesn't seem a question of what we have lost or gained in Ireland by the censorship . . . but a question of how long intelligent people are going to stand this pompous, ignorant, impudent, and silly practice that is making Ireland a laughing-stock among the intelligent of all lands" (O'Casey, "Censorship" 404).

O'Casey's own plays of this period provided a comic critique of this state of affairs. These plays, usually published before they were staged in London or New York, were poorly reviewed by Irish critics determined to lament the falling-off in O'Casey's drama since he left old Erin's isle. But the poet Austin Clarke, about to find his courage once again and recreate himself as a latter-day Dean Swift, saw in O'Casey's fantasy–satire *Cock-a-Doodle Dandy* (1949) something original and valuable: "In this new comedy Mr. O'Casey has found, I think, the symbolic form for which he has searched with such assiduity. His rapid technique is as brilliant as that of Saroyan and other up-to-date playwrights; but integrity replaces sentimentality." This play, Clarke opined, if given "months of rehearsal at the Abbey," might provide "a lesson to our younger dramatists and save us from the now pernicious influence of Boucicault. There might be a few unholy scuffles in the pit, but the risk would be worth taking" (6). The challenge was not taken up. And when a new O'Casey play, *The Bishop's Bonfire* (1955), was staged in Dublin at the Gaiety Theatre and not at the Abbey, it was predictably slaughtered by the Irish (but not the English) critics, who had been lying in wait for just this opportunity.

So, of course, the question arises and presents itself with some force as to why O'Casey offered his new play, *The Drums of Father Ned*, for production in Dublin in 1958. Shakir Mustafa takes the earlier O'Casey to task elsewhere in this volume for what he sees as O'Casey's "refusal to engage nationalism as an ideological and historical phenomenon." The result "is usually the presentation of Irish nationalism as detrimental to progress and modernity and the call for an unscrupulous dismantling of its heritage." This analysis overlooks the radical nature of O'Casey's dramaturgy. Far from "saying no to politics," O'Casey from the outset (i.e., from the unstaged plays, of which *The Harvest Festival* alone survives) forced readers and spectators alike to respond with what we would now have to call Brechtian alienation. In the three Dublin plays, the working class is foregrounded and their fate deplored. What is this dialectic if it is not a political technique? A playwright does not have to recommend political action in order for his/her plays to be political; the politics is in the representation. *The Plough and the Stars* (1926) caused violent controversy, and controversies, Lucy McDiarmid reminds us, are "micro-units of social change." O'Casey wanted controversy; he wanted social change. Although his later plays are more reliant on satire and fantasy than the three Dublin plays of the 1920s, O'Casey continued to favor a radical use of dramatic form. In short, he courted controversy as bravely in 1958 as in 1926.

The Drums of Father Ned is the third in a trilogy, the others being *Cock-a-Doodle Dandy* and *The Bishop's Bonfire* (Kosok 233). Each is an exposé of the conditions of Irish life. In none of these plays is the analysis provided within a framework of realism; Rabelaisian fantasy reduces the serious to the ludicrous. Bakhtinian carnival rules the day. Transferred into practical terms, this means that *The Drums of Father Ned* opens with an expressionistic scene (the "Prerumble") set in 1920, with the War of Independence raging in the Irish countryside, just as it raged in the city in *The Shadow of a Gunman* (1923). Here history is employed to point up the absurdity of destructive division in Irish society. Two men, McGilligan and Binnington, taken prisoner by the Black-and-Tans, would rather be shot by the enemy than shake hands with each other. The Black-and-Tans decide that to allow these two to live will do more damage to Ireland than executing them would. The play then moves into the mid-1950s, where we catch up on the fortunes of these representatives of post–civil war Ireland. They have done well financially; between them they own the town of Doonavale (Gaelic for "close his mouth"), of which one is lord mayor and the other his deputy. They are veritable Ibsenite pillars of society, although they persist in showing mutual animosity. However, their children think differently. And they are encouraged to think differently by Father Ned.

Here O'Casey was developing two ideas which energize his later plays. Both ideas were radical and ahead of their time. On the one hand, O'Casey saw youth as the great sign of hope in the modern world. Put like that, the idea may appear fatuous in its banality, but if we consider for a moment the pessimism which, with some justification, pervaded Western society following World War II, O'Casey's emphasis on youth may be seen as a deliberate, somewhat Shavian act of faith in *élan vital*. He had always, in fact, celebrated Rabelaisian energy in the face of immediate death: one sees this in the glorious one-act *Nannie's Night Out* (1924), in which the alcohol-addicted Nannie flings caution to the winds and dances in spite of her heart condition and, in one version of the play, at least, dies dancing.[2] Ten years later O'Casey inducted this character into the broader social concerns of *Within the Gates*, where the prostitute Jannice, afflicted with a similar heart condition, asserts "I'll go game, and die dancing!" (O'Casey *CP* 2: 228). Jannice, too, dances herself to death, this time, significantly, in the arms of the Dreamer, the voice of romantic recklessness and revolt. Perhaps one should turn to *The Silver Tassie* for the implications of this doctrine in favor of defiance in order to underline that far from being sentimental, it was brutal and harsh. Act 4 of *The Silver Tassie* is set at a dance. Harry Heegan, now crippled after his service in the war, is in a wheelchair, furiously pursuing and being rejected by Jessie, the woman who conspicuously gave him all her love in act 1. In one sense, audience sympathy is elicited for Harry, whose passion for life is as cruelly crushed as the silver trophy he helped to win is symbolically crushed beneath the wheels of his chair. But in another sense, this audience sympathy is suddenly and cruelly withdrawn as the nurse Susie relegates him to the sidelines of life while all the able-bodied are swept into the dance: "For he is a life on the ebb, / Ours a full life on the flow!" (*CP* 2: 103). It seems heartless, this rejection of those whose disabilities result from their sacrifice in war, but the point being made is that so long as people make wars, there will be such tragic marginalization, and the remedy lies not in crocodile tears but in confrontation of the nature of things. Again, O'Casey is alienating his audience. The final joyous dance which excludes Harry, Teddy, and the old folk, is ironic in the extreme. So, there is celebration of youth and energy as a kind of Strindbergian "Dance of Death" (a play, incidentally, which O'Casey greatly admired).

During World War II and in its aftermath, however, O'Casey more positively celebrated youthful energy in its fruitful, sexual, renovative associations. It is almost as if he were reading Northrop Frye in advance, when it is more likely he was reading Shakespeare's last plays. For now O'Casey was offering a *mythos* of spring in a context of cold war, and he was saying that it is to the next generation one must look for reconciliation and redress of those historic ills which create differences and divisions in the present. If it be asked what had Ireland, controversially neutral in World War II, to do with the cold war or the cold war to do with Ireland, the answer is blindingly simple: the fear of communism. Does anybody need to be reminded at this stage of the notorious mother-and-child scheme of 1951, when a leftish minister for health, Nöel Browne, found himself up to his neck in opposition from the Catholic hierarchy that suspected this was the thin edge of a communist wedge? The recent version, by Michael Yeats (son of the poet), of this story will refresh some memories; the topic is well covered by Browne himself and by Deeny, Lee, and Keogh, among others. As O'Casey read the dispute (and his one-act *Hall of Healing* is an intervention in it), this fear of communism was characteristic of a nation which had lost its nerve. There was no fight left in the older generation, which was too eager to comply with authoritarian sanctification of poverty. Only the young could create change, once they had the right kind of guidance.

Here is where the second idea, mentioned above, enters the picture. Whereas the clergy as such, the institutionalized Roman Catholic Church, was hegemonic, there were individual priests who sidestepped the dominant ideology and who, out of concern for the poor economic, social, and psychological conditions suffered by huge sections of the Irish population (particularly in the western half of the country), put various cooperative schemes and community programs in place. These men O'Casey regarded as visionaries. He dedicated *The Drums of Father Ned*, significantly subtitled *A Mickrocosm [sic] of Ireland*, to some of them, namely Canon Hayes, "Founder of Muintir na Tíre, bringing a sense of community life and cooperation to rural Ireland, and brightness with them," and Father O'Flanagan, who risked removal by his bishop in Sligo for urging the poor to help themselves. "Each in his time was a Drummer for Father Ned, and the echoes of their drumming sound in Ireland still," O'Casey wrote in the first edition (1960). But he had introduced just such a rebel priest in *The Bishop's Bonfire* in 1955 in the role of Father Boheroe, who urged the young people to "refuse to be frightened" by the trappings of power in the new Ireland (*CP* 5: 81). That power was shared between the businessmen and the church and was based on repression and class differentiation. The master image for all of this negativity lay in the "Bishop's Bonfire," a plan to honor a visit to the town by a newly created bishop with a bonfire of books. This takes place at the play's end, where it provides an image as ominous in its own way as the fires which mark the burning of Dublin in 1916 as *The Plough and the Stars* fades out (for closure is not a factor in O'Casey's dramaturgy). The bonfire, which is actually enacted in the earlier *Cock-a-Doodle Dandy*, eloquently concedes the anti-intellectualism of this brow-beaten community. The opposition mounted against *The Bishop's Bonfire* in Dublin, however, ironically claimed that the play was anti-clerical (Schrank, *Sean O'Casey* 19). Within the play, O'Casey conceded that the Father Boheroes could do little to challenge this mindset. Yet when he drafted *The*

Drums of Father Ned, first entitled "The Night is Whispering," O'Casey decided to empower this Boheroe figure and to transform him into an enabling influence.

Father Ned is never seen on stage. His presence offstage is denoted by a rumbling of drums, but he is named so often as man of action that he assumes a presence onstage also. Whether O'Casey was in any way indebted to his fellow Dubliner Behan for this idea is a question worth posing: *The Quare Fellow* (1954) made quite a stir when Joan Littlewood gave it its London premiere in 1956. The eponymous "Quare Fellow," the murderer who is to be executed, is at the heart of Behan's play, but he never enters the stage. One might say the same for Beckett's Godot. Yet years earlier, in 1922, even before a play of his was staged at the Abbey, O'Casey had told Lennox Robinson that he had an idea for a play about Jim Larkin, "in which he would never appear [on stage] though [he would be] responsible for all the action" (Krause, *The Letters of Sean O'Casey* 1: 105). It is likely, then, that O'Casey, in quite a revolutionary move, independently decided to transform his Jim Larkin figure (written about, in any case, in *The Star Turns Red* [1940], with Red Jim very much present on stage) into an inspirational priest. For Father Ned is more a spirit of the age than a character. It is he who galvanizes the young people of Doonavale and, in particular, the son and daughter, respectively, of the old enemies Binnington and McGilligan, into painters, singers, dancers, and performers in a play produced in celebration of the *Tóstal* festivities in the town. This is a history play, set in Wexford in 1798, and its theme is rebellion.

The *Tóstal* (Gaelic for "hosting") was a national cultural event inaugurated in 1953 by *Bord Fáilte,* the Irish Tourist Board. The purpose of the festival, according to the government minister who launched it, was to showcase Ireland in forms which would revive cultural nationalism: "The programme of cultural, social, and sporting events which has been prepared has been designed to express the Irish way of life and to revive the spirit which animated the traditional Gaelic festivals for which Ireland was famous when Europe was young" (Lemass n.p.). This annual spring celebration was expanded in 1957 to include the newly established International (subsequently, Dublin) Theatre Festival. After a successful inauguration in 1957, the director of the Theatre Festival wrote to O'Casey and asked for a play for 1958. Quite fortuitously, O'Casey was working on a play in which he incorporated the *Tóstal* as image and symbol, and so *The Drums of Father Ned* was actually a most appropriate text for inclusion in the program. Its purpose was, as O'Casey put it in lines prefatory to the published text,

> To wake up drowsy girl and drowsier boy,
> To snatch from Erin's back the sable shawl,
> And clothe her as she was before her fall. . . . (*CP* 5: 134)

The "fall" O'Casey referred to was the fall into puritanism. It is in this context that *Drums* may be seen as a pendant to *Cock-a-Doodle Dandy,*

intended, O'Casey said in 1947, to "hit at the present tendency of Éire
to return to primitive beliefs, & Éire's pre-occupation with Puritanism"
(Krause, *The Letters of Sean O'Casey* 2: 477).

The controversy—in Lucy McDiarmid's sense of the word—which
ensued over *Drums of Father Ned* indicates the complexity of this puritanism. It had been established in 1957 that the Catholic archbishop of Dublin
should be asked to inaugurate the Theatre Festival by presiding at a solemn
votive mass in the pro-Cathedral. He was invited to do so again for the 1958
festival. However, Archbishop John Charles McQuaid, rather like Cardinal
Logue in 1899, when he condemned unread Yeats's *The Countess Cathleen*,
ignited a controversy by refusing the invitation to preside at this special
mass because the Theatre Festival program featured a dramatization of
Ulysses and a play by O'Casey. Of course, this meant no mass was to be
allowed. McQuaid offered no explanations, no critique, no details of any
kind. He did not have to. He had merely to sit back and let the *Tóstal*
Committee work itself into a lather over the bad publicity that the archbishop's disapproval would bring. The only direct comment I have been
able to find by McQuaid on the festival program is in a letter to a priest
whom he rebuked for appearing to defend the choice of *Ulysses*. He insisted
that this priest should make it clear that this view was not the "opinion of
Archbishop's House," and added: "I would like you to take means to remove any such misunderstanding, for I shall feel obliged to take very definite action if either Ulysses or O'Casey's play be chosen by the Tóstal. The
'Rose Tattoo' ought to have been a lesson to the Tóstal." The reference
here was to Alan Simpson's production of Tennessee Williams's play at the
Pike Theatre during the 1957 Theatre Festival. Simpson was arrested and
imprisoned on an indecency charge, which caused a great stir—another
controversy, in fact. The case went all the way to the Irish Supreme Court
before Simpson was discharged (Swift, *Stage by Stage* 240–304). McQuaid
implies that imprisonment and charges of obscenity could well await members of the festival committee itself in 1958.

The director of the Dublin Theatre Festival at the time has given his
own version of events (Hickey and Smith 136–151). In that version, Mc-
Quaid's main target was Joyce and not O'Casey. Certainly, the *Tóstal* Council withdrew Alan McClelland's adaptation of *Ulysses* early in 1958, and it
may well be that Smith had nothing directly to do with the developments
which led to O'Casey's withdrawing *Drums* on 29 January. The production
of the play was in the hands of the Globe Company, which had recently
been founded by actors Godfrey Quigley and Norman Rodway and director Jim Fitzgerald. Fitzgerald obviously had problems with the text of
Drums: he arrived in Torquay, Devon, to discuss these concerns. He and
O'Casey didn't get on: it seems clear that Fitzgerald thought it acceptable
to ask O'Casey to revise his text, and O'Casey, senior dramatist that he was,
balked. O'Casey's letters on this topic are revealing (Krause, *The Letters of
Sean O'Casey* 3: 445–559). He formed the view that Smith, the festival

committee, the Globe Company, and the *Tóstal* Committee were in collusion and were looking for a pretext for the removal of the play from the program. They were all scared. It is clear from the very fact that a copy of the minutes of the festival committee appears in the McQuaid Archive at Archbishop's House that the archbishop was monitoring the whole affair. On 3 February, that committee recommended that O'Casey be asked to "permit some alterations [to *Drums*] on technical grounds (sneer at peasants in country districts in the play)." Ignorant of the fact that O'Casey had already withdrawn, the *Tóstal* Council then decided to send an emissary to London [*sic*] to "get O'Casey to allow amendments." The presumption was that O'Casey would refuse. While it is diverting to picture this emissary roaming the streets of London in search of O'Casey, who had left London for Devon in 1939, it is obvious that the *Tóstal* was acting exactly in that spirit of hypocrisy which O'Casey had targeted over and over in his later plays.

It is to be noted that O'Casey withdrew his play before the two committees met to decide to ask him for changes. And the main reason he withdrew was because of the Globe Company's blundering. On 29 January 1958, he wrote to Smith to report that he had just received a letter from Norman Rodway and Godfrey Quigley on behalf of the Globe, "which assumes that I have submitted my play to that Theater [*sic*, for Company] for consideration. You know that this isnt so. I wouldnt give a play of mine under any circumstances to them." He then quotes from their letter, asking O'Casey to give the director, Jim Fitzgerald, the authority to make "such alterations as he requires" in the text before "committing ourselves to any definite action with the Tóstal authorities." O'Casey was infuriated by this request, rapidly called an unprecedented "demand," to which he as playwright would never agree. "It is plain to me now that there is no theater into which O'Casey can be allowed to fit, which is all OK by me; and that Mr. Fitzgerald doesnt understand what I am aiming at in the theater, and also, that the manner of my playmaking frightens him. Indeed, this demand left me with little to say: there is no answer to it, save silence" (Krause, *The Letters of Sean O'Casey* 3: 530).

It may be, of course, that the issue of the Globe Company's unease with the play as play was independent of the growing controversy surrounding it. Innocence may have survived and been thriving still in de Valera's Ireland, as Brian Fallon (1998) would have us believe. But O'Casey preferred to believe otherwise and quickly decided that he had been "banned" by the archbishop. That put an end to the "silence" he promised above; O'Casey spread the word world-wide. Even if O'Casey's charge was never strictly true, the web of events surrounding the handling of *Drums* surely justified his intuitive sense that McQuaid was behind the whole controversy. His belief that Ireland was in the grip of a stultifying conspiracy was being borne out. Life was imitating art. He who had penned grotesque caricatures of Irish clerical domination (Father Domineer in the *Cock*, Canon Burren in *The Bishop's Bonfire*) lived to find himself confronted by a real embodiment, too subtle to be openly engaged. One of McQuaid's current biographers revealingly refers to his admiration for J. Edgar Hoover: "On being told by a New York monsignor of McQuaid's admiration for the FBI's espionage work against suspected communist trade unionists, Hoover sent McQuaid a note thanking him for his 'highly valued support.' By separate post Hoover sent McQuaid a copy of his book, *Masters of Deceit*" (Cooney 1). The context that *Drums* demands is thus a complex weave, inscribed with diverse narratives and conflicting discourses. But the wider drama the text establishes is the story of Ireland in the 1950s, a story of secrecy, pretence, acquiescence, and oppression.

When O'Casey withdrew his play from the festival, Beckett, three of whose mime plays were also on the program, withdrew in sympathy and as a mark of respect to Joyce. As a result of all this publicity, the Dublin Theatre Festival for 1958 was cancelled. A dead silence on the matter emanated from the Tourist Board, which celebrated the *Tóstal* with "a military tattoo, athletics and folk dancing," as if nothing had happened (Hickey and Smith 135). But the whole affair was a disaster for O'Casey. All he could do as a gesture of contempt was to refuse professional production of all of his plays in Ireland. To his cost, O'Casey preserved this particular "ban" until pressed to allow the Abbey Company to stage *Juno* and *The Plough* for the 1964 World Theatre Festival in London.

As time went on, O'Casey focused on the failure of the intellectuals in Ireland to lend him support. He mocked and at the same time was hurt by what one might call "the silence of the lambs." He wrote a three-act play on the theme entitled *Behind the Green Curtains* (published 1961), which was reminiscent of the later satires of Austin Clarke. Although an embittered play, it remains part of the wider narrative context in which *Drums* must be read.

The great irony of this whole affair is that *Drums* was not in the least anti-clerical, nor could it be construed as morally dangerous. Its positive message, its celebratory thrust, leads on in the text to a spirit of reconciliation and unity. When one attempts to put all of this into perspective, what is the result? The controversy shows clearly that in the 1950s it was not possible for an Irish playwright to take a stance which challenged the authority of the Catholic Church. The Irish plays which were successful at the time, Behan's and Beckett's excepted (since both authors were, in different senses, outcasts and members of the avant-garde), were marked either by piousness, like Frank Carney's play about demonic possession (*The Righteous Are Bold*, 1946), or cynicism, as in Louis D'Alton's bitter condemnation of Irish hypocrisy in *This Other Eden* (1953). Even good plays, such as Molloy's *The Wood of the Whispering* (1953) and John Murphy's *The Country Boy* (1959), bent to Ernest Blythe's demand for innocuousness. What was really wanted were well-made comedies with recognizable Irish stereotypes and happy endings.

The controversy surrounding *Drums* did not introduce immediate change in terms of the reception and liberalization of production of plays in Ireland. Two years later came the equally infamous case over the dramatization of *The Ginger Man* (in 1959). J. P. Donleavy's play went on for three nights at the Gaiety Theatre until the management closed the production because of supposed public outcry against its sexual explicitness. Donleavy plainly says in his introduction to the text of the play that Archbishop McQuaid's secretary, one Father Nolan, made a visit to the office of the theatre manager, Louis Elliman, who then canceled the show (43–49). As a Jew, Donleavy argues, Elliman was anxious to maintain good relations with the Catholic authorities. Ironically, the company producing *The Ginger Man* was the Globe, the company selected to do O'Casey's *Drums*. The Globe was ruined by the collapse of *The Ginger Man*, and it folded soon after.

Yet Ireland was entering a period of massive social, economic, and cultural change. The drums of Father Ned, silenced in Dublin, were sounding loudly in Rome with the advent of Pope John XXIII. McQuaid's fall, it was said twenty-five years after his death, "came about because of his disastrous pastoral failure to adapt to the reforms of the Second Vatican Council. The Irish Catholic church today is paying a heavy price for the McQuaid legacy" (Cooney 2.7). As Ireland began to change, as new ideas penetrated the "green curtains" that O'Casey complained of, the theatre became emboldened. The voices of John B. Keane, Hugh Leonard, Tom Murphy, and Brian Friel were raised in passionate dissent because of the conditions imprisoning mid-century Ireland. Writers were arriving of whom it could again be said, in Eric Bentley's sense, "they *are* Ireland" (315). In the meantime, it was the drama surrounding *Drums* which was the Ireland of the 1950s.

In 1962, when Hugh Leonard's skillful adaptation of Joyce's fictional confessions (in prose) was staged at the Dublin Theatre Festival under the title *Stephen D*, a significant breakthrough was made in the kind of cultural correctness, to coin a phrase, which had ensured the subjection of Irish theatre at mid-century. The play went ahead without controversy. There was no objection from the Archbishop's palace (possibly because by this time, the *Tóstal* was dead, and the Dublin Theatre Festival had no need to invite the Archbishop to say mass). *Stephen D* was a major hit and traveled to London for an extended run. Staged experimentally by Jim Fitzgerald, who might have been the director of *The Drums of Father Ned*, this was Hugh Leonard's first international success. It launched him as major playwright; it prefigured in important ways the arrival of Friel's *Philadelphia, Here I Come!* (1964); it marked the coming of age of Irish drama in a new era. Without O'Casey, that arrival would certainly have been postponed.

NOTES

1. File of letters and clippings in possession of Mrs. Roger McHugh (Dublin). I am grateful to Mrs. McHugh for allowing me to read this file.

2. See *Feathers from the Green Crow: Sean O'Casey, 1905–1925*, Robert Hogan, ed. (Columbia, Missouri: University of Missouri Press, 1962), 301–302. Three versions are in the Berg Collection at the New York Public Library.

—8—

Love and Death: A Reconsideration of Behan and Genet

STEPHEN WATT

[Behan's] plays are O'Caseyesque in their sharp critique of idealism, so sharp that they come perilously close to downright nihilism. Ultimately, they owe more to the absurdist theatre of Ionesco, Genet and Beckett than to their forerunners in the Irish dramatic movement.
— Declan Kiberd, *Inventing Ireland* 513

In a less civilised country, [Genet] would have been engaged in the production of mailbags, four stitches to the inch. [. . .] I had extracts of his autobiography read to me, some of which rose the hair on my head. And, as my mother once remarked, that which would shock Brendan Behan would turn thousands grey.
— Brendan Behan, *Confessions of an Irish Rebel* 146–147

This essay is, in many respects, about as conventional in aim as it gets: the interpretive equivalent of soup before dinner, coffee and dessert after. Indeed, it is based upon a perhaps musty *raison d'être* originating in my sense of what *must* be included, what *cannot* be overlooked, in a volume that reassesses the past century of Irish drama. For such a project promises not only a predictable historical narrative, however revised or troubled that narrative becomes, but also the consideration of a cast of prominent characters that are central to it. Some of these — Bernard Shaw, W. B. Yeats, Sean O'Casey — contributed dozens of plays to the Irish and world theatres; others like Brendan Behan offered but three full-length dramatic works, only two of which were performed during his lifetime. Happily, theatre and literary histories do not operate like accounting ledgers; more is not always more. If they did, someone of Behan's unique significance, or even of James Joyce's — after all, how many "novels" did he write, if *Finnegans Wake* can even be described by this word? — might be passed by.

Stated alternatively, while scores of critics and theatre historians are engaged with the beginning or end of the past hundred years of Irish theatre history, the post-war Irish theatre at mid-century generates considerably less critical enthusiasm. Without too much difficulty one might draw up a list of distinguished commentators on the work of Yeats, Lady Gregory, Shaw, O'Casey, and J. M. Synge, or assemble a similarly impressive roster of scholars interested in Brian Friel, Marina Carr, Sebastian Barry, or Frank McGuinness. But save for Gerry Smyth's sustained reading of Irish literary criticism of the 1950s in *Decolonisation and Criticism: The Construction of Irish Literature* (1998), Michael O'Sullivan's 1997 biography of Behan, the substantial chapters of such recent books as Anthony Roche's *Contemporary Irish Drama: From Beckett to McGuinness* (1994), Declan Kiberd's *Inventing Ireland* (1995), and Christopher Murray's *Twentieth-Century Irish Drama: Mirror Up to Nation* (1997), there seems to exist a kind of critical lacuna smack-dab in the middle of the century. Or, rather, the gap appears in our collective interest in the period between, say, Denis Johnston's *Moon in the Yellow River* (1931) and the rise of that great wave of writers in the 1960s: Brian Friel, Tom Murphy, Thomas Kilroy, John B. Keane, and Hugh Leonard. Murray describes the 1960s as bringing with them a "second renaissance" of Irish drama (*Twentieth-Century Irish Drama* 162), and there is little doubt that this is so. This second renaissance has given way to what Fintan O'Toole calls a "third wave in 20th-century Irish theatre" ("Shadows" 17): namely, the recent successes of Martin McDonagh, Conor McPherson, Carr, Barry, and other playwrights, who have been coming into their own as the millennium draws to a close. Yet, as Smyth charges, the 1950s in particular are so "unfashionable" in Irish studies as to constitute "a sort of Dark Ages between the classicism of cultural nationalism and the Renaissance of post-nationalism" (*Decolonisation and Criticism* 1). Drama from the middle of the century, in short — O'Casey's later plays, for example, as Murray discusses earlier in this volume, and those Shaw wrote at the end of his career — too often gets left out.

And when it isn't omitted, mid-century Irish drama often gets transposed into the registers peculiar to our own interpretive agendas, re-read by way of the preoccupations of academic criticism of the 1990s rather than within the post-war context that I hope to explore here (a readerly project which emerges from my own preoccupation with, among other things, cultural studies). Such re-reading is, to be sure, both inevitable and not entirely undesirable, and one contemporary issue — the performative nature of gender and sexuality — runs as a thread throughout this essay. But, as further evidence of the point I'm stumbling about to make, I would return to the epigraph from *Inventing Ireland*, in which Declan Kiberd claims that Behan's plays "owe more to the absurdist theatre of Ionesco, Genet and Beckett than to their forerunners in the Irish dramatic movement" (513). He's right. Yet this sentence marks the only occasion on which Ionesco and Genet appear in Kiberd's mammoth study.[1] Why? Because, as the title of Kiberd's chapter "The Empire Writes Back — Brendan Behan" implies, his project has little to do with assessing Behan's indebtedness to a European avant-garde but is rather more concerned with casting Behan as a postcolonial dramatist. It is thus hardly surprising that, by the end of his chapter, Kiberd contends that Behan was "one of the first post-colonial writers to impinge on the consciousness of post-war Britain" (529) and, further, that as a "bisexual male who wrote in Irish as well as English, Behan cheerfully embraced his own hybridity" (529). Nothing these days is more postcolonial or, in the case of Guillermo Gómez-Peña's performance art, more "post-NAFTA" than hybridity. Behan embraces it; Gómez-Peña's Chicano/a border-crossers and speakers of "Spanglish" embody it.

Anthony Roche's understanding of Beckett and Behan in *Contemporary Irish Drama: From Beckett to McGuinness*, a purchase conveyed through his thoughtful comparison of *The Quare Fellow* and *Waiting for Godot*, resembles Kiberd's, or perhaps it's the other way around: Kiberd's understanding resembles Roche's. Hence, the lack of a "leading man" in both plays reveals the "anti-hierarchical nature of a post-colonialist Irish drama" (Roche, *Contemporary Irish Drama* 59), and the "absence of a traditional plot" is "particularly prevalent in Irish and post-colonial drama" (62). More important, from this vantage point, the "official" hanging in *The Quare Fellow* represents "the persistence of colonial acts of legislation," while the "unofficial" effect on Behan's prisoners includes "the incorporation within the individual colonised subject's psyche of that legacy of hanging as a mode of escape from an intolerable situation" (54). The thrust of such a reading, as Roche clarifies, is not only to underscore Behan's postcoloniality but also to reclaim Beckett as an Irish, not an international, writer. And, had he wished to do so, Roche might have identified even more overt allusions to Ireland's colonial subjugation in *The Hostage*, as troublesome a text as it is.[2] On several occasions early and late in the play, the British presence in Ireland is compared with British imperialism around the world: "in Kenya, in Cyprus!," for example.[3] More voracious in its bloodlust than the executioner in *The Quare Fellow*, England is reviled in *The Hostage* as the "hangman of thousands" (179) and, as such, the progenitor of thousands of martyrs and "quare fellows."

Without quarreling with such recastings of Behan within a postcolonial frame, I want to speculate a bit more about hanging in *The Quare Fellow* and *Waiting for Godot*, beginning with the same prediction that Beckett's Didi makes: it could — in fact, Didi claims it *would* — lead to an erection and all that follows. What difference would it make if we suspended our understanding of this exchange in *Godot* as either "comic knockabout" or a "comically subversive, self-defeating pantomime" in which Vladimir and Estragon fail to hang themselves (Roche, *Contemporary Irish Drama* 55–56) and took Didi's prediction seriously? What would it mean that the condemned man in Behan and Beckett would achieve an erection with all that follows? In a postcolonial context, it might signify one last display of masculine agency; the feminized subaltern defies his colonial executioner by being "made a man" (recall Joyce's phrasing of his first sexual encounter with Nora) in death. But in a different register, one informed by discourse on death and sexuality after World War II, the condemned man's act *performs*, in the process remaking his identity as he approaches death and the oneness it implies. To be sure, death can signal escape in Genet's work, as Claire's suicide in the closing moments of *The Maids* (1947) suggests, but it also intimates so many other things: joy, beauty, and an ascent to mythic, even godly, dimensions. This is especially true, as is the case with the misguided Lefranc in Genet's *Deathwatch* (1949), in the death of a murderer. The disempowered prisoner obtains power in death; the impotent reach climax; the murderous "quare fellow" exchanges his bestial past for sainthood, for what Lefranc calls the "luminous place" of his enamoratum, the criminal Green Eyes. The "under-world" of criminals and prisoners becomes imaginatively relocated to an upper world of monarchs — and gods.

It is this *performative* dimension of Behan's and Genet's plays that I hope to juxtapose here, restoring for the moment Behan's moniker as "the Irish Jean Genet," the term with which journalists greeted him upon his arrival in New York in 1960 for the American premiere of *The Hostage*.[4] What exactly might it mean to be an "Irish Jean Genet," and why should this label be of interest to students of Irish drama? Again, attempting to answer both questions, especially the latter, will pose no challenge to postcolonial readings of Behan. In fact, the colonized subaltern bears much in common with the subject positions that most interest me here: those of the prisoner and of the bisexual, both driven into a kind of underworld by the law and the hypermasculinist, heterosexual ideologies and conventions of Irish nationalism.[5] And in the later pages of this essay, I want to revisit allusions in *The Hostage* and *Richard's Cork Leg* to the Wolfenden and Kinsey Reports and — more broadly — to reposition Behan's representations of sexuality alongside both of these groundbreaking mid-century studies and such theoretical ruminations on death and sensuality as Georges Bataille's *L'Erotisme* (*Erotism: Death and Sensuality* 1957). For it is my conviction that Behan's plays perform important cultural work in the wake of World War II and the dawn of the atomic age in representing sexual desire (in many of its myriad forms) and in suggesting the broader social need for greater tolerance and understanding of difference.

Without belaboring the obvious or privileging biography as crucial to my argument, it might prove useful to recall two parallels between Behan's and Genet's lives: both writers' incarcerations as adolescents — Behan was arrested in Liverpool and sentenced to a borstal at sixteen; Genet, confined to the Mettray Reformatory Colony at fifteen — and both men's sexuality. Genet is both more direct about his homosexuality and more contemplative than Behan about matters of homoerotic attraction and subjectivity (though both matters might be read in, among other places, *The Borstal Boy*). Equally important, the sense of theatricality or performativity that constitutes self-hood and sexuality, queer or straight, in Genet's prose seems muted in Behan's. This same sense of the performative, however, is much more apparent in *The Quare Fellow*, *The Hostage*, and *Richard's Cork Leg*, especially when juxtaposed to Genet's *The Maids*, *The Balcony* (1958), and *The Blacks: A Clown Show* (1959). One further motive for this comparison is my desire to promote *Richard's Cork Leg*, that unwanted child of Behan and Alan Simpson, as more than a "poor thing" and "self-parody on Behan's part" (Murray, *Twentieth-Century Irish Drama* 160). "Self-parody," after all, often involves significant playing or mirroring as well as the imaginative construction of worlds, the creation of a space of selfhood that is protected from the scrutiny of an outside world. So, in the institutional vernacular of *The Borstal Boy* and *The Quare Fellow*, the cell is a "flowery dell"; in *The Hostage*, a chair and circle of light become both a prison cell and site of sexual assignation between Teresa and the captive soldier, Leslie Williams; in *Richard's Cork Leg*, a gravestone becomes a bed in which the sexually voracious Cronin attempts — and fails — to achieve sexual congress with Deirdre.

Compare, for example, Genet's account of his attraction for a fellow inmate at Fontevrault in *Miracle of the Rose* (1951) with Behan's descriptions of romps at Dublin's Catacombs Club (another underworld in both name and ambience) in the late 1940s or of his at times sexually playful relationship with Freddie May earlier in the decade. First, Genet recalling his youthful infatuation with Bulkaen, who was already committed to another man:

> The exact vision that made a man of me, that is, a creature living solely on earth, corresponded with the fact that my femininity, or the ambiguity and haziness of my male desires, seemed to have ended. [. . .] And though my meeting Bulkaen revives dormant charms, I shall preserve that march toward maleness, for Bulkaen's beauty is, above all, delicate. I no longer yearned to resemble the hoodlums. I felt I had achieved self-fulfillment. (*Miracle of the Rose* 26)

> [L'exacte vision qui faisait de moi un homme, c'est-à-dire un être vivant uniquement sur terre, correspondait avec ceci que semblait cesser ma féminité ou l'ambiguité et le flou de mes désirs males. [. . .] Et si la rencontre de Bulkaen redonne vie à des charmes sommeillants, je garderai le bénéfice de cette marche vers l'homme, car la beauté de Bulkaen est, d'abord, délicate. Je ne désirais plus ressembler aux voyous. J'avais le sentiment d'avoir réalisé la plénitude de moi-même.[6] (*Ouevres Complètes* 2: 204)]

Writing some fifteen years after his initial sentence, Genet realized that before this epiphany, his "moral substance" was "soft" and "without sharpness." A subject in process, his "personalité prenait toutes sortes de formes" (*Ouevres Complètes* 2: 204) so that "any male could squeeze my sides [. . .] could contain me" (*Miracle of the Rose* 26). Then, he was not "completely at ease unless I could completely take his place, take on his qualities, his virtues; when I imagined I was he making his gestures, uttering his words: When I *was* he" (*Miracle of the Rose* 27) — "lorsque j'étais lui" (*Oeuvres Complètes* 2: 204). Impersonation, playing, and the accoutrements of performance thus lead directly to a fuller self, to a "plénitude de moi-même."

Interrupting his narrative with thoughts of the outside world and his life as a thief, Genet identifies the final touch that completes the performing or becoming of the Other: the burglar's "jimmy" or "pen," a device used to gain entry to a building, the importance of which, in terms of the performance and of the subject, can hardly be overestimated. He explains:

> I had always needed that steel penis in order to free myself completely from my faggotry, from my humble attitudes, and to attain the clear simplicity of manliness. (*Miracle of the Rose* 27)

> [J'avais, depuis toujours, besoin de cette verge d'acier pour me libérer complètement de mes bourbeuses dispositions, de mes humbles attitudes et pour atteindre à la clair simplicité de la virilité. (*Oeuvres Complètes* 2: 205)]

While walking to a job, this steel penis, among other devices, had to be concealed in his trousers, dangling against his thigh: they were steely hard even if the psyche was not. A jimmy was the "weapon" of a "warrior"; thus, Genet regarded it with "mysterious veneration" (*Miracle of the Rose* 28). It contributed to the nobility and "glamour" of a criminal realm located far above the shameful sub-world of prostitution and begging in which Genet once languished (*Miracle of the Rose* 29). Love for Bulkaen thus meant, for Genet, manliness, a rise in status, and residence in an ennobled imaginative world.

But that's not all. For Genet's epiphany is not only inherently performative — involving role-playing and the props of a thief — but it is also connected to death and the French equivalent of a "quare fellow." That is to say, the fifteen-year-old inmate was affected almost equally by both Bulkaen's delicate beauty *and* the presence of the brutal Harcamone, sentenced to death for murdering a young girl and, later, a prison guard. Before Genet was transferred to Fontevrault, he had heard of Harcamone and his impending ascent of the scaffold/stage/altar. To the young Genet, the prospect of execution was not so much fearful as it was "glorious": like a Christian martyr's final sacrifice, Harcamone's end would illuminate him "with a glory more somber and gentle than the shimmering, silvery velvet of great funerals" (*Miracle of the Rose* 2). Like Lefranc in *Deathwatch*, who longs to take the "radiant" Green Eyes's place, the young Genet of *Miracle of the Rose* aspired to Harcamone's "heavenly glory" (3). Genet felt "the weight" of the condemned man's presence (14), and this "burden of saintliness" prompted his and other inmates' fervid admiration of Harcamone (15). They strained to get a glimpse of him, and when the warder opened Harcamone's cell, the younger inmates were like children at mass, gazing in awe "quand le prêtre ouvre le tabernacle" (*Oeuvres Complètes* 2: 197). Writing years later, the more mature Genet vows to express his "worship of the murderer" (17), of the man who had become his idol. Yet for teenagers, idols come and go; the day after finally meeting Harcamone, Genet spies Bulkaen, and one icon is supplanted by another, a hagiography replaced by a *bildungsroman* and its *frisson* of nascent desire. Still, the juxtaposition is of importance to our ends here: to echo an irreverent headline in the fracas following the publication of Ulick O'Connor's 1970 biography of Behan — "Quare fellow; Queer; Query?" — what relationship obtains between the quare fellow and the queer or bisexual fellow (not necessarily Behan himself)?[7]

By contrast to Genet's psychologically resonant and complex articulation of sexuality with death and the performative in *Miracle of the Rose* — topics of central importance, most obviously, to a play like *The Balcony* — Behan's comments on homoeroticism seem unreflective, even flippant. And, in this important respect, his prose differs markedly both from Genet's and from that of *The Quare Fellow*, *The Hostage*, and *Richard's Cork Leg*, in which this triad proves to be of central importance. Perhaps the most quoted passage on the homoerotic from Behan's prose involves his characterization of nightlife at the Catacombs, a basement gathering place in a Dublin flat that was famous for its bohemianism and unrestrained soirées. Rented free of charge to a young homosexual named Cecil, in the late 1940s the Catacombs was the site of "some sort of a party practically every night" (*Confessions* 138). In *Confessions of an Irish Rebel* (1965), Behan provides a definition of the word "party" that even such mavens as Hugh Heffner would be pressed to match: "A crowd of people would assemble in the flat, each one bringing a bottle of gin, or whiskey, or a dozen of stout. There would be men having women, men having men and women having women; a fair field and no favour. It was all highly entertaining" (138–139). According to O'Sullivan, Behan was similarly impassive about his "limited sexual conduct" with Frederick May, musical director at the Abbey and a devoted supporter of Behan while he served time in the Hollesley Bay Colony Borstal and thereafter. "After all, it's only sex," Behan is said to have remarked (O'Sullivan 91), a kind of variation on his later theme of nights at the Catacombs as "a fair field and no favour." Entertainment is mere entertainment.

Such entertainment and performance, however, accrue richer significance in Behan's drama, as do death and the condemned man. As the time of execution nears in *The Quare Fellow*, Jenkinson sings a hymn while the

Hangman calculates the force necessary to break the quare fellow's neck, and Prisoner C acts as a "choir," singing in Irish for the doomed man. To be sure, there is nothing in *The Quare Fellow* to rival the proximity of glorious death and sexual ardor in Genet's *Miracle of the Rose*. Quite the opposite is the case in *The Hostage*, particularly with the first half of the articulation, where the sanctity of the nationalist cause is concerned. One exchange between Pat, proprietor of the "brockel" in *The Hostage*, and an IRA officer who is disdainful of the brockel clarifies the point, which is rendered more forcefully in the play's 1958 production:

> *Officer.* [I]f it was my doings, there'd be no such thing as us coming here at all.
> *Pat.* Isn't it good enough for your prisoner?
> *Officer.* It's not good enough for the Irish Republican Army.
> *Pat.* Isn't it now?
> *Officer.* Patrick Pearse said, "To serve a cause which is splendid and holy, men must themselves be splendid and holy."
> *Pat.* Are you splendid or just holy? (26)

The Officer views Pat's establishment as "filthy," a denigration reserved in the opening lines of the 1958 production for the two "queers," Rio Rita and Princess Grace. After two whores and the two queers "dance a jig" to open the play, one of the whores shouts, "Get off the stage, you dirty low things" (1). Hence, the locations of death and sexual "being," a cartography so central to the two "worlds" of *The Balcony*, appear in reverse in *The Hostage*: in the former, revolution rages outside the brothel, while inside sexuality and subjectivity are realized through impersonation and performance; in the latter, the hostage and death occupy a "circle" of confinement inside the public house, surrounded by cavorting prostitutes and "queers," a crucial symbolic mapping to which I shall return in a moment.

To state the point differently, in *Miracle of the Rose*, Genet's love for Bulkaen and the fate of Harcamone are equally ennobling. In *The Hostage* (both the 1958 and 1959 versions), Behan introduces the glory of execution through Pearse-like metaphors of religiosity and martyrdom only to undercut them later. When death and sexuality, especially queer sexuality, are juxtaposed, neither appears glorious, but then again, neither is dismissed as filthy. Leslie Williams, the hostage, is neither Harcamone nor Green Eyes; he is hardly luminous or "radiant." But particularly in the 1959 version of *The Hostage*, he grows to become associated with "all the outcasts of the world," which include the whores and queers who dance around him. His parodic duet with Miss Gilchrist helps concretize this association:

> *Miss Gilchrist.* Did you read the Wolfenden Report on whores and queers?
> *Soldier.* Yeah, gorblimey, it was moving. I collapsed meself in tears. (*The Complete Plays* 226)

The condemned man, the nationalist hero, and homosexuality become most conspicuously linked in the figure of Roger Casement, who is "outed" by the aptly named Mrs. Mallarkey in a response to Cronin in *Richard's Cork Leg:*

> *Casement (to Cronin).* You know that he was a homosexual was proved by the British government. The Committee were all Etonians who knew about it. *(CP* 266)

Hence, the ideological purity and excessive prudishness of the IRA officer, who is too "holy" to set foot in the brothel, are challenged by the end of *The Hostage,* and in the process, sexual "outcasts," including queer fellows, are linked to quare fellows.

Admittedly, there is nothing in Behan's work quite like the triangulation of death, sexuality, and the performance of selfhood in the mirrors and on the balconies of *The Maids* and *The Balcony.*[8] Recall that the "Balcony" is the name of a brothel in Genet's play, a place where men in costume assume specific parts en route to their various sexual fulfillments; all the while, as I have mentioned, a revolution is raging outside, one which punctuates the dramas inside with gunfire and chaos. Genet himself regarded this cartography as fundamental to the play, and he despised productions that ignored — or sublated — the violence outside. As a consequence, he criticized a London production at the Arts Theatre in which the director made a "satire de la guerre" and a New York production in which the director deliberately minimized the war outside ["le metteur en scène a carrément fait disparaître tout ce qui concernait la révolution" ("Comment Jouet *Le Balcon*" 139).] Both productions, Genet asserted, were examples of ways in which *The Balcony* had been "mal joué."

Before the outside world intrudes noisily into the inner world of costume and performance, it is not in fact the violence outside but rather the mirrors inside that capture the men's attention, for in the mirror one is able to assess the image's "ornamental purity" that becomes the self. Like Gilles Deleuze's masochists, who fetishize photographs, poses, and statues to "exorcise the dangerous consequences of movement,"[9] the costumed patrons of Genet's Balcony seek "immobility" and the "purity" of the image. "Brothel tricks are mainly mirror tricks" (48), Genet's Chief of Police concludes, which is as much to say that brothels are places of impersonation and performance. Death puts an end to the incessant role-playing near the end of *The Balcony;* it thereby functions as a final space in which role-playing and performance, costume and impersonation, cease.

Subjectivity — or, rather, a plenitudinous, "secret" subject-position — is realized in performance in *The Balcony,* then caught by the Genetian mirror in what Jean-Paul Sartre calls "consciousness in reverse": "If Genet looks at himself in the mirror, it is not primarily out of homosexual coquetry; he wants to understand his secret" (73). As "personal as the eye" (74), the mirror captures every nuance of appearance. (So, by the way, does the other, who, in the act of male-to-male coupling, doubles the maleness of the self [Sartre 75].) Irma, proprietress of *The Balcony*, knows that the more killing that occurs outside her establishment, the more men frequent her "studio." Some men, she explains, are "drawn by mirrors and chandeliers"; others — here we might think of Yeats's Michael Gillane or Sean O'Casey's Jack Clitheroe — allow "heroism" to take "the place of women" (31). One of those so well described by Irma, her client who assumes the role of a bishop, must don all the accoutrements of the sacred office while he abuses young women. For him, the mirror relates to the costume, to the ornaments of holy office, and, finally, to the more authentic self in performance:

> Ornaments, laces, through you I re-enter myself. [. . .] I beleaguer a very ancient *place* from which I was driven. I install myself *in a clearing* where suicide becomes possible. The judgment depends on me, and here I stand, face to face with death.[10] (13, emphasis added)

The mirror and the performance, the performance and the mirror: are they one and the same?

And the mirror and the Other? In the next scene, the Judge looks at the Executioner, a flunky Irma hires to play the part, as if he were a mirror: "Mirror that glorifies me! Image that I can touch, I love you" (18–19). But this mirror, the Executioner, is also a part of the performance with a third player, the Thief (a beautiful young girl). The Thief, as the Judge acknowledges, plays the prior, privileged role in the drama: before the Executioner can punish, a judge must judge. And before a judge can judge, a criminal or suspected criminal must be arrested and bound over for trial. Mirrors, costume and performance, Others, selfhood and image — all form that space, that "domain," over which the Bishop rhapsodizes. Once its "ornamental purity" is violated by the outside world, the place of this being is "gone forever" (80). Or, recalling Sartre's notion, the "secret" inside both self and mirror is lost.

To return to a topic addressed earlier, what about space, performance, and sexuality — gay or straight — in Behan? Is performing not only a process of re-entry to a lost or secret self, as it becomes for Genet's Bishop, but also a method of world building? And what of death — "radiant," ignominious, or otherwise — in Behan's plays? In *The Quare Fellow*, the condemned man clearly occupies a place of radiance, to continue with Genet's metaphors of luminosity. The quare fellow's domain is marked by the freshly dug grave in the yard, which is juxtaposed to the cells in which two new prisoners will be housed: a lifer, "Silver-top," who bludgeoned his wife with a silver-topped cane, and the other, a "dirty beast" who has been sentenced for two years. The prisoners maintain a kind of backhanded respect for the Lifer, who, after all, unlike the quare fellow, didn't chop anyone to pieces: a "man with a silver-topped cane, that's a man that's a cut above meat-choppers whichever way you look at it" (*CP* 42). After Dunlavin, Behan's most opinionated prisoner or "lag," learns about the other man's bestial crimes from a card newly inserted in the cell door, he jibes, "I hope it's not another of that persuasion" (42). At this point in Behan's writing, the quare fellow is in no way a queer fellow; the quare fellow must be respected and fed well, even if he slaughtered his own brother. The queer fellow is no better than a beast, the "low, dirty" thing the whores in *The Hostage* denigrate.

Yet in *The Hostage*, especially in the 1958 version, and in *Richard's Cork Leg*, issues of sexuality and performance grow more complicated. So do the "worlds" or concentric circles of death and life in both plays. As I have mentioned, Williams occupies a "circle" of death in *The Hostage*; Teresa enters this world offering herself (their bed occupies the center of the circle), and the queers, whores, and other denizens of Pat's brothel dance around this bed. IRA men stand guard around them and the perimeter of the brothel, even though, as is the case in *The Balcony*, nothing can finally prevent death (or policemen) from entering. Given the allusions through-out the play to Britain's colonial dominations, Pat's establishment forms a microcosm of the colonized world, even a mirror. Yet all of this occurs within perhaps the largest circle of death: one inscribed by the H-bomb, which Pat calls the "big bomb" that scares him. By comparison, the IRA's "little bombs" are "out of date" (*CP* 133). In addition to delivering a sharp slap to the IRA, Pat's line — and others which make mass destruction by atomic bombs a motif in the play — places death, perhaps total annihilation, in the foreground of post–World War II consciousness. Similar to the desert outside of Hamm's bomb (?) shelter in Beckett's *Endgame* (1957) or the hill of sand which confines Winnie in *Happy Days* (1962), the H-bomb looms on the horizon, bringing with it the vista that Clov surveys in *Endgame:* "Nothing. Nothing. Nothing." Final immobility.

All of these factors combine to make *Richard's Cork Leg*, however silly at times, such an intriguing play. Its narrative, in some ways like that of *Waiting for Godot*, is constructed of role-playing and "bits," comic interchanges and quips, songs and lascivious talk. Most of it occurs in a cemetery, and the play's final tableau features Cronin, whom Simpson, correctly, I believe, designates as a stand-in for Behan (*CP* 24), hanging over his coffin while other characters sing of death:

> It's my old Irish tomb
> I'll be in there soon
> But first you must kiss me
> Beneath the harvest moon. (*CP* 312)

Actually, like Williams in *The Hostage*, Cronin dies and still has more to do; he walks into a mist and then is suspended over his own coffin, "rather like the sort of religious kitsch frequently seen on the front of a mass card" (312).

The play's "self-parody," recalling Murray's term, is thus also a parody of the Christ-like "quare fellow," who in *Richard's Cork Leg* quite literally rises from the dead, thereby forming the comic counterpart to the glorious Harcamone and Green Eyes in Genet. Yet if Cronin is the quare fellow in *Richard's Cork Leg*, he isn't quite a "queer fellow" as well. He's far more pansexual than this, as a partial list of his performances would include advising the Hero that he "missed a damned good thing" by never masturbating (271); playing the "Cynical European Intellectual" when attempting to seduce Deirdre (272), and later her accuser, by suggesting that she goes around with her mother "in a condition well-nigh bordering on incestuous lesbianism" after declining his offers (274); and so on. Deirdre's reticence leads Cronin both into self-criticism of his unsuccessful "technique" of seducing women and into a flood of "queer" jokes. Where could he learn about the techniques of seducing women? "Five years with the Christian Brothers — nearly as bad as Eton or Harrow" (278). He asks his companion the Hero, "Would you expect she'd know about queers?," which prompts the following exchange:

> *The Hero.* She wasn't brought up in America?
> *Cronin (with interest).* Don't they have them there?
> *The Hero.* Only in the police force and on the Senate. They are not permitted in the Armed Forces [because of Section Eight]. [. . .] Pity they haven't got it in other armies. There'd be no more war! (*CP* 279)

Such political banter in no way affects Cronin's pansexuality. For later in the play, after the Hero explains that in England "a pervert is a man who has sex relations with other men," Cronin quickly replies, "Well, I might have a go at that too" (*CP* 305).

These and a host of other references to various sexual practices and orientations dominate act 1 of *Richard's Cork Leg*, the action of which begins in a Dublin cemetery, with two bawds visiting the grave of a prostitute, and ends with Cronin's attempted seduction of Deirdre. He fetches a rubber mattress, which he places on top of a tomb, and might have achieved his goal were it not for the meta-theatrical imagination of his creator. A bright spotlight breaks the mood, prompting Cronin's retort, "When the author wrote this you weren't allowed to do it on stage" (281). But Cronin, whom Mrs. Mallarkey calls a "sex maniac" in act 2, is as irrepressible as Behan's penchant for low humor. Significantly, one of the most absurd plays on words in act 2 follows Cronin's ballad of a Wexford hero: " 'Twas in the town of Wexford they sentenced him to die / 'Twas in the town of Wexford they built their gallows high." Mrs. Mallarkey orders him to stop, demurring that the man was probably just shot in a non-vital part. Cronin's response:

> *Cronin.* He was shot in the arse hole.
> *Mrs Mallarkey.* Rectum, rectum.
> *Cronin.* Wrecked him. . . . it near killed him. (*CP* 301)

Here the quare fellow, violated anally, becomes a different kind of queer fellow and, at the same time, more than merely the forced partner of the colonizer's buggery. He is the principal vehicle for Behan's ruminations about sexual difference, status, and death in all three of his major plays.

Quare fellows and queer fellows, performance and subjectivity, self-parodies and that self which is being parodied — and questions, lots of questions. Do both Behan's and Genet's representations of an internal/external opposition or subjective space that can never finally be maintained anticipate the gender theory of someone like Judith Butler, who articulates bodies with spaces and contemplates the socio-sexual meaning of their boundaries:

> Regardless of the compelling metaphors of the spatial distinctions of inner and outer, they remain linguistic terms that facilitate and articulate a set of fantasies, feared and desired. "Inner" and "outer" make sense only with a mediating boundary that strives for stability. . . . Hence, "inner" and "outer" constitute a binary distinction that stabilizes and consolidates the coherent subject. (134)

Genet shows us a subject who becomes a "man" only by internalizing the male love object, one who breaks down the binarism by forming a mirror until it is shattered and its image is no longer available to be incorporated. Particularly in *The Hostage* and *Richard's Cork Leg*, Behan creates quare fellows — Williams and Cronin — who operate in proximity to queer fellows who, if not quite constituting mirrors of the self, are fellow "outcasts of the world."

In such motifs as those of H-bombs and nuclear annihilation in *The Hostage* and the circle of violence that surrounds Irma's Balcony in Genet, one wonders if, or to what extent, the devastations of World War II are responsible for these writers' visions. And this inquiry is *not* intended as an echo of Theodor Adorno's well-known coupling of the horrors of Auschwitz with the "austerity" (his term) of Beckett's *Endgame*. Rather, Behan's plays quite clearly respond to a post-war Britain and Ireland that is far more complexly international, even contemporary, than the colonialist rubric will allow. Among the most volatile traces of post-war discourse are allusions in both *The Hostage* and *Richard's Cork Leg* to the Wolfenden Report, published in Britain in September 1957, and the first Kinsey Report, *Sexual Behavior in the Human Male* (1948). The former report, published by a parliamentary committee appointed in 1954 (and chaired by Sir John Wolfenden) to study both homosexuality and prostitution in Britain (which it did for over three years), seems particularly relevant to our concerns here.

The publication of the committee's liberalizing, hence controversial, recommendations occurred, ironically enough, at nearly the same time disarmament talks broke down between the United States and the Soviet Union and Russian officials announced that they had tested an intercontinental ballistic missile. Commenting on these events in his defense of the

Wolfenden Report, Eustace Chesser suggested that "a visitor from Mars would doubtless be surprised" that the committee's recommendations elicited a stronger reaction from the British public than the "enormously greater danger of atomic warfare" did (14–15).

What were these recommendations that led, in some quarters, to the report being denigrated as "The Pansies' Charter" (14)? Contrary to the line (in *The Hostage*) suggesting its emotional power, the report possesses the meager excitements of statistics and legal argument to advance two principal theses insofar as homosexual *activity* (not desire) is concerned: 1) consensual homosexual relations conducted in privacy between adult males should *not* be illegal, as it was when the committee was empaneled; and 2) the maximum penalty for homosexual anal intercourse, or "buggery," consensual or otherwise — life in prison — was both extreme and disproportionate in relation to all other penalties for other illegal sexual behaviors. The committee argued that consensual relations among adults conducted in private exist "beyond the proper sphere of the law's concern"; thus, the law should not interfere "with what a man does in private unless it can be shown to be so contrary to the public good that the law ought to intervene [. . .]" (21). On the second point, the excessive penalty for male sodomy (heterosexual sodomy was a far different matter), the committee was even more direct: "[I]t is ludicrous that two consenting parties should be liable for imprisonment for life simply because the act of indecency takes a particular form [. . .]" (33–34). These two recommendations, more so than any other topics upon which the committee deliberated, aroused the lion's share of controversy.

And Behan knew this, and must have been sympathetic with the Committee's recommendations.[11] Like Genet and perhaps an equally prescient commentator on such matters, Georges Bataille, Behan writes in the shadows of both Hiroshima and Alfred Kinsey's research on human sexuality, in the dawn of nuclear destruction *and* the dawn of unprecedented conversation about sexual diversity. And like both Genet and Bataille, Behan understands the relationships between what Bataille calls the "underworld" and a kind of almost monarchical privilege enjoyed by certain powerful criminals, especially where sexual matters are concerned. Further, unemployed or unemployable characters like Cronin in *Richard's Cork Leg*, whether a figure for Behan or not, replicate Bataille's thesis that "sexuality given free rein lessens our appetite for work, just as sustained work lessens our sexual appetite" (161). Here, Bataille is responding to those parts of Kinsey's 1948 report that correlate the frequency of male sexual activity with class and economic status. And throughout the play Cronin is, in effect, defined by both his sexual predilections, which are certainly given "free rein," and his marked aversion to work.[12] "A job is death without the dignity" (*CP* 252), he asserts in act 1, and later, paralleling Bataille's skepticism about the quantifying impulse in Kinsey's findings, he advises Deirdre that scientists going round "parked cars with tape recorders" really cannot inform readers about tactics of seduction and the finer points of sexual play. For Bataille, while certain sexual acts — masturbation, for example, which Cronin endorses so heartily — might be observed "objectively," the "essential thing," something inherently "unamenable" to statistical description, "eludes definition" (*CP* 154).

In such a context, I believe, references to the H-bomb in *The Hostage* take on greater meaning. And, in the context of the Wolfenden Report, so too does the simple line uttered by Princess Grace, one of the cavorting "queers" at the beginning of the 1958 production of the play: "What we need round here is a bit of tolerance" (*Hostage* 1). The British, Irish, and American publics were wrestling with such calls for tolerance and greater understanding at this historical moment, even as more refined weapons of mass destruction were being tested and stockpiled on both sides of the Atlantic. The "Irish Jean Genet" could not avoid implication in such discourses, and, of course, he contributed significantly to them — or parodied them, as the case may be — in his plays.

NOTES

1. Two historical facts might be mentioned here. One, as Alan Simpson makes clear in *Beckett and Behan and a Theatre in Dublin*, the Pike Theatre staged Beckett and Behan in a repertory that prominently included Ionesco, in whom Simpson was very interested. Simpson was taken by the "the emergence of the new non-realistic drama" of the "theatre of the fifties" (18–19); indeed, he termed it this theatre's most "outstanding feature." Ionesco's *Victimes du Devoir* had its first English-language production at the Pike, which also produced *The Bald Prima Donna* in 1956. Two, Behan is quoted as not liking Genet much, a view which Michael O'Sullivan attributes to his high regard for Camus, who disliked Genet intensely. Nonetheless, when Behan arrived in Paris in the late 1940s, Genet was "the talk of literary Paris" (O'Sullivan 146), and Behan's announced view of him, as captured in my second epigraph, matters little to the case I wish to make here.

2. See Murray's *Twentieth-Century Irish Drama* for a useful review of the well-known textual complications of both *The Quare Fellow* and *The Hostage*, which is, as Murray notes, a far different play from *An Giall*, the play from which *The Hostage* was born. The Brechtian and modernist style of the latter, as Murray explains, results in part from Behan's unhappiness with "the style" of the former, which Behan declared originated in "the school of the Abbey Theatre naturalism," of which he was not "a pupil." Many of the epic elements of *The Hostage* were contributed by Joan Littlewood, with whom Behan, as Murray terms it, was a "willing collaborator in staging it" (158).

3. An indication of subtle yet significant differences between the 1959 revised version of *The Hostage*, as presented at Wyndham's Theatre (the version that Alan Simpson includes in *The Complete Plays*), and the 1958 Theatre Workshop version produced by Joan Littlewood (as published by Grove) can be seen in this single line. In the 1958 version, "In India. The World!" (44) is added to this line, thus suggesting that British imperialism forms a worldwide domain, within which Ireland and other countries are subjected.

4. For a brief discussion of Behan's arrival in New York for the premiere of *The Hostage*, see O'Sullivan (264–270).

5. While Behan's own sexuality is of no importance to my argument — his views of sexuality and the attitudes of his characters are far more significant — I will assume that my friend Séamus de Búrca's staunch defense of his cousin's heterosexuality (41) might not be entirely accurate.

6. Especially significant quotations from Genet will be rendered in both English and French.

7. For a brief discussion of the controversy prompted by O'Connor's biography — and its speculations about Behan's sexuality — see O'Sullivan (136–144).

8. This is not to suggest that mirrors and balconies operate in identical ways in both plays. In *The Maids*, the balcony is clearly a place of public performance — Solange castigates the despised Madame for "strutting on the balcony at two in the morning and greeting the populace" (51) — whereas the mirror simply reflects back one's own image. In this arrangement, the populace thus functions as a mirror to reflect one's public image; as such, the balcony in *The Maids* functions differently than the Balcony in *The Balcony*. There, inside the Balcony, patrons can contemplate their ornamental images in relative privacy.

9. See Deleuze (31–33) for a discussion of the importance of fetishism to masochism, especially the fetishistic desire for stasis: "The fetish is therefore not a symbol at all, but as it were a frozen, arrested, two-dimensional image, a photograph to which one returns repeatedly to exorcise the dangerous consequences of movement [. . .]" (31).

10. Acting and costume serve different purposes in plays like *The Blacks: A Clown Show*. If such factors allow the Bishop to re-enter or rediscover the self, acting and costume also enable actors to distance themselves from audiences, as Archibald explains to the audience: "We shall increase the distance that separates us — a distance that is basic — by our pomp, our manners, our insolence — for we are also actors." By doing so, Archibald and the others create a new world — "a delicate world of reprobation" — within which to exist (12).

11. In this regard, recall Behan's kindness to British coal miners accused of homosexual intimacy in the mining "pits" whom he met while jailed in Manchester: " 'Look,' I said to one of them, 'nothing that you have done, except that you interfere with a little child, is shameful' " (*Confessions* 115). He regarded prison as a site of further sexual "temptation" for these miners, suggesting strongly that they had done nothing to warrant this punishment.

12. This distaste for work is also shared by Behan: "I'm inclined to have a contemptuous attitude to work of any description" (*Confessions* 122).

—9—

Playing Outside with Samuel Beckett

JUDITH ROOF

"When you are in the last ditch, only one thing is left-to sing," Samuel Beckett said when railing against the act of censorship that had, in the late 1950s, caused him to refuse to allow his plays to be produced in Ireland. The annual Tóstal festival of plays and music had scheduled works by Joyce and O'Casey, and Beckett had agreed to contribute the two mime plays and *Krapp's Last Tape* to the program. When the archbishop of Dublin declined to perform the traditional votive mass unless Joyce's and O'Casey's works were changed and the authors refused to change them, the plays were banned. In light of this outrage, Beckett withdrew his offering and took the further step of depriving Ireland of all future performances.[1] Incensed equally at the Catholic Church and the British government, Beckett completed the protracted process by which he had, for the previous twenty-five years, been slowly cutting his ties with his native country. But he would not do so without a last word that in itself provides an insightful portrait of the effects of nation on art: "Il nous ailes en culer à la gloire," he said. "They have buggered us into glory" (Bair 493).

Such biographical anecdotes often haunt discussions of identity and nation in literature, especially in cases such as Beckett's, where even the Modern Language Association is not quite sure where to locate him, indexing his work at one time or another as French, English, and Irish.[2] While we may be fairly certain that a writer's nationality has some bearing on his or her writing, Beckett's example makes nation an operative part of his theory of theatre itself, as enacted in his plays. Beckett's work challenges traditional national and linguistic alignments, the assumptions of biographical criticism, and notions of the relations between literature and culture. In Beckett's dramatic *oeuvre*, nation — things Irish — and nationality — Irish identity (whatever that may be) — form parts of the complex apparatus of his theatrical dynamic.

While students of his plays are quick to observe the Irish cadence in Beckett's language as well as the Irish references, names, place names, folk songs, and stories — in other words, the Irish detritus — that sometimes mark the imaginary world of his characters, things Irish also garrison the structurally crucial sites of distance and memory in Beckett's theatre.[3] These two elements constitute the exteriorized otherness paradoxically central to Beckett's dramatic practice and are, through the life of his work, progressively contained in less and less obvious apparatuses. These apparatuses — whistles, clocks, tape recorders, and lights — are synecdoches of theatre itself, as a device for bringing time back at a remove. They function as machines for preserving distance within an identical space. If, in such plays as *Krapp's Last Tape* (1958), *That Time* (1976), and *Rockaby* (1982), characters are confronted with their pasts in a highly condensed form, and if this confrontation, staged as if between present and absent, then and now, is the paradigmatic dynamic of Beckett's dramatic practice, then nation — Ireland — as it persists in Beckett's plays among the shards, shreds, and scraps of "canned" memory, attests to the structural rather than the substantial function of nationality. Things Irish in Beckett's plays are neither setting nor subject, but rather they function as structure in a dramatic practice that depends upon exteriorization, distance, removal, and alienation. Beckett's structural deployment of things Irish suggests that nationality is a tool, one of several mechanisms for enabling and defining alienations. What this ultimately implies is that on Beckett's stage, nation is bound up with the theatrical as part of the very mode of its operation, but nation is neither a defining locus nor the platform for celebration, identity, social question, or apology. Beckett's drama is emphatically not an Irish theatre but a theatre where both Ireland's distance and one's distance from Ireland become enabling relations.

The Apparatus

Many of Beckett's plays contain a signaling apparatus that in some way directs action on the stage. In many plays this apparatus is merely mechanical; in *Endgame* and *Act Without Words I* it is the whistle; in *Happy Days*, the alarm clock; in *Act Without Words II*, the goad; in *Play*, the light. But in *Krapp's Last Tape*, *That Time*, and *Rockaby*, it consists of a recording machine, present on stage in *Krapp's Last Tape*, merely implied in *That Time* and *Rockaby*. What all of these apparatuses do is "wake up" characters and force their confrontation with otherness, whether that otherness takes the form of another person, as in *Endgame*, another state of being, as in *Act*

Without Words II, *Happy Days*, and *Play*, and/or some narrative from a different time and place, as in *Krapp's Last Tape*, *That Time*, and *Rockaby*. This apparatus is more than a mere device; its operation bespeaks the very essence of Beckett's theatrical practice.

Since *Waiting for Godot*, Beckett's drama has seemed to depart from more traditional theatrical styles. On the first page of the introduction to his influential *The Theatre of the Absurd*, Martin Esslin calls *Godot* "a highly obscure, intellectual play" (1); and pioneer critic Ruby Cohn works hard to correlate what she describes as Beckett's "imaginative shrinking of the human horizon" with more traditional formulations of dramatic action (4). Jan Kott, countering Esslin, suggests that even the label "theatre of the absurd" became a way to avoid understanding the theoretical challenges of the new French theatre of the 1950s — an "altogether different theater than had existed up to that time" — by containing unfamiliar linguistic and theatrical practices within the rubric of an "absurd" that as an entity "had now found itself on the stage and was exhibited via nonverbal means of expression" (131). Beckett's drama offers these theoretical challenges, working steadfastly toward the ever-more purely abstract performance of a dramatic theory. In a later essay, Esslin acknowledges this evolution: "In Beckett's more recent plays, this movement to stricter and stricter patterns seems to have carried him towards a new and far more austere form of drama: not only have his plays become more and more concise, they have also shed the notion of *characters in action* which is so often regarded as the basic minimum definition of drama itself" (*Mediations* 118).

Beckett's deployment of the "absurd" is very much an enactment of questions involving the basic possibilities of theatre (and via the example of theatre, communication and existence in general). In considering Beckett's unfinished prose manuscript, *Long Observation of the Ray*, Steven Connor defines the process of that work as emblematic of the developmental direction of Beckett's theatre: "*Long Observation of the Ray* may suggest a movement away from the theatrical, which is to say away from the actualities of space, position and performance, of time, change and progression, and towards the pure self-presence of theory, especially when theatre has traditionally been defined (and often condemned) according to its non-self-identity, its coordination of radically heterogeneous elements . . ." ("Between Theatre and Theory" 87). If Beckett's later plays, like *Long Observation of the Ray*, "traverse, or [. . .] uneasily inhabit, a threshold between fiction and theatre, the page and the stage, virtual and actual space" (79), then the theoretical processes of *Long Observation of the Ray* also describe a theatre in which a departure from the actualities of space and time — a definite location and context — leaves protagonists progressively alone on the stage in performances of non-performance and attitudes of auto-audience.

But when a theory of non-theatrical theatre becomes the essence of a theatrical practice that has worked progressively toward a minimalist economy, as Beckett's has, it produces the paradoxical effect of a meta-theatrical theatre, which, rather than being less theatrical, becomes more so. Connor notes this paradox, saying, "If it is true that much of Beckett's work is rightly seen and explicated as an attempt to create 'pure' theatre, to eliminate theatricality from theatre itself, then it is also the case that his work bears witness to the impossibility of achieving this elimination, whether in prose or in drama" ("Between Theatre and Theory" 87). And Esslin sees the shrinking world of Beckett's stage as evidence of an even more condensed theatricality: "The stasis of these plays, far from being an absence of action, can thus be seen as, on the contrary, a concentration, condensation, and therefore maximal intensification of the tensions that make conventional plays dramatic" (*Mediations* 120).

The Ireland of Magnetic Residue

Beckett's three recording-apparatus plays — *Krapp's Last Tape*, *That Time*, and *Rockaby* — demonstrate this trend toward "the pure self-presence of theory" by exposing, via the relation of the character with the apparatus, the architecture of distancing, reception, and alienation that organizes sound and image, actions and temporality, self and other-self that enact in increasingly starker *gestalt* the passage toward non-being in Beckett's dramatic *oeuvre*. *Krapp's Last Tape*, a play set in "the future," features the birthday encounter of the character Krapp, a "wearish old man," with the thoughts and voice of his younger self through the medium of a tape recorder and a box of previously recorded "spooools" of tape. The material on the tape is, by virtue of the recording apparatus, from another time; by listening to the tape, Krapp ponders the disparity between himself and this former self, a self of which he no longer approves: "Just been listening to that stupid bastard I took myself for thirty years ago, hard to believe I was ever as bad as that" (62). While some critics read this comparison between past and present, in the future, as "an ironic comment on the insignificance of the passing of time" (Cohn, *Samuel Beckett* 249), I would suggest that the layering of time, memory, and self indicates just how central and crucial a condition is the passage of time. In Beckett's drama, passing time is everything.

The complexity of the temporal frames in *Krapp's Last Tape* is enabled by the apparatus of the tape recorder, which represents the space and means by which not only past speech but also the magnetically fixed sound waves of the past's ambience and location can potentially repeat endlessly. The apparatus guarantees that certain portions of the past are never lost, but remain accrued in boxes or a drawer, to be recalled and replayed at will. But the tapes already represent a layered time, performed and recorded at one time and place but referring to times and places other than the scene of their recording. And listening to the tapes is never simply a repetition of a past scene. Since Krapp himself is never the same from moment to moment, he himself constitutes multiple different audiences through time; the possibility of multiple audiences complicates the layering already contained on the tape by adding to it not only Krapp's non-recorded memory but also the memories of the other times he has listened to the tape (parts of the tape are even heard more than once in the play). As Connor astutely observes, "Krapp's recordings are intended to provide a firm and unambiguous record of a moment of time, but instead show how every utterance can be taken up or enveloped by some other occasion, some other context of understanding. Krapp's recorded life then comes to seem less like a logically continuous series of discrete utterances, each located firmly in its intentional context, than a web of mutually enveloping, self-quoting moments, each endlessly displaced from its originating context, and regrafted elsewhere" (*Samuel Beckett* 130).

The apparatus in *Krapp's Last Tape* performs the relation of self to self through time by providing a means of saving, and hence distancing, the words of one time from any other time at which they are heard. While the apparatus would thus seem to function as a conservative device, salvaging time, it also, and more importantly, is a device for performing the distance between one time and another. The clash of these times on stage, through the vehicle of the tape recorder, is a capsule version — a mechanized, minimalist, de-psychologized version — of fairly traditional Western theatre as the encounter of the present and the past (i.e., *Oedipus Rex*, *The Cherry Orchard*, *The Wild Duck*). But Beckett's deployment of the apparatus as an "objective" source of the past denaturalizes and de-psychologizes the process of memory, making its appearance sudden and selective. Displacing memory from mind to machine enables Krapp to distance himself from his own past and recall it as if it were both self and other. This distance is manifested not only in his literal control over the past as an object — a spool — that he can manipulate, but also in the graphic differences between the scenes he listens to on the tape and the scene of his listening in the circumscribed pool of light on the stage. The difference between past and present is the difference between here and there, where "there" opens out into locales other than the scene of taping; hence, "there" may become a physical distance as well as a temporal one.

There, then, is where things Irish come into play. "There" consists of the details, described on the spool, that refer to another place, a place linked both linguistically and referentially to Ireland. Ruby Cohn notes that Beckett's interest in the work of actor Patrick McGee's "voice like an elevated whisper," inspired Beckett's return to his native language and to his native Ireland in *Krapp's Last Tape* (*Just Play* 23–24). But defamiliarized, along with his former self, things Irish work simultaneously as a way to define Krapp further and provide a contrast to his present situation. Suggesting a concrete, nationally identified past through references to things Irish on the tapes hints at a material and social history for Krapp, one that contrasts with the more narrow, isolated presence of the stage's ambiguous future/present. The tape includes specific details — "Old Miss McGlome," "Kedar Street" — that, though small, are enough to evoke an existence as certain as the one taking place on a stage that is as unmarked by geographic detail as the tape is pocked with it. If the audience of *Krapp's Last Tape* grasps onto spool numbers, banana peels, and the sounds of imbibing to characterize the Krapp who is present, then both Krapp and the audience grasp onto the details of name and place to define the past Krapp. The contrast between the two sets of details produces a shifting between two "kinds" of Krapp. Nation, evoked through a few details on the tape, stands for one side of the oscillating conditions of identification and alienation that define Krapp's experience of listening to the tape. On the one hand, Krapp identifies this former self in its former place as himself, and late in the play he seeks to relive a particular moment on a boat with a girl; on the other hand, the tape bears a version of himself that Krapp rejects, sometimes violently, and the tape is evidence of a time past that he can never regain.

The combination of here and there, then and now, identification and alienation, enabled by the tape recordings structures Krapp's drama of the ambivalent consumption of ambivalent memories, indexed both by year (on tape) and by ambivalently regarded loci of action. This ambivalence characterizes an emotional oscillation between extremes (love/hate, feeling/nonfeeling), a physical alternation between dark and light, time and place, closed and open, and their imagistic contrasts on stage. Perhaps more important, this ambivalence provides the structure for the flickering oscillations that ultimately enact a theory of theatre as the place for replaying a drama of distance and proximity, clarity and ambiguity, hope and despair, a drama that defines existence and produces meaning. Ultimately the play's ambivalence is a desire machine, wherein oscillations between extremes enact a Sisyphian scenario of desire/fulfillment, circling around the same object or locus in time.

That Krapp is impatient with most of his thirty-year-old tape yet willingly seeks and hears the episode on the boat twice suggests a nostalgia, a desire to return to the boat's moment of bliss.[4] When the listening Krapp hears "the stupid bastard" claim he doesn't want his best years back and ends the play sitting "motionless staring before him," the play performs the ultimate irony of temporality. Even if Krapp does want them back and even if they seem to return via the tapes, he cannot have them back. The play's final tableau is a scene of desire; the inevitable distance of time itself produces the impossibility of fulfillment that defines both desire and Beckett's theatre. The tape finally illustrates more than anything Krapp's removal from the scene itself as he sits contemplating his contemplations.

The apparatus is thus an ambivalence machine, orchestrating the play of oscillations between acceptance and rejection, bliss and despair, present surface and historical depth, then/there and now/here, and what Beckett himself calls "mind" and "anti-mind," which define his theatre as a rapid shifting among states, catalyzed by memory, that constantly reenact the production of desire. Governed, as Eyal Amiran suggests, "by a notion of temporal periodicity and by literalized metaphors," Beckett's theatre and its "literalized metaphor" of the apparatus figures what Amiran identifies as the dichotomy of "wandering and home" that organizes the metaphysics of Beckett's structure (5). "Wandering and home" embodies the paradoxes resident in *Krapp's Last Tape;* home is never what it was, wandering is inevitable. Home is regained only through a wandering, as Krapp sorts through his tapes, but the home found is itself only a wandering, a contemplation of a past that has disappeared into the narration of its memory. Indeed, it is often difficult to discern what in Beckett's plays constitutes wandering and what constitutes home; what is important is the figure of alternation, of oscillation between states of being, that structures many of his plays (*Act Without Words II* is perhaps the archetypal example). And even if many critics are quick to link home autobiographically to Dublin, in its sparse detail, Dublin itself functions as a site of ambivalence and alienation.

In a theatre whose dynamic is the twinkling oscillation between states of mind and being, mental images of physical location provide, along with the specifics of recalled individuals, the imagery that secures the illusion of a certain locale on one side of the oscillation. Things Irish thus constitute not home but the fleeting specificity which permits the continued vibrant wavering that characterizes Beckett's theatre not as an encounter with another or with a simple past but rather as a complex and continually layered process of going round. This vertiginous layering enacts the infinite play of desire which gets worse and more intricate as time (and the play) goes on. In this sense, Beckett's theatre imitates existence but is located in a metaphysical rather than a physical plane — the site of exchange among memory, image, consciousness, and temporality projected and literalized in stage space.

Krapp's ambivalent oscillations and circular layerings are further complicated in *That Time,* where the recording apparatus has disappeared from the stage, evoked only by "Voices A B C . . . his own coming to him from both sides and above" (228). Where Krapp moves in and out of the pool of light that illuminates the table, the central figure or "Listener" in *That Time* is static, "10 feet above stage level midstage off centre," while the voices play around him from the darkness. The play consists of repeated and circular narratives from the three voices focusing on three different scenes from the past, scenes moored by "the ruin," "Foley's Folly" (Voice A), "the Portrait Gallery" (Voice C), and "the stone at the edge of the little wood" (Voice B). The narratives depict scenes from three different times, A narrating the return to a nettle-covered childhood haunt, C narrating the older man's taking shelter in the Portrait Gallery, and B narrating a bucolic love scene. The play is quite formal, the three voices arranged, as many critics have observed, in a strict pattern:

ACB ACB ACB CAB
CBA CBA CBA BCA
BAC BAC BAC BAC[5]

The apparent formalism of this patterning combines the circular repetition of three different voice orders, but the order of the voices is less of an indicator of repetitions and echoes than the repetition of words and phrases within the narrations. The word "time" chimes throughout the piece, as do phrases such as "another time," "talking" or "muttering" "to yourself who else," "making up," and "on to hell out of there," which emanate from different voices. While the narratives delivered by each voice circle on themselves, they reverberate with the others, producing a layering, or chiming, that makes each voice seem to come back from where the others had been.

The three scenes that the voices narrate are all stories about the impossibility of "going back" and the psychic functions of such histories of return and its failure. Voice A, narrating the return to the childhood scene, describes the change in the landscape: "not a curse for the old scenes the old names straight up the rise from the wharf to the high street and there not a wire to be seen only the old rails all rust . . ." (229). But even if the scene has changed, the narration constantly performs a return to "the ruin still there where you hid as a child." Voice C narrates a habitual experience in the Portrait Gallery, where, having sought dryness and warmth, voice C contemplates a portrait, trying to make out its face, when after that, "never the same after that never quite the same but that was nothing new if it wasn't this it was that common occurrence . . ." (230). Voice B tells the story of an assignation but ends by thinking that the story might be false: " . . . hard to believe harder and harder to believe you ever told anyone you loved them or anyone you till just one of those things you kept making up to keep the void out . . ." (230). It doesn't matter if the loving ur-moment ever occurred. What matters is its memory, the narrative of which never quite fills the void to which it is assigned.

Like *Krapp's Last Tape*, *That Time* enacts the disjuncture between now and then, here and there, but makes the impossibility of return more its subject as it paradoxically returns to phrases and images that produce layerings and memories within the piece itself. And perhaps more overtly than *Krapp's Last Tape*, *That Time* evokes place as a signifier of return and of its impossibility by narrating the experience of change in place as the essence of the failed return. The places evoked, which have been laboriously traced in various biographies, are all sites in Ireland linked to points in Beckett's life.[6] Ireland never makes an overt appearance in the play, but the descriptions of changed landscape are the palimpsest of a nation lurking within memory, and impossible to regain. The admonition to "on to hell out of there," voiced by both A and C, is analogous to Krapp's saying that he "wouldn't want them back." That is, despite the failure of memory to revivify the past, a past is nonetheless evoked by memory's failure. In *That Time*, the Listener, like Krapp, knows what he is missing, and he misses it even as he fills in with tales of how one can't go back. At the heart of this dilemma is an Ireland that stands both as an unrecoverable past (like childhood and lost love) and the Ireland of the Portrait Gallery, which has supplanted a more euphoric past.

As in *Krapp's Last Tape*, *That Time* performs a disjuncture between word and image, between the places described and the places the audience sees on the stage. This disjuncture constitutes another layer which enacts again the difference between here and there, now and then, a difference already evoked by the voices. Ireland is hidden in sound but again provides the specificity necessary to counter the image of the stage's "old white face" by providing the scant shreds of detail that focus the memories and render the narration more visually varied than the stage scene. *That Time*'s trios would seem to counter the dualistic oscillations of *Krapp's Last Tape*, but what they enable is a magnification of those oscillations among the voices and between seen (scene) and said. By reinforcing repetitions among the voices, the trios amplify the oscillations between past and return within the narratives, which literally oscillate as the source of sound shifts from side to side and above, accompanied by the Listener's opening and closing of his eyes. While *Krapp's Last Tape* has more physical action, *That Time*, in its greater abstraction, becomes even more complex in its layering, as each Voice plays with the impossibility of return. The narratives reverberate and layer the paradox of that impossibility, and the play's order and visual disparity inveigle the audience into its own memory game. Our position as listeners of the Listener reproduces on some level the Listener's ambivalent experience of the impossibility of going back conjoined with a going back, a desire to return with its simultaneous fulfillment and frustration in the layered iterations which enact the lesson that despite constant repetition, nothing is ever the same twice.

The abstractions of *That Time* are abstracted again in *Rockaby*. The oscillations of voice, light and dark, and word repetition are condensed into the rocking motion of W as she listens to "her recorded voice" (275). W prods the apparatus, uttering the word "more" four times to get the offstage recorder going. Unlike Krapp's spools, W's recording seems to have lost all of its temporal and spacial markers, referring only to a very undefined locale of windows, with their blinds down, a room, and a rocking chair. Pronouns are even more ambiguous in their reference, the ubiquitous "her" and "she" referring maybe to W, maybe to someone else — "Another creature like herself" (275). The language of the recording is reminiscent of *That Time* in tone and phrase, particularly in the repetition of "who else" and "time," and in the melodic recircling of repetition in the piece. Like *That Time*, *Rockaby*'s repetitions represent a complex layering and relayering whose iterations illustrate the non-identity of any repetition. *Rockaby*'s words wind around windows and blinds and eyes and gradually accrue through repetition the image of a woman rocking alone, ending with the phrases "fuck Life" and "rock her off."

But while *Rockaby* would seem to spiral toward an end, or at least the cessation of movement as the chair stops rocking and the voice ceases to speak, the play's oscillations between self and other, then and now, here and there, enact in balder form the very splits that structure Beckett's theatre. The narrated action juxtaposed with the action we see on stage combined with the ambiguous identity/non-identity of W and the figure in the narration produce a structure which plays out the essence of drama as a constant shifting, emblematized most graphically by the image of W's head rocking in and out of the light. As Leslie Hill notes, "Rocking [. . .] works as a kind of metatextual shorthand for the oscillating uncertainties created by the instability of structural oppositions in Beckett's play; it is a graphic embodiment of the continual oscillation between extremes that Beckett thematizes here — as he does elsewhere — as a ceaseless coming and going [. . .] between light and dark" (20). The tape's use of the third-person pronoun simultaneously suggests both difference and identity between the W we see and the "she" to which the voice refers, producing reverberating multiple referents which are layered onto the image. Hill sees this as a kind of undermining: "Throughout Beckett's play, one is confronted not with a series of stable characters, voices, or bodies, but rather an irredeemable proliferation of doubles or simulacra, with the result that relations of sameness are constantly undermined by difference, and relations of difference are thrown off balance by apparent similarity" (22). I see it as a condensed and repeated version of a theatrical essence which comes and goes from here to there both then and now, circling and layering into the complex simplicity of the repeated last line, "rock her off," producing desire as the by-product of its oscillations and frustrating it again in its uncertain and ambivalent ending.

The palimpsest of Ireland has finally disappeared in *Rockaby*, except for its faint whisper in the cadence of the language. But the absence of any definitive markers of context shows the progression of Beckett's theatre from one that is still attached to those irretrievable old places to one that is a complete rewriting of past sites as windows with their blinds down. The window in *Rockaby* is the emblem of a process of memory which is forever separated from the view it seeks; the window is the same as the failed return to childhood sites voice A narrates in *That Time*, and it is the same as the section of the tape Krapp replays that focuses on his experience in the boat, moving up and down and side to side, watching the woman's eyes open and close. The window is the metonymy that substitutes the structure of memory's failure to return time (a window with the blind down) for the images that mark the memories (ruins, rusted rails, nettles, paintings in a gallery, Kedar Street). In *Rockaby* we can no longer see behind the blinds; the blind — like Hamm's "old Stancher," the closed ash bins, and the closed eye — becomes a signifier of a past that is closed off and no longer desired. Without the specific details, the sense of the past as distinct from the present, as well as the distinctions between there and here, dissolves. The image of a woman rocking together with the narrative of a woman rocking and searching and looking becomes a far more densely layered version of the problem of presenting the meaning of time's passage.

If *Rockaby* condenses the essence of theatre to the juxtaposition of an image of rocking with a description of rocking, then the theatre whose theorization has long lurked finally is almost (but not quite) reduced to its own terms, moving, as Connor says, "towards the pure self-presence of theory" ("Between Theatre and Theory" 87). Its condensation has rendered all terms — image, detail, context — to less and less specific manifestations, except for W, whose image is still quite definitively drawn. The details of the images described in *Krapp's Last Tape* and *That Time* are condensed in *Rockaby* to the single specific image of the rocking W in "Black lacy high-necked evening gown. Long sleeves, jet sequins to glitter when rocking. Incongruous flimsy head-dress set askew with extravagant trimming to catch light when rocking" (273). The specificity of W's costume is a detail designed to make W herself function as a twinkler, a site of visual oscillations that match the movement of the chair, the oscillations between she and she and all of the other differences and layerings evoked on stage by the combination of sound and image. The playing outside that seemed part of both Krapp's and the Listener's relation to a past contained somewhere else has moved inside. The lack of distinction between present and past, here and there, has been displaced into the play's drama of intersubjective splitting, into the minute structurally defined differences between voice and image, she and her, this repetition and that, which both localize and universalize efforts to come to an end.

Outsiders

The nation that lurks decreasingly prominently in Beckett's theatre is nonetheless still a necessary locus, functional in its absence. Nation as "home" and "wandering": both make the concept of Ireland itself a necessary pole against which and in relation to which the impossibility of writing exists. Ireland itself is perfect as this kind of home, since Beckett's relation to Ireland is as full of contradictions as his plays are replete with oscillations. This is not to suggest that biographical evidence of his self-exile necessarily defines a playwright's practice but rather that the particular situation of Ireland provides a model of internal contradiction and oscillation that renders Beckett's literal "home" a fairly good example of the

contradictions his plays enact. As a middle-class Protestant in a predominantly Catholic country, Beckett grew up in a society where national identity was a fractured site. While Beckett detested the Catholic Church and
the English equally (reportedly because they both censored art and made
innovation difficult), the class and religious differences between Protestant
and Catholic Irish defined marital alliances, neighborhoods, schools, and
friendships. Finding a place beyond this splitting where one's alterity was
immediately accounted for provided the distance intrinsic to Beckett's theatrical project in general. I am not claiming that Beckett's status as a Protestant Irishman produced a need for and model of distanced difference but
rather that the various internal dramas of nations and the general status of
foreigners in France provided the imaginary loci for an idea of theatre as an
exteriorizing, distancing machine.

Exile and/or difference — or even, as in the cases of Brendan Behan and
Jean Genet, imprisonment, as Stephen Watt's essay elucidates — seem to
produce many playwrights in both Ireland and France. Many of Ireland's
most prominent playwrights were Protestants (Synge, Yeats, O'Casey), England's dominant playwright was a Protestant Irishman (Shaw), while many
of France's theatrical innovators were foreigners who wrote in French
(Beckett, Ionesco, Adamov, Arrabal). This is not to imply that these writers
had a privileged view because of their alterity nor is it to argue that national
or other differences are necessarily intrinsic to innovative theatre. Rather, it
is to suggest that in the twentieth century, distance, manifested in any
number of ways, becomes increasingly central to the conceptualization of
theatre and that national origin becomes one element of an experience of
distance that works its way into the structure of drama.

The idea that drama is linked to nation is not new. Alexis de Tocqueville noted in the mid-nineteenth century that "the love of drama is, of all
literary tastes, that which is most natural to democratic nations" and that
such democracies substitute their own taste for conventions (482). A half-
century later, W. B. Yeats set forth his idea of a "People's Theatre" as one
where the plays "are to some extent a part of that popular imagination" but
where the theatre is "objective with the objectivity of the office and the
workshop, of the newspaper and the street, of mechanism and politics"
(331). Both Yeats and Romain Rolland, who also formulated a "People's
Theatre," envisioned a people's theatre as responsive to class divisions,
representing popular experience as defined by popular imagination to the
populace (rather than to an elite). Working against what Georg Lukács
identifies as the "bourgeois" and "individualist" character of theatre, both
Piscator and Brecht develop these ideas, but within the unacknowledged
frame of nation. For them, the people's theatre becomes a revolutionary
theatre, openly appealing to class problems but only covertly assuming any
national basis. Popular imaginations, however, are presumed to be local,
even though Brecht, for example, imagines "the people" as a European

population.[7] If the theatre is to be responsive to the people, it of necessity reflects national identity. Because we premise most of our ideas of the theatre on Aristotelian notions of imitation of action, then nation (what is, in a sense, at stake already in *Oedipus Rex* and Shakespeare's history plays) is an intrinsic part of the context for action.

The tendency to universalize theatre — to make theatrical action not only the literal drama of specific place and time but also, at the same time, a more metaphorical action that presumably works beyond its context — means, however, that theatre is also not tied either to nation or context at all and that it can be transferred easily from one context, time, or nation to another. Insofar as theatre depicts characters at all mimetically, it depends upon the subtle character of nation for verisimilitude, motive, context. Insofar as theatre exists beyond the details of setting and character, which depend upon language and national identity, theatre exists beyond nation. But even if the details are removed and the plot universalized, the founding mark of the idea of nation as a defining quality is still present as a palimpsest — if not as the subject or content of drama, then as part of its structure of division. In other words, nation provides one archetypal spatial locus, in relation to which spatial and temporal dislocations operate.

If theatre, even a "People's" theatre, is to be strong and permanent, it should, according to Eugène Ionesco, extend beyond its own time and locale. Like every era, it "needs something 'out of period' and incommunicable to be introduced into what is 'period' and communicable" (21). This difference gives psychology a "metaphysical dimension," where "drama lies in extreme exaggeration of the feelings, an exaggeration that dislocates flat everyday reality. Dislocation, disarticulation of language too" (26). This dislocation, of course, can only occur in covert reference to a location, the disarticulation of language in reference to language. Playing outside, therefore, means producing a theatre of dislocation and disarticulation. Dislocation might mean anything from exteriorizing and distancing to interiorizing claustrophobia in relation to what we know to be the normative sites for action. Beckett's plays do both — exteriorizing and distancing material by manifesting internal mental processes as relations with objects in space (which arguably occur in almost all of his plays) and interiorizing by manifesting larger social relations as enclosed and isolated (most notably in *Play*, *Not I*, and *Rockaby*). Both exteriorizing and interiorizing produce the distancing exaggeration that constitutes drama by reference to the proportion that is missing and, ultimately, only implied.

The perspective that enables such distancing as the very premise of drama, however, may be a by-product of expatriatism. Ionesco (who never much admired Brecht) intimates that Brecht is not distant enough from his own time and locale, writing what is too much a national theatre immersed in local ideology. While this assumes that physical dislocations produce a practice of dramatic dislocation, I maintain that this is less a psychological process than a cultural positioning that for some coheres with what are already certain artistic or philosophical inclinations. Since physical travel through time is currently unavailable (except, of course, only in one direction and at time's normal pace), geographic relocations are the primary way such dislocation can occur, especially if relocation also involves moving into another linguistic culture. One is always an outsider in such a culture, forced constantly to look at oneself as if from the perspective of the other culture in which one is immersed. This enacts a splitting, a *distancing* between self and self, then and now, there and here, as an effect of such dislocation.

Beckett's drama, then, is less about nationality and is more focused around nation as a lost site and a site of loss. Ireland is *Rockaby*'s window with a closed blind, a very necessary place, for the more it is hidden as a subject, the closer Beckett's plays come to being pure expressions of a theory of theatre. Ireland's suppression as a dramatic object results in the elegant architecture of a drama whose tensions reenact the expatriatism of time and the very structure of desire.

NOTES

1. As it turned out, this refusal was only temporary, but the gesture, with its air of permanence, was dramatic.

2. The first *MLA Bibliography* entry on Beckett was located in the "French Literature" section in 1955. Accompanying the entry was a note explaining Beckett's inclusion in the French section: "[B was born in Ireland in 1906. In France since 1938, and his recent work has all been in Fr. *En attendant Godot* was pub. in 1952, staged in 1953]." From 1959 through the 1960s, most of the work was located in the "French Literature" section, with cross-references in the "British Literature" section. Beginning in 1981, the MLA reorganized its categories to include a section on Irish literature. From that point on, essays on Beckett's *oeuvre* were located both in the Irish and the French "Literature Bibliographies."

3. In "Beckett's Irish Rhythm Embodied in his Polyphony," Johanneke Van Sloten lists the ways Irishness comes out in Beckett's plays — Irish music, oral transmission, allusions and quotes, patronyms, place-names, historical and literary references, explicit examples of dialect, "typical turns of thought," turns of phrase, cadences of speech, and the way of storytelling. She observes that "The Irishness in Beckett's work seems part of its vital core; he himself sees it as constituting the 'condensing spiral of need' in any work of art" (45). Noting that Beckett "has not called attention to his Irish nationality as Yeats and Joyce did," Richard Ellmann hypothesizes that "The geographical change" involved in living outside of Ireland "symbolized for all four of them [Yeats, Wilde, Joyce, Beckett] an attempt to proceed from the known to the unknown, to remake themselves in unfamiliar air" (91–92).

4. Ironically, Beckett's biographers locate the boat scene in Germany. See Deirdre Bair, *Samuel Beckett: A Biography* (87).

5. Both James Acheson, *Samuel Beckett's Artistic Theory and Practice*, and Antoni Libera map out the play's pattern.

6. See, for example, Bair (636).

7. As in many of Brecht's writings. See specifically *Brecht on Theatre*.

Part IV

CONTEMPORARY
THEATRE COMPANIES
AND REVIVALS

—10—

Translating Women into Irish Theatre History

MARY TROTTER

A century ago, one of the central goals of the Irish Literary Theatre, the Gaelic League, and other nationalist cultural organizations was to advance representations of Irish character which would contest British stereotypes of the Irish people. The stage was the logical site for this challenge, and a century later, many Irish playwrights still seek to dramatize realistic Irish experiences. For example, as Lauren Onkey underscores in her contribution to this volume, Roddy Doyle, Paul Mercier, and the other collaborators in the Passion Machine Theatre Company have explored the experiences of, and, thus, have given a voice to, Dublin's young, postmodern, male-dominated working class. Considering the history behind such initiatives, it seems doubly important to ask, "Where are the women's voices in contemporary Irish theatre?" This essay critiques when and how women's voices are heard in contemporary Irish drama and examines one way in which two women playwrights have forced their powerful work outside Ireland's theatrical margins.

While women have played vital roles in the Irish dramatic movement over the past century as playwrights, actors, managers, editors, and critics, their involvement has often entailed a hard-fought struggle. Practically, biases within the theatre community often make it difficult for women to get employed in theatres—a typical problem in theatre communities around the world, but one which women like Garry Hynes and Pam Brighton are helping to change in the Republic and in Northern Ireland.[1] Critically, writing by women playwrights is routinely overlooked, ignored, or marginalized. Often written and/or performed by collaborative groups or in smaller, independent spaces, plays by women frequently go under-reviewed and unpublished. Too often, the absence of major productions translates into very short lives for dramas by women, with no published versions of their plays and few, if any, international stagings of their work.[2]

While American audiences may equate contemporary Irish drama with the highly acclaimed and excellently marketed innovations of writers like Brian Friel, Connal Morrison, and Martin McDonagh, Irish women play-wrights are also transforming Ireland's theatrical landscape, at least in per-formance, if not often enough in print, and they are doing so through a variety of methods. For example, Charabanc's collaborative pieces in the 1980s used historical research and ethnography to explore Northern Irish women's experiences throughout the twentieth century. Emma Donahue radicalizes Dublin stages with her portrayals of lesbian experience. And Patricia Burke Brogan's play, *Eclipsed* (1992), one of the plays staged during the conference (as noted in this collection's introduction), dramatizes the silenced stories of a group of Magdalene women, misfits in their commu-nity who were forced into servitude as laundresses in a convent.

Each of these examples points to the familiar feminist strategy of plac-ing female characters and their stories in the subject position of the drama, reclaiming an aspect of the Irish experience — women's — which has been alternately idealized and ignored in the Irish mainstream tradition. The nationalist dramatic tradition was founded on the premise that this tradi-tion would seek to rid the theatre of the stage Irishman, but far less atten-tion was paid to rewriting the long-suffering mother figure or the idealized Colleen. And from Yeats and Gregory's *Kathleen ni Houlihan* (1902) to McDonagh's virgin/whore "Girleen" in *The Lonesome West* (1997), Irish female characters have embodied the nation, the land, the desires or re-sponsibilities of male characters, but rarely have they been authentic, com-plex, autonomous women.[3]

To write women into Irish theatre history, women playwrights write *outside* of Irish theatre history, finding new subjects (real Irish women) and alternative forms (street performance, cross-gender casting, contiguous narratives) to break out of the male-centered traditions of Irish drama and to develop Ireland's increasingly heterogeneous theatre scene. Likewise, by referring to popular Irish performance forms like the Irish melodrama and the *ceilidh*, they in fact broaden the mainstream memory of Irish drama beyond the horizons of the formal traditions founded and perpetuated by the Abbey Theatre. Rejecting a version of history is an effective way to advance a new tradition, and these writers are certainly enriching Ireland's theatrical future by rejecting elements of its mainstream theatrical past.[4]

Regrettably, such playwrights — in Ireland and around the world — often find themselves in an economic and artistic catch-22. Audiences, trained to understand and appreciate male discourses, are often reluctant to embrace feminist forms, or they regard dramas with female protagonists as the theatrical equivalent of "chick flicks," designed for a solely female clientele. Such an attitude can only change by increasing audiences' exposure to alternative, gynocentric forms, but most theatres are reluctant to risk productions that do not have an established audience base. Thus, theatre by and about women remains ghettoized to the point where some women playwrights shun the term "feminist"—or even "feminine"—in descriptions of their work for fear of such marginalization. In Ireland, feminist playwrights find themselves on the margin of a theatre on the margins.

But there is progress. This essay looks at how Marina Carr and Christina Reid—two successful, mainstream playwrights—have subverted one of the central tropes of Irish realism, a convention which I will call the "family memory play," to place women's experience in the narrative foreground. Usually, the family memory play's male protagonist, who narrates his story outside the frame of the action, recalls his childhood. In his remembering, he tries to reconcile his youthful desire for autonomy with his connections to family, history, and land. Female characters provide the protagonist with emotional support, a source of conflict, or a sexual interest, but the real attention in the family memory drama centers on the patrilineal relationships. Even avant-garde Irish dramas, like Yeats's *Purgatory* and Beckett's *Endgame*, focus on the trope of the patrilineal family memory, and the trope continues to be found in some of contemporary Irish drama's most famous plays. In Hugh Leonard's *Da*, for example, an Irish emigrant returns to his hometown to bury his foster father, whose ghost takes him on a journey through his childhood. He remembers his first attempt at heavy petting with a local girl, but his mother, while mentioned, never appears. The two formative characters for the boy were his foster father and his (father figure) male employer. In Brian Friel's *Philadelphia, Here I Come!*, a young man, Gar, spends his last night in his father's home (before emigrating to America) by remembering the significant moments of his youth, thus confronting the still-unresolved relationship with his father that ties him to home. And in Connall Morrison's adaptation of the Patrick Kavanagh novel *Tarry Flynn*, beautifully staged at the Abbey Theatre in 1997, the audience follows the everyday experiences of the hero until he decides to leave his rural community to become a writer. The play glosses over the fact that he leaves his mother and sister to run their struggling farm and abandons a woman he may have impregnated.

Brian Friel adapted the family memory play's patrilineal narrative somewhat in his 1990 drama *Dancing at Lughnasa*. In that play, the adult male protagonist/narrator—who is onstage but outside the frame of the story throughout the drama—recalls his youth as an illegitimate child in 1930s rural Ireland, where he grew up in a house with his mother and her four sisters. While Friel's play gives us five vivid, colorful, and sympathetically drawn female characters, we see these women through the eyes of a man who is nostalgically remembering their experiences through the lens of childhood experience. The women may seem the center of the story, but the male narrator is firmly in control of the narrative, and we see the women exclusively through his eyes.

Employing the form of the family memory play to explore Irish women's struggles for personal identities amid the weight of family ties and cultural forces, Carr and Reid's work may, at first glance, look like the family memory dramas of Leonard and Friel. But they actually appropriate that traditional form to make a distinctly matrilineal narrative, revealing a great deal about women's experience in Ireland while simulteaneously subverting several of the stereotypical representations of women that are usually found in mainstream Irish drama.[5] In other words, these dramas reflect how Carr and Reid have mastered a prominent dramatic form only to subvert it in ways that reveal Irish women's perspectives in contemporary Ireland. Elin Diamond has remarked that "feminists, in our different constituencies [. . .] with our different objects of analysis, want to intervene in symbolic systems, linguistic, theatrical, political, psychological — and intervention requires assuming a subject position, however provisional, and making truth claims, however flexible, concerning one's own representations" (vii). While Reid's and Carr's reappropriations of Irish realism do little to radicalize an audience's understanding of gender or performance (their plays are, after all, predominantly realist, and, especially in the case of Carr's work, they lean more toward liberal than material or radical feminist ideology), they do show a way in which a form that is traditionally exclusive to women may be co-opted to provide a legitimate vehicle for expressing women's experience.[6] These reappropriations are not so much imitations — or even emulations — of preceding works but are rather kinds of translations of a traditionally male-centered Irish dramatic discourse.

Translation has been a key trope — and point of cultural critique — in Ireland throughout the twentieth century. In *Inventing Ireland*, Declan Kiberd discusses the political and cultural role of the act of translation in Ireland — the array of methods individuals use to reject the imposition of one language by carrying the spirit of their own language into the translation. He cites Walter Benjamin, who wrote:

> It is the task of the translator to release in his own language that pure language which is under the spell of another, to liberate the language imprisoned in a work in his recreation of that work. For the sake of pure language, he breaks through the decayed barriers of his own language. (628)

Kiberd goes on to historicize his theory in terms of Irish writers who resisted colonialism during the Irish literary renaissance, "by writing their own history and then rewriting it. This would be a literal re-membering — not a making whole of what was never whole to begin with, but a gluing together of fragments in a dynamic recasting" (629). Kiberd uses an example from theatre: the nonverbal courtship of Yolland and Maire in Friel's *Translations*. "[I]n a strict sense," he writes, "it embodies the achievement of the higher ideal underlying every act of translation, for in a language of silence which has no need of recasting is the hope of a privileged space in which resistance to all degrading systems may be possible" (627).

While Kiberd is correct that Yolland and Maire's transcendent love "escape[s] the entrapments of language, being contained between the lines rather than in them" (627), he does not mention the noisy, non-verbal languages of the stage that are constantly at work throughout the play. In theatre, translation can function not only at the textual level but also at the semiotic level: traditional ways of reading performance can be upstaged by new acting styles, new stagings, new points of view. As *Belle Reprieve* still attests, a casting choice can foreground or alter the interstice between the original and translated dramas as elegantly as any textual rewrite.[7]

Since before Douglas Hyde called for the "deanglicisation" of Irish literature and before Lady Gregory translated Irish epic and Molière's *The Imaginary Invalid* into Kiltartan dialect, translation of Irish and European classics into a contemporary Irish idiom has been an ideological tool in the nationalist community. Even Yeats's poetic, highly formal theatre required (and requires) actors with a deep familiarity with Irish dialect and Gaelic pronunciations. Along with a translation of language and dialect among nationalist theatre practitioners was a translation of representations, as playwrights and actors strove to replace the stage Irishman performance tropes with nobler representations of the national character. The tales of heroes like Cuchulain and Deirdre became emblems of Ireland's noble past and models for the national character: the melodramatic gestures of the London stage Irishman were translated into Willie and Frank Fay's understated Irish realism.

Ireland's contemporary crisis, especially the hunger strike in Long Kesh Prison in 1980, inspired playwrights to turn to translation in a new way, adapting Greek classical dramas as metaphors for the contemporary troubles.[8] Tom Paulin's conversion of *Antigone* into a parable about partition and Seamus Heaney's rewriting of Sophocles' *Philoctotes* as a drama of reconciliation in *The Cure at Troy* simultaneously addressed Ireland's current situation through ancient Greek "classics" while politicizing and interpreting them in new ways. As the twenty-first century — and the Irish dramatic movement's second century — begins, these dramas from the 1980s are well on their way to assuming a position as "classics" themselves in the Irish dramatic tradition; that is to say, the Field Day Theatre's position in theatre history is secure. Yet most of the women playwrights writing during that period, like those from other decades of this century, remain for the most part on the historical margins, outside the mainstream dramatic tradition. Part of Carr's and Reid's success and acceptance within mainstream Irish theatre practice stems from their keen ability to translate within both the textual languages of the Irish tradition and the semiotic languages of the realist stage, taking those traditionally patriarchal discourses and re-membering them to make room for Irish women's lives.[9]

A Century of Stories: Marina Carr's The Mai

After only a decade of dramatic writing, Marina Carr has already estab-lished herself as a leader among contemporary Irish playwrights. She was appointed Ansbacher writer-in-residence at the Abbey in 1995, and within eight years, the Abbey produced four of her works: *Ullaloo* (1991), *The Mai* (1994), *Portia Coughlan* (1996), and *By the Bog of Cats* (1998). Her work has also appeared in such venues as The Project Arts Centre (Dublin), San Francisco's Magic Theatre, and the Milwaukee Repertory Theatre.

Carr's work often toys with different aspects of the Irish dramatic tradi-tion. Her earliest published work, *Low in the Dark* (1990), appropriates Beckett's absurdist use of language and space to discuss childbirth, meno-pause, and women's sexuality. Her 1996 drama *Portia Coughlan* seems, on the one hand, an example of late-twentieth-century realism, but on the other hand it reflects an almost Yeatsian fascination with the transcendent, liminality, spirituality, myth, and the occult. The title character's obsession with abandoning her husband and children to drown herself in the Belmont River and to join her dead brother, who drowned himself fifteen years before, echoes Yeats's play, written a century earlier, *The Land of Heart's Desire*. Frank McGuinness compares this play to Japanese Noh, thus point-ing to another link between this play and Yeats's work ("Introduction" ix); yet Carr's characters possess a simultaneously raw and sensual tone that Yeats would have envied. Carr's most fascinating feminization of the tropes of Irish theatre history, though, occur in her 1994 play *The Mai*.

The Mai explores the relationships among four generations of Irish women: from a 100-year-old opium-smoking fisherwoman from the West of Ireland to her sixteen-year-old great-granddaughter, who eventually em-igrates to the United States. Each of these fiercely strong women is torn between the power of her matrilineal bonds and her desire for personal autonomy. The actress who plays the great-granddaughter, Millie, is on stage for the entire play, as she performs the roles of both the sixteen-year-old girl in the action and the thirty-year-old narrator who recalls the story and who frames the narrative with her commentary. Millie's mother, Mai, is the central figure in the drama, just as her age places her in the middle of the extended family tree. The other characters in the play call her "the Mai," adapting the Irish tradition of adding "the" before the last name of the (male) head of a clan.

There is even an aspect of magical realism in this drama, as the women make sense of their lives through inventing mythic stories about their expe-riences or by finding parallels in Irish myth and folklore. Before the action of the play, Mai's husband, Robert, leaves her and their four children, and Mai proceeds to save every penny to build a magnificent house on Owl Lake, which she hopes will beckon her husband back. Owl Lake, according to a folktale told in the play, was created when a Celtic goddess wept a lake of tears after her lover was taken away from her by a witch. In his absence, the goddess drowned in the lake of tears, killing herself in her own sorrow. The Mai, like this goddess, is a waiting woman, and like the goddess, she too will drown in the lake of tears.

In the opening scene of the play, Robert, a cellist, does return, announcing his arrival by playing music in the house. When the Mai enters, he rises and runs his bow across her neck, her arms, her breasts, suggesting that as great as their love may be, there remains an element of manipulation on Robert's part, as he "plays" Mai, just as he had played his cello. While Robert has returned to his family, he continues to be unfaithful, so Mai gets her real support from her female relatives. When Grandma Fraochlán, the 100-year-old matriarch of the family, berates Robert for treating her granddaughter so badly, Robert weakly pins the blame on her: "Well, maybe if you and the rest of the Mai's family weren't livin' in our ear." Grandma Fraochlán retorts, "I'm here as an invihed guest in Tha Mai's new house, an' I'll lave whin Tha Mai axes me to lave an' noh before!" (23).

Traditionally, the husband prepares a house for his bride, who enters into his home and becomes a member of the patriarchal family line.[10] Carr turns the tables in *The Mai*, however, translating the tradition of the bride crossing her husband's threshold into a situation in which Robert enters the house built by Mai. Because he enters Mai's home, Robert must accept the dominance of *her* family line, represented by the matriarch, Grandma Fraochlán.

And, unlike the traditional rendering of love relationships in Irish drama, the women's sexuality is not repressed (for most of the characters) nor ignored in Carr's play but rather is openly acknowledged and explored. Men are important to the women for physical and emotional love and for the purposes of begetting children, not to uphold a moral code or to fulfill an economic need. Grandma Fraochlán, for example, still remembers the deep sexual passion between herself and her husband, "the nine-fingered fisherman."

> Ya're born, y'ave sex, an' thin ya die. An' if ya're wan a thim lucky few whom tha gods has blesst, tha will send ta ya a lover wud whom ya will partake a thah most rare an' sublime love there is ta partake a an this wild an lonely planeh. I have bin wana thim privileged few an' I know a no higher love in this worlt or tha next. (38)

But while celebrating female sexuality and desire, *The Mai* depicts women's relationships to men in ways that subsume them to the primary issue of the drama — the relationships among four generations of Irish women.

Grandma Fraochlán's still-passionate love for her fifty-odd years dead husband and the Mai's mystical tie to Robert magnify aspects of these women's complex psychological and emotional makeup, but we do not understand these women strictly in light of those particular relationships.

Also, by focusing on the matrilineal relationships in the play, *The Mai* points out how historical and cultural developments in the Republic of Ireland over the last century have shaped Irishwomen's experience. The first generation, represented by Grandma Fraochlán, evokes the mythic images of Ireland's west, which were celebrated by pre-Republic writers during the Irish Literary Renaissance. Born on Inis Fraochlán, an island off Connemara, Grandma Fraochlán functions as an emblem of the imaginative, passionate world of the turn-of-the-century Gaeltacht. She is the product of a one-time tryst between "an ageing island spinster" (18) and a Spanish or Moroccan sailor, and she uses this romantic parentage to account for (or excuse) her outrageous behavior. After she lashes out cruelly at one of her daughters, she apologizes, saying, "Sorry, Julie, sorry, *a stóir*, it's me filthy foreign tongue" (39). Despite being a century old, she continues to smoke opium as she did in her youth, using a pipe left by her mysterious father. That habit may explain the conversations she picks up with imaginary figures like the ghost of her dead husband or "the sultan of Spain." She argues with the sultan, "Now Sultan! You give me wan good reason why women can't own harems full a men whin ih is quihe obvious thah men owns harems full a women! G'wan! I'm listenin'! G'wan!" (22). This imaginary argument not only reflects Grandmother F's robust sexuality but also comments upon Robert's adultery against Mai's monogamy.

The second generation, Grandma Fraochlán's daughters Julie and Agnes, represents a more repressed period for women in Irish history, the deeply moralistic years of the Free State in the 1920s and 1930s. When the Mai's sister, Beck, announces that her very brief marriage will end in divorce (she was married in Australia — divorce was still illegal in Ireland during the play's setting in 1979), the two aunts appear at Mai's house, "armed with novenas, scapulars and leaflets on the horrors of premarital sex which they distributed amongst us children along with crisp twenty-pound notes. Births, marriages and deaths were their forte and by Christ, if they had anything to do with it, Beck would stay married even if it was to a tree" (32–33). It is hard to believe that these two prim women, with their matching handbags, are descendents of an opium-smoking, half-Spanish island woman. In the 1996 revival of the play on the Peacock Stage at the Abbey Theatre, Julie and Agnes, in their tweed suits and gray permanent waves, actually *looked* and behaved as if they were older than their century-old mother, who dressed in a flowing skirt and still had long, dark curls. But these women represent the period in Ireland when the state insisted that its citizens recognize deeply conservative Catholic mores and the sanctity of the family.

Agnes and Julie embody the dominant female role for their generation. But Carr also expresses Agnes and Julie's pain, dealing with a fiery mother whose force of personality had such power over their lives. Julie and Agnes find themselves trapped between their opium-addicted mother and a political state that is founded on moral absolutes. Neither position gives them many choices in their own lives. "I'm seventy-five years of age, Mai, and I'm still not over my childhood," Julie tells her niece. "It's not fair they should teach us desperation so young or if they do they should never mention hope" (40–41). Mai's mother, Ellen, nearly escaped Julie and Agnes's fate when she became a pre-med student at Trinity College, but pregnancy forced her out of university and into marriage. She died giving birth to her third child.

The third generation — Mai and her sisters, Connie and Beck — however, is trapped between their desires for autonomy and fulfillment and the mores and expectations of the previous generation. The Mai fights desperately to make her unfaithful husband faithful, while Connie finds herself bored in a stable marriage and wishes she had slept with other men before she married. Beck, the youngest, has traveled the world and slept with so many men that she claims she has lost count, but she longs for the sense of belonging that her sisters have found in their marriages and careers. She tells Mai, "you don't know what it's like out there when you're nothing and you have nothing, because . . . you've always been somebody's favourite or somebody's star pupil or somebody's wife, or somebody's mother or somebody's teacher. Imagine a place where you are none of those things" (30). The real sadness of Beck's story (and of that of her sisters) is her inability to see herself in any role outside of a subordinate one: her desire to belong to someone else keeps her from finding and fulfilling herself sexually, intellectually, or spiritually.

Despite Mai's professional, economic, and (partial) romantic success, she realizes that her commitment and duties to others — building the house, keeping Robert, caring for her family — have also forced her to make sacrifices. "And I started off so well," Mai tells Beck. "The more I think about it, the more I begin to realise that, one by one, I have to let go of all the beautiful things in my life, though I didn't mean to" (55). Although it is not depicted in the play, Millie informs the audience that the Mai's struggle to balance her family, to stitch these four generations together, and to make Robert a faithful husband led her to despair, and she committed suicide. There is a long lineage of women who die for love or transcendence in Irish drama, like the heroines of Yeats's *The Land of Heart's Desire*, of Edward Martyn's *Maeve*, several *Deirdres*, and, more recently, the heroine of Paulin's *The Riot Act*. In Carr's play, selflessness leads to death but not transcendence for the Mai. Her death is not the stuff of tragedy, but rather a sad and senseless act that only produces grounds for fierce screaming fights between the traumatized Millie and her embittered father.

Millie, the fourth generation in this line of what Beck called "proud, mad women," struggles to create meaning in her own life outside the weight of this matrilineal history. She emigrates to New York and while unmarried gives birth to a son, Jimmie. Millie states that she tricked the father into conceiving a child "because [she] wanted something that didn't stink of Owl Lake" (56). Yet the history of the women who came before her haunts Millie's current life, and her actions echo those of her foremothers. She protects her son by creating a romantic story about his father:

> I say your Daddy is an El Salvadorian drummer who swept me off my feet
> when I was lost in New York . . . I tell him that high on hash or marijuana
> or god-knows-what we danced on the roof of a tenement building in
> Brooklyn to one of Robert's cello recordings.(56)

She does not tell Jimmie that his father was already married with two sons or that he refused to acknowledge paternity. And the El Salvadorian drummer sounds strangely like the Spanish sailor who swept Grandma Fraochlán's mother off her feet over a century before, leaving behind his unborn daughter, an opium pipe, and stories.

Millie has moved beyond her childhood at Owl Lake, although she remains haunted by it. But like Grandma Fraochlán, Millie has learned to create a narrative based on the past and the present, reality and myth, in order to create a sense of meaning, purpose, and wonder in her life and in order to continue the history of women from which she came. Her narrative control is presented semiotically—as it is in the work of Friel and Leonard—as the actor portraying Millie literally moves in and out of the drama's narrative. At times she stands outside the set and addresses the audience directly; at other times she enters the set space and interacts with the characters in their frame of reference. Also, Millie is the first woman of the four generations to be truly independent. The play presented before the audience is indeed Millie's narrative of her matrilineal heritage. This family memory play is now her family memory, and she is the controller of the narrative, the keeper of these women's history, a woman protagonist.

Women across Borders: Christina Reid's
Tea in a China Cup *and* The Belle of the Belfast City

While *The Mai* records women's social and personal experience in the Republic of Ireland, Christina Reid's *Tea in a China Cup* and *The Belle of the Belfast City* explore women's relationships to family and community in Northern Ireland. A Northern Irishwoman with a Protestant background, Reid began writing plays after returning to university in the early 1980s. The success of *Tea in a China Cup* in 1982 led her to drop her formal studies so that she could write full-time. Since Reid's plays are set during The Troubles, one can read them in the tradition of the war dramas of Sean

O'Casey and contemporary playwrights like John Boyd and Martin Lynch (Murray, *Twentieth-Century Irish Drama* 189–191). But while many playwrights have used the domestic sphere as a microcosm for the war-torn nation, Reid, like her contemporary Anne Devlin, examines the domestic sphere as a part of the nation; the activities in the household are as important and unique as the events in the streets.

Reid's plays over the past two decades have foregrounded the hybridity of Northern Irish culture and the need for change across class and gender as well as religious and political boundaries. Her drama *Joyriders* (1986), for example, examines how the social violence of joblessness and poor education exacerbates the political violence confronting Belfast's working-class youth, whether Catholic or Protestant. *Tea in a China Cup* and *The Belle of the Belfast City* (1989) also look at the ways in which class, gender, religion, and nationalism shape Northern Irish lives, predominantly through the lens of women's experiences, using the trope of the matrilineal narrative.

Tea in a China Cup is the simplest of Reid's matrilineal narratives. It examines three generations of Northern Irish Protestant women — Grandmother and Aunt Maisie, Mother Sarah, and narrator Beth — whose lives have been shaped by either the legacy or the experience of war. Two of the wars, World Wars I and II, injured or killed men in the family, causing economic and emotional hardship for the women. The third war, The Troubles, is fought on the women's home ground, and they find themselves defending their own lives as well as their property. Throughout the play, we see how the women's cultural and economic situation makes them defenders of their home in both war and peacetime. On the periphery of the drama, the women's husbands may drink too much or disappear, but the leadership, friendship, and support of mothers and daughters sustain the women and enable them to put on a strong public front, despite the desperation of their situations. Traditionally, Northern Irish women have had a duty, as keepers of the hearth, never to show any kind of weakness in the family fabric. "No matter how hard times are," Grandmother tells Beth, "you don't let yourself down in front of the neighbors" (25). The public silence of Northern Irish Protestant women's private and domestic struggles has historically translated into an absence of representation of those struggles on the stage. *Tea in a China Cup* corrects this by revealing just how difficult "keeping the homefires burning" can be.

Particular semiotic gestures foreground how this play records a historical narrative that is usually marginalized in accounts of Northern Irish culture and the conflict. As the three generations of women interact in the family living room, time is marked in that room by the appearance of portraits of three generations of men in the family, generations who served king (or queen) and country in the military. Underneath the portraits stands the china cabinet, holding the family heirlooms passed from mother to daughter for over a century. Both the portraits and the china chest reflect family tradition, but the portraits represent the patrilineal and the public aspect of the family history, while the china cabinet represents the family's matrilineal and domestic history.

The representative of the second generation, Sarah, points to both these signs of her family history during The Troubles in 1971. In the midst of a riot, Sarah's daughter Beth begs her mother to leave the house before they are burned out, but Sarah refuses to leave the china, linens, and devon grate that her foremothers had "worked [their] fingers to the bone" (56) to acquire. When an Army sergeant enters the house, however, he notices not the china — the female sign of a proud, Protestant household — but the portraits of British soldiers on the wall, commenting, "I see you're on our side, anyway" (57). Sarah's response proves that, despite her die-hard Protestant sensibility, her first loyalty is to her family: "[. . .] three generations of my family have fought in your army, and for what? That's my father, gassed in the First World War, that's my brother, killed in the Second, and that's my son, my only son, and he can't even come home on leave any more in case he gets a bullet in his back" (57). But while Sarah can explain the patriarchal symbols to the soldier, her first loyalties are to her foremothers' things and her daughter's future. Sarah may hold on to tradition, and she may love to hear the Protestant marchers pass her door, but she accepts that her daughter's best friend is a Catholic. The importance of the women's objects appears again at the end of the play when Beth, after her mother's death, sells the family china but holds on to one cup and saucer. She keeps for herself — and perhaps for her daughters — a symbol of her foremothers' tradition without being bound to every aspect of it.

Reid creates a more complicated exploration of Northern Irish Protestant tradition and change through the mother–daughter relationships in her 1989 play *The Belle of the Belfast City*. The grandmother in this play, Dolly, is a retired music-hall star, billed on the circuit in the 1920s as "The Belle of the Belfast City." Even in her eighties, Dolly can still perform a music-hall turn at the drop of a hat, to the embarrassment of her ultra-loyalist nephew, Jack. Her children, Vi, born in 1929, and Rose, born in 1950, actually reflect two generations of Northern Irishwomen. Vi obediently abandons her own dreams by leaving school to help her mother in the family shop and to raise her little sister, Rose, and her cousin, Janet. Janet grows up to rebel against her Protestant heritage by marrying a Catholic who is equally committed to transgressing borders: he is a member of the almost all-Protestant police force, the Royal Ulster Constabulary. Janet and her husband marry not for love but to escape the aspects of themselves that they fear. Janet tries to erase the fierce Protestant lessons her mother taught her before she moved in with her Aunt Dolly; her husband is running away from his homosexuality. When Janet has an affair after fifteen years of celibate marriage, the foundations of both her early Protestant upbringing and her idealist marriage are shaken utterly. Rose rejects the ideological repressions and oppressions of her nation and culture by leaving Ireland to become a photojournalist, but she remains committed enough to her home country to take undercover photos of loyalist paramilitaries.

The third generation of women in this family is represented by Belle, Rose's illegitimate daughter by an African-American Baptist preacher. Only half Irish and raised in England, Belle's identity as a Northern Irish Protestant is defined for her almost exclusively by her relationships with her mother, aunts, and grandmother. Despite Belle's age and her distance from her grandmother, Dolly feels a kindred spirit with her namesake, one that she does not feel with her daughters or her niece and nephew. She tells Belle that she does not want life-extending measures to be taken if she becomes too ill to live on her own: "I can cope with not bein' able to dance with my feet no more. But I couldn't cope with not bein' able to dance with my head" (197). But when Dolly does collapse, the other women in the family submit to Jack's leadership, and he resuscitates her, despite Belle's protestations. Dolly's body survives, but she is left completely incapacitated by a stroke.

Narrator Belle, however, continues the family line in her own way. Like Millie in *The Mai*, she controls the way in which this matrilineal narrative is relayed to the audience, but she tells it in a way which both builds upon and reflects the stories of her foremothers. Belle steps in and out of the frame of the play, observing contemporary scenes in which she is not involved and flashbacks of events from before she was born, and interacting within the frame of the play in other scenes.

The conclusion of *The Belle of the Belfast City*, however, puts Belle in a liminal place between her roles as character and narrator. Dolly stares at a picture that dominates her room, a concert-hall poster of herself in 1925. She can no longer burst into song, as she did before her stroke, so it is her granddaughter, her namesake, her likeness, Belle, who puts music to Dolly's remembering. But instead of a 1920s concert-hall tune, this Belle of the Belfast City sings a contemporary political ballad:

> . . . O the bricks they will bleed and the rain it will weep
> And the damp Lagan fog lull the city to sleep
> It's to hell with the future and live on the past
> May the Lord in His mercy be kind to Belfast. (250)

Since this song, "Ballad to a Traditional Refrain," by Maurice James Craig, is an ironic politicization of a jingoistic song tradition, Reid ends the play with two "translations." Craig's song translates the literary/music genre of the sectarian ballad into a call for the end of sectarian violence. She also semiotically translates Dolly's now-silenced voice into the body of her half-Irish, half–African-American granddaughter. A song protesting Belfast sectarianism sung by a body with both Irish and African-American identity markers becomes a Brechtian gestus, a call to the audience to think critically about the historical conditions which have led to the constructions of identities in Ireland and around the world.

In a 1993 issue of *Theatre Ireland*, Caroline Williams critiqued the absence of women playwrights in Ireland's mainstream theatre. "One of the difficulties in this area is that we are so used to men's images of men, and men's images of women on stage, that a play written by a woman is regularly criticised or rejected for not complying to these norms" (6). In an unrelated critique of Irish writing and culture, Tom Paulin notes that Irish writers conquered the colonizer by taking the English language forced upon them and translating it into the superb eloquence of the Irish dialect.[11] I believe that Irish women dramatists find themselves in a double bind, as the very forms of Irish realism traditionally used against hostile representations of Irish culture are themselves often hostile, or at least indifferent, to the realities of Irish women. W. B. Worthen notes that in many postcolonial dramas, playwrights use translation as a mode of cultural resistance, through which "the 'classic' is both presented and represented, doubled in ways that foreground the original's position as classic, and also interrogate the work that translation can be made to do in refiguring the relation between the classic and contemporary culture" (22). For those contemporary writers who have translated classical works (like Greek tragedies) into an Irish milieu, the "classic" is a work outside the national tradition, yet this work is influential in terms of the ways in which the national culture defines itself. For Marina Carr and Christina Reid, translating the Irish "classic" means refiguring the male-centered discourse of Irish theatrical realism and women's marginalized experience in that tradition. Carr and Reid take the structure of the Irish realist family memory play, and its assumptions and stereotypes about women, and translate them into a vehicle for staging a century of Irish women's lives. Perhaps these translations will widen the Irish mainstream to include more female protagonists and more radically feminist performance modes.

NOTES

1. Garry Hynes, a founder of the Druid Theatre Company in Galway, has directed at the Druid, the Abbey Theatre, and the RSC and directed on Broadway in the spring of 1999. She has also served as artistic director of both the Druid Theatre Company and the Abbey. Pam Brighton made her mark directing Charabanc productions and has directed for stage and television in Ireland, Canada, and England.

2. Women playwrights are harder to find in print than are their male counterparts, but they are out there. Anne Devlin, Christina Reid, and Marina Carr have plays published by Faber and Faber; Marie Jones has published plays with Nick Hern Books. Margaretta D'Arcy's work is collected in a Methuen series. Smaller

Irish presses, like the Attic Press, Salmon Publishing, and the Gallery Press, have put several women playwrights into print, including Patricia Burke Brogan. *The Dazzling Dark: New Irish Plays*, edited by Frank McGuinness, includes plays by Marina Carr and Gina Moxley. *The Crack in the Emerald*, edited by David Grant, contains plays by Marina Carr and Marie Jones. While Charlotte Canning, Lizbeth Goodman, Elaine Aston, Michelene Wandor, and Sue-Ellen Case, among others, have performed invaluable work in recording the histories and theories of feminist theatre practice in Britain and the United States, a record of Irish feminist theatre practice has yet to be written.

3. Arguably, for much of the twentieth century, actual Irishwomen found themselves equally idealized or ignored by the gender pressures of Irish post-revolutionary politics. Women in the North and in the Republic found themselves cast into the very auxiliary roles in everyday life that were being portrayed on the stage. Although women had fought in the revolution, the conservative faction which rose to power after the civil war pushed many women out of the public sphere and back into the home. Those who remained in the public eye often manipulated the idealization of women's domestic roles. Maud Gonne, a violent revolutionary, took to wearing widow's weeds and using the last name of her husband, even though she had separated from John MacBride years before his death in the 1916 Easter Rising. Her husband was an alcoholic who abused her, but he also became one of the martyrs of the fight for independence, and the title "Mrs. Maud Gonne MacBride" gave her a credibility and a right to a public voice which would have been denied Gonne in Ireland's post-war climate.

For critical examinations of contemporary feminism in the Republic of Ireland, see Pat O'Conor, *Emerging Voices: Women in Contemporary Irish Society*. Northern Irish women and feminism are thoughtfully analyzed in Begoña Aretxaga's *Shattering Silence: Women, Nationalism, and Political Subjectivity in Northern Ireland* and in Margaret Ward's "The Women's Movement in Ireland: Twenty Years On." Several essays on twentieth-century feminism in the Republic and the North can be found in Bradley and Valiulis's *Gender and Sexuality in Modern Ireland*.

4. For a thorough theoretical overview of the feminist use of alternative theatrical forms, see Elin Diamond, *Unmaking Mimesis: Essays on Feminism and Theatre*.

5. Matrilineal narratives that provide a feminist revisionist history by describing several generations of women have been used to great effect by a range of contemporary playwrights and performance artists in the United States. Some of the best examples include Glenda Dickerson and Breena Clarke's *Re/Membering Aunt Jemima: A Travelling Menstrual Show*, Louella Dizon's *Till Voices Wake Us*, and Leeny Sacks's *The Poet and the Translator*. Each of these dramas, I would argue, plays not only with assumptions of history but also with theatrical preconceptions and representations of that history.

6. Other contemporary female playwrights who write outside of the Abbey/ realist tradition are Gina Moxley, Marie Jones, and Emma Donahue. It is noteworthy that even more so than in the United States and Britain, the farther a woman writer works outside the mainstream discourse, the harder it is to find records of her work.

7. For the classic interpretation of *Belle Reprieve*, Bette Bourne, Paul Shaw, Peggy Shaw, and Lois Weaver's gender-bending reinterpretation of Tennessee Williams's *A Streetcar Named Desire*, see Sue-Ellen Case, "From Split Subject to Split Britches."

8. W. B. Worthen articulates the politics of the Field Day Theatre's translations of classical texts in his essay "Homeless Words: Field Day and the Politics of Translation." While Field Day plays like Tom Paulin's *The Riot Act: A Version of Sophocles'*

Antigone and Seamus Heaney's *The Cure at Troy* explore the pathos of the Irish troubles, Worthen argues, they also actually retrench the nationalist/unionist debate linguistically, semiotically, and ideologically. Other Field Day dramas, however, like Tom Kilroy's *Double Cross*, actually blur the binaries between nationality and identity in modern Ireland. Other excellent essays on the Irish translation of classical texts in the 1980s include Eamonn Hughes's "'To Define Your Dissent': The Plays and Polemics of the Field Day Theatre Company" and Anthony Roche's "Ireland's Antigones: Tragedy North and South." Elizabeth Cullingford examines another translation of a classic conflict into an Irish idiom in contemporary drama in "British Romans and Irish Carthaginians: Anticolonial Metaphor in Heaney, Friel, and McGuinness."

9. I am grateful to Christopher Murray who, in a discussion of this paper, pointed out how Paula Meehan's mythopoetic comedy *Mrs. Sweeney* re-frames the pastoral, heroic myth of Finn McCool in contemporary working-class Dublin, thus translating across time and class as well as across gender lines.

10. Anthony Roche discusses how this cultural notion translates into Irish drama in his essay "Woman on the Threshold: J. M. Synge's *In the Shadow of the Glen*, Teresa Deevy's *Katie Roche* and Marina Carr's *The Mai*."

11. Tom Paulin, "A New Look at the Language Question."

—11—

"I've Never Been Just Me": Rethinking Women's Positions in the Plays of Christina Reid

CARLA J. McDONOUGH

> The majority of playwrights [in Ireland] are men, and women in their plays tend to be presented only in relationship to one man; they are not explored in depth.
> —Reid, qtd. in Roll-Hansen 394

> *Beth.* I'm getting married tomorrow, I'm moving from my mother's house to Stephen's house . . . I've been my mother's daughter and now I'm going to be Stephen's wife . . . I've never been just me.
> —Reid, *Tea in a China Cup* 50

Women playwrights are not scarce in Ireland, but they are scarcely produced, especially in the major, high-profile venues like the Abbey Theatre.[1] In examining "women's theatre in Ireland" in 1991, Steve Wilmer noted that between 1984 and 1989, the Abbey Theatre had produced only one play by a woman (and not an Irish woman at that) on their main stage. He quotes Caroline Swift, a play reader at the Abbey in the 1980s, who commented:

> I saw a number of plays written by women that struck me as having particularly good characterization. Without exception the comments of the male readers in rejecting them included the phrase "implausible characterization." I may say that they recommended many plays in which the women's parts were the usual stereotypes we are used to seeing on the stage in this country. These give little scope to our actresses, trying to

invest some reality into characters put in purely to off-set the male hero, and which can be described in terms such as "the mother to whose apron strings he is tied" or "the bitch that blighted his life." (357–358)

In examining the plays of Christina Reid, my objective is not to establish a "woman's theatre" tradition but rather to underscore that a male-dominated, male-focused national theatre is at best telling only half the nation's story.

The overriding male bias in Irish theatre is easily apparent in the number of plays by male playwrights that are produced, reviewed, and studied; not surprisingly, even this volume devotes more space to Irish men than women, though several of the contributors acknowledge and seek to redress this imbalance. The bias is also evident in the focus that Irish men's plays give to male characters. When concentrating on a female character, moreover, male playwrights have tended to present them as symbolic representations of abstract ideas or as stereotypes.[2] Yeats's work perhaps can serve as an arresting example of such unrealistic depictions. Writing to Katharine Tynan in 1889, Yeats admitted that his interest in a specific woman to whom Tynan had referred was "only as a myth and a symbol" (qtd. in Wade 117–118). Woman as myth and symbol is an apt description of women's positioning within his plays as well, particularly those that explore the (male) poet's relationship with his (female) muse, such as *A Full Moon in March*, *The Herne's Egg*, and *The Player Queen*. Even Yeats's most potent muse, Maud Gonne, seemed to agree with him about woman as symbol, given, for example, her performance as the title character in *Kathleen ni Houlihan*; with this performance she both electrified the audience at the Abbey Theatre and helped to establish that theatre's reputation as a national theatre by playing the emblem of Mother Ireland.[3]

Although we could compile a list of male characters who might also fall into stereotype, it is clear that, while striving to avoid the Stage Irishman, too often the Irish theatrical scene has continued to embrace the Stage Irishwoman. The history of the Charabanc Theatre Company is quite pertinent in this regard. The company was founded by five out-of-work actresses who were appalled by the conditions of Irish women on the stage; not only were there few roles written for them (other than what they describe as "ciphers" or stereotypical "Noras or Kathleens"), but there was also a custom of flying English actresses in to play paltry three-line parts. These women recognized that if they wanted "real" roles, they would have to write them for themselves. Interestingly, their realization that they needed a theatre of their own resembles the impetus for the founding of an Irish national theatre. Charabanc's outstanding success with plays such as *Lay Up Your Ends* (1983) and *Somewhere over a Balcony* (1988) reflects the need for stories that were not being told elsewhere in the Irish theatre.

One hundred years after the founding of the Irish national theatre, it is important to consider that the roster of Irish playwrights is a bit more diverse than it used to be. Marina Carr, Christina Reid, Anne Devlin, and Marie Jones are currently familiar names on the theatre scene. These women, however, are in the definite minority; there is a much longer list of well-known male playwrights whose plays have been staged at prominent venues and who have received generous support for their failures as well as their successes. Why does it matter that plays by and about women rarely get staged? The answer is fairly obvious: The theatre is a public realm where a people perform themselves to themselves, a part of cultural and national self-presentation; erasing the complexity of women's lives from this arena is, therefore, tantamount to erasing them from public life. In fact, the theatre in many ways reflects how women's stories are often erased elsewhere in the public arena.

In writing about women's political roles in Northern Ireland, Elizabeth Shannon argues that women have been silent too long. She chastises women for the minor and supportive roles that they have taken in place of the active public roles she would like to see them take, even as she praises the strength that women have shown in keeping the family (and by implication, the country) from falling apart in the face of at times devastating economic and personal hardship. Shannon notes that when her interviewees referred to the important roles women played in the troubles, all they ultimately came up with was "banging garbage lids to signal the arrival of British troops, or making sandwiches and tea for the lads" (248). This portrait of Irish women as playing minor, supporting roles in the public arena while being chiefly housewives and mothers reproduces the traditional view of their lives and work. Other recent studies of women in Northern Ireland paint a different picture; for instance, Margaret Ward discusses the "unmanageable revolutionaries" within several women's movements in Ireland from 1881 to the 1940s, prefacing her discussion with the following:

> Generally, the importance of women's contribution has been dismissed in a few sentences as historians itemise what they consider to be the important events; events which have been evaluated in male terms. (*Unmanageable Revolutionaries* 1)

Similarly, in her 1997 ethnographic study of republican women, *Shattering Silence: Women, Nationalism, and Political Subjectivity in Northern Ireland*, Begoña Aretxaga questions the traditional stereotypes of women as peace-loving homemakers or victims of political strife by noting how such narratives have erased women's active involvement in the politics of Northern Ireland. As she says, "[w]omen have been left out [of the stories of political conflict] not because analysts have recognized their subversive potential but because, by not fitting existing discourses, they have not been recognized at all as socially relevant" (4). In other words, because the efforts of women have exposed the simplifications of stereotypes and of the received political narratives, they have been largely ignored. In the previous essay, Mary Trotter examined how contemporary female playwrights such as Christina Reid and Marina Carr use drama to reclaim matrilineal histories and explore women's lives and thus go against the grain of traditional Irish theatre. I am similarly concerned with the way in which theatre in Ireland has often contributed to the reification of traditional narratives, reinforcing male bias in public discourse and relegating women to the sidelines. My particular concern, though, is that Irish theatre has in some sense exacerbated the political turmoil in Northern Ireland since the late 1960s by casting political struggle as something inherently consumed with manhood.[4]

In examining Northern Irish political theatre in 1990, D. E. S. Maxwell lists twenty-four plays, to which Christopher Murray, in his 1997 study, adds seventeen more. Out of these lists, the work of a total of three women playwrights appears.[5] What is interesting here is not only the maleness of the list but also the way in which many of these political plays by men conflate the political struggle with maleness. Mary Trotter's essay discusses the focus on the patrilineal family, the father–son conflict, that is at the heart of so many Irish plays, many of which appear on the list of political plays mentioned above. This melding of the domestic with the political is fitting in regard to Northern Ireland, since the conflict is frequently fought in the domestic sphere — in neighborhoods, in houses, between families. A mixed marriage is seen as a political act, and the location of one's home is almost always a political marker. Yet, while the domestic sphere traditionally defines a woman's life, in rhetoric especially, the political struggle in Ireland has been repeatedly framed as an issue of manhood.

One Northern Irish play that illustrates this point effectively is Graham Reid's *The Death of Humpty Dumpty* (1979), which examines the effects of paramilitary violence on an individual man who was not actually involved in the political conflict. He is shot on his own doorstep and paralyzed from the neck down simply for having witnessed paramilitary activity. The play chronicles his recuperation and his battle to restructure his life after he is paralyzed. He fails miserably because he believes that he is worthless, not simply because he is a burden to his family but also because he cannot dominate his family or perform sexually as he believes Irish men should. In a perceptive reading of *Humpty Dumpty*, Lionel Pilkington argues that

> what unsettles [Graham] Reid's portrayal of Northern Ireland's paramilitary violence as a dangerous madness is the similarity between what is presented as the principal attributes of this violence and the natural attributes of male sexual identity. Both, in this play, involve a view of individuals as commodities. (22)

Pilkington further compares this play to Bill Morrison's 1977 farcical *Flying Blind* by asserting that in both plays, "individual identity is equated with male sexual identity and this in turn is assumed to be synonymous with men's natural authority over women" (23).

Although Pilkington does not place "natural" in quotation marks in the previous phrase, the naturalness of male authority over women should, of course, be questioned. Yet this sense that men are destined to be rulers over women has long pervaded male-dominated religion and politics and is in fact the basis of male identity in many cultures. What is often overlooked, though, is that basing their self-worth on the subjugation and compliance of women puts men in a precarious position. Discussing involvement by men in paramilitary groups, Elizabeth Shannon describes how men in Northern Ireland have been "easily turned toward political violence" because of a "sense of inferiority bred by generations of frustration. [. . .] The gun and the bomb, or close proximity to them, gave them a sense of machismo that their everyday life had denied them" (11). Mary Condren further emphasizes this connection when she opens her discussion of myth and history surrounding women in Ireland by stating that "The Irish male's obsession with history has given him a place to stand, a fortress of certainty: the stories of heroes, warriors, and saints have created a sacred space in the world where men could feel free of the humiliations and trivialities of daily life imposed by their own or a conquering race or by the weight of economic necessity" (xvii).[6]

If further illustration of the gendering of the political struggle in Northern Ireland is needed, we have only to consider that the political story of Northern Ireland is a colonial story, and as postcolonial theory has pointed out, colonial discourse is a gendered discourse.[7] The relationship between the colonizer and the colonized is that between dominator and dominated, a relationship that mirrors the vision of male/female intercourse in a patriarchal society. Thus, the colonized subject is a feminized subject in the sexist sense of being weak and in need of subjugation, while the colonizer is presented as masculine in the sexist sense of being powerful and a natural leader. The traditional narrative of colonial politics presents a clash between men — with those in power striving to maintain their control and thus protect their manliness and those without power seeking to attain manhood by gaining power and control. Often this battle is fought symbolically or literally over the body of woman. Gayatri Spivak's well-known discussion "Can the Subaltern Speak?," which examines the debates about the practice of widow sacrifice in India, reveals how the sati emblematizes the subaltern in colonial discourse and thus reflects how women's bodies are the sites upon which conflicts, discussions, arguments, and wars of national identity, independence, and autonomy are symbolically fought. Spivak points out that the subaltern does not speak in this discourse but rather is spoken for. Thus, it would seem that within colonial politics, the truly radical act would be to have the feminized subaltern speak — or more accurately within the colonial landscape of Ireland, to listen to the voice of women who have spoken but whose stories too often get ignored or erased.

Patricia Burke Brogan's play *Eclipsed*, about the Catholic Church's practice of imprisoning unwed mothers or sexually active young women in the Magdalene laundries, offers pertinent historical examples of Irish women's lives getting "eclipsed" by a male-dominated culture that prefers to sweep into obscurity women who do not fit narrow definitions of acceptable female behavior.

Christina Reid's plays are particularly interesting to explore in the context of the gendering of political discourse. As the opening passage from *Tea in a China Cup* indicates, many of her female characters seek to redress this problem of inadequate representation of women, and they seek to do so amid the myriad expectations of behavior dictated by family, religion, society, and politics. While I do not want to hold Reid up as being symbolic of Woman's Voice, something she herself would object to since she believes that "labels diminish good art" (Kerry Campbell 25), I do want to consider how her portraits of life among Northern Irish families in the 1980s offer a rich tapestry of women's experience that is relevant to the theatrical task of cultural and national presentation and self-examination.

Tea in a China Cup, which launched Reid's career in 1983, focuses on the development of one woman, Beth, from an obedient daughter and unhappy wife, who "faithfully repeated [her] mother's mistakes" by marrying a gambler, into a woman who is ready to make her own choices. While this first staged play establishes Reid's commitment to exploring the complexities of women's lives and choices, *The Belle of the Belfast City* (1989) offers her most powerful portraits not only of women's lives but also of the many layers of politics and social limitations that often entrap the people of Northern Ireland. Most of Reid's plays deal in some way with family issues, particularly with the younger generation as it tries to cope with prejudice and economic disadvantage, which have been institutionalized by politics both outside and within the family.

Reid's plays offer portraits of life in working-class Protestant families, and they examine how religious ideology affects a woman's upbringing. It could be argued that fundamentalist Protestant ideology in many ways fosters an even more disadvantageous position for women than Catholic ideology does. At least the Virgin Mary of Catholicism offers a powerful female figure, even if it is an impossible role model for women to follow — a virgin mother. Protestantism has no equivalent, although it often furthers repressive Calvinistic ideas about the evils of sex (E. Shannon 214). In fact, in this ideology, woman is the temptress Eve, the fallen woman. The desire to keep sexuality enshrouded in mystery or to keep young people, especially girls, "innocent" of the knowledge of sexuality is a move which Catholicism shares with Protestantism, at least as Reid experienced it. Reid herself tells of sneaking into a documentary about natural childbirth, a movie that had been determined "pornographic" by the Irish censors. It was at this movie, at the age of fifteen, that she learned how babies are born. She says she knew how babies got into women because a boy on her street had told her when she was about eleven or twelve years old, but she had always wondered how they "got out" (qtd. in E. Shannon 214). This comment brings up the question of how, if a woman is not allowed to know her own body's functioning, she is to make reasonable and responsible choices in the world.

Ignorance about sex and reproduction is documented in *Tea in a China Cup* in a scene in which an embarrassed Protestant mother tries to explain menstruation to her daughter. The terms she uses are so vague and euphemistic that the daughter, Beth, is left more puzzled than informed. Beth's Catholic friend Theresa is similarly ignorant, and the two ten-year-olds have the following conversation:

> *Beth.* You have to be married to get a baby.
> *Theresa.* I have a cousin who's not married and she got a baby.
> *Beth.* How?
> *Theresa.* I don't know. I asked my mammy about that too, and she hit me again. (27–28)

After both girls begin to menstruate, they meet again to share stories:

> *Theresa.* [My mammy] told me I wasn't to wash my hair while I had it or put my feet in cold water or the blood would all rush to my head and I'd die. Did your mammy cry?
> *Beth.* A wee bit. She said, "God help you child, this is the start of all your troubles."
> *Theresa.* My mammy calls it the curse.
> *Beth.* I wish somebody would tell us what it's all about. I mean if it's going to bring us some sort of trouble, do you not think we should know?
> *Theresa.* Sure they never tell you anything. (30)

When the two girls finish school and are applying for jobs, they meet again; soon they are reminiscing about the confused talks they used to have about sex. Now they have the facts, the theory, but they are confused about the practice:

> *Beth.* Do you ever wonder what it's like?
> *Theresa.* All the time. When my eldest sister got married, I thought she'd tell me all about it, we were very close.
> *Beth.* And did she not?
> *Theresa.* She came back from the honeymoon with such a stunned look on her face that I hadn't the nerve to ask her. (42)

As these excerpts indicate, *Tea in a China Cup* directly confronts the real issues so many women struggle with while growing up, as they come to terms with their womanhood amid the myths and mystification of a repressive culture. Both Beth and Theresa, kept ignorant about their bodies and sexuality, end up making bad decisions about marriage and relationships.

The discussion of menstruation and sex within this play is itself quite radical in light of the lingering taboo (in Irish culture) surrounding women's bodily functions. When Sarah talks to her daughter about menstruation, she finishes with a command that she speak little about it, especially noting that "you don't talk to men about that sort of thing, it's not nice" (29).

This desire to erase women's experiences is apparent in the response to the "dirty protests" by women prisoners in Armagh prison in 1980. Aretxaga offers an extended analysis of the reaction to, and the semiotic significance of, the dirty protests: Women's menstrual blood became a mark of gender that denied them recognition as political subjects and instead turned them into "girls" who needed to learn to behave properly. Aretxaga quotes one of the women prisoners who took part in the dirty protests describing how

> Sinn Fein would say "Don't do that. It's easier on men." They didn't want us on dirty protest because of our periods. They didn't say that; they said we were women, that we were different. But we knew it was because of our periods. These were men who had killed, had been imprisoned and they couldn't say the word "period"! (127)

The level of embarrassment that the women prisoners themselves felt about their menstrual cycles and about sexuality, an embarrassment that was often used as a terrorist tactic against them to get confessions or simply to humiliate them, is indicative of attitudes toward women's bodies in Northern Ireland. Aretxaga notes that in her interviews with women in Northern Ireland, "Many women commented, sometimes with resentment, about the painful process of learning from scratch about sex and childbearing" (129). Mentioning this issue herself in an interview, Reid presents on stage women's discussions of sexuality and their bodies, thus becoming another way, as Aretxaga puts it, to "shatter silence" regarding women's lives.

Although *Tea in a China Cup* focuses on the mother–daughter relationship between Sarah and Beth, their story is not told in isolation. Reid employs flashbacks of events that occurred much earlier in the lives of this family in order to show how the history of the family's beliefs and way of life have been handed down to Beth. Chief among those beliefs is a patriotism for Ulster as an English state and a fervently held line of demarcation between themselves as Protestants and those "dirty" Catholics, who are always letting themselves down "in front of the neighbours" (23, 25). Beth's friend Theresa serves to dispel any ideas that the play actually advocates Protestant prejudices about Catholics, particularly as we witness that the young women's lives are all too similar. Both ultimately make mistakes about men—Theresa becoming pregnant by an Irishman while in England, and staying there to raise her daughter alone, and Beth dutifully marrying a wealthy Protestant man only to find that he neither really loves nor cares for her and that he is every bit as reckless about money as her own gambling father. While both women recognize that the ignorance in which they were raised led to their mistakes, neither blames her family or the men in her life. In their cheerful determination to move beyond their mistakes and to make the best of things, they capture the strong spirit that so many sociological studies of Northern Irish women document, the philosophy that we'd better laugh so as not to cry.[8] In evincing this attitude, these characters offer a refreshing change from the politics of blame and the image of tragedy that pervades so many Irish plays.

Reid's most layered examination of the entrenched and damaging politics of church and state within the family and the unique responses of individual women to these damaging influences is found in the 1989 play *The Belle of the Belfast City*. While *Tea* presents an almost prototypical Ulster family — proudly sending their sons to fight and die in British wars and terrified at seeing the Protestant Ascendancy in their working-class neighborhood eroded by the changes in economics as much as by the politics of the early 1970s — *The Belle of the Belfast City* on many accounts offers an unusual family. *Belle* again examines the matriarchal core of a Northern Irish family, but in contrast not only to *Tea* but also to so many plays that portray the Irish family, *Belle* offers a good marriage between the eldest couple. We are given every indication that the matriarch Dolly and her husband Joe (now dead) loved each other dearly and lived for one another. Dolly explains that she was never a housewife: "[my Joe] was a rare bird. An Ulsterman who could cook" (195). In this play, Reid examines three generations of women — the elderly mother/grandmother Dolly, her two grown daughters (Vi and Rose), and Rose's illegitimate daughter Belle. Dolly is a former vaudeville star, who, when she trod the boards, was known as "The Belle of the Belfast City," an unusual life for a woman in the early years of the twentieth century. Also unusual is the fact that her two daughters, Vi and Rose, were born twenty-one years apart. Vi tells of being scandalized by finding out that her mother was pregnant at such an advanced age, since it was unseemly for a woman in her forties to still be sexually active. Here, Reid emphasizes the fact that a woman's life does not end once she marries and becomes a mother, nor is she completely defined by motherhood.

The family is working-class Protestant, but it is clear that neither Dolly nor her late husband Joe put much stock in religion or in nationality per se. Dolly is not eagerly awaiting the Twelfth of July parades, as did Sarah in *Tea in a China Cup*, but she does surround herself with music, continually singing songs from her vaudeville past, many of which are both religiously and politically irreverent. The family is also a blended family in that Dolly and Joe took in his brother's children — Jack and Janet — after they were orphaned at the ages of ten and eight, respectively. In contrast to the happy and fun-loving household of Dolly and Joe, Jack and Janet were raised by rabidly fundamentalist Presbyterians who warped their children's psyches before they died. The play is set in a family shop run by Vi and takes place in the late 1980s, with flashbacks to previous days when the children were young. While Vi has continued to run the family shop, taking care of Dolly as she ages, Rose went off to London, where she started a career as a photographer and is currently quite involved in liberal politics. Her concern about right-wing politics in both England and Ireland, and more generally, her concerns about racism, stem in part from her worries about her daughter Belle, who is not only fatherless, Rose having refused to marry the man who fathered Belle, but who is also of mixed race, her father being African-American and, interestingly enough, a Baptist preacher. The play opens with Rose bringing her now college-age daughter Belle to Belfast for her first trip, thus allowing the audience, through Belle, to encounter the problems in Belfast through fresh eyes and to see the abnormality of what has become normalcy for citizens of Northern Ireland. For instance, Belle comments on the complacent reaction to shoppers at Marks and Spencer's during a bomb scare, telling Dolly, "I was frightened . . . by their irritated acceptance that it's a normal part of everyday life, like being searched before entering the shops" (213). The trip is not solely a family reunion for Rose, however, as we eventually learn that she is also in Belfast to photograph the political rally (that is to be led by her cousin Jack) and to document the connections between the Democratic Unionist Party that Jack works for and the National Front in England. Jack has become a Bible-thumping fundamentalist preacher/politician on the order of Ian Paisley and is currently working to form an alliance with the National Front in Britain, represented by a suave, gentlemanly Englishman named Thomas Bailey. In contrast, Jack's sister Janet married a Catholic man who is, of all things, a policeman in the Royal Ulster Constabulary, a job that helps to define his tolerant and saintly nature.

While Rose is the strong voice of women's independence and professional and political advancement, it is her older sister, the seemingly more conservative Vi, who ends up being the moral center of this play. On the surface it seems that Vi is not as politically adept as Rose, since Rose chastises her for selling propagandist newspapers and for paying protection money to Ulster Defence Association (UDA) thugs. But Vi is no simpleton. She tells Rose that she is driven by the necessity of economics and of personal security to play the game as the paramilitaries have laid it out for citizens such as herself. On another level, Vi seems at times to be the classic supportive mother figure. Although she is childless herself, she helped to raise her much younger sister and cousins, and she continues to defend Jack to the rest of the family, who have long since dismissed him as hopeless in his infatuation with Ian Paisley and in his fundamentalist and fascistic religion. Vi's excuses for Jack at first seem similar to those of the women in *Tea in a China Cup*, who, as Beth pointed out, always defend the bad behavior of men by blaming the women in their lives (*Tea* 38). But there is more going on here. The real conflict of the play arises between Jack and the women of the family, and it is through this conflict that Reid demonstrates the divide that often arises between the lives of women and men who are fueled by religious politics.

The damaging effects of right-wing Protestantism are examined through the characters of Janet and Jack. Dolly explains to her granddaughter Belle how Jack and Janet came to be raised by Dolly and her husband Joe:

> *Dolly.* Their father was a Presbyterian Minister you know. Joe's only brother, Martin. Martin died young an' the mother took the two children back to Scotland where she came from. An oul targe of a schoolteacher she was. You know the sort. Goes to church on Sunday, an' prays to God to give her strength to beat the kids on Monday.
> *Belle.* She beat them?
> *Dolly.* Into the ground. Not with a big stick. With words. Words like sin, the world and the devil. And the worst sins were the sinful lusts of the flesh. Jack's job as the man of the house, was to protect his sister from temptation. . . . May God forgive her an' Jack for the way they scared that wee girl, for I know I never will. (196)

We are shown further evidence of how this upbringing affected Jack and Janet when, as a teenager, Jack finds out that his sister has bought a statue of the Virgin Mary. Janet purchased the statue on a trip she took to the Republic with her aunt and cousins, and apparently, she had no idea of its religious implications. Here we see an attempt to separate symbol from physical reality, as Dolly had let the child buy the "pretty lady" because she liked it so much. But Jack can see only the symbol. He tells Janet that she has to be punished for this "blasphemous Popish statue," and then in anger he exclaims: "Women! Women! Temptation! Deception! You're the instruments of the devil! The root of all evil!" (202–205).

Jack's reaction to Janet demonstrates how women in general, and his sister in particular, have for him been turned into symbols by his religious upbringing. Jack shares this desire to shape Janet into a symbol with Janet's Catholic husband Peter, and even with the Englishman, Martin, with whom Janet has had an affair. As Rose points out to Janet, "Martin, like Peter, fell in love with your innocence" (208). Janet, long since cowed by her parents' and Jack's treatment of her, married a man who was so saintly (the play never openly considers other reasons for his behavior) that he kept their marriage celibate for all of its seventeen years. But on a recent trip to visit Rose in London, Janet lost her virginity in a brief affair with a married man, and she returned a changed woman. While other characters in the play remain fairly static, Janet is the only one who truly changes, rejecting the role she had been forced into accepting for so many years. She states simply, "I'm tired of being the sister of a devil and the wife of a saint" (208), and later she comments that for her, "[a] devil and a saint are the same thing. Afraid of women. Afraid we'll tempt you. Afraid we won't. They say there are no women in Ireland. Only mothers and sisters and wives" (208–209). Janet gives a firsthand account of what it is like to be treated as a symbol rather than as a person, demonstrating the effect both on her and on the men in her life whose world rests on their image of her.

Dolly and Rose and even Belle are firmly supportive of Janet and her decision to break from Peter and from Jack. They also view Jack as the one who has warped Janet's life, but Reid refuses to simplify her story into an us/them polarization. In response to Rose's questioning of Vi (about why she always defends Jack), Vi replies, "Have you ever stopped to wonder what *their* mother and father done to Jack? . . . He was that lost and lonely, I felt heart sorry for him" (220). Thus, rather than demonizing Jack, who is hardly a likeable character in this play, Reid works, through Vi, to show him as a victim of the dangerous mix of politics and religion. It is clear from the context of this play that Jack has picked up cruelty and hatred from his religion, but even Vi has her limits of tolerance for his hatred. When Jack and his friend from the National Front subtly threaten Belle because of her mixed racial heritage, Vi tells them in no uncertain terms to leave: "I know a threat when I hear one. Even when it's made by a well-spoken gentleman. And nobody threatens our Belle, nobody!" (229). Rose then follows up with a comment to Thomas Bailey — "never forget that loyalty to one's immediate family will always take precedence over loyalty to the Unionist family" (229) — which is obviously true for the women in this play, though not necessarily for the men. In the diverse choices of Jack and the women of the family, who choose love and liberty over hatred and hierarchy, this play demonstrates the limitations and the dead-end results of Jack's religion and politics. He is a lonely, cold man, afraid even to touch hands with another person, a man whose only warmth comes in the violent fervor of his speeches, which themselves incite others to violence, as the riot that ensues at his party's rally against the Anglo-Irish Agreement indicates.

While Jack remains loyal to the hard-line religion of his childhood, which affirms for him male dominance over women, Janet manages to break from her upbringing and make her own choices at last, refusing to be an emblem of purity and inspiration for her husband and for her brother. She tells her brother that she is leaving her husband and Belfast because "I want a life of my own. My own! Nobody else's! Not his, not Peter's. Not yours. Most of all not yours. I am walking away from this violence." And when Jack asserts defiantly, "I am not a violent man. I abhor violence," Janet tells him what is obvious to everyone else: "You love it Jack. You need it. It excites you. Violence is the woman you never had" (244). This last comment is a telling one in light of the gendering of political discourse discussed earlier in this essay.

What makes women like Janet and Beth able to walk away from the myths they were raised to believe, while men like Jack remain trapped in

them, is a question that Reid's plays raise but never answer. We can speculate that the old tradition continues to give men a sense of importance,
however misdirected, that they lack otherwise, bringing us back to Mary
Condren's comment that "The Irish male's obsession with history has given
him a place to stand, a fortress of certainty" amid "the humiliations and
trivialities of daily life" (xvii). That these traditions are ultimately dead-
ends seems to be the implication of Reid's plays. The younger generation of
women in Reid's plays are every bit as beset by their country's and their
families' history and tradition as characters in Irish plays always seem to be.
However, both the plays themselves and specifically these younger women
are willing to question those traditions and to forge new definitions for
themselves. Reid explores the delicate balance of both accepting the past
and moving beyond it to a better way of life, of neither embracing the
martyrdom of foremothers nor validating the oppressive authority of fore-
fathers. In doing so, she shows us that characters who are unable to rethink
their beliefs, to adapt, to change, and to show understanding or compassion
for others are the ones who become destructive forces in their own lives and
in the lives of those around them. In a culture inundated with labels, Reid
extols the truly radical act of an individual learning to reject exterior labels
and to take the first step toward self-definition by being "just me." That she
does so through developed portraits of women that reflect the complexities
of women's lives reveals that there are rich stories yet to be mined in the
theatrical project of presenting a nation's history, struggles, and conflicts to
and for itself.

NOTES

1. In her presentation at the seminar, Claudia Harris noted that during the year
in which Reid's *Tea* was selected by the Lyric Theatre (1983), there were some 200
submissions of plays by women.

2. For instance, Friel's *Dancing at Lughnasa* was a topic of one respondent's
comments; the respondent noted that the play is not about the five women but is
instead about the boy, Michael, and his memories. Even when writing female characters, it seems that male playwrights often use them to convey a man's story.

3. An excellent discussion of Maud Gonne's use of this role to call for national-
ism can be found in Antoinette Quinn's "Cathleen ni Houlihan Writes Back: Maude
Gonne and the Irish Nationalist Theatre," in Bradley and Valiulis's *Gender and
Sexuality in Modern Ireland*.

4. Various sociological studies that consider gender in light of Northern Ireland's political conflict note how traditional ideas of manliness fuel participation in
that conflict, especially in the form of paramilitary groups. See, especially, Fairweather, McDonough, and McFadyean's *Only the Rivers Run Free*, Elizabeth Shannon's *I Am of Ireland*, and Aretxaga's *Shattering Silence: Women, Nationalism, and
Political Subjectivity in Northern Ireland*.

5. Four female playwrights appear if you count Charabanc Theatre Company

as being different from Marie Jones, who was the Company's chief writer. The other two playwrights are Christina Reid and Anne Devlin.

6. A recent portrait of this behavior can be found in Frank McCourt's *Angela's Ashes: A Memoir,* in which McCourt recalls that his idle, drunken father passionately told stories of Cuchulain and other legendary heroes, the only things that his father had to give him.

7. For further discussions of the gendering of colonial issues and discourse, see Ania Loomba's lucid overview in *Colonialism/Postcolonialism*, especially 151–172 and 215–245.

8. See especially Elizabeth Shannon and Fairweather, McDonough, and McFadyean.

12

Neither Here nor There:
The Liminal Position of Teresa Deevy
and Her Female Characters

CHRISTIE FOX

Be brave. Be strong. Serve your country. In the 1930s, Irish women were still being told that the best way they could serve the country was to serve as wives and mothers: to make dinners for their husbands was the pinnacle of Irish womanhood. Caught between the wars and in a state that was struggling to define itself as independent despite its dominion status, male and female playwrights sought to express the emergent nation on stage, yet their representations were extremely selective. Irish women's conditions, for example, were rarely the focus of their plays; in fact, most dramas from the post-independence period simply replicated the traditional view that women's principal arenas were kitchens and birthing rooms, and that satisfying their domestic duties was the path to their personal fulfillment. The plays of Teresa Deevy broke with this convention and thus provide a fuller sense of women's experiences during this transitional period.

The women of Deevy's plays of the 1930s—Katie Roche and Amelia Gregg from *Katie Roche* and Annie Kinsella from *The King of Spain's Daughter*—are all caught in a changing world not of their own making, a world that seeks to control, limit, and shape Irish womanhood. Just as Ireland was caught between constitutions and without a clear image of the future, so Irish women were stuck in a liminal stage between their brief freedom in the nationalist era and their enforced domesticity, as codified in the 1937 Constitution. While women fought in the 1916 Easter Rising, were granted the vote (in the British government) in 1918, and were part of the first Dáil, their political activity declined after the War of Independence and the Civil War. In other words, in the 1920s and 1930s many women were sent back to the home to resume their traditional roles.

Deevy's heroines reflect this liminality, as they, like the women around them, are caught betwixt and between these eras. At the center of the issue lies marriage as a ritual that is not always completed, that is often scorned, but that is eventually reluctantly accepted. Like the women of their day, Deevy's characters are tempted with great freedoms, but they are caught in the mores of Irish society, mores which thrust them back to the homes and hearths. Looking at Deevy's plays in light of her historical circumstances provides fresh insight both into her characters and into women in times of nation-building, in large measure because Deevy's heroines make choices which reflect the kinds of choices Irish women were making in the 1930s. Much like the 1950s, discussed by both Stephen Watt and Christopher Murray earlier in this volume, the 1930s themselves seem to be an area of critical neglect for scholars. This essay attempts to redress this situation, in part by revisiting some of the work of this era which laid the groundwork for plays which have garnered more academic attention. In particular, I hope to offer here an alternative reading of Deevy's plays both by historicizing them and by applying Arnold Van Gennep's theory of ritual, thereby affording both a feminist view of the plays and a re-interpretation of their endings as ironic.

Despite her status as one of the few female Abbey playwrights, Deevy has been largely neglected by both theatre companies and scholars. Her plays have not been revived with the same frequency as other early Abbey productions. In fact, only the most successful of her plays, *Katie Roche*, has been revived, in 1975 on the Abbey main stage and in 1994 at the Peacock. The 1994 production of *Katie Roche* did, however, renew interest in Deevy, which resulted in an *Irish University Review* issue dedicated to "Teresa Deevy and Irish Women Playwrights." While this is commendable, the initiative nevertheless seems belated. In his introduction to that issue, Christopher Murray explains why Deevy's plays were neglected at mid-century: because the reigning Abbey director, Ernest Blythe, whose tenure Eileen Morgan reviews in this volume's introduction, did not welcome work by women writers.

If hostile management was the reason *Katie Roche* did not receive more attention earlier, problematic endings are one obstacle to producing Deevy's plays today, as Murray notes. In *Katie Roche*, Katie's husband forces her to move to Dublin. She is dismayed at the thought but seems to find "courage" and hopefulness at the last minute: she can be fulfilled through service to her husband. According to Murray, "Deevy's task as a playwright is to reconcile subjectivity with authority perceived as patriarchal. . . . In a sense what is searched for in Deevy is legitimacy itself, the space to be free. It is achieved only ironically, a feature of her work not commented on in her own day and felt to be too compromised by conventional endings in our day" ("Introduction: The Stifled Voice" 9). I will come back to Deevy's endings later in this essay, but for now I want to consider the "space to be free." And while Murray contends that identity is problematic in Deevy's work (9), I will argue that this identity was a reflection of the status and condition of women in the 1930s, as their identity was changing.

Elements of Deevy's own biography seep into her characters, and while she worked hard to portray female characters who reflected Irish women's experiences, like her, they had to negotiate life around the edicts of the Catholic Church and the government. Deevy was convent-educated and raised by a widowed mother who emphasized religion in her home. She had seven sisters and five brothers; two sisters became nuns and one brother became a priest, and Deevy herself took communion daily until her death (Judy Friel 117). After contracting Ménière's syndrome (a disease of the labyrinth of the ear) while at university, Deevy lost her hearing but continued to write. Her close attention to pacing, emphasizing silences and pauses, may be a result of this hearing loss. Deevy wrote characters who were like herself and, probably, like the women around her: Amelia Gregg, for instance. In fact, characters like Amelia are ever-present in Irish writing, suggesting that the single Irish woman, living alone, with another female companion, or with a mother or father to care for, was a sight common enough in the early twentieth century that it persisted into more recent drama and fiction. Other well-known literary examples might include William Trevor's "The Ballroom of Romance," Martin McDonagh's *The Beauty Queen of Leenane*, and Jennifer Johnston's *The Railway Station Man*. The women in these works, and indeed Deevy herself, had limited options: marriage, the convent, or seclusion in single life. While marriage and the convent offer ritualized induction into adulthood, women who lived with their families remained in a state of incompletion, of perpetual societal adolescence.

Ireland and Irish Women between the Wars

Ireland in the 1930s was perched not only between the wars but also between constitutions. The last of three constitutions would be the one under which Ireland operates today, the 1937 Constitution, written by Eamon de Valera with considerable assistance from Archbishop Croke. Some of the major differences between that constitution and both the 1922 Constitution and the 1916 Declaration concerned the Treaty (which ended the War of Independence and confirmed Northern Ireland as part of the United Kingdom) and the status of women. Scholars such as Margaret Ward and Maryann G. Valiulis have shown that the 1930s were a time when the political gains that women made before and during the Rising were eroded. As the men in government forged a new nation, it became important for them to reassert their masculinity through the imposition of traditional views of Irish femininity. Women who once fought for the franchise, women's equality, and Ireland's freedom were now asked to return home and take their "proper" place as wives and mothers. Although many had trained as sharpshooters or served in the Citizen's Army or the First Dáil, they found that their voices were no longer heeded.

Meanwhile, the 1930s provided increased employment opportunities for women. In Deevy's most successful play, *Katie Roche*, Katie finds her husband through work—she marries her employer. As Mary E. Daly observes, in 1936, 53.3 percent of single women (aged fourteen and over) were employed (Daly, "Women in the Irish Free State" 101). Katie is, in this sense, a reflection of her time. Amelia Gregg, also Katie's employer and future sister-in-law, similarly reflects a reality of the time. According to Daly, nearly one in four women aged forty-five to fifty-four were single in 1926 and were unlikely to marry (103). Perhaps out of economic necessity, women increasingly were moving into the work force. Many were not, as the 1937 Constitution would seem to imply, chained to the house or dependent on a male provider. By 1936 women "accounted for 31.3 percent of the manufacturing workforce, compared with 26.6 percent in 1926" (110). Deevy's heroines, especially Katie, are caught between this tantalizing freedom and tradition. Katie works for her living and hopes for a good match in marriage, her preferred route to societal acceptability and maturity. What she gets with that marriage, however, is not freedom but further constrictions of her movement and, eventually, her life, as she is forced to move to Dublin with Stanislaus Gregg.

While economic advancements provided some opportunities for young Irish women (if manufacturing jobs can be seen as a gain), the political climate worked specifically against such developments. Valiulis observes that there was much that the Free State government could not control, bound by lack of resources, dominion status, and the like, it "could, however, control women" (127). Throughout the 1920s, with a series of government acts and measures, the government banned women from some civil service exams, outlawed divorce, and prohibited the distribution of birth control (133).[1] This kind of legislative conservatism ensured that the government maintained control over women's public activity and helped to build an image of the Irish woman as chaste, pure, and homebound—an image that was essential in showing that the Irish had a right to an independent government and a superiority over their former colonizer, whose women were gaining political rights. While there was a vocal feminist minority who opposed the government at every turn, the majority of Irish women were not working toward increased women's public participation. Rather, they were, like Katie and Amelia, working and living from day to day with little knowledge or care of what happened in the Dáil.

While feminists maintained that women could be citizens in addition to mothers and wives, they simultaneously used the government's own rhetoric to show that it was women's motherly nature that necessitated their inclusion in public affairs (Valiulis 130). Deevy's characters do not display this mothering instinct: the young women are intent on improving themselves through marriage but seem disinclined to motherhood. Perhaps this is one way in which Deevy subverts the nationalist view of womankind; perhaps she is simply reflecting her own reality. Deevy's women do not value marriage and motherhood above all else. Generally young, they want to enjoy the freedom that their youth might allow, and in this respect, they stand in contrast to the women of Gregory, Yeats, and the nationalist project. This subversion may represent Deevy's writing from her own experience, as a woman living under the new legislation of the 1920s and 1930s. Her heroines, however, also express a profound ambivalence about the position of women in the Irish society of the 1930s.

Katie Roche

In other words, Deevy's characters, like Irish women of the time, remain neither here nor there. They are betrothed but not married, or they are married in name only. This extends beyond the title character in *Katie Roche*, as Amelia Gregg too is single, living a "spinster" life not unlike Deevy's own yet also transgressing norms and fearing displacement from her home if she refuses to marry.

Furthering her indeterminate status by being born an "illegitimate" child, Katie is an outsider in town: her mother, Mary Halnan, is known, but the identity of her father remains concealed. While there is much discussion of Katie's father (who is revealed to be Holy Reuben, the pilgrim), the person who would give her a name of her own, Katie is essentially motherless. Her mother died and only Mrs. Roche would take a nameless child in and raise her. But Mrs. Roche was not a surrogate mother, and we get the impression that theirs was a loveless house. Katie was raised without a mother figure, without an example of womanly behavior and mores. While being fatherless is more of a legal disadvantage for a child, a girl without a mother is left without a heritage, without a feminine inheritance.[2]

As the play begins, Katie is unmarried and considering the convent. She tells Stan, "Wouldn't it be a good thing to save my soul — and to more than save it — so what else can I do?" (10). While it is tempting to dismiss this as hyperbole, the religious life remains a real option to Katie throughout the play, and in the 1930s the convent offered one route by which an unmarried woman might ritually accede to adulthood. In an environment constricted by church and state, many would see marriage — the second, more common ritual induction into adulthood — as a means to a stable life. It is, in fact, a rite that Katie welcomes, but one which Annie Kinsella in Deevy's later play, *The King of Spain's Daughter*, fears.

Stan is perturbed by the news that Katie is considering the convent, as he has come home to propose to her. If there is ambivalence in the lives of Deevy's heroines, it is nowhere more present than in Stan's proposal to Katie, as he was actually in love with her mother, Mary Halnan: "A crowd of them, long ago, were in love with her. I loved her; I could have knocked down the world for her. But — she said I was too young" (14). Stan, seeing in Katie all that is left of the beguiling Halnan, thinks to make this "child" (as Stan refers to Katie throughout the play; see Leeney) his wife and helpmate. Katie herself is confused by Stan's reminiscence in the middle of his proposal.

> *Stan.* Would you think of marrying me?
> *Katie.* Now is it . . . or . . . or then? (15)

After some reluctance, Katie agrees. She is willing to accept Stan's condescension, perhaps out of the complacency that it is her lot in life, or perhaps out of a larger understanding that this marriage offers a way out of her employment and her status as a somewhat unrespectable "adolescent."

However, once married, Katie is not initiated completely into the community or married life; as she says to Stan, "Three months now since we stood at the altar, and three times you drew from me" (50). Her marriage is not complete. It appears to be unconsummated, or at least not frequently so. In addition, Katie's social life seems to have shrunk rather than expanded, further restricting her to the house, as she is denied the social benefits of marriage while her husband is away. In sum, she has not progressed into married life and remains in what Arnold Van Gennep refers to as the "liminal transition state" — not incorporation but betwixt and between betrothal and marriage, adolescence and adulthood.

Van Gennep observes that most — if not all — societies have three classes of rites: separation, transition, and incorporation. These can also be described as, respectively, preliminal, liminal, and postliminal rites (11). Moving from adolescence to marriage involves a series of rites combining all three classes, which now can be considered stages. "A betrothal forms a liminal period between adolescence and marriage, but the passage from adolescence to betrothal itself involves a special series of rites of separation, a transition and an incorporation into the betrothed condition," which is a transitional period (11). There follows a series of rites that move the woman from betrothal to marriage. These are the rites that Katie has not completed; she remains in the midst of an unfinished rite.

The other primary female character in the play, Amelia Gregg, is caught between different worlds than Katie, but she, too, finds comfort in neither. Amelia lives as a "spinster" in the home that her brother shares with Katie, seemingly content to make tea and go to church — a small, if not fulfilling, existence — until Stan's plans upset that life. Stan, it turns out, could evict her, a theme which will also arise in *The King of Spain's Daughter*. Stan therefore suggests that Amelia marry Frank Lloyd, an old suitor. Again, the proposal is an odd one, as Lloyd declares his long-standing love, proposes, recants, and then restates it, all within two pages. Yet the betrothal remains unanswered at the end of the play: nothing has been resolved.

Deevy's obsession with marriage is, I think, a reflection of the attempted control over women's lives that was being legislated in Dublin. The legislation pertaining to women in the 1920s and 1930s sought to keep them at home, out of the workforce. The laws regulated women's public activity and, in some instances, represented a clear attack on women's sexuality. Similarly, Deevy's characters fight for control of their own sexuality. Amelia Gregg moves into the betrothal stage, one normally associated with transitional biological periods, yet she has not been a biological adolescent for some time. Socially and legally, her status has not kept pace with her age, and marriage offers her stability, security, and sexual and legal maturity. As a single woman, Amelia stands to lose her house and even her servants. Katie, on the other hand, seeks freedom through marriage, but she is physically punished by both Stan (father figure) and Reuben (actual father) for her (or their, in the case of her father) sexual indiscretions. The kind of control wielded by Stan and Reuben over Katie's public behavior mirrors the control sought and achieved by the Dáil.

At the end of the play, Stan forces Katie to go to Dublin.

> *Stan (to Katie, furious).* Get your case.
> *Katie.* We're going away! He says we must — this very minute — though I want to stop here!
> *Amelia.* This very minute . . . oh dear . . . Won't you stay for tea?
> *Stan.* We must get the seven-ten. I've ordered the car.
> *Katie (with a cry).* And I'll never be here in my life again! (*Covers her face with her hands, sobs*). (111)

According to the stage directions, for the next few minutes, Katie sobs, looks sorrowful, shakes "her head as at something that has failed her," is angry, resentful, and "full of self-pity" (112–113). Then, in the last moments of the play, Amelia tells Katie to be brave, and Katie seems to undergo a transformation, as if the very word "brave" rekindles the real goal of an Irishwoman — to satisfy her husband:

> *Katie.* I think you're right! . . . (*Pause*) I'm a great beauty . . . after all my talk — crying now . . . (*grows exultant*). I *will* be brave! (113)

This ending has proved problematic for contemporary readers and directors. Regarding rehearsals for the 1994 revival, director Judy Friel said "there was a sense of disbelief at Katie's predicament here" (J. Friel 122). In light of late twentieth-century options such as divorce and emigration, the players had difficulty in finding redemption in this ending. Friel dismisses the ending as a "whitewash" because it is too abrupt and discordant with the tone of the play: "Deevy's experience as a woman in the nineteen thirties told her to survive by submission and do it with grace" (123). But I am not certain that Friel has exhausted the possibilities of this ending; she is imbuing it with a one-dimensional, 1990s view of feminism and of women's positions in post-independence society.

Throughout the play, Katie teeters between worlds: single life, the

convent, and marriage. Implicitly she rejected emigration. I think one possible interpretation is that Katie chose to be brave because Dublin offered
an adventure. If she were dissatisfied with her life, maybe she could find in
the city whatever it was that was so clearly missing in her small-town life.
She is innocent, and Dublin can offer her a world about which she knows
nothing. In Dublin, no one knows or cares that she is fatherless. She will
have the appearance of a respectable marriage; she and Stan will at least
cohabitate. More importantly, in Dublin, Katie can move out of transition
and into incorporation — the completion of the marriage rite (Van Gennep
11). In fact, the journey to Dublin may finally be the separation which,
according to Van Gennep, must precede incorporation: without it, the rite
cannot be complete. The trip to Dublin, which many find so problematic,
may in fact be the ritual resolution of the play as well as the plot resolution.
I offer this alternative interpretation, one that foresees choices in Katie's
future, based on Katie's facile understandings of the world and on her
stubborn search for freedom.

The King of Spain's Daughter

Admittedly, my reading of the end of *Katie Roche* may be influenced by my
reading of the end of Deevy's *The King of Spain's Daughter*. Somewhat like
the alternatives facing Katie, with their limited routes to recognized adulthood, in *The King of Spain's Daughter*, Annie has to choose between working
at the factory (essentially indentured servitude) or marrying Jim, whom she
finds boring. Again, in the last moments of the play, Annie suddenly faces
marriage enthusiastically, despite her previous objections that a match
would curtail her freedom.

> *Mrs. Marks.* A good, sensible boy.
> *Annie.* Boy! (*She laughs exultantly*). I think he is a man might cut your
>   throat!
> *Mrs. Marks.* God save us all!
> *Annie.* He put by two shillin's every week for two hundred weeks. I think
>   he is a man that — supposin' he was jealous — might cut your throat.
>   (*Quiet, exultant, she goes*)
> *Mrs. Marks.* The Lord preserve us! That she'd find joy in such a thought!
>   (141–142)

Annie Kinsella and Katie Roche, therefore, are much alike: both are dissatisfied with the options before them, limited by their time and place in rural
1930s Ireland, and both work to glean whatever excitement they can from
dismal circumstances.

   In fact, *The King of Spain's Daughter* and *Katie Roche* are more alike than
different in that Annie also has a questionable reputation in town because of
her perceived sexual improprieties. Mrs. Marks, who represents a more

stereotypical view of Irish womanhood than Amelia Gregg but who performs the same function in the play, continually speaks badly of Annie,
encouraging Jim to find a "better" woman. Mrs. Marks may be the most
interesting character in the play. She in some ways exemplifies idealized
womanhood — she is married and has children — but she remains fundamentally dissatisfied with her life. Mrs. Marks shows that even the ideal is
greatly flawed and that the path for women is neither easy nor satisfying.
Here may be the proto-feminist writing that some modern feminists seek in
Deevy's work: Mrs. Marks shows symptoms of what Betty Friedan would
write about thirty years later in *The Feminine Mystique*.

> *Mrs. Marks.* I was thinking of my marriage day when I was looking at them
>   two. It is a thought would sadden anyone.
> *Jim.* How is that, Mrs. Marks?
> *Mrs. Marks.* That's how it is; the truth is the best to be told in the end.
> *Jim.* Haven't you Bill and Mary, and the little place? You didn't fare bad.
> *Mrs. Marks.* Bad? What have bad or good to do with it? That is outside of
>   the question. For twenty years you're thinking of that day, an' for
>   thirty years you're lookin' back at it. After that you don't mind — you
>   haven't the feelin' — exceptin' maybe the odd day, like to-day. (126)

Although Mrs. Marks articulates reason and propriety in the play, this small
speech speaks directly to women's experiences and to what she — and perhaps Deevy — saw as the limited opportunities for women's happiness. Her
words establish the obsession with marriage that is also seen in *Katie Roche*.
As a result of exercising her own sexuality, Annie must marry Jim, whom
she has already rejected, or sign on at the factory for five years.

While this narrative may suggest nascent feminist writing on Deevy's
part, it may also be a reflection of women's lives at the time, when options
were limited and opportunities were disappearing with each legislative act.
Through her emphasis on women's roles, Deevy thus reveals a segment
of Irish society that was previously invisible to most people and which,
through critical neglect of her plays, remains largely so to contemporary
playgoers. Annie, like Katie and the women of their time, is locked into
limited options. Annie must not be allowed to exert her sexual freedom: she
must choose immediately between factory work and marriage. She reluctantly agrees to marriage, perhaps hoping for a glint of freedom not open to
her in her role as a factory drone. Her turnaround is as confusing as Katie's
when viewed from a modern perspective. Suddenly faced with everlast-
ing marriage to a determined and stubborn man, she twists his obstinacy
into excitement, finding fulfillment not in the prospect of being a wife or
mother but rather in danger. She can maintain her role as provocateur by
creating a unique place for herself, while tradition and contemporary ethics
might prescribe a very different life. Ultimately, she chooses the ritual
which will take her into recognized adulthood. Annie maintains the hope

that her marriage will be happier than Mrs. Marks's, that her separation
from home and incorporation into Jim's will contain an element of thrill.

Both Katie and Annie reject traditional norms of womanhood in favor of
finding solace, or at least satisfaction, in unusual results. These plot twists
make a contemporary reading troublesome — or, rather, they lead contemporary feminists to shy away, seeing in the conclusions more entrapment
for the heroines and a capitulation by Deevy. However, looking at the
historical predicament of Irish women in the 1930s sheds considerable light
on Deevy's plot resolutions. Irish women were teetering between increased
public roles and stronger restrictions than they had seen under British rule.
Moreover, women in the government were often at odds with the administration (a holdover from the Civil War),[3] another motive for the government's restrictions on women. As women faced diminishing choices, Deevy
wrote characters whose choices were forced, or at least limited, by their
circumstances. Further complicating her position, Deevy was an Abbey
playwright who could not write against the nationalist sentiment of the
time. Synge might be able to, but Synge was male and hearing. A "deaf
spinster from County Waterford," as Hugh Hunt called her, could not risk
writing plays in which women ran away with tramps or rejected Irish ideals
outright (143). Instead, Deevy's plays turn at the very end, making her
characters more complex, and in some ways confusing, for the modern
reader. Curiously enough, she created characters who emulated the Irish
ideal — passive, self-effacing, meek, sacrificial, passionless, and bland (Valiulis 117) — but these were not her heroines. On the contrary, Deevy's
heroines challenge the nationalist worldview and undermine it. Whether
or not Deevy intended to be controversial, her women create rebellion
in small ways, forging lives for themselves in spite of the societal pressure against them, leaving the contemporary reader to speculate that Irish
women of Deevy's time might have created similar subtle rebellions in their
own lives.
  Deevy is an enduring, yet oft-forgotten Abbey playwright. That is to
say, although her attention to tone and pacing would seem to lead to rich
productions, her character reversals have led feminist directors to shy away
from her. This is singularly unfortunate, for attention to the plays' dialogue
about women and women's position at the time might lead us to better
understand the dearth of female playwrights today. In addition, more critical attention to her work would lead to a greater understanding of Irish
writing and life in the "forgotten" middle of the century. With modern
attention to feminist coding (Radner) and a desire to understand our present through our past, it is a shame that Deevy has been largely rejected
(when she has not been simply ignored). We might look to her plays for an
understanding of women who are caught between worlds — between the
public and private, religious and secular, single and married. We might see

in her work a way to enact difficult realities while nations are being rebuilt and a way to make quiet critiques when the stakes are high.

NOTES

1. These government acts included the 1924 and 1927 Juries Bills, the 1925 Civil Service Amendment Act, the 1929 Censorship Act (regarding distribution of birth control information), a 1934 act that prohibited the sale of contraceptives, and a 1935 limit on the number of women in any given profession. See Valiulis (133).

2. See Luce Irigaray's work on *Antigone* for her analysis of the motherless daughter and its reconstruction of patriarchal oppression.

3. For more information on this era and on women's involvement in it, see the work of Maryann G. Valiulis and Margaret Ward.

13

Playwrights of the Western World: Synge, Murphy, McDonagh

JOSÉ LANTERS

In a well-known exchange of words in James Joyce's "The Dead," Molly Ivors encourages a reluctant Gabriel Conroy to come on an excursion to the Aran Islands the coming summer and to bring his wife Gretta, who is originally from Galway in the West of Ireland. Miss Ivors's sentiments reflect those of the Gaelic League around the turn of the century, as its leaders encouraged people to rediscover their own language and culture by "going West." The West of Ireland thus came to stand for a nationalist "myth of simplicity, nobility, and endurance as the characteristics of Irishness at its best" (O'Dwyer, "Play-Acting and Myth-Making" 31). In 1896 Yeats, at least by his own account, advised Synge to give up Paris and to visit the West of Ireland instead, and the latter's summer visits to the Aran Islands between 1898 and 1902 famously influenced his dramatic art. *Riders to the Sea* was set on the Aran Islands, and Mayo became the backdrop to *The Playboy of the Western World*. At the same time, Synge's depiction of the West never fit in with the romantic, nationalist ideal; he was accused of unfairly representing Irish life in a negative light, and his work evoked highly critical, even violent responses in his own time, as Susan Cannon Harris's essay in this volume attests. The playwright was not unfamiliar with the less than romantic reality of rural Ireland, having traveled in Mayo and having written articles about the appalling poverty he encountered there, but as numerous commentators have pointed out, it is absurd to see Synge's work as a naturalistic mirror held up to the West of Ireland. In his plays, he distanced himself creatively from his material: they are "as much about the intense, personal preoccupations of the artist as about the portrayal of a peasant community" (Thomas Kilroy, "A Generation" 138).

Within the Abbey Theatre, of which he became a director in 1905, Synge was always a somewhat controversial figure who never fit comfortably into the parameters that Yeats and Lady Gregory had formulated for the national theatre as an instrument of cultural emancipation: to show that Ireland was "the home of an ancient idealism" (qtd. in Murray, *Twentieth-Century Irish Drama* 2). While Synge firmly opposed the inclusion of foreign plays in the Abbey repertoire, in order to encourage the development of an Irish creative school of drama, he was also a man of many contradictions, and his work is a reflection of these complexities of character. As Nicholas Grene has argued, Synge's dark comedies lack the underpinning security of viewpoint upon which conventional comedies rely. Synge leads his audience through several different sorts of sometimes contradictory reactions; whereas conventional comedy "rests ultimately on a confident belief in the organisation of society [. . .] Synge's deliberate manipulation of audience response results in a sceptical and ironic attitude towards the laws society imposes upon the individual" (149–150). Synge's plays always contain an element of danger; his work, even at its funniest, is also "deeply disturbing" (Grene, *A Critical Study of the Plays* 185). That disturbing quality also informs his portrayal of the West of Ireland. Declan Kiberd contends that "the so-called exoticism of Synge's language is related to the remoteness of his characters from the 'big world,'" and the greater that displacement, "the more untamed the life and the more colourful its deviations from the linguistic norm" (*Synge and the Irish Language* 173). But since poetry and violence thus spring from a common source, Synge challenges nationalists who would see the Western peasant "as a secular saint and Gaelic mystic" to concede "the savagery as well as the glamour at the heart of their cultural enterprise" (Kiberd, *Synge and the Irish Language* 171).

After Synge's death in 1909, the Abbey gradually caved in under the public protests against such disturbing messages; danger and subversion gave way to complacency and conventionality. Yeats sadly noted in 1919 that "we did not set out to create this sort of theatre, and its success has been to me a discouragement and a defeat" (qtd. in Jeffares 186). The emphasis on Irish traditionalism very soon led to the predominance of the "peasant play," a tamer, more conventional version of the "Western" genre that Synge had pioneered, particularly under Yeats's successor as managing director, Ernest Blythe. In the decades after Yeats's death, the Abbey presented, from a predominantly Catholic perspective, safe, realistic drama depicting life in small towns and rural areas. This was the era of Archbishop McQuaid, censorship, and sexual repression, and, as Christopher Murray's essay on Sean O'Casey in this volume shows, to do other than provide these safe, realistic dramas was to invite problems.

It was not until the early 1960s that Ireland saw "the stirrings of what would be the first significant shift in sensibility in the Irish theatre since the early days of the Abbey Theatre" (T. Kilroy 135). One of the playwrights to bring this shift about was from the West of Ireland: Tom Murphy from Tuam in Galway. Murphy's generation reacted sharply against the Abbey tradition of the "peasant play." When he was contemplating the subject matter of his first play with Noel O'Donoghue, the latter told him: "One thing is fucking sure, it's not going to be set in a kitchen." That, according to Murphy, "was the most progressive thing anybody had ever said to me" (qtd. in T. Kilroy 139). The dislike between Murphy and the Abbey was mutual: in 1961 Ernest Blythe rejected *The Iron Men* (later revised for London's Royal Court Theatre as *A Whistle in the Dark*) by pointing out "that the characters in [Murphy's] play were not real, nor its atmosphere credible. He did not believe that such people existed in Ireland" (qtd. in Toibín, "Thomas Murphy's Volcanic Ireland" 24). Similar criticism had been leveled at Synge for *The Playboy of the Western World* some fifty-five years previously.

After Blythe's departure in 1967, the Abbey's attitude toward Murphy changed; in fact, the playwright served as a member of the Abbey's board of directors from 1973 to 1983, as Synge had done before him, and Murphy was also writer-in-association with the Abbey for a time. Meanwhile, the geography of Irish theatre was also changing. The Abbey Theatre's Dublin-based focus on the West of Ireland had always been something of a paradox, one which Nelson Ó Ceallaigh Ritschel's essay emphasizes was directly challenged by other theatre companies as early as 1906. In 1975, however, the West of Ireland came into its own when Druid became the first professional theatre company outside Dublin to open its doors and stage its very first production in Galway. It was, fittingly, Synge's *The Playboy of the Western World* (which Druid would take on tour to the Aran Islands in 1998 to mark the centenary of Synge's first visit there). Tom Murphy was well aware that "something was happening in Galway, something stirring there, and I have a very strong tribal instinct within me, a very strong homing instinct" (qtd. in Roche, "Bailegangaire" 116). Murphy was writer-in-association with Druid from 1983 to 1985, and their affiliation produced *Conversations on a Homecoming* and *Bailegangaire*. Most of Murphy's plays, however, have premiered at the Abbey.

Affinities between Synge and Murphy abound. The controversy that accompanied the performance of Murphy's *The Sanctuary Lamp* in 1975 was reminiscent of the riots that broke out on the first night of *Playboy*, but that was not the only reason why Brian Friel called Murphy's play "an achievement that Synge would have been proud of" (qtd. in Harry White, "*The Sanctuary Lamp*: An Assessment" 78). In terms of language and characterization, there are similarities between Murphy's work — especially plays such as *The Morning After Optimism, The Sanctuary Lamp,* and *Bailegan-*

gaire — and Synge's *Playboy* or *The Well of the Saints*, the latter of which Murphy directed at the Abbey in 1979; in that same year, Murphy also wrote and directed *Epitaph under Ether*, a dramatic compilation based on Synge's life and works.

Lady Gregory was convinced that one of the reasons Ireland was inclined toward drama, rather than the novel, as an art form was because "it's a great country for conversation," and "drama is conversation arranged" (Mikhail, *Lady Gregory* 58–59). Indeed, the verbal nature of Irish drama has been much commented upon, in that playwrights such as Synge and Murphy "have created language plays where words tend to predetermine character, action and plot" (Kearney, "Language Play" 78). In the preface to *Playboy*, Synge declared that in a good play, "every speech should be as fully flavoured as a nut or an apple," and he claimed that he himself had used "one or two words only" that he had not heard among the country people of Ireland, or in his own nursery before he could read, or spoken by the servants he overheard through a chink in the floor of the old Wicklow house where he was staying (*J. M. Synge: Plays* 103). Many commentators have pointed out that Synge's language is in actuality as artificial as it is naturalistic; Nicholas Grene has shown that his dialogue is synthetic, "in that he brings together dialect features from various parts of the country to suit his dramatic purposes," and that Synge invented phrases and expressions to fit his poetic needs (*Synge: A Critical Study* 62). As Grene points out, however, such words and phrases "may appear superficially picturesque; but at the highest level of Synge's craftsmanship they serve to renew the very springs of meaning" (64).

Language in Tom Murphy's work, too, goes beyond being merely a means of communication. Walter Ong has defined the spoken word as "a mode of action and not simply a countersign of thought" (*Orality and Literacy* 32), as "something that happens, an event in the world of sound through which the mind is enabled to relate actuality to itself" (Ong, *The Presence of the Word* 22). Murphy's background may provide a first clue to the way in which he perceives the relationship between word and world. Originally from Tuam in County Galway, as I have mentioned, Murphy seems fascinated by Tuam's unique form of slang, a mixture of archaic and standard phrases, and by the town's vibrant attitude toward life (Carney 3). He has acknowledged that the place and its language are of great importance in his work and that everything he writes is processed through his background there: "It's my microcosm — all the types and characters in my work have been filtered through people I knew in Tuam" (Boland 21). The language of Murphy's plays — Brian Friel in a program note calls it "a factitious speech, almost a private dialect" — has attracted a great deal of critical comment, especially regarding its "copiousness" (a characteristic, according to Ong, of cultures with a high degree of residual orality). According to David Nowlan, for example, *The Morning After Optimism* "suffers at times from a plethora of words apparently for their own sake" (10); Gus Smith observes that in *The Sanctuary Lamp*, "the author indulges himself in a torrent of words" (16); and the language of *The Gigli Concert*, according to Kate Kellaway, "is on a sort of inspired bender. It surfeits on its own potency" (44). Christopher Murray cautions readers unfamiliar with Murphy that "the plays may appear obscure or the level of feeling inexplicably intense, and the language (Murphy's strongest weapon) perhaps in excess of the apparent facts" ("Thomas Murphy" 392). A tentative but important connection between Murphy's language and the word as action or event is made by Gerald Dawe: "The energy of the language is almost dramatic compensation for the inactivity and stasis that enfolds Murphy's people. Words become alternatives to living" (26).

Words in these plays are verbal acts, and the stories told by the characters function as individual myths. Myths explain the origins of things; the telling of a myth not only recreates the event of the myth, but it also gives the believers in that myth the power to control and manipulate their existence. Language in *Playboy* "is used to make the actual phenomena of life more categorical, more interesting and more wonderful" (Grene, *Synge: A Critical Study* 80), but it is also used to manipulate those phenomena: "*The Playboy* is a drama about the power of words to transform oneself and one's world," and at its end, "Pegeen is compelled tragically to acknowledge that what she has lost is not the 'small, low fellow, dark and dirty' that Christy *was*, but the playboy of the western world he has *become* through the power of a lie" (Kearney, "Language Play" 78). Identifying with a fictitious "other" through lies or stories is a form of denial of the self, but it is also a performative act of empowerment: saying it is so makes it so. For oral societies, reality resides in what is said or heard: a person becomes the thing he says he is by an act of faith. In Tom Murphy's plays, characters are frequently torn between regarding such behavior as dangerously deluded, on the one hand, and conceding the possibility for positive transformation on the other.

Murphy's characters are caught between two responses to the word: they are in danger of going mad unless they speak out, but they are prevented from speaking out by self-consciousness and guilt. As a consequence, characters frequently relate stories about other people that are of particular relevance to themselves or that are later revealed to be *about* themselves. In *The Morning After Optimism*, Rosie speaks of "a person who, when she found out that things are really what they seem and not what they are supposed to be, instead of manifesting her reaction in a little tear, held back and clung to her pain" (12). In the same play, James tells the story of a little boy who was given balloons by everyone so that he floated above the ground and "never had to walk a step anywhere. Until, one day, one of them burst, and it was the beautiful blue one. And he was not prepared for this" (48). In *Conversations on a Homecoming*, Michael tells of a man — whom Tom rightly identifies as Michael himself — who went berserk, took off his clothes, and danced on the table, and when the words would not come for him to tell his message to the world, "he tried to set himself on fire" (29). Michael also defends JJ, the owner of the White House pub, who identified so much with John F. Kennedy that he came to believe that he *was* Kennedy: "And, in a way, he was" (52). Tom, however, accuses JJ of dangerously deluding himself and others:

> *Tom.* Oh yes, they hated him — Why wouldn't they: Puppetry, mimicry, rhetoric! What had he to offer anyone? Where were the facts, the definitions?
>
> *Michael.* Why are you getting so excited?
>
> *Tom.* I'm not getting excited. He-fed-people's-fantasies. That['s] all he did. Fed-people's-fantasies.
>
> *Michael.* People are afraid of realising themselves. (101)

Is verbal magic a schizophrenic denial of self, as Tom suggests, or a creative realization of self, as Michael argues? Or is it perhaps a combination of the two, given that Tom and Michael "together might make up one decent man" (107)? In *The Gigli Concert*, JPW King tells the Irish Man that he is in the business of "Self-realisation, you know?" (4), but he initially dismisses the Man's identification with Gigli — "Sing us a song, Benimillo, the people used to say" (8) — as psychotic "Fiction. Fantasy" (10). Eventually, however, he comes to realize the Man's dream — to sing like Gigli — for himself. Murphy's plays suggest that creative transformation of self is indeed possible, but only after initial denial of self has been confronted and transcended.

Bailegangaire is perhaps Tom Murphy's most self-consciously "Western" play in that it was written during his time as writer-in-association with Druid, is set in the *"country kitchen in the old style"* of a traditional thatched house (43) — but with a Japanese electronics factory down the road, which provides the deliberate echoes of the peasant play with ironic overtones — and has the healing and transforming power of storytelling as its central concern. Thomas Kilroy calls it a "very knowing" text in its reverberations, especially in its "extraordinarily resonant re-echo of *Riders to the Sea* in Mommo's enumeration of her own bereavements." He sees these as not simply modish references but rather as evidence of a larger awareness, "an ability to lift the purely personal on to a plane of wider implication" (140). Mommo in *Bailegangaire* is very old and therefore especially given to a traditional mode of expression that is typical of predominantly oral cultures. Her speech patterns and even some of her vocabulary are derived from Irish, in much the same way characters speak in a Synge play. Mommo's story is about "how the place called Bochtán [. . .] came by its new appellation, Bailegangaire, the place without laughter" (43). The town's original name implies poverty (the Irish word *bochtán* means "a poor person"): "The land there so poor [. .]. 'twas credited with bein' seven times worse than elsewhere in the kingdom. And so hard they had it, to keep life itself in them, whenever Bochtán was mentioned the old people in their wisdom would add in precaution, go bhfóire Dia orainn, may God protect us" (43). The tramp in Synge's *In the Shadow of the Glen* expresses himself in much the same way when he tells Nora, "You'll be saying one time, 'It's a grand evening, by the grace of God,' and another time, 'It's a wild night, God help us, but it'll pass surely'" (*Plays* 29). His language is replete with formulaic phrases "which are like spell-words against disaster" (Grene, *Synge: A Critical Study* 81). In a similar way, in *Bailegangaire*, the name Bochtán is credited with the power to provoke the poverty that it describes, an effect that may be warded off by the force of a protective formula. Elsewhere in the play, the importance of such benedictions is emphasized: "Now as all do know the world over the custom when entering the house of another [. . .] is to invoke our Maker's benediction on all present" (55). The inhabitants of Bailegangaire blame their misfortunes in part on the strangers' alleged ignoring of this rule: "no mention of our Maker, or His Blessed Son, was mentioned as the strangers came 'cross that threshel" (55). An omitted blessing also spells disaster in *Riders to the Sea*, where Maurya foresees Bartley's death when she tries to say "God speed you" but the words choke in her throat (*Plays* 10).

Mommo rambles on interminably, but, as her granddaughter Mary points out, she never finishes her story. Her sister Dolly calls Mommo's story her "confession" and believes that "that's why she goes on like a gramophone. Guilty" (65). The guilt stems from the fact that it was Mommo who both encouraged her husband to take part in the Bochtán laughing competition and suggested that they laugh at "Misfortunes . . . *She* supplied them with the topic" (74):

> Nothin' was sacred an' nothing a secret. [. . .] The stories kept on comin' an' the volleys and cheers. All of them present, their heads thrown back abandoned in festivities of guffaws: the wretched and neglected dilapidated an' forlorn, the forgotten an' tormented, the lonely an' despairing, ragged an' dirty, impoverished, hungry, emaciated and unhealthy, eyes big as saucers, ridiculing an' defying of their lot on earth below — glintin' their defiance — their defiance an' rejection, inviting of what else might come or *care* to come! — driving bellows of refusal at the sky through the roof. Och hona ho gus hah-haa! . . . The nicest night ever. (74–75)

Having verbally invited the worst, Mommo feels responsible when the worst does indeed happen: her grandchild Tom, home alone with his sisters Mary and Dolly while Mommo and her husband are on the road, dies in an accident when he throws paraffin on the fire, and her husband dies at the child's graveside two days later. Mommo represses her grief, never crying for her husband; unable to acknowledge that Tom is dead, she keeps telling herself that he is "in Galway" (46, 58).

Mommo's unfinished story negates the past. It is emphatically about "strangers, ye understand" (44), and her refusal to recognize her own granddaughter Mary by addressing her as "Miss" is a way of continuing her denial of the past into the present. Mary herself has come to realize that her whole career as a nurse was a form of pretense, too, a veiled response to atone for her childhood failure to save the life of her injured brother. Dolly, meanwhile, is creating another fiction that will deny her unwanted pregnancy: Mary will pretend the child is hers and will take it away with her, and "if it's a boy [she] can call it Tom, and if it's a girl [she] can call it Tom" (67). The child is the link between the past and the future. In the end, the sisters realize that the time has come to break the cycle of denial, and Mary decides to help Mommo finish the story. When this is accomplished, tears of mourning for the dead child of the past double as tears of gratitude for the living present; laughter in the face of misfortunes turns into laughter of relief (77). Once the guilt of the past has been exorcized by being put into words and spoken out loud, Mommo no longer needs devious language strategies and addresses Mary by her own name for the first time. The story's end is also the beginning of a new, happier story:

> *Mary.* . . . To conclude. It's a strange old place alright, in whatever wisdom He has to have made it this way. But in whatever wisdom there is, in the year 1984, it was decided to give that—fambly [*sic*] . . . of strangers another chance, and a brand new baby to gladden their home. (77)

Myths can be as liberating as they are confining, but the upbeat ending inevitably raises the question of "whether this is more than a consoling fiction, another false vision which will obscure reality" (O'Dwyer, "Play-Acting and Myth-Making" 40).

Thomas Kilroy writes that anyone looking into the Irish playwriting tradition "is faced with a tri-furcated past with such tenuous connections between the three strands that the very notion of tradition becomes questionable" ("A Generation" 135): the Irish-born playwrights of the eighteenth and nineteenth centuries who turned to London; the small group of Anglo-Irish and mainly Protestant playwrights around Yeats (including Synge); and the writers of the thirties, forties, and fifties, who wrote realistic "peasant plays" from a predominantly Catholic perspective. Kilroy sees his own generation of playwrights, which arrived on the scene in the early sixties and which includes Friel and Murphy, as transitional. Having been born into a traditional culture and seeing it undergo massive change, they faced a problem in bridging the present and the past. A play like *Bailegangaire* fits, on one level, the conventional peasant play of times past, but at the same time, "is something of a hybrid" in that it uses the material "for effects that transcend the material itself" (137). Kilroy suspects that his generation may be the last "with such a sense of continuity with the past, particularly the immediate past" (136). He wrote this in 1992, four years before Martin McDonagh arrived on the scene, and in that light his concluding paragraph is especially interesting:

> A place apart, a place retaining some of the innocence of the pre-modern, a kind of literary environmentalism, a version of greenery, some Irish writing has always answered this appeal, sometimes shamelessly, from readers and audiences outside Ireland. Certain stereotypes of Irish writing and the Irish writer have thereby become entrenched, the Irish writer as roaring boyo, for example, or as untutored, natural genius and Irish writing as a pure, natural flow of words, untouched by a contaminating intelligence. As traditional Ireland fades into the past these stereotypes become even more absurd and are best consigned to pulp fiction. And as it does, nostalgia may no longer be enough, indeed it may not even be necessary as Irish drama begins to locate itself more in the present. (141)

The Irish writer as untutored, natural genius, and traditional Ireland as pulp fiction: Kilroy may not have reckoned with the McDonagh phenomenon, but ironically, he manages to presage and dismiss it at the same time.

Martin McDonagh's brief career (to date) has been extraordinarily triumphant and international in scope. His success story began, however, in the West of Ireland: the plays of the Leenane trilogy (*The Beauty Queen of Leenane, A Skull in Connemara, The Lonesome West*) were first performed in Galway by Druid before they moved on to London and Dublin. In the winter of 1996, Druid took *The Beauty Queen of Leenane* to each of the three Aran Islands; in June 1998, the same play's Broadway production won four Tony Awards. McDonagh's vision, in Michael Billington's words, "is not wholly original. Indeed, he shows a post-modern delight in asking you to recognise his sources. . . . McDonagh constantly plunders the past. But he has a talent for excess, for taking a situation and pushing it to surreal extremes" (26). The intertextual nature of Martin McDonagh's plays is reflected by many of the reviews of his successful Leenane trilogy and of *The Cripple of Inishmaan*. John Peter of the *Sunday Times* asks us to imagine the trilogy as "J. M. Synge's plays rewritten by an Irish Joe Orton," and according to Eileen Battersby in the *Irish Times*, in McDonagh's plays, "a surreal variation of Pinter meets a present-day J. M. Synge." Like Synge and Murphy, McDonagh has provoked controversy. *The Financial Times* dubbed him "the Quentin Tarantino of the Emerald Isle" but called his talent "old-fashioned" and his Ireland "more artificial, more sentimental, more silly, more slow, more melodramatic, and light-years more cute" than the real Ireland (qtd. in Joseph Feeney 24). That kind of criticism of Irish drama has been around since the time of Synge, and Garry Hynes rightly observed that McDonagh is "no more authentic, if you want to use that word, than was Synge, who also mythologised this part of Ireland. It's the imagination of him that counts" (qtd. in J. Feeney 29).

Martin McDonagh grew up in London, but since both his parents are from the West of Ireland, he spent his summer holidays in Connemara. When his parents returned to live there, he stayed behind in London with his older brother. McDonagh left school at sixteen and by his own admission spent most of his time watching television and films; books and theatre were very much secondary influences on his early attempts to write. He claims to come to theatre from "a film fan's perspective" (qtd. in O'Toole, "Nowhere Man"), although the influence of his reading of Borges, Pinter, and Mamet is also apparent, as is that of Beckett (*vide* the title of *A Skull in Connemara*, from Lucky's speech in *Waiting for Godot*). He also read *The Playboy of the Western World* and was amazed by its darkness, and while he claims that he based the rhythm and the structure of the language of his characters on the way his uncles spoke back in Galway, the idiosyncratic Irish flavor of their speech is, at least in its effect, not unlike the poetically artificial Hiberno-English of his theatrical predecessor: "In Connemara and Galway, the natural dialogue style is to invert sentences and use strange inflections. Of course, my stuff is a heightening of that, but there is a core of strangeness of speech, especially in Galway" (qtd. in J. Feeney 28). The association that Synge creates between the West of Ireland and violence, lawlessness, and madness also informs McDonagh's work, and part of the plot of *A Skull in Connemara*, in which a murdered man returns from the dead with blood dripping from his head, only to be hit over the head again, is obviously derived from Synge. In *Playboy*, Michael proclaims that "there's sainted glory this day in the lonesome west" (*J. M. Synge: Plays* 111), thus providing McDonagh with both the title of the third play of his trilogy and an ironic reflection on the appalling lack of "sainted glory" on the part of any of its characters. Given such deliberate echoes, Christina Hunt Mahony believes that McDonagh is more sophisticated in his knowledge of theatre than he admits and that his intention is "not to shock us, but to subvert theatrical memory, with Synge as his easiest and most frequent target" (7).

McDonagh's affinity with Synge, particularly with *Playboy*, then, is undeniable in terms of both the form and content of McDonagh's work, but there are clear differences as well. McDonagh works within a postmodernist framework, and his plays are characterized by the four general symptoms of postmodernism, as listed by Fredric Jameson—the suspension of subjective inwardness, referential depth, historical time, and coherent human expression (Kearney, *The Wake of Imagination* 5). As such, McDonagh's plays have as much in common with films like Quentin Tarantino's *Pulp Fiction* as they do with Synge's *Playboy*. Indeed, critical reactions to *Pulp Fiction* and the Leenane trilogy have been somewhat similar: noting the influences on McDonagh of at least four other writers, Fintan O'Toole nevertheless hailed him as "a true original" ("Début"), just as one reviewer of *Pulp Fiction*, while observing that the film "smacks of the second-hand," went on to say that "this film itself is absolutely new" (Maslin). Like McDonagh's, Tarantino's earlier years were spent surrounded by film and television (Tarantino was a clerk in a video store before he started making films), and the pervasive impact of the image industry on modern life is a crucial factor in both *Pulp Fiction* and the Leenane trilogy.

The relationship between reality and fiction is, of course, a central thematic concern of *The Playboy of the Western World*. Christy Mahon becomes the defender of Pegeen Mike and of her father's public house on the strength of his story that he has killed his father by hitting him over the head with a loy. Encouraged by the warm reception given to murderers and outlaws in this particular township, where "Daneen Sullivan knocked the eye from a peeler" and "Marcus Quin [. . .] got six months for maiming ewes" (*Plays* 108), Christy embroiders on his story until he eventually almost comes to believe it himself; and on the wings of "the power of a lie" (*Plays* 159), he becomes the most successful man in the place, winning the local races as well as the promise of marriage to Pegeen. When his father turns up, the fiction is exposed, and the community, including Pegeen, turns against him; initially Pegeen is angry at having been taken in by "an ugly liar [. . .] playing off the hero and the fright of men" (*Plays* 158), but when Christy attempts to turn fiction into reality by again hitting his father with the loy, she has him tied up and tells him, "I'll say a strange man is a marvel with his mighty talk; but what's a squabble in your back-yard and the blow of a loy, have taught me that there's a great gap between a gallous story and a dirty deed" (*Plays* 161). Christy alone has come to recognize the power of a story to transform reality and to turn him from a coward into "a likely gaffer" (*J. M. Synge: Plays* 163): as Seamus Deane puts it, "in discovering this degree of eloquence he also discovers for the first time a degree of personal identity" ("Irish Theatre" 167). Because all the other characters insist that there is a "great gap" between truth and fiction, however, Christy is expelled from the community, and Pegeen is left disillusioned and alone.

The relationship between truth, imagination, and identity, then, lies at the heart of *Playboy*, the tragedy being, in a sense, that reality fails to live up to the possibilities of the imagination. In McDonagh's plays, however, the relationship between reality, fiction, and identity is much more problematic and reflects a crisis of representation and imagination that is characteristic of much postmodernist drama and fiction. In McDonagh's plays, images of television and film intrude inescapably into the characters' lives, while language has lost the ability to capture reality — if there is such a thing — let alone recreate it. As Richard Kearney points out in *The Wake of Imagination: Toward a Postmodern Culture*, it is almost impossible in a world dominated by the mass media "to contemplate a so-called natural setting, without some consumerist media image lurking in the back of one's mind" (1); in today's world, *pace* Jean Baudrillard, "the image *precedes* the reality it is supposed to represent. Or to put it another way, reality has become a pale reflection of the image" (2). In an artistic climate of reproduction rather than one of "original" creation, where the gap between high art and popular culture has virtually disappeared, we are no longer certain "who exactly produces or controls the images which condition our consciousness. We are at an impasse where the very rapport between *imagination* and *reality* seems not only inverted but subverted altogether. We cannot be sure which is which" (3).

McDonagh's plays have this quality about them. They are set in the West of Ireland, or rather, in a familiar image of the West of Ireland; his characters have names like Johnnypateenmike and Maryjohnny; they live in cottages, burn turf, and drink poteen; they are surrounded by farm implements, crucifixes, holy statues, and pictures of the Kennedys; and they have relatives who work in England or America. This Ireland is a stereotype built around traditional clichés, a throwback untouched by even the feeblest of Celtic Tigers. This anachronistic setting is juxtaposed with the media world of pop culture that invades it through the television screen: there are references to Australian and American soaps, Bugs Bunny, *The Quiet Man*, *Star Wars*, *Hill Street Blues*, *Alias Smith and Jones*, and Eurovision Song Contest winner Dana. Few if any of these media references are contemporary, however, and their datedness suggests a television world of endless reruns. On all levels of reality or fiction, then, McDonagh's world is stuck in an image of the past and unable to move beyond it.

In *The Beauty Queen of Leenane*, the television is on at the beginning of the two scenes with Mag and Ray, in the middle of the day; in the first scene, it shows an old episode of *The Sullivans*, in the second, an episode of *Sons and Daughters*. Mag is not watching: she is waiting for the news (the real world) to come on. Ray is waiting for Maureen, and he becomes increasingly frustrated when she does not appear. Bored with the next show, *A Country Practice*, he switches the television off. Irritated, he tells Mag, "A whole afternoon I'm wasting here. (*Pause.*) When I could be at home watching telly" (40). Television is an escape from the boredom of reality, and the Australian shows appeal to Ray because "Everybody's always killing each other and a lot of the girls do have swimsuits" (37). This in contrast to Ireland: "Who wants to see Ireland on telly? . . . All you have to do is look out your window to see Ireland. And it's soon bored you'd be. 'There goes a calf'" (53). Yet in McDonagh's Leenane, people are constantly betraying, framing, torturing, and murdering each other when they are not mutilating dogs, destroying each other's property, or killing themselves. The "reality" of Leenane is nothing like *A Country Practice* and everything like *Sons and Daughters*: Ray is living in a soap opera world, but he is unable to see it, because it does not conform to his image of Ireland.

Thomas Hanlon, the ineffective guard in *A Skull in Connemara*, perpetually tries and fails to live up to the police image created by television.

His brother Mairtin accuses him behind his back of believing "he's Starsky and Hutch" (46), and Mairtin derisively calls Thomas *"Macmillan and Wife"* to his face (60). When Thomas complains about the job of supervising the grave-digging, Mick counters, "I thought the way you do talk about it, just like *Hill Street Blues* your job is. Bodies flying about everywhere" (29). Thomas counters that he "would *like* there to be bodies flying about everywhere, but there never is" (29) — disregarding the fact that he lives in what Father Welsh in *The Lonesome West* calls "the murder capital of fecking Europe" (34). His real interest, Thomas claims, is in detective work, "like *Quincy*" (29): "going hunting down clues, and never letting a case drop no matter what the odds stacked against you, no matter how many years old. . . . Like *Petrocelli*" (57).

Thomas, however, is a postmodernist example of an anti-detective; the difference between circumstantial evidence and hearsay has to be explained to him by the man he is trying to incriminate, and rather than solving the three blatant murders in Leenane, he clumsily attempts to fabricate evidence against Mick in order to implicate him in the murder of his wife, only to be found out and betrayed by his own brother Mairtin. In *The Lonesome West*, Thomas ends up drowning himself in the lake. Fittingly, Valene and Coleman can only respond to the tragic death of Thomas, a real person of their acquaintance, by relating it to a media image, which immediately comes to dominate the conversation, to the exclusion of Thomas. According to Father Welsh, Thomas is now in hell, that being the fate of every suicide in Catholic doctrine:

> *Valene.* Well I didn't know that. That's a turn-up for the books. (*Pause.*) So
>   the fella from *Alias Smith and Jones*, he'd be in hell?
> *Welsh.* I don't know the fella from *Alias Smith and Jones*.
> *Valene.* Not the blond one, now, the other one.
> *Welsh.* I don't know the fella.
> *Valene.* He killed himself, and at the height of his fame.
> *Welsh.* Well if he killed himself, aye, he'll be in hell too. . . .
> *Valene.* That sounds awful harsh. (*Pause.*) So Tom'll be in hell now, he will?
>   Jeez. (*Pause.*) I wonder if he's met the fella from *Alias Smith and Jones*
>   yet? Ah, that fella must be old be now. Tom probably wouldn't even
>   recognise him. That's if he saw *Alias Smith and Jones* at all. I only saw
>   it in England. It mightn't've been on telly here at all. (26)

In the Leenane trilogy, reality always loops back into popular media images; it is merely a reflection of old television reruns, just as art in the postmodern era is no longer "a leap into the Future but a replay of quotations from the Past" (Kearney, *The Wake of Imagination* 25) — in McDonagh's case, quotations from cultural icons like Synge.

The prevalence of the image results in a lack of emotional depth; this is particularly apparent in the language crisis from which McDonagh's characters suffer. All speak in short, paratactic sentences and are prone to repetition, banal pronouncements, and stating the obvious:

> *Mary.* Mick.
> *Mick.* Maryjohnny.
> *Mary.* Cold.
> *Mick.* I suppose it's cold.
> *Mary.* Cold, aye. It's turning.
> *Mick.* Is it turning?
> *Mary.* It's turning now, Mick. The summer is going. (*A Skull in Connemara* 3)

Without a stable, meaningful world in which context can act as a guide to interpretation, simple words turn into potential booby traps. When Mairtin, in *A Skull in Connemara*, rants on about Thomas digging up Mick's wife, his brother eventually asks him, "Are you finished, Mairtin?" whereupon Mairtin pauses and asks, confused, "Am I Finnish?" (61). The treacherous surface of words keeps drawing attention to itself and hence prevents true depth of feeling. After Thomas's funeral in *The Lonesome West*, Father Welsh asks, "Did you ever hear such crying, Valene?," and the latter answers,

> *Valene.* You could've filled a lake with the tears that family cried. Or a russaway at minimum.
> *Welsh.* (*Pause*) A wha?
> *Valene.* A russaway. One of them russaways.
> *Welsh.* Reservoir?
> *Valene.* Russaway, aye. (24)

A detachment between signifier and signified also affects the identity of the characters. In the Leenane trilogy this is apparent in the perpetual confusion over names. In *The Beauty Queen*, Mag confuses Ray Dooley with his brother Pato, as does Maureen later on. Ray himself has trouble remembering the name of Pato's new fiancée:

> *Ray.* It won't be much of a change for her anyways, from Hooley to Dooley. Only one letter. The "h." That'll be a good thing. (*Pause.*) Unless it's Healey that she is. I can't remember. (*Pause.*) If it's Healey, it'll be three letters. The "h," the "e" and the "a." (57)

Nobody ever gets Father Welsh's name right because, as Girleen tells him, "It's just Walsh is so close to Welsh, Father" (36). The religious conventionality of Girleen's real name, Mary, makes her cringe, because "Mary's the name of the mammy of Our Lord. . . . It's the reason she never got anywhere for herself" (36–37), the suggestion being that she "never got anywhere" because her name was Mary rather than because she was Christ's mother. Father Welsh's unusual first name merely draws attention to itself, not to the personality or the convictions of its bearer. When the priest kills himself in despair, Valene and Coleman resolve to honor his last wishes, but even as they do so, Valene asks his brother, "Did you see 'Roderick' his name is?," and Coleman snorts in derision (50).

Because in McDonagh's plays language is detached from any underlying or inherent psychological or moral reality, social and moral conventions become mere games to play: they have certain superficial formal rules that can be followed and abandoned at will. As Berger and Luckmann put it in *The Social Construction of Reality*,

> A society in which discrepant worlds are generally available on a market basis entails specific constellations of subjective reality and identity. There will be an increasingly general consciousness of the relativity of *all* worlds, including one's own, which is now subjectively apprehended as "*a* world," rather than "*the* world." It follows that one's own institutionalized conduct may be apprehended as "a role" from which one may detach oneself in one's own consciousness, and which one may "act out" with manipulative control. (192)

We see this when Coleman and Valene decide to honor Father Welsh's last request to list all the wrongs they have done each other over the years and to forgive each other for them. They begin apologizing and forgiving, and Valene soon concludes that "This is a great oul game, this is, apologising" (53). Before long, the game turns into a bidding war, with Coleman telling Valene, "I'm winning" (57) and "You're too slow" (58). Valene counters with a particularly heinous crime and asks his brother to "top that one" (60): Coleman does and they nearly end up killing each other. Having concluded the apologizing game, they decide that they like a good fight, because "It does show you care, fighting does. That's what oul sissy Welsh doesn't understand" (67).

Because the characters are confused about language, identity, and values, they tend to invest their emotional capital in consumer items and in the concrete, unchanging reality of inanimate objects. In *The Cripple of Inishmaan*, for example, Bartley (another echo from Synge) cares more about Mintos, Yella-mallows, and Fripple-Frapples than about the fact that Billy is still alive after his American adventure. In *The Beauty Queen*, Mag's world revolves around soup, porridge, and the lumps in the Complan she hates, and she is prepared to betray her daughter to maintain this tedious but reliable routine. In the middle of a fight, during which Maureen revels in the idea of her mother's death and Mag gloats at her daughter's perpetual virginity, they manage to argue about the relative merits of Kimberley biscuits. In *The Lonesome West*, Valene may be guilty of the murder, mayhem, and miserliness of which Father Welsh accuses him, but he possesses forty-six holy figurines, and he is "sure to be getting into heaven with this many figurines" in his house (43). Valene cares little for his own life, that of his brother, his father, or Father Welsh, but he nearly cries when Coleman threatens to crush a packet of Tayto crisps worth 17 p., and he is positively heartbroken when Coleman blows his expensive stove to smithereens and smashes his holy statuettes. For this reason, it is difficult to see Valene's inability to burn Father Welsh's letter at the end of the play, and his careful arrangement of the letter on the crucifix with Girleen's heart-shaped pendant, as being indicative of anything more profound than his obsession with the preservation and surface value of material objects.

In *The Playboy of the Western World*, the moral is located within the play and the characters ("there's a great gap between a gallous story and a dirty deed"), but Synge's manipulation of his audience's response problematizes the issue. As Christopher Murray has argued, in the opening scene of the *Playboy*, "nobody on stage picks up on the incongruities in Christy's language. The absurdity of a law-abiding murderer is left for the audience to perceive." Shawn Keogh, the only one to express moral scruples and to protest Christy's appointment as pot-boy, is ridiculed and discredited as a despicable coward. "Thus the audience's orthodox moral position, which would normally incline towards Shawn's, is undercut and the audience is left little choice but to rejoice with the others on stage at Christy's disclosure. A moral issue is brazenly made fun of and the audience is implicated in the conspiracy. This technique is used repeatedly" (*Twentieth-Century Irish Drama* 85). In McDonagh's trilogy, audience manipulation is pushed a step further. McDonagh shifts the moral center from the play to the audience; the plays are effective only because they rely on the audience to be able to perceive and feel what the characters do not. We know we are watching a gallous story about dirty deeds, and we know that there is something wrong with this world. Perhaps influenced by Borges's brand of postmodernism, McDonagh presents a distorted world in which characters are imprisoned, but this very distortion, in Gerald Graff's words, "implicitly affirms a concept of the normal, if only as a concept which has been tragically lost" (qtd. in Bertens 39). The characters are largely unaware of the difference between the mundane and the meaningful, the trivial and the tragic — and the only ones with a sense of morality kill themselves in despair — but we are not unaware. We recognize the symbolism behind the crucifix and the heart, even if Valene does not. We may laugh at the ludicrous incongruity of smashing the skulls of the dearly departed with a mallet to the tune of Dana's "All Kinds of Everything" (a method used, incidentally, by Jeffrey Dahmer to destroy the evidence of his crimes) or of killing your father because he criticized your hairstyle and trod on your Scalectrix when you were eight, just as we laugh in spite of ourselves in *Pulp Fiction* when Vincent and Jules squabble about cleaning up the mess in the car after Vincent accidentally shoots Marvin in the head. But we recognize the appalling and inappropriate nature of these deeds. As John Peter puts it, laughter in the face of such events "is both unsettling and liberating: a combination of terror and the sense of relief that lurks in all comedy that all this is happening to other people."

If there is one thing we share with the plays' characters, it is a degree of uncertainty. The ambiguity of the plays' events leaves the audience with many questions. Did Maureen really have a last-minute reconciliation with Pato at the train station (where they kissed "like they do in films" [51]), as she believes, or do we believe Ray's version, in which there was no reconciliation (Pato left by taxi and has since become engaged to Dolores Healey/Hooley)? Or did Ray make this up in revenge for Maureen's confiscation of his tennis ball all those years ago? Did Mick really kill Oona? At the end of *A Skull in Connemara*, Mick swears he did not kill his wife while rubbing Oona's skull against his cheek, *"trying to remember"* what really happened (66); at the end of *The Beauty Queen*, Maureen responds in a dazed manner to Ray's accusations that she is "a fecking loon" (58) and begins to fall into the same irritating habits as her hated mother whom she killed with a poker. In an incoherent world, confusion is not an ignoble condition; in the case of McDonagh's characters, it is their only saving grace.

Confusion and ambiguity are central to McDonagh's dramatic aims, and he admits to finding them more interesting than "choosing a strict path and following it" (O'Toole, "Nowhere Man"). The epistemological doubts he raises in his plays also inform his artistic method and raise the question of whether the means are ultimately different from the end: "Do not the very postmodern efforts to contest the dominance of a fetishized system of representation themselves fall victim to the system? Do they not confirm, despite themselves, the culture of pastiche they intend to mock?" (Kearney, *The Wake of Imagination* 32). In McDonagh's case, the answer depends on the extent to which one is willing to read beyond the surface of the plays and construct a meaning for them. Richard Harris refused to do so, proclaiming *The Beauty Queen* to be "Irish cliché after cliché. An old story rehashed rather badly" (qtd. in Dening). *The Village Voice* reviewer had much the same opinion of *The Cripple of Inishmaan*, seeing its islanders merely as "updated stage Oirishmen" (qtd. in Mulkerns). Most positive reviews, however, see the plays, particularly the trilogy, as postmodernist, postcolonialist critiques of the human condition in general and of the Irish condition in particular. Michael Billington sees the characters all as victims, "of history, of climate and of rural Ireland's peculiar tension between a suffocating, mythical past and the banalities of the global village where American soaps hold sway." John Peter takes a similar view in which Ireland, as one of those countries that was "battered, colonised, exploited, corrupt or insecure," produces plays "of conscience and self-examination," asking questions such as, "Who are we as a nation? Have we an identity?" Maria Tymoczko sees the themes of "image and reality, abuser and abused" in these plays as "timely analogues of the national Irish discourse at present: What is it to be really Irish? How does this image relate to the reality?" (16).

These are interesting readings, given that McDonagh describes himself in an interview with Fintan O'Toole as "somewhere kind of in-between" Irish and English and as "not into any kind of definition, any kind of -ism, politically, socially, religiously, all that stuff" ("Nowhere Man"). This does not stop Fintan O'Toole himself from reading the trilogy as, on the one hand, "the culmination of a long demythologisation of the West" (and, hence, "a final reversal of Romanticism") and, on the other, "a version of one of the great mythic landscapes — the world before morality. It is the ancient Greece of The Oresteia — a cycle of death and revenge before the invention of justice," as well as "the wild west [. . .] a raw frontier beyond civilisation" ("Murderous Laughter"). McDonagh himself dislikes too much analysis: " 'All I want to do,' he once said, 'is to tell stories' " (qtd. in J. Feeney 27). So far, McDonagh's lack of definition appears to have benefited from critics who were all too willing to provide meanings for his ambiguities; given his phenomenal success under these circumstances, one can understand why he would hope that he could "just continue with the stories rather than achieve some kind of position where you feel you have to say something" (O'Toole, "Nowhere Man").

Storytelling as a "Western" device is what ties Synge, Murphy, and McDonagh together, but through that device, each dramatist reflects the concerns and anxieties of his age. As a precursor to modernism, Synge is aware that identity is not a stable given but rather a construct. Central to his work is a concern with the transformative qualities of language: telling stories is both a way of facing the self in all its aspects and a way of transforming the self. As Declan Kiberd puts it, there is violence in Pegeen, "as in many persons, and it has not been assuaged by the gallous story: this becomes clear when she lights a sod of turf to cripple her former lover. [. . .] Emphasizing this scene, the original production underscored Synge's brilliant insight: that those who make rhetorical denials of their own violence invariably end up committing even more" (*Synge and the Irish Language* 171). Tom Murphy's plays also focus on identity, but they do so in a more intensely personal way: they are concerned with psychological crisis and breakdown and with the overcoming of that crisis. Harry, in *The Sanctuary Lamp*, wants "Someone to talk to" (10), and Francisco reminds him of "the talking we used to do in bed in the old days . . . one big bed" (75); the man who knocks on JPW King's door in *The Gigli Concert* wants "To talk. . . . To sing" (3); Mommo in *Bailegangaire* wants to finish the story of her guilt. The transition to healing is marked by storytelling, speaking out, or giving voice in song, which is "yourself alive in time. . . . Great singing is prayer" (O'Toole, "Tribune Portrait"). By contrast, McDonagh's postmodernism does not allow for such healing transformations: if language and identity are at the center of his plays, it is because language and identity themselves are in crisis. For McDonagh, storytelling is not a means but an end in itself: "We're all here and we have our time on earth. The Brothers Grimm had their time and they left these stories behind them. Leaving little things behind that nobody else could is much more interesting than saying things in general about human nature which most people can do if they try" (qtd. in J. Feeney 345).

For Synge, Murphy, and McDonagh, being a playwright of the Western world does not involve representing its "simplicity, nobility, and endurance": rather, their focus on the West of Ireland as a locus of displacement from the center and the norm allows them to act as agent provocateurs in the national debate. What makes them part of a "Western" tradition is an attitude of contrariness to accepted pieties and an ability to use the Irish arts of controversy and conversation ("arranged," in Lady Gregory's phrase, as drama and myth-making) to raise questions about the representation of identity, including Irish national identity.

—14—

The Passion Machine Theatre
Company's Everyday Life

LAUREN ONKEY

In his introduction to *Brownbread* and *War!*, the plays he wrote for the Passion Machine Theatre Company, Roddy Doyle recounts the night he first saw Paul Mercier's *Wasters* in 1985 at the SFX Centre, a "smelly old hall behind Cranby Row." He describes the surprise and joy he felt upon watching familiar characters on stage:

> [. . .] for the first time in my life I saw characters I recognised, people I met every day, the language I heard every day. It was like watching an old cine-film; I could point out people I knew and remember them saying what they said. The way they dressed, walked, held their cans of lager — it was all very familiar. I'll never forget it. (1)

Doyle goes on to distinguish the space of the SFX from that of traditional theatres: the SFX Centre "wasn't a theatre. It was used for heavy-metal gigs, bingo, martial arts competition, talent shows, civil service exams, auctions, Irish dancing. It had none of the things we expect to see in a good theatre — clean toilets, spacious bars, young men and women dressed in black talking meaningful shite during the intermission" (1). Because the SFX was imbedded in everyday life experience, he argues, it freed theatre from elitist associations and made it available to those viewers who weren't speaking "meaningful shite."

Passion Machine's critical reception similarly celebrates their representation of authentic real-life or "everyday" experiences and the non-traditional theatre audiences it has attracted. In a review of *Spacers* (1986), a writer for *The Sunday Tribune* described Mercier as "an explorer of a world that has been all but written out of Irish literature and theatre" ("A Voice" 19). In a review of the rock musical *Drowning* (1984), Thomas Myler echoed Doyle's comments about the lack of typical theatrical trappings in a Passion Machine project: "It means you don't get a glossy theatrical production but what you lose there, you gain in being able to participate with the comedy of real life." Other responses emphasize the importance of the new audiences that the Passion Machine brought to the theatre. Francine Cunningham's 1990 description of Passion Machine's achievement is typical: "The company's popular success with plays about everyday Dublin life [. . .] has won for it an audience that does not usually frequent the theatre [. . .]. The Passion Machine has helped put contemporary Dublin back into Irish theatre" (8). In a survey of developments in the theatre in 1989, Anthony Roche trumpeted Passion Machine's effect on Dublin's theatrical "apartheid": "The Passion Machine, a group from North Dublin which has done much to draw a nontraditional audience, scored with *War!* by Roddy Doyle [. . .] With *War!* which takes the arena of pub quizzes as its site of conflict, the Passion Machine breached Dublin apartheid by transferring southside to the Olympia Theatre and holding it against all comers" ("Against Nostalgia" 114). By the early 1990s, Passion Machine's reputation as a theatre of the everyday was well established.

Paul Mercier formed the Passion Machine Theatre Company in 1983 with John Sutton and John Donne. They have produced seventeen plays since then, ten of which were staged at the SFX Centre and eight of which were written and directed by Mercier. The company became successful enough that by 1988, Mercier was able to quit his job as a schoolteacher and work with the theatre full time.[1] In interviews, Mercier uses the term "everyday life" like a mantra to describe Passion Machine's project: "I'm trying to create a theatre that reflects, celebrates and comments on everyday life as it is. It is indigenous in every respect, from ourselves, about ourselves, for ourselves" (Cunningham 8). He argues further that theatre can function like a social service, but only if it is indigenous, accessible, and "popular":

> Theatre should be doing something for people, liberating them and helping them come to terms with aspects of their lives. [. . .] So many influences from abroad have crept into our culture. We are trying to create our own heroes at home and we have begun to do that on a popular, not an elitist, level. [. . .] We don't go in for high drama, high art, political drama, obscure drama, foreign work. Our main aim is to develop a theatre that is about what we think is important in everyday life. (Cunningham 8)

He asserts, as did Doyle, that such experience was previously unavailable on the Irish stage: "We wanted plays that were relevant, entertaining and reflecting Modern Irish society as it hadn't been reflected before" (Hickey). He wears the commitment to representing "the everyday" like a badge of honor, thereby aligning himself with people who don't go in for high culture. In 1988, for example, he told Colin Kerr: "If theatre is going to be important, it should reflect the lives of people. That's what we're aiming for. [. . .] If you take your ordinary punter who comes to see a play, he or she does not think of alternative theatre, does not think of fringe, doesn't even think of the Dublin Theatre Festival. They just come to be entertained, to see something about themselves" (Kerr).

At the same time that he privileges such "simple" values, Mercier also establishes complex and contradictory terms for Passion Machine: to be a social service in people's liberation yet not to go in for "political drama"; to represent indigenous Irish life that is deeply influenced by Western pop culture but to resist "foreign influences."[2] Certainly part of the motivation behind Mercier's rhetoric originates in his desire to establish street credibility. But, less cynically, it can also be argued that by valuing a notion of the "everyday," Mercier attempts to refine a theatrical practice that is not already overdetermined by Irish nationalist theatre and its sometimes cumbersome notions of "Irishness" and "nation." Mercier defines the "everyday" as residing outside the discourses of politics and art, and, therefore, as a naturally liberating force. Alan Read defines the everyday in similar terms in *Theatre and Everyday Life: An Ethics of Performance:* "There is no 'language' or single critical stance associated with everyday life, it is precisely a term which is thought to be outside the domain of specialist vocabulary and is therefore the milieu which is least likely to conceal the object under scrutiny with its own historically mediated languages" (106). This notion of the everyday as an escape from politics and other "historically mediated languages" is a problematic one. Terms such as "indigenous" and "ordinary punter," as well as an audience's desire for authenticity, are deeply imbedded in many ideological discourses, including the national. In this essay, I want to analyze Passion Machine's construction of "the everyday" in three plays: Doyle's *Brownbread* (1987) and *War!* (1989), and Mercier's *Buddleia* (1995). I plan to address the following questions: What constitutes "the everyday" for Passion Machine? Whose everyday experience does Passion Machine recreate? How is their "real Dublin" created/articulated/celebrated? What is the cultural work, the "social service," as Mercier would put it, that such a deployment of "the everyday" achieves?

Early Passion Machine: Pop Culture and Community

In some of the earliest Passion Machine productions, such as *Studs, Wasters, Brownbread,* and *War!,* Passion Machine defined "everyday" experience as participation in popular culture practices such as football teams, pub quiz games, and rock-and-roll fandom.[3] Communities are constituted by characters' participation in these practices, which are not marked as particularly "Irish." Mercier's and Doyle's characters thus define themselves not by religion or politics, traditional subject-positions in Irish drama, but rather by their engagement with "the popular." O'Toole argues that such use of the popular complicates Passion Machine's reputation as a "realist" theatre company; he says that Mercier has found forms "which break down almost completely the distinction between the real and the imagined, ways of moving and acting on stage that makes [sic] the dreams real and visible" ("'Studs' Scores Again in the Replay"). These plays suggest that people — especially men — live their "everyday" lives through television, sports, and music. The plays do not create an opposition between mediated experience and authentic experience, as in Martin McDonagh's plays (discussed in José Lanters's essay in this volume); mediated experience in these Passion Machine plays is authentic experience.

For example, in *Studs*, the weekend soccer players move on stage as if they are part of a slow-motion television replay; during the quiz show in *War!*, a televised boxing match suddenly frames the scene. In his introduction to *War!*, Doyle describes how he consumed "real" news only as a means to win the pub quiz: "For about a year I read the papers and watched The News only with next Monday in mind. There was a volcano in Columbia [sic]; I didn't give a shite about the dead, I just wanted to remember the name of the mountain" ("Introduction" 2). What is recognizably real and "everyday," therefore, is the characters' engagement with the popular practices of a post-nationalist, urban Ireland (there are almost no references to an Ireland outside of Dublin in Passion Machine's work), where the corporation kids do not participate in economic booms. Most obviously, viewers and critics recognize the language of Mercier's and Doyle's characters as authentic contemporary North Dublin vernacular. In his review of *Wasters*, O'Toole describes Mercier's language as "a densely woven texture of slang, vulgarity, metaphor and wisecrack that establishes the world of the corporation better than any amount of 'realistic' setting and design" ("Lives of Noisy Desperation"). But Passion Machine does not simply get the accents or the jokes right. Their characters' speech is also drenched in references to popular culture, especially sports, pop music, and American television.[4] In *Brownbread*, for example, three young guys kidnap a bishop and rely on a pastiche of American television and politics for their dialogue: "Book him, Danno! Hands against the wall, mutherfucker" (83). In his analysis of Doyle's fiction, Gerry Smyth describes Doyle's characters as "poised between total immersion in the local and invocation of a multinational, postmodern world. [. . .] much of the experience of working-class life on housing estates on the edge of a big city like Dublin cannot be explained with reference to Ireland or Irishness" (*Novel and Nation* 70). The same can be said for Doyle's and Mercier's early plays. Paradoxically, postmodern, international culture is recognized as most "real" by the audience and critics of this "indigenous" theatre company. And their work celebrates Ireland's participation in such a culture.

Although Passion Machine's early work conveys hipness, comedy, and a less limiting national identity, their plays do not simply celebrate a new postmodern Irish self. At their best, these plays function as an important method of critiquing the effects of economic conditions, church, and family structure in contemporary Dublin.[5]

In *Brownbread* (1987), one of Passion Machine's wildest and funniest plays, three nineteen-year-old boys who live in corporation homes in Barrytown kidnap a bishop and hold him hostage for several days — for no particular reason.[6] Their boredom is funny, exciting, and frightening. After a decade of Irish clerical scandals, we may miss the thrill or freshness of a bishop being attacked in this way.[7] But a blindfolded bishop, whom the boys — and the audience — taunt throughout the play is a powerful anti-clerical joke. More than anything else, the bishop seems irrelevant to the boys' lives; he has no physical or moral power over them.

The play simultaneously suggests that economic conditions cause the boys' behavior and mocks such a simple explanation (one boy could go to university if he wanted to, for example).

The bishop asks, "But d'you mind me asking—. Why did you, eh, kidnap me?"

Ao. "Well, we had the gun, an' you were in Barrytown doin' the confirmations, an' there was nothin' on the telly; yeh know, snooker or cricket—" (40).

"So, Ao, you did it because you had nothing else to do. Is that right?"

Ao. "No; not really" (40).

The bishop looks lost. He likes the idea that they're bored because it gives him some sort of plausible explanation for the kidnapping. But the boys deny that their actions are a result of unemployment. They try to explain to him that they just want thrills: "Did yeh ever rob ann'thin'?" Ao asks him (42), and they get the bishop to admit to robbing apples; Ao says, "it was great, wasn't it?" (43).

It turns out that the bishop is American, and his kidnapping causes a hilarious U.S. invasion, carried out to The Doors' "The End"; the news announces that "Reports are coming in that an advance force of United States Marines has occupied Bull Island in Dublin Bay. Earlier today President Reagan, speaking from the White House, said that America could not and would not stand by and watch Americans being mauled by Libyan-backed agents of terror" (45). The army destroys the Barrytown community center, and when the Americans realize their mistake, Reagan stages an international broadcast with the boys, sponsored by Budweiser. The boys prove to be expert at staging and manipulating a media event. After the invasion, they reposition the bishop in front of the window, with his arms spread out, covering as much of the window as possible. After telling Reagan to "fuck off" on the air, the boys release the bishop and describe the event as "brilliant crack." The "brilliance" of the event for the boys, their pleasure and sense of identity, is the creation of a media event, complete with radio and television coverage, crowds, and chip vendors. The play celebrates this rollicking everyday life.

In *War!*, Doyle uses a pub quiz to dramatize tensions within a family that arise over money, authority, and, especially, challenges to a father's masculinity.[8] There is tension between two different kinds of "everyday" experience here. The play takes place in The Hiker's Rest (also called "The Gaza Strip" by its patrons) and in the kitchen of one of the quiz show players, George Finnegan. The pub, a modern place where Budweiser, Heineken, and fancy mixed drinks are as popular as Guinness, is the site of arguments, flirtations, drunkenness, jokes — in short, a place of vitality. The quiz tests participants on pop music, world history, and sports — typical "trivia" without much specific reference to Ireland or Irish culture. In contrast, the kitchen scenes between George and his wife Briget are cramped, tense, and violent. The pub scenes feature violence, too, but that violence is for entertainment purposes and does not, therefore, cause the serious consequences that Briget faces. It is in the kitchen that we discover George's financial problems: though he now has a job (after being on the dole), he still has trouble paying the children's school registration fees. As in Doyle's other works, the pub is a social site for young women, divorced women, and men of all ages, but it is not a place for wives and mothers (except during important football matches). Briget wants to be asked to play for George's quiz team, and her skill at crossword puzzles, which she works on constantly in the kitchen, suggests that she would be a useful member of the team, but George does not want her. Sports and games create community and provide escape from the responsibilities and tensions of family — the other kind of everyday life; therefore, if Briget were to join the team, she would break down the distinction between those worlds for George. His pub quiz competition and pitch and putt games must remain in a public, masculine world in order to retain their importance. Writing about Mercier's *Studs*, Fintan O'Toole notes the connection in that play between everyday local sporting activity and male identity: "The carefully balanced pun in the play's title, linking football and male sexual fantasy, says it all. It is about the irony that those who have little to lose have most riding on the need to win, even if the win is only in a football match" ("'*Studs*' Scores Again in the Replay"). The same issues are at work in *War!*. Winning at the quiz war gives George some sense of mastery, which he feels is under siege everywhere else. (Interestingly, his winnings from the games are domestic items: Christmas turkeys from the pitch and putt, a teakettle from the pub quiz.)

Most of the time, George is a joking man, but he often erupts in violence at both the pub (when he fears the team will lose) and at home (when Briget asserts herself). He fights bitterly with his friend Bertie over the quiz, and he nearly strangles Leo, the bartender, over his demand for the master of ceremonies to reread a question. The battle between George and Bertie's team gets more heated, until Bertie calls George "a fuckin' eejit, compadre," and George declares, "It's not a game anymore, lads. This is war, righ'. War!" (165). But the violence at the pub is played for laughs; the violence at home is deadly serious.

Briget, always onstage in the kitchen while action is taking place in the pub, works her crossword puzzles and has begun to write a journal. There is some communication in the kitchen—in particular, a warm discussion about boyfriends between Briget and her daughter Yvonne—but Briget is not part of any real sense of community. George enters her space, the kitchen, to practice his quiz answers and to ask Briget to sew a button on his shirt. But primarily he functions as a threat to her: he gets jealous when he comes in and finds her talking with a young neighbor, Tommy; when they argue, he pins her to her seat, brandishes a golf club for a moment, and shouts: "I'll kill yeh; I'll split your fuckin' head for yeh!" (190). Everyday life for Briget means a constant threat of violence.[9] Briget stands up to George, describing his violence as a way to prevent her from acting on her own: "It's always the same. [. . .] Always, it is. When I wanted tha' job. When—when I wanted to go to Liverpool with the girls. When I did tha' English night class. (Triumphantly.) An' I passed it, yeh bastard. Even when I just have a bit o' crack with someone else, yeh put me down" (191).

The scenes between George and Briget are interspersed with the pub quiz scenes, but they have all taken place during the week before the quiz begins. It appears, then, that George brings a great deal of pent-up violence to the quiz. At the end of the play, after George has won the war and his kettle, Briget cowers at home, petitioning for divine intervention: "Please God, he didn't lose again. Please" (215). While the quiz scenes provide humor and community, the scenes with Briget suggest that the fun (even the fun of "*War!*") at the pub, is a desperate escape from "the everyday." The divisions George has created between the two worlds have undermined his marriage and driven him to violence. The play finally questions the ideology of the male "everyday life" of war.

Passion Machine Leaves the SFX: Paul Mercier's Buddleia

In Paul Mercier's more recent work, he has kept the "authentic" language and Dublin settings, but he has more overtly addressed urban social concerns. Everyday life has gotten more serious and more mundane. His "Dublin Trilogy"—*Buddleia* (1995), *Kitchensink* (1996), and *Native City* (1998)—depicts the problems of contemporary Dublin's housing "development."[10] Christopher Murray notes that the theme of home runs throughout Mercier's work (and the work of other such "Northside realists" as Doyle and Dermot Bolger): "It is this sense of home, nostalgic but problematic, which unites Mercier's work with that of many of his young contemporaries. There is a search for re-definition of place, a destination for a new kind of pilgrim in Irish society" (*Twentieth-Century Irish Drama* 242).

Relations between people in a communal space, and the use of that space, constitute everyday life in *Buddleia*. The play takes place entirely in the basement/downstairs floor of an old terraced artisan house in Dublin's north inner city. After the owner of the house dies at the beginning of the play (from a heart attack brought on by a robbery), the house becomes an ever-changing "home" for an impermanent and decayed city life: a political campaign, drug deals, a rave. The play is performed in one act with fifteen scenes, each of which contains different characters.

The play is named after a shrub that grows especially well on waste ground. Moran, a real estate developer, explains how it grows: "Feed it a bag of cement and you'll know all about it. It'll get up and walk" (49). Moran tells a story about a failed car park deal; when he goes to clear the land three years later, he finds more buddleia than rubble: "you couldn't see the rubble anymore. All you saw was this thing. . . with flowers to beat the band. And it's been followin' me ever since" (50). The buddleia functions as a symbol for the community: can anything productive or healthy grow in an environment in which "real estate" seems the only marker of value? Do these disparate characters share any sense of community outside of the physical space of the dilapidated house? Is buddleia a symbol of possible rebirth or just a pretty gas station built on top of the decay?

Mercier uses a series of birth and death scenes to pose this last question and the urban legend which runs throughout the play: the story of Jordan, a young homeless boy who is hanging around the house. The play opens with an old man who finds himself being robbed by two "youths" who threaten to "shove a needle in [his] fuckin' neck" (3) if he doesn't give up his money. Jordan is a friend of the old man, and he is forced by the youths to help with the robbery. After this scene, Frank Sinatra's "Rain (Falling from the Skies)" plays, as it will throughout, reminding the audience that it is indeed raining in every scene. The song, a beautiful ballad, sets a dark, melancholy, and sentimental tone of loss.

Wasted lives are everywhere. John, the old man's son, who is home for the funeral, and his ex-wife Ruth discuss their wayward son, a "waster" who is currently knocking around Europe, his whereabouts unknown. The mother is pregnant with another child, a sign of new possibility or simply a marker of new buddleia. Hannah, the neighbor who found the old man, comes by and meets John, and they reminisce about the old man's experiences during the war. John asks Hannah when various neighbors left: "I know who lives there now. As you can see he gave up on the garden. And these houses beyond have been bought up to make way for the new road" (25). The house has no future as a family residence, as it will be the site for a new road. Like the old man, the neighborhood is being robbed and killed.

In the next scene, Kernaghan, the estate agent at the center of the new real estate economy, appears, as he will in several scenes, displaying his power and importance. Kernaghan is meeting with Jane, John's sister, about the potential sale of their father's house; she emphasizes how much work her father did to add unique individual features to the house, while Kernaghan insists that such things don't matter now that the neighborhood has declined. He tells her, "Look, you have to be realistic. There are flats either side of you. There is a major road a hundred yards away. And this is a bad locality and it's not getting any better. Any auctioneer is going to tell you the same" (30). Kernaghan wants to buy the house himself and rent it out to young single mothers or crack addicts, because "the state takes good care of its dependents" (47).

To underscore the importance of land development in the play, Passion Machine included in its program for the "Dublin Trilogy" performance reprints of a 1987 *Irish Times* article on re-zoning in Dublin, in which Frank McDonald decries the kind of urban planning that wipes out neighborhoods like *Buddleia's*:

> Is there no way of halting the relentless sprawl of Dublin? Certainly not if we are to leave it in the hands of local councilors whose apparent rush to rezone every piece of land in sight — at the behest of landowners intent on making windfall gains — appears unstoppable. Week after week, or so it seems, more agricultural land on the city's periphery falls prey to this frenzy of rezoning. Fortunes are made by the beneficiaries of these decisions — and the public is left to pick up the tab for new roads, schools, sewers and water supplies.

The program also includes a response in the form of a letter to the editor from Terry O'Regan of Landscape Alliance Ireland, who argues that unless people make alliances, they "will ruefully reflect on what might have been if we had taken the time to work together as a community to develop appropriate master plans, policies and strategies, which focused on the quality of life, rather than facilitating windfall property gains, property developers, and house builders replicating cloned housing units." By including this material in the program, Passion Machine intervenes directly into the "everyday life" of Dublin city politics, using the theatre space to create the very community that is absent in the play.

Buddleia suggests that no such community exists. Family relationships are fragmented and bitter, and politicians are in developers' pockets. As Dessie Fitzgerald, the local political candidate in the play, tells one of his campaign workers, "It's got nothing to do with me. Listen, off the record now, but I'm only along for the crack here. In fact, and they don't know this, but the real candidate kept putting his foot in the door, so they kneecapped him" (61). The campaign cynically uses the flat so that it appears as if Fitzgerald cares about the neighborhood. One campaign worker asks another "Tom, where did you get the dive?" to which he responds, "It has what they call street cred, Patricia" (62). Fitzgerald does not oppose the new road but feels that he must appear to do so in order to win votes. His aide Mulligan tells him, "You're going to get flack over this new road," and Fitzgerald practices his response: "I am concerned and taking a personal interest" (69).

In his analysis of theatre and "the everyday," Alan Read uses Gaston Bachelard's notion of "the blahs" to define the everyday as something that is distinct from the simulacra of media consumption:

> The everyday is covered by a surface: that of modernity. News stories and the turbulent affectations of art, fashion and event, veil without ever eradicating the everyday blahs. Images, the cinema and television divert the everyday by at times offering up to its own spectacle, or sometimes the spectacle of the distinctly non-everyday; violence, death, catastrophe, the lives of kings and stars—those who we are led to believe defy everydayness.

Read argues that "These 'blahs' are the narratives which in the absence of metanarratives will have to provide the discourse of a localised and politicised expression" (127). In *Buddleia*, the blahs are the daily care of home and neighborhood, which Dublin's citizens ignore at their peril.

The community shares one thing: the story of Jordan, a baby pulled out of the river (he is the boy we meet in the first scene). We first hear the story from Gus and Les, *Waiting for Godot*-like characters who appear in several scenes—as firemen, undertakers, demolition men. They talk about all that has been discarded in the river: "Washing machines, mattresses, three piece suites, carpets, shopping trolleys, a convenience store at your own doorstep" (35). Then Gus tells the story of the boy. In his version, a man is tossed out by his wife and mistress and comes down to the canal to kill himself. He finds a baby in a box in the canal, and he rescues the child. "I mean this baby is a godsend. Heaven sent. No way would he sin again. He would clean up his act. He was now a daddy" (37). But the story ends in a joke: the man calls his wife and says, " 'I've something for ye. Your one and only wish." And she says, "If I see another box of them fuckin' After Eights, I'll give you somethin' ye miserable cheatin' bastard" (37). In the next version of the story, which is related by a man who uses the flat to rent out porn videos, a man is waiting under the canal bridge to engage in some kind of shady deal. The man jumps in to save the baby and has to ward off a conger eel in the canal. The story continues beyond the punch line about the wife. The couple keeps the child, names him Jordan, and one day a girl appears to work as their nanny; she breastfeeds him, revealing that she is the child's mother. When Jordan turns 13, the girl's father turns up at the house, revealing that he is Jordan's father. They are all involved in some sort of vague drug deal, and Jordan's mother kills herself in the canal. Jordan remains "around."

The program from the "Dublin Trilogy" production also includes a short article on "Urban Legends" by UCD folklorist Bairbre Ni Fhloinn.

She describes the urban legend's roots in an ancient past and its contemporary everyday use:

> Today's legends reflect the same underlying human fears and hopes and dreams and anxieties as in the past, but transposed to a modern setting. So legends today will be told about things like crime and violence, illness, the safety of our children, foreign foods and people, the goings-on of celebrities, etc., and they can feature anything from baby-sitters to aliens, from Gay Byrne to microwaves to the ghosts of the past.

The urban legend of Jordan, and the jokes it inspires, are part of "everyday" conversation in this house; Jordan, a product of one of the culture's sicknesses — incest — is the society's "waste," and he is the waste that the community is making of its future. Everyone feels free to "waste" Jordan. In one scene, Harry, who is hired to watch the place and guard against looters, finds Jordan living in the house because he has no place else to go and tries to rape him. In the final scene, a demolition workforce appears. Construction of the new road is underway, as is an American-style gas station/convenience store/car wash. Accidentally hit by the excavating machine and dying at the play's end, while Sinatra sings "Rain," Jordan is this community's product and its future. It is a powerful, probably oversentimental and even didactic ending. But if urban legends exist, perhaps community still exists.

Mercier has moved from defining the theatre of everyday life as apolitical to writing consciously political plays. But the politics that concern Passion Machine the most are the politics of "the blahs," those experiences seen as existing outside larger national narratives. Unless the politics of the "blahs" are tended to, there will be no community or "home." One wonders if Mercier's new interest in a more overtly politicized everyday life can be reconciled with his earlier representation of popular culture practices as a vital communal force. At the moment, Passion Machine's work oscillates between the seriousness of the new work and the raucousness of the earlier material. To fulfill Mercier's vision, Passion Machine may need to define the everyday in terms that can accommodate both tendencies.

NOTES

1. Mercier has written and directed *Drowning* (1984); *Wasters* (1985); *Studs* (1986); *Spacers* (1986); *Home* (1988); *Pilgrims* (1993); *Buddleia* (1995); and *Kitchensink* (1996). Mercier also directed Roddy Doyle's *Brownbread* (1987) and *War!* (1989). The company's other productions include *The Birdtable* (1987) and *Breaking Up* (1988), written and directed by Brendan Gleeson; *Going Places* (1988), written and directed by Aidan Parkinson; *Too Much Too Young* (1995) and *Fully Recovered* (1998),

written and directed by Anto Nolan; and *Massive Damages* (1997), written by Declan Lynch and directed by Gerard Stembridge.

2. As John P. Harrington points out earlier (in the first essay of this volume), the tension between resisting "foreign" influences and being influenced by them was at work in the early years of the Abbey as well; while the rhetoric of the Irish Literary Theatre claimed "a fully formed and wholly autonomous 'Celtic and Irish school,' in practice the project would continue to reveal the culture and consciousness elided from the statement—all those insinuating influences represented by Germany, Constantinople, Madrid, and farther abroad."

3. Christopher Murray pointed out in a discussion at the "Nationalism and a National Theatre: 100 Years of Irish Drama" conference that Passion Machine did a survey of its audience in 1985 and discovered that most audience members were under twenty-five years old. The subject matter of the earliest work clearly reflected the interests of their young audience.

4. In her essay on Synge, Murphy, and McDonagh (earlier in this volume), José Lanters notes Martin McDonagh's use of popular culture and suggests that his characters are stuck in the past. She suggests that his characters' obsession with popular culture shows their confusion about "language, identity, and values" (218) and an obsession "with the preservation and surface value of material objects" (219). In Doyle's and Mercier's early work, however, popular culture practices are not marked as outdated or symbolic of bankruptcy. Rather, the plays celebrate the characters' engagement with the popular.

5. Doyle's career suggests the possibilities and problems of this reliance on the popular. It has been said that Doyle's work received acclaim because it was thought to be accurate, a "true" representation of contemporary Irish life. It is a character-ization he seems rather uncomfortable with, especially since the uproar over the television show *The Family*, on which he was taken to task by residents of Ballymun for misrepresenting them. In an interview with Charles Foran, Ballymun residents offered sharp critiques of Doyle: "At the end of the day when Roddy Doyle is on a beach in Spain with his nest egg, he doesn't care that he's slandered and categorized this community. Grand enough for him to make a few bob, but not off the backs of working class people" (62). "We really didn't need the bad press"; "you have to read a Roddy Doyle book to hear such foul language in Dublin" (62). Doyle was startled by the response: "Listening to the radio the day after the first episode, I thought, Jesus, what the fuck have I done? I'll have to emigrate now" (60).

6. *Brownbread* premiered at the SFX Centre in September 1987; it was staged again in November 1987, January 1988, and August 1994 at the Olympia Theatre.

7. In Colm Toibín's essay for *The New Yorker* ("Dublin's Epiphany: on Ireland's massive cultural changes"), Toibín discusses the impact of such "bishop bashing":

> I remember a concert in Galway by the blues singer Mary Coughlan in 1987. Between songs, she mentioned that in the sixties girls in Galway had been forbid-den to wear bikinis by the archconservative Bishop Michael Browne. She wanted, she said, to dedicate the song she had just sung to him. She looked at us all and grinned, and since the last song had been about debauchery and shamelessness, this got a huge cheer. Mary Coughlan was laughing at a dead bishop [. . .] and then she went further. 'This next song,' she said, in her West of Ireland drawl, 'is for the bishop we have now. The one who drinks and drives.' A louder cheer went up, and there was laughter. Eamonn Casey, the Bishop of Galway, had recently been found guilty, in London, of driving while drunk. At blues concerts, bishops, suddenly, were fair game. (45)

8. *War!* premiered at the SFX Centre in September 1989 and was staged again in October 1989 at the Olympia Theatre.

9. In an interview with Gerry Smyth, Doyle commented on his depiction of Briget: "In an earlier play I'd done called *War!* about a pub quiz team, it didn't really work, because inevitably all the action and humour was in the pub scenes. But there were quieter scenes in between with the husband and wife, and basically she was a good deal brighter than him, she had more information, she would have been far more useful on any quiz team but nobody noticed, and she was stuck at home. But it didn't quite work on stage. I think it was asking too much of lighting or something, and I was never happy with it" (*Novel and the Nation* 105).

10. *Buddleia* debuted in October 1995 during the Irish Life Dublin Theatre Festival at the Project Arts Center and ran again in March 1996 at the Donmar Warehouse in London. And it also got reviews that used the same discourse as earlier descriptions of Passion Machine, emphasizing their accuracy; for example, Joe Jackson described the play as a "mercilessly accurate representation of contemporary life in the nation's capital in 1995" ("Machine Heads," *Hot Press* 19 [November 1995]).

Part V

IRISH HISTORY ON THE
CONTEMPORARY STAGE

The Book at the Center of the Stage: Friel's Making History and The Field Day Anthology of Irish Writing

KATHLEEN HOHENLEITNER

> Another history! Jesus, if we had as many scones of
> bread as we have historians!
> — Red Hugh O'Donnell, in Brian Friel,
> *Making History*

First performed in 1988, Brian Friel's last Field Day play, *Making History*, reaches back to the 1590s, the last days of the Gaelic chieftains. The play chronicles the life of Hugh O'Neill, earl of Tyrone, hailed by many nationalist histories as the only man who could have been king of Ireland, the last man who defended the "One True Faith" against the Reformation of the Elizabethan era. The fact that such legends surround this national hero render him a highly appropriate subject for a Field Day play, given the company's stated commitment to recognizing the political implications of cultural narratives and images. In *Making History*, Friel juxtaposes the received nationalist myth of O'Neill with historical documents from his life in order to consider the role of the historian in shaping national culture, both past and present.

As is often his custom, in writing *Making History* Friel relied primarily on one historical source, Sean O'Faoláin's biography of Hugh O'Neill, entitled *The Great O'Neill: A Biography of Hugh O'Neill, Earl of Tyrone, 1550–1616.*[1] Published in 1942, this text illustrates the revisionist trend in Irish historiography by painting a less heroic image of O'Neill.[2] O'Faoláin's revisionist approach, in other words, attempts to demythologize this emblem of a romanticized Gaelic civilization.[3] O'Faoláin recuperates a utilitarian O'Neill who recognized the usefulness of an Irish political allegiance with England and who sought to unify the Irish clans so that they could confront the powerful English army. O'Faoláin sees efficiency as the key to Britain's imperial strength; he also recognizes national unity and subscription to the Enlightenment concept of progress as attributes and explains Ireland's underdevelopment as a function of their absence. For example, O'Faoláin characterizes Irish culture in the 1590s as backward: "[I]t still held its attraction, powerfully nostalgic, atavistically resurgent, long after the rest of Europe had begun to move forward to new ideas, new inventions, new codes, greater and finer elaborations in every branch of life — manner, education, architecture, social organization, politics, dress, food, philosophy, methods of war, letters" (42). This atavism persists particularly fiercely in Ulster, O'Faoláin insists, where it is manifested as a kind of "racial psychosis" which hinders the "reforming, modernizing mind of our Hugh O'Neill" (42). O'Faoláin's unwillingness to romanticize O'Neill indicates his deep investment in an Enlightenment ideal of an accessible historical "truth" which, once arrived at, would debunk the constructed "mythology" that had been masquerading as truth. Because O'Faoláin wrote during the de Valera administration, we could read his commendation of O'Neill as an implicit attack on the anti-modernization of de Valera's isolationist policies.

The Great O'Neill clearly influences Friel's depiction of O'Neill as a modern, "renaissance" man whose foresight and English education enabled him to recognize that the future of Western civilization lay with the English monarchy, its unified army, and its newly reformed Church. But Friel complicates this depiction by addressing the larger question of historiography. Friel wrote the play for the Field Day Theatre Company, which was an initiative undertaken to give Northern Ireland a voice in both cultural production and cultural critique. The company produced plays and cultural criticism which grappled with Irish nationalism rather than eschewing it in the name of Enlightenment logic. Making History unites a number of Field Day's areas of inquiry: it brings a historical figure to the stage and examines the popular, heroic accounts of his deeds as well as their influence on historical interpretation. In addition, the play dramatizes, quite literally, the making of history, as Archbishop Peter Lombard attempts to assemble the events of O'Neill's life into a narrative that can be read as heroic in years to come. What Lombard chooses to omit from his friend's life story is as important as what he includes in his effort to produce an edifying narrative. In underlining how history is reconstructed for political ends, Friel acknowledges that both O'Faoláin's biography of O'Neill and his own dramatic adaptation are motivated by twentieth-century needs, specifically, in Friel's case, the need to clarify conditions in Northern Ireland by re-examining received views of Irish history.

Declan Kiberd sees Friel's work as targeting revisionist historiography: "Friel's plays are implicit critiques of the value-free approach to history taken by most contemporary Irish historians: and reminders that it is human nature to name as truth what is usually the narrative most flattering to current ruling vanity" (*Inventing Ireland* 633). My reading of *Making History* concurs with Kiberd's, while still marking the great extent to which Friel's characterization of O'Neill is drawn from O'Faoláin's depiction of him. In the tension between these two seemingly contradictory readings lies the force of this play. I propose reading this widely criticized play in conjunction with a consideration of the the equally dramatic furor surrounding the compiling of the *Field Day Anthology of Irish Writing*, which had begun at the time of the play's premiere (despite the fact that the three-volume text did not appear until 1991). I compare "the Book," Lombard's biography of O'Neill, which occupied center stage throughout the play, to the anthology, which occupies center stage of so many contemporary debates on Irish identity, arguing that each text refuses fixity in order to define "O'Neill" and "Irishness" from multiple perspectives.

Field Day's programs are known for tying drama to intellectual work and, thus, for involving the audience in the work of the production. The program for *Translations* was attacked by critics such as Ulf Dantanus for creating the illusion of historical accuracy.[4] In the program for *Making History*, Friel specifically chose quotations from historical sources which include accounts of O'Neill's life that were provided by eyewitnesses, contemporary histories, and correspondences. Each quotation renders an element of O'Neill's life that does not correspond exactly with the way it has been represented in recent Irish history. A reproduction of an engraving of O'Neill's surrender to Mountjoy provides the most prominent example of this discrepancy, ironically depicting the Irish nationalist hero at the ignominious moment of his surrender of the Gaels to the English.

So as to avoid the kinds of outrage prompted by historical inaccuracies in *Translations*, Friel includes a mission statement, in which he admits to having tampered with historical data in order to tell a better story. He specifies that the play is a "dramatic fiction," one which attempts to keep faith with the empirical method of history, but he adds:

> But when there was tension between historical 'fact' and the imperative of the fiction, I'm glad to say I kept faith with the narrative. For example, even though Mabel, Hugh's wife, died in 1591, it suited my story to keep her alive for another ten years. Part of me regrets taking these occasional liberties. But then I remind myself that history and fiction are related and comparable forms of discourse and that a historical text is a kind of literary artifact.

This time, Friel refuses to allow the audience the convenience of pretending that his narrative is historically accurate; he refuses even to allow them the comfort of a single interpretation of Hugh O'Neill. At the play's end, we are faced with two stories that have been told in counterpoint, each

somewhat contradicting the other.[5] Friel's process of "making history" is
one of telling a story that can be owned by a comprehensive Irish audience;
that is, he consciously creates art from history, producing a cultural text
that reaches across boundaries of religion, class, and politics. If the nation is
defined by its history, then Friel sets out to define a history that accommodates multiple perspectives of O'Neill and, consequently, of Ireland. Christopher Murray has observed,

> The self-reflexive form of the play thus makes redundant any charge of
> historical accuracy. As Friel dramatizes this question, there is only the
> invention, the making process, and this is something which Irish and
> English audiences, variously inheritors of the situation O'Neill brought
> about, are necessarily implicated in. ("Brian Friel's *Making History*" 76)

The final portion of the program situates *Making History* within the
context of the Field Day Company, which by 1988 had published five series
of pamphlets and had commissioned the massive *Anthology of Irish Writing*.
In addition to advertising its recent publications, the program also includes
excerpted quotations of the company's reception by the academic world,
the media, and theatre-going public. These citations illustrate the variety of
audiences that Field Day reaches and the positive reception that the company has received across sectarian, class, and cultural divides. I emphasize
the context that Field Day creates for the production because the play, in
my view, affected the critical reception of the anthology and Field Day's
larger project. *Making History* investigates history itself, specifically the
period in Irish history when the Gaelic aristocracy fell, because it is from
this era that so many contemporary concepts of Irish nationalism derive.
For this reason, Field Day found this play appropriate to produce at a time
when multiple contradictory historical narratives threaten the stability of
life in Northern Ireland.

The final segment of O'Faoláin's biography describes the kindly old
Archbishop Lombard of Armagh laboring to organize the events of Hugh
O'Neill's life into a heroic national narrative, while O'Neill, now exiled in
Italy under the protection of the pope, lives out his final years, drowning in
regret and drink. O'Faoláin describes Lombard's history writing as advancing "ideal pictures of men who never existed, and of motives so pure that
only angels could have been stirred by them" (352). Friel derives his plot
from this image of the priest–historian working assiduously to salvage a
victory from O'Neill's exile.

O'Faoláin's portrait of O'Neill seeks the balance that is absent in Lombard's account but which is in some regards no less subjective. O'Faoláin
credits O'Neill with realizing the stakes of the wars with Elizabeth. He does
not pretend to know why O'Neill made specific tactical choices, but he
insists that O'Neill's knowledge of English society afforded him a heightened sense of England's goals and of Ireland's apparent barbarism com-

pared to other nations of Europe. He argues that compared to England, "[t]he spirit of Ireland was not articulated in the same way [. . .] because it was too disparate and individual and politically unformed" (21). He continues by making the distinction that "[t]here *was* a Gaelic race. There *was not* a Gaelic nation. O'Neill was the first man who gave that race a form, by giving it a speech that it could understand and which made it realize itself intelligently" (21–22, emphasis in original). Thus, O'Faoláin sees O'Neill's war with England as a clash between civilizations, as a defense of the Gaelic way of life, which he clearly finds outdated compared to the ways of life of the rest of Europe at the time. While the English were fighting to defend their queen and the unified national government that she represented, the Irish had only their way of life to defend; Ireland as a concept had not yet cohered to the same degree.

O'Faoláin assumes that O'Neill had access to the Enlightenment concepts of the State and the Nation. His representation of O'Neill anachronistically applies the Enlightenment ideal of the secular state to the early seventeenth century, which reveals O'Faoláin's own interest in proposing the secular state as an ideal for Ireland. Writing in 1942, O'Faoláin had seen enough of nationalist Ireland and the violence and nostalgia associated with it. Rather than seeing O'Neill as a defender of Catholicism and of essential Gaelic culture, O'Faoláin required a hero who was in tune with modernity, a hero who was recuperable for the secular society that was O'Faoláin's ideal for the South at mid-century.

As a result, O'Faoláin blames O'Neill's defeat on the inability of the Gaels to "break through the tribal concept." They lost, writes O'Faoláin, because they were "pure Gael" (111). He argues that such tribalism kept all of the Gaels but O'Neill from realizing what was at stake in the Irish wars. He explains: "In short O'Neill the 999th was too busy watching O'Neill the 998th to have any time for Gregory XIII or Philip II or the plans of Elizabeth I" (113). O'Faoláin contrasts such tribalism with the more advanced condition of England, which had learned in the Wars of the Roses the value of having a central authority and which had replaced the Blessed Mother with Queen Elizabeth at the center of government and trade (112). O'Faoláin's analysis is rooted in the Enlightenment concept of history as progress, a concept which he applies retrospectively to the sixteenth century. His O'Neill was one who saw the path of the future and chose progress for Ireland, thus placing himself in the central position of authority, not necessarily out of lust for power but instead because he recognized that the tribal, decentralized culture of the Gaels would not survive in modern Europe.

O'Faoláin was not the first to "revise" the myth of a coherent, precolonial Ireland. Luke Gibbons cites Sir George Baden-Powell, who wrote to justify imperialism during the Home Rule controversy: "Ireland does not contain the necessary elements of a separate nationality—for among the inhabitants there is no unity or individuality of blood, religion, laws, occupations, sentiments, history, or even tradition" (Baden-Powell 221; Gibbons, *Transformations* 137). Gibbons connects Baden-Powell's dismissal of Ireland to the kind of historical revisionism O'Faoláin performs in *The Great O'Neill*, arguing that:

> Such mythic accounts of Ireland as 'the oldest nation in Europe' can be seen as part of an attempt to smuggle into Irish culture the continuity and permanence of English tradition as venerated by Edmund Burke, but while notions of stability and security come readily to colonial powers, they hardly make sense in societies uprooted by the expansionist designs of the West. (137)

Gibbons argues, rather, that Ireland's diffusion prevented England from colonizing the island at one blow; the diversity among the clans enabled a form of resistance, not unified in itself but rather unifying in its objection to colonization. Gibbons' comparison illustrates the futility of applying modern European theories of nationalism to sixteenth-century Ireland, largely because of Ireland's own historical specificity. Similarly, O'Faoláin's forced reading of O'Neill as a proto-Enlightenment thinker backfires because of Ireland's complicated historical situation in 1600.

Against the earl of Tyrone's "modernizing mind," O'Faoláin pits another Gaelic hero, Ulster chieftain Red Hugh O'Donnell. In O'Faoláin's account, O'Donnell represents not only the fighting Irish personality, complete with blustering single-mindedness and red-headed temper (Friel's portrayal adds fondness for drink), but also the epitome of atavism, in contrast to O'Neill's pragmatism. According to O'Faoláin, "Red Hugh represented Gaelic resistance at its most obstinate and inspiring, fired the imagination of the clansman as a soldier, and gave the people what the more cold and aloof Tyrone could never give them — the image of a popular hero, as rooted in their own traditional life as some flashing figure out of the sagas," and he describes O'Neill's efforts "to get control of Red Hugh" as a trying part of the battle to bring Ireland into modernity (60).

Friel adopts O'Faoláin's characterization of O'Donnell in its entirety, casting him as a comic semi-Falstaffian figure whose loyal devotion to Gaeldom and Catholicism sends him enthusiastically into battle, into exile for further negotiation with Spain, and into awkward social situations with Hugh's "New English" wife. For example, O'Donnell lives up to the Gaelic stereotype assigned to him by O'Faoláin (during a war council) by using dismissive phrases in reference to people and places unfamiliar to him during a war council meeting. The most egregious of these is his comment regarding the town of Kinsale, far to the south of Ulster, where the Spanish are reported to have landed. To the mention of Kinsale, O'Donnell responds impatiently, "Wherever that is. Never heard of it" (32). The tragedy of this offhand comment indicates the lack of communication between the Gaelic chieftains and their Spanish allies, the poor military strategy that resulted from such miscommunication, as well as the absence of a sense of nationhood, to which Baden-Powell refers. Friel's representation of Red Hugh O'Donnell as an impetuously volatile yet ill-informed warrior attests to the influence of O'Faoláin's Gaelic stereotypes. This scene contrasts Lombard's obsessive concern with maintaining O'Neill as a hero in the eyes of the Church. The direct opposite of O'Donnell, Lombard is so fixated on Europe and the Vatican that he has difficulty relating to O'Neill's more immediate concerns, such as cattle raiders and the English colonists who are trespassing on his territory. O'Neill, then, appears in both portrayals as a pawn who has been manipulated by advisers who put their own concerns first.

While O'Faoláin constructs Lombard as a straw man, against whom he offers his ostensibly "value-free" version of O'Neill, both Friel and O'Faoláin depict Lombard as being motivated primarily by loyalty to the pope, whose power he seeks to increase. The Reformation had recently threatened the pope's power, both politically and spiritually, so it would be to Lombard's advantage to help retain Ireland for Catholicism. Both the Church of Rome and the Crown of England sought O'Neill's support in governing Ireland, and O'Neill was forced to side with whomever could better secure his title. O'Faoláin and Friel both make clear that to ally himself with the queen would bring O'Neill into conflict with neighboring clans and would also require him to take an oath of loyalty to England, while Spain ultimately offered him sovereignty over Ireland. In rationalizing O'Neill's choice after the fact, Lombard privileges the earl's commitment to Catholicism as one of the unifying features of Gaeldom, while Friel and O'Faoláin vigorously resist the notion that Catholicism is the strongest unifying cultural agency in Ireland. Friel's foregrounding of Lombard's attempt to manipulate the story illustrates the deep political implications of language in history and national consciousness.

Making History opens with a preoccupied earl of Tyrone dashing restlessly about Tullyhogue, meeting with his fellow chief O'Donnell and Archbishop Lombard to discuss the state of Ulster. O'Neill's sudden announcement of his marriage takes O'Donnell and Lombard by surprise. The fact of O'Neill's marriage, after the relatively recent death of his second wife, does not surprise his friends as much as the fact that his new wife is Mabel Bagenal, daughter of their English enemy, the colonist Upstart. Lombard struggles to process this information, wondering how it will fit into the heroic narrative of O'Neill's life, while O'Donnell ponders the political consequences of the match.

In true Field Day fashion, Friel calls language into question on the stage through the terminology the characters use to refer to the marriage. Mabel's brother sends a statement of indignation, which Friel appears to have lifted directly from O'Faoláin. What O'Neill and Mabel see as their elopement Bagenal calls an "abduction," because Mabel is under twenty-one years of age. Lombard, in his shock upon hearing the news of the marriage, refers to it as an "association," only to be immediately corrected by O'Neill. Lombard's concern as a patriot, a historian, and an archbishop is O'Neill's standing with the pope, because in order for the native Irish to win military support from Spain and the Vatican, O'Neill must be made to appear a defender of the Catholic faith. The uncertainty of terms illustrates the larger project for Lombard's character, namely the narrating of the story to create the most politically positive reading of Hugh O'Neill. Words are the primary tool of historians, and the words they choose to represent an event, be it a marriage, an abduction, or an association, reveal their perspective on the event. Lombard tries to see it as a political tactic, carefully plotted to achieve the ultimate goal of a unified Ireland; Bagenal sees it as an attack on his bloodline; and Friel's O'Neill, as the end of this scene illustrates, merely adores his young wife and wants his friends to love her as well.

Lombard assures O'Neill that he will not "interpret" the events of his life but rather will "just describe" them. In response to O'Neill's anxious petitions that he will "tell the truth," Lombard admits that the kind of objectivity O'Neill requests is impossible. Rather, he asks whether or not truth is the proper criterion: "Isn't that what history is, a kind of story-telling? . . . Imposing a pattern on events that were mostly casual and haphazard and shaping them into a narrative that is logical and interesting" (8). Perhaps Lombard saw that Catholicism would provide a useful narrative at the time, and perhaps O'Faoláin's biography responds to the 1940s historical situation, where the illusion of unbiased objectivity appeals to a people who are trying to distance themselves from the passionate nationalism that fueled not only the 1916 Easter Rising and the War of Independence, but also the Civil War of 1922–1923. But what Friel admittedly responds to is the present's need not for value-free history but for a recognition of the value of history to the self-consciousness of a community. If any historical narrative is to represent a diverse community such as Ireland, it must tell a story that will accommodate vastly different perspectives. Friel's metaphor of a marriage provides a story that shows O'Neill and Mabel compromising to build a life together that incorporates two cultures while preserving the unique identity of each. Historical evidence that their marriage was not nearly so idyllic as Friel depicts further emphasizes the importance of the drama as fiction. I propose that Friel flaunts the departures he takes from historical records in order to celebrate his freedom to do so. Field Day's project involves not only creating cultural texts but also claiming the volition to conduct cultural criticism. Independence from England means freedom of representation, in fiction and in history—the power to narrate stories that confer a sense of identity on the culture, which, in turn, draws its sense of identity from these stories.

Friel's representation of the contrast between the ancient Gaelic past and the modern European world complicates O'Faoláin's clear-cut analysis of the Gaelic past as atavistic and of modernity as positive. Friel changes the focus by dwelling at length on the relationship between O'Neill and Mabel. Friel's placement of O'Neill's marriage to Mabel at the center of the action of *Making History* enables the audience to consider the earl's political and military choices as being motivated by something other than patriotic love for a united Ireland. The marriage alliance allows the play to explore the conflict between cultures on a more personal level and to supplant the power imbalance of the parent/child metaphor that colonialism offers.

Mabel also offers Friel a dramatic means to explore the contrast between the traditional Gaelic lifestyle of husbandry, Catholicism, and tribal government and the English, Protestant, agrarian society, governed by Elizabeth I. In act I, scene 2, when Mabel is visited by her sister Mary, Friel recreates the culture shock that Mabel suffered upon her marriage. Having bought into the stereotypes, Mary believes that the superstitious Gaels are doomed to extinction unless they acquire "Reason." Mary's anachronistic Enlightenment teleology of progress through technology and economic development demonstrates how O'Neill could have seen as much validity in his own Gaelic civilization as in the civilization of the emergent British Empire. By seeing history as teleological, the Enlightenment cooperates with a Christian view of history as one narrative, all of which leads up to the culmination of progress and time — the present. O'Faoláin's argument that O'Neill recognized the shift toward English politics, religion, and society as an inevitable outcome for Ireland invests O'Neill with a modern view of progress, one that he could hardly have held in the way we understand it today. Whereas O'Faoláin's O'Neill appears to equivocate so as to further his own political interests, Friel's O'Neill insists on taking responsibility for his life and for the way he will be represented in history as a national hero. He refuses to be written into the progressive narrative of Irish patriotism that will end with the survival of the "Hidden Ireland."[6]

Friel's O'Neill finds himself caught between two civilizations, one Irish and traditional, one English and progressive. Friel makes his clearest connections between historical and contemporary Ireland in the scenes in which O'Neill ponders his role as intermediary. In act 3, O'Neill castigates his neighbor, Maguire, whose clan attempted rebellion to defend their ideals: "Their noble souls couldn't breathe another second under 'tyranny.' And where are they now? Wiped out. And what did they accomplish? Nothing. But because of their nobility, survival — basic, crude, day-to-day survival — is made infinitely more difficult for the rest of us" (30). This cynical view of idealistic rebels condemns the contemporary republican groups who campaign to "restore" a united Ireland that, as O'Faoláin insists, was never united in the first place.[7] Ironically enough, the "Hidden Ireland" that militant nationalists seek to restore and the utterly "value-free" history that the most zealous revisionist historians seek are equally impossible. While acknowledging his debt to O'Faoláin's interpretation, Friel nonetheless points out with these oblique references to the present that while O'Faoláin's assumptions may be valid, they, like Lombard's, are made for a specific historical moment.

When O'Neill receives the news that Spain has sent an army, he decides that he now must join the Spanish, who have agreed to support him in the interest of the Vatican. When Lombard reads the Bull of Indulgence from Pope Clement VIII, which promises remission of sins to all who join O'Neill's forces, it becomes clear — before Lombard announces it — that this "mere war" has become a holy crusade. Lombard explains, "Which means, too, that we are no longer a casual grouping of tribes but a nation state united under the Papal colours" (33). The ironic use of the modern term "nation state" suggests that O'Neill has achieved modernity for Ireland by fighting to preserve a life characterized by antiquity. If Ireland is no longer a casual grouping of tribes but a united force, then it has moved into the modern era, because the very concept of a united national community is also a product of imperialism and the Enlightenment.[8] The term "nation state," which would not have been thought of as such until the twentieth century, reveals the anachronism of that phrase.[9] While the concept of uniting as a nation would be understood in 1600, fighting in a crusade under the papal colors was a medieval concept, one that had become outdated long before that time.[10] Historian Sean Connolly objects to what he sees as Friel's underlying assumption that "what was going on in the 1590s was understood by those involved as a national conflict between the English and the Irish" (161). On the contrary, it is precisely Friel's use of anachronistic words such as "nation state" that indicates how this play consciously addresses history to analyze the present.

Mabel urges her husband not to proceed with the vigorous Spanish invasion but rather to persist with his own carefully planned guerrilla strategies. Mabel, like O'Faoláin himself, blames the hotheaded Hugh O'Donnell and his "typically Gaelic" belligerence for the downfall of the Spanish and the clans at Kinsale. She reminds him that although he and Spain are manipulating each other, he stands to lose more: "It's not Spain's war. It's your war. And you're taking on a nation state that is united and determined and powerful and led by a very resolute woman" (38).[11] With this argument, Mabel intends to point out the military and political advantage of England's unity against tribes who often disagree among themselves. As little as Mabel trusts Spain, she also remains wary of Lombard, who appears to be committed to O'Neill's "leading Europe in a glorious Catholic Counter-Reformation," mainly for the purpose of augmenting papal political power.

Mabel's warning upsets O'Neill, who corroborates another Irish national stereotype by launching into a proclamation. Like an earlier Friel character with the same first name, O'Neill waxes eloquent on his predicament, alluding to the issue first raised in *Translations*, namely the issue of economic prosperity versus an elusive Gaelic heritage:

> I have spent my life attempting to . . . hold together a harassed and a confused people by trying to keep them in touch with the life they knew before they were overrun. It wasn't a life of material ease but it had its assurances and it had its dignity. And I have done that by acknowledging . . . beliefs these people have practised since before history, long before the God of Christianity was ever heard of. And at the same time I have tried to open these people to the strange new ways of Europe. . . . Two pursuits that can scarcely be followed simultaneously. Two tasks that are almost self-cancelling. But they have got to be attempted because the formation of nations and civilizations is a willed act, not a product of fate or accident. And for you to suggest that religion is the only coagulant that holds us together is to grossly and ignorantly overlook an age-old civilization. (40)

By identifying the "assurances" and "dignity" that get lost through colonization, Friel illustrates the effect of the loss of power and identity that was suffered by colonized people. The tragedy of the Flight of the Earls becomes less a moment of the loss of the culture itself than a moment of the erosion of identity and self-determination that Gaelic culture conferred on members of its community. Mabel's suggestion that religion was the one coagulant that bound the Gaelic clans together offends O'Neill because it deems Gaelic society to be uncivilized and denies it legitimacy. By pronouncing the Gaels barbaric, Mabel justifies colonization. This speech represents an O'Neill who has tried to honor his oath of loyalty to the queen by trying to modernize his society to bring it into step with the rest of Western Europe. It also depicts the impossibility of such an attempt to simultaneously preserve and modernize without becoming "self-cancelling." Claiming that religion is the one "coagulant" only adds to the futility by ignoring the other cultural, political, and economic forces at work in the history of any community.

The refusal to read O'Neill as an Irish crusader, a refusal shared by both O'Faoláin and Friel, is important to any analysis of Irish history and politics. Lombard's deliberate construction of O'Neill as defender of the faith does attempt to unite the various clans, and it seems that the clans largely did have Catholicism in common. When de Valera's government revised the Irish Constitution in the 1930s, they identified Catholicism as one of the distinctive characteristics of Irishness. For example, the Preamble of the 1937 Constitution reads:

> In the name of the Most Holy Trinity, from Whom is all authority and to Whom, as our final end, all actions both of men and States must be referred, We the people of Éire, Humbly acknowledging all our obliga-

tions to our Divine Lord, Jesus Christ, Who sustained our fathers through
centuries of trial, Gratefully remembering their heroic and unremitting
struggle to regain the rightful independence of our Nation, and seeking to
promote the common good, . . . so that the dignity and freedom of the
individual may be assured, true social order attained, the unity of our
country restored, and concord established with other nations, Do hereby
adopt, enact, and give to ourselves this Constitution.

While not specifically Catholic, this preamble does position Christianity as
the foundation of the State. It also illustrates the teleological view of history, with its references to a "struggle to regain the rightful independence
of our Nation" and to "restore" the unity of the country, implying the
resurgence of a hidden but vibrant cultural nationalism, one that has been
suppressed by English imperialism.

Similarly, to understand the recurring violence in Northern Ireland as
merely a religious struggle would be to ignore centuries of economic injustice and political subordination. No "Hidden Ireland" lurks behind this
play, waiting for O'Neill (or de Valera) to usher it in. Conflict between the
political and the religious in this play complicates the work of nationalist
historians. Like O'Faoláin, Friel objects to patriotic historians who focus
on the Catholic element in order to render the story heroic. Unlike O'Faoláin, Friel's anachronisms and conflations of the contemporary situation
with the historic one do not pretend to undo the damage of nationalist
historians but rather seek to investigate how the story has become part of
the contemporary understanding of history. Through O'Neill's refusal to
see religion as the only coagulant, Friel characterizes history as a cultural
product shared by the community that defines it as Irish.

In act 2, scene 1, O'Neill shares with O'Donnell the most controversial
document in this play, his submission to Queen Elizabeth, his last chance to
remain in Ireland without being a fugitive. His armies defeated, his cause
humiliated, his Spanish defenders in hasty retreat, O'Neill constructs a text
entirely contrary to everything he values, but one which he believes might
be enough to convince the queen to use him to aid her in "taming" Ireland.
O'Donnell incredulously reads his friend's promise of loyalty to the queen
and his renunciation of Spain:

Particularly will I help in the abolishing of all barbarous Gaelic customs
which are the seeds of all incivility. And for the clearing of all difficult
passages and places which are the nurseries of rebellion. And I will endeavor to erect civil habitations for myself and for the people of my country to preserve us against any force but the power of the state . . . as long as
we continue in our loyal and faithful duties to Her Majesty. . . . (50)

Submitting his people to the power of the State might be the worst of
O'Neill's offenses to the present, and at this point Friel differs from O'Fao-

láin in his interpretation of this event. Friel's O'Neill at this point comprehends fully that the queen will not accept him, although she might exploit his influence to get the Irish savages under control. O'Donnell's ambition to return from exile to reclaim his sheep back from "the shit O'Doherty" itself indicates that O'Neill's efforts to "modernize" the Gaels have failed if they persist in seeing each other as enemies rather than as neighbors who should unite against the powerful English threat. O'Neill realizes that the queen will bring the State into effect and that he might as well procure for himself a say in its formation. This enforcement of the Enlightenment State is part of the problematic legacy that O'Neill bequeathed to his successors.

At the beginning of the final scene, the contested history book sits prominently at the center of the stage, thereby centering the action around the idea of the historical text. Lombard's task has become increasingly challenging; to heroicize the morose, drunken, impoverished emigré requires no small amount of fabrication. Lombard's theory of history involves simple construction of heroes; he argues, "You lost a battle — that has to be said. But the telling of it can still be a triumph" (65). Disgusted by such manipulation, O'Neill decides that his last battle will be for truth in history; he will campaign until Lombard represents him accurately. Furious that Lombard has glossed over his formative years in England, his marriage to Mabel, and his declarations of loyalty to the queen, he realizes that the hero Lombard has written bears his name but not his history. He rages at his friend, "Don't embalm me in pieties" (63). The battle between O'Neill and future generations' image of him is waged within the text. O'Neill refuses the story, and with it, he refuses the role of the hero, which is almost a rejection of his own people, who, in turn, he feels have betrayed him. He challenges Lombard to explain why the six years after Kinsale are not represented: "When I lived like a criminal, skulking round the countryside — my countryside! — hiding from the English, from the Upstarts, from the Old English, but most assiduously hiding from my brother Gaels who couldn't wait to strip me of every blade of grass I ever owned . . . If these were 'my people' then to hell with my people! The Flight of the Earls — you make it sound like a lap of honour. We ran away just as we ran away at Kinsale" (66). Friel gives us history from a different angle while simultaneously calling into question how history gets narrated.

The play's final scene juxtaposes O'Neill and Lombard, each reciting the text which he feels best represents the life of Hugh O'Neill. Lombard recites his history's opening sentences, while O'Neill whispers, *"almost in counterpoint"* to the opposing text, his own statement of submission to the queen after the defeat at Kinsale ended his hopes for regaining power in Tyrone (70). The stage directions specify that O'Neill's accent fades from the elite English he generally speaks to a Tyrone inflection that he would have learned in childhood. The effect of this accent shift does not suggest a reversion to the "real" O'Neill that he was as a child, because he himself would not deny his upbringing in England and his English wife. Rather, it enables the drama to enact a play of meaning between the two O'Neills: one a heroic Gaelic leader, the other a remorseful exile, begging for the forgiveness of his wife for having failed at a cause for which she renounced everything to support him. Both O'Neills are entirely fictional; neither has any more claim to reality than the other, as each exists only in the words of the playwright and the action of the drama. Both are based on historical legend and have been created by men who have studied existing historical documents in search of facts on which to base their stories. The significance of each O'Neill gets expressed in reference to the other; the audience derives an image of each from the play of meaning between the two texts which represent Hugh O'Neill. Somewhere between Lombard's "God-like prince [who] will be king for the span of his life" and O'Neill's petition for Mabel to forgive him in his defeat we see a man whom some historians have used to symbolize Ireland at its most glorious and one other whom historians have accused of failing to become the first king of Ireland, thereby dooming Ireland to centuries of colonization and internal violence.

The problem with this play of meaning for the audience is whether or not these two representations of O'Neill are self-canceling. Friel dramatizes the tension between the two so that no cross-fertilization occurs, no hybrid version of the figure emerges that is "neither one nor the other." Rather, two representations of O'Neill play themselves out here, both of which are supported by historical data. Because history becomes the cultural product of a community, the fact that two conflicting representations can be drawn illustrates the importance of recognizing history less as objective truth and more as narration, especially amid the highly contested debate about revisionism that rages in Irish scholarship today.

Making History suggests that revisionism's stake in refusing to recognize the political element in history indicates a refusal to recognize history's role in shaping the consciousness of a modern nation.[12] In the Field Day's project of anthologizing Irish writing, the group has been accused, by critics such as Edna Longley, John Gray, and Francis Mulhern, of the self-contradictory gesture of attempting to create a canon while simultaneously resisting a rigid definition of Irish literature.[13] Director Seamus Deane admits the difficulty of reconciling these positions, but he refuses to agree that "by trying to inhabit two unreconcilable positions, one is therefore caught in a state of paralyzing contradiction" (Callaghan 41). In this sense, Field Day's inquiry into that impossible category of "Irishness" can only be resolved the way Friel refuses to resolve the historical ambiguity of *Making History*. To restrict an interpretation of O'Neill to that of loyal defender of Gaelic Catholicism would be to ignore the contradictions in his life, namely that he was educated in England, married Mabel Bagenal, and took an oath of loyalty to the queen. Similarly, to see him only as O'Faoláin's forward-looking modern man, one who sought to bring Ireland into step with proto-Enlightenment Europe, would be to deny any validity to the Gaelic civilization which he led until the Flight of the Earls. While the pitfalls of Lombard's religious patriotism include violent nationalism, the danger of the reverse, O'Faoláin's revisionism, is that it rationalizes colonialism by characterizing Gaelic Ireland as superstitious, backward, and doomed to eventual decay. Field Day resists this, as it resists the separation between culture and politics. By dramatizing the play of meaning between the two contradictory texts — Lombard's biography and O'Neill's own letter of submission — Friel puts on stage the intersections among religion, language, politics, and history that continue to structure Irish communities.[14]

Theorists of nationalism and revisionist historians like O'Faoláin rely on the teleology of progress in order to understand Ireland in terms of modern-day Europe. We have seen how this paradigm does not accommodate the diversity of a nation such as Ireland. Luke Gibbons compares the concreteness of a traditional symbol of national identity, a monument, to the more fluid expressions of Irish cultural identity — ballads, stories, and allegorical images which operate on multiple levels and change with each performance. Gibbons posits that the less fixed representations of nationalism prove more appropriate to colonized nations, while the formerly imperial European nations identify with the fixity of monuments which "bear witness to the power of the state to legitimize its triumphant version of the past" (*Transformations* 145). In the same way, the emphasis on performance in Field Day productions allows for a kind of national expression that is more in keeping with the resistant, oral culture of Ireland. Friel's refusal to narrow the representation of O'Neill — and consequently, that of Ireland — to one calcified image allows multiple meanings to emerge from each performance.

To conclude, any confusion caused by this argument, with all its different representations of O'Neill, will precisely illustrate the point that the stage is an ideal space to allow for play between various historical texts, because on the stage, the tension between competing narratives is illustrated simply by visual images. The most striking image in *Making History* is that of the book, Lombard's manuscript-in-progress, which sits at the center of the stage. In the same way that Western European nations center their national history around epics, *Making History* positions Lombard's history book at the center of the stage throughout the play. Although the book itself is concrete, rival interpretations persist in challenging its fixity throughout the production. In the context of the Field Day project, the huge book evokes the images of the controversial *Anthology of Irish Writing* and of the contested histories within the loose metanarrative that the anthology creates. Field Day produced the anthology, like the plays, in an attempt to articulate Irishness, to investigate what it means to be Irish — with the intention of broadening the definition — and to resist narrow stereotypes. Like O'Faoláin's biography, the anthology also exudes an ostensibly value-free aura, because it appears to present merely the literature that comprises the cultural heritage of the community. The outraged responses to the anthology illustrate just how "value-laden" any such anthology inevitably is, because the compilers make decisions to include texts based on what they think is important to the construction of Irishness.

With that in mind, I want to resist reading *Making History* as a play that offends no one in its refusal to toe any particular political line, because the whole effect of dramatizing the play between the competing narratives is achieved with the acknowledgment that political agendas are built into interpretations of culture. *Making History* expresses the orality and multiplicity of Irish history without exclusion or calcification while centering the performance around the text in question. Friel's play performs the story of Hugh the way that the anthology performs the nation. Both productions place the text at the center of the stage, and both refuse to limit their subject to what the text dictates, but rather, they find the expression of their subject in the competing narratives about the subject that each performance generates.

Making History has been accused of being a bad play, a boring play, an overly intellectual play, a dramatized Field Day pamphlet. The irony that a number of Field Day plays work better on the page than on the stage lies in the fact that their aim is to conduct cultural critique through artistic expression. The company's political agenda is to recognize how various representations derive their perspectives and to hold them in tension with other views. So rather than expecting Field Day's stage to be a value-free "fifth province" which decontaminates culture, we can read the company as one that is self-consciously making histories in the plural sense, not excluding the representation of them to the written words in the book but rather allowing for the play of different interpretations on the stage, while the book remains present on stage, perpetually deconstructed by the performances that surround it.

NOTES

1. In *Twentieth-Century Irish Drama: Mirror Up to Nation*, Christopher Murray calls attention to the existence of another precursor text, Thomas Kilroy's play *O'Neill* (1969), and suggests that Kilroy's play may have "paved the way" for Friel's *Making History*. For this reason, Murray recommends studying the plays in tandem (184).

2. I am grateful to Mary Burgess at the University of Notre Dame for her own critique of O'Faoláin's text, which led me to think about O'Neill's biography in this manner.

3. Shakir Mustafa's dissertation, particularly its second chapter, contains a useful, thorough analysis of the growth of historical revisionism and its trends throughout the twentieth century.

4. See Richtarik and Dantanus.

5. Sean Connolly objects to the last scene's ambiguous representation of O'Neill: "Our image of Hugh O'Neill remains that which he himself outlines: a man caught between two opposing worlds, seeking to act as mediator between a defeated Gaelic culture and an advancing English civilization" (163). I would argue that the dramatic tension between the two versions of O'Neill accommodates context in a manner that a quest for the "real" story cannot provide. For this reason, I find the public, dramatic depiction of multiple stories a revolutionary way of resisting the polarizing dichotomy that vexes debates about the anthology and the ceasefire talks as well.

6. Daniel Corkery's book of this title is the best known example of this patriotic view of Irish history. It is precisely such "biased" history that O'Faoláin seeks to displace in favor of the "value-free" history promoted by historical revisionists in the twentieth century.

7. Robert Welch calls O'Neill's fellow chieftains "casualties of language" — victims of such abstract nouns as "tyranny," "nobility," and "soul"; their faith in and loyalty to such highly contested terms is their eventual downfall ("Isn't This Your Job?" 147).

8. See Anderson, for example, "Old Language, New Models," in *Imagined Communities* (67–82).

9. The word "nation" itself would have been used as early as the twelfth century. But the term "nation-state," although Friel does not hyphenate it here, would not have been used until 1918, according to the *Oxford English Dictionary*.

10. Later in Lombard's history, the archbishop embellishes O'Neill's foresight as he tells O'Neill how he has written about "those early intimations you must have had of an emerging nation state" (64). Here again Friel marks the similarities between the historian and the storyteller, as each employs the language and perspective of the present to narrate the past.

11. I am grateful to Marilynn Richtarik for suggesting that this quotation is an example of history speaking to the present, which could as easily refer to the Thatcher administration as to the reign of Elizabeth I.

12. See Bradshaw.

13. See Gray, Longley, and Mulhern.

14. Richard Pine writes, of the ambiguity of the ending of *Making History*, "In order to be Irish, it is necessary to reject 'either/or' in favor of 'both/and'; it means to suffer the uncertainties of life in the gap, to allow the life sentences of our conflicting and potentially lethal versions of time to run concurrently" (219).

—16—

"Ireland, the Continuous Past": Stewart Parker's Belfast History Plays

MARILYNN RICHTARIK

In an author's note to the Samuel French edition of his play *Catchpenny Twist* (1977), Stewart Parker emphasized the relevance of Irish history to the headlines of the present:

> When Americans talk about "the past," they might mean Watergate, or Chappaquiddick, or maybe Dallas in 1963. When the Irish say "the past," they're gesturing back at least three hundred years to Cromwell and King Billy, and often beyond. . . . Grow up in Northern Ireland today, and your every step is dogged by whichever of the two camps you were born into. You can surrender to it, react against it, run away from it . . . you can't ignore it. The past is alive and well and killing people in Belfast. (Parker 92–93)

Born in East Belfast in 1941, Parker shared with many of his Northern Irish contemporaries (including Seamus Heaney, Michael Longley, and Seamus Deane) a sense of obligation to respond to the cultural and political peculiarities of the province. As a student at Queen's University, Parker had been eager to escape Belfast, but the Troubles that began in the late 1960s solidified his commitment to the city in complex ways. As a writer, he felt keenly the duty thrust upon him by a particular time and place to bring insight rather than obfuscation to public perceptions of what often seemed a hopeless situation. At the same time, he resisted the compulsion to make the violence itself the subject of his drama, preferring the excavation of causes to the mere portrayal of symptoms. Taking as his exemplar Sam Thompson, a member of the previous generation of Belfast playwrights with whose working-class Protestant roots and socialist politics he could identify, Parker conceived of the dramatist as "a truth-teller, a sceptic in a credulous world." Playwrights had a solemn responsibility because, he wrote, "a play which reinforces complacent assumptions, which confirms lazy preconceptions, which fails to combine emotional honesty with coherent analysis, which goes in short for the easy answer, is in my view actually harmful" (Parker, *Dramatis Personae* 18–19). Throughout his career, from his earliest radio features to his final stage play, Parker's work was distinguished by its intense engagement with the history of his native city, and in his most enduring dramas Belfast becomes a character in its own right, with its quest for a viable identity placed squarely at the center of the stage.

Even before the start of The Troubles, Parker had recognized the importance of history to the Northern stalemate, but for a time, the problem remained to find a way to represent it. Parker's work for the British Broadcasting Corporation (BBC) Northern Ireland's Schools Department in the early 1970s provided him with a crucial apprenticeship. The BBC's charter included an educational mission, and a central Schools Department in London produced programs on history, literature, science, and even physical education, which were broadcast weekly in a format aimed at the classrooms of the United Kingdom. Each region of the BBC also had a certain number of slots that it could fill with its own programming. It was not until 1960, however, that Northern Ireland had acquired its own Schools Department, like those established many years earlier in Scotland and Wales, to produce programs of mainly local interest (Cathcart 200). The reason for the delay was political: Unionist officials opposed the creation of a broadcasting entity whose *raison d'être* would be to focus on "Irish" subjects, which were associated in their minds with republican views; Nationalists, on the other hand, regarded with suspicion the offerings of a Broadcasting Corporation with the prefix "British" attached to its name. The formation of the Northern Irish Schools Department reflected the easing of communal tensions in the province that would continue through the first half of the 1960s, but by the time Parker was writing for it, violence had erupted in the province and the Schools Department had become, in effect, an "emergency service," providing a more "consistent and coherent" treatment of things Irish than any other department in the region (Carson 1998). A small team of educators-turned-producers ran the Northern Irish Schools Department from their offices in Belfast, annually producing several series of programs on Irish history, Irish geography, Irish writing, and Northern Irish history and culture. Parker himself worked most often for a program called *Today and Yesterday in Northern Ireland*, a miscellany of history, legend, folklore, social geography, storytelling, music, and contemporary culture (McAuley). The local Schools broadcasts were enjoyed by the general population as well as by the captive audiences in classrooms, and those who tuned in were given an opportunity, in the anonymous space provided by radio, to enrich their understanding of Northern Ireland and its complex relationship with the rest of Ireland, Britain, Europe, and the world. At a time when many other outlets for creative expression were cut off, BBC Schools Northern Ireland also provided steady employment for local writers and actors, who had a chance, through frequent production sessions, to meet and get to know each other.

The social commitment of the Northern Irish Schools Department — its aim of inducing the future decision-makers of the province to acknowledge, respect, and even appreciate Northern Ireland's diversity and to recognize the intertwining strands of a shared Northern Irish culture — underlay everything that it produced. A young writer could also imbibe a great deal about professionalism through working for the BBC. Accuracy was always of paramount importance, and producers and writers collaborated on the research that went into any Schools program. Writers had to present their work under a deadline; they usually had about a month to write any given script, which would then be subject to (sometimes extensive) revision before being sent on to the studio for recording and editing. Moreover, most Schools programs used a semi-dramatized format, with a narrator and actors, and were treated by the producers and technical support people as serious radio drama. Thus, they provided particularly useful experience for aspiring playwrights. Writing for Schools honed the writers' skills of selection, exposition, clarity, and concision. In some respects, the challenges faced by a writer for, say, *Today and Yesterday in Northern Ireland* were virtually unique: to present material of substance about, for example, the first Catholic parish priest of Belfast (one of Parker's subjects), material that would certainly be regarded as controversial in certain quarters; to do this with political aims that must never appear to be partisan or too overt; to ensure the accuracy of said material; to balance factual narration and more engaging dramatization; to capture and hold the attention of children ranging from ten to thirteen years of age, from all sorts of backgrounds — and to do all this in twenty minutes.

Parker's on-the-job training as a Schools writer left its mark on his interests, strategies, and craftsmanship as a playwright. His radio play *The Iceberg*, produced by BBC Northern Ireland in 1974 and first transmitted in January 1975, was, Parker said later, the first of his plays that he felt he wanted to keep a copy of (Allen 9). In it he tells a story about the *Titanic*, a story that does not focus on its sinking on 15 April 1912. Everyone knows that the sinking happened, and throughout Parker plays on the audience's knowledge in a textbook application of dramatic irony, but the action centers on Hugh and Danny, workers from the Belfast shipyard that built what was then "the largest vessel in the world" (Bardon, *Belfast: An Illustrated History* 176). The audience does not even have the usual suspense of wondering whether the two protagonists will live or die, because they are already dead — ghosts haunting the ship on its maiden voyage. Parker got the idea for the play while reading the Irish socialist James Connolly, who made the point that while the world was shocked and horrified by the deaths of millionaires on board the *Titanic*, no one seemed to give a thought to the seventeen Belfast shipyard workers who were killed during its construction (Gardner 8). People can see and hear Hugh and Danny, and the two men are subject to emotions and sensations, but their fate has already been sealed. They are beyond harm, or, as they put it, "home and dry." The destiny of the other passengers, though, has yet to be decided. In the closing moments of the play, as the ship approaches and hits the iceberg, Hugh and Danny's description of the scene (windless, dark, the sea calm and "black as gas") echoes the language they used earlier to describe the instant before their own accident. Parker suggests in this way that what is about to happen to the ship as a whole is no worse than what happened to them individually. In writing the play he rescues their deaths from inconsequence.

Parker was also struck by the coincidence in time between the shipwreck and the debate in the British House of Commons on the Third Irish Home Rule Bill, "a moment long awaited by the Nationalists of the Irish Party and long feared by the Unionists" (Bardon, *Belfast* 177). Organized Unionist resistance to the idea of Home Rule for the whole of Ireland would result directly in partition and indirectly in the political impasse and renewed violence experienced by Parker and his contemporaries. In *The Iceberg*, Parker makes the doomed ship a metaphor for the equally ill-fated "statelet" of Northern Ireland. The ship's grand staircase and first-class dining saloon are designed and decorated "in the style of the time of William and Mary," the very time when the original Protestant planters were solidifying their control of Ulster, and it represents the province's "proudest offering — to the Empire — and to the world" (Parker, "The Iceberg" 3, 28). What had been intended as a monument to Belfast ingenuity, however, would be remembered as a tragic vessel whose short career was marred by the *hubris* that allowed it to set sail with 2,201 people and only twenty lifeboats on board (Bardon, *Belfast* 177). Throughout the play, Parker implies an ironic contrast between the ship's luxurious appointments (private promenade decks, stained-glass windows, gymnasium, Turkish baths, and so forth) and its ignominious end.

Characters at two different social levels debate the extent to which Belfast (and, by extension, Northern Ireland) has been made or hampered by its association with the British Empire. In the first-class lounge, Thomas Andrews, managing director of the Harland & Wolff shipyard and chief designer of the *Titanic*, encounters Dr. O'Loughlin, a Southern Irishman and Home Ruler. Andrews is characterized by Parker as the stereotypical honest Ulsterman. He is unemotional and relentlessly hardworking, a perfectionist and a philistine. Naturally, he is also a Unionist who opposes Home Rule because it will mean "Dublin taxes on Northern industry to prop up its own peasant economy." "We're simply rationalists up in the North, doctor," he explains: "We look at Belfast today, a city close to half a million souls employed in manufacturing industries that can compete with any in the world. Yet what was it before the Act of Union made us part and parcel of Britain? A scruffy provincial village" (Parker, "The Iceberg" 55).

Andrews's views are parroted by Danny, who is convinced that a ship like the *Titanic* could never have been built by the "shiftless" people of Cork. Hugh, older and more experienced, is of the opinion that "if they had the chance to get the jobs in the South, they'd work as blindly as us poor gets." Soon the two are embroiled in an argument about whether Belfast is servant or master, with Danny taking pride in the fact that "Belfast-built" is a phrase that means "workmanship" the world over. Hugh retorts that the ship was paid for by English magnates and built for "Yankee" millionaires: "I didn't notice them inviting the mayor of Belfast on the maiden voyage. Take a walk round the decks and ask all the tycoons you meet where the ship was built. . . . I guarantee you that nine out of ten of them won't have a notion" (40). Later, Hugh and Danny read in the ship's newspaper about protests in Belfast against the Home Rule Bill and German plans to build an even bigger ocean liner than the *Titanic*. Through this juxtaposition Parker makes the point that Belfast's fate is being decided in the context of imperial competition that has little to do with its best interests (four years later, 5500 men of the Ulster Division would be killed or wounded on the first day of the Battle of the Somme). Danny is crestfallen but sure that "Harland's 'ill build a bigger one again." "Certainly they will," Hugh agrees facetiously, "they'll put a slipway under Belfast and launch the whole cursed city into the river — after the people have all been shot by the Army — for refusing to obey orders and abandon ship" (43). When a bigoted English stoker asks them if they are Irish, Danny replies defensively that they "come from the shipyard," but the man makes no distinction between them and the other "paddies" he has persecuted over the years (50–51).

Danny is portrayed as being in some ways more intellectual than Hugh — he is always quoting poetry and musing over the meanings, sounds, and associations of words, for example, and he is commended for his work by Thomas Andrews himself — but he is more naive politically. Although he mouths clichés about the Southern Irish, it is obvious that he feels more at home with third-class Cork passengers Molly and Rosaleen than with any-one else that they encounter on the ship, and he cites Thomas Moore and Shakespeare with equal facility. Hugh, who maintains that — unlike Danny, who "would have gone far" — he himself was "only fit to drive rivets" (37), is nonetheless feeling his way toward a radical critique of the interlocked systems of capitalism, imperialism, and Unionism, envisioning a unity of interest among working men of all sorts. "If you've four or five thousand men building a ship," Danny argues, "it stands to reason some of them'll have accidents. There's men killed on every ship." "Why? For what?" asks

Hugh (58). His questions hang unanswered over the end of the play, but perhaps the meeting of ship and iceberg is what the two men have been expecting all along, the "something" that will "happen to clear it all up" (15). For if the *Titanic* is the ship of state, a microcosm of an unjust society, then all that the wealthy passengers on board can see is the tip of the iceberg, and sooner or later the vessel is doomed to founder on the submerged aspirations of the mass of the population.

Parker's first professionally produced stage play, *Spokesong*, was directed by Michael Heffernan, the director of *The Iceberg*, and premiered at the 1975 Dublin Theatre Festival. In it, as in the radio play, Parker drew on local history, though *Spokesong* also deals explicitly with the violence of the early 1970s in Belfast. In trying "to isolate what is at the heart of the turbulence in Ireland at the moment," he deliberately "decided against writing a play about Protestants and Catholics fighting each other, or another play about the I.R.A." Parker felt that that would only be dealing with the surface; the "core," he believed, had to do with how people perceive their history, the past, and what sort of relationship they establish with it (Berkvist 5). "The thing that obsesses me," he told an interviewer in 1976, "is the link between the past and the present. How do you cope with the present when the past is still unfinished?" (Gardner 8).

The first challenge that Parker faced was a formal one. As he recalled in 1979, "I had to make manageable the subject of contemporary Irish politics and the nature of the violence I've lived through in Belfast for the past 10 years. . . . And I wanted to do it in such a way that the audience would be taken completely by surprise, caught without its preconceptions. I decided that the way to do that was to write a play about the history of the bicycle — because that is the most unlikely way in the world to get into the subject of Northern Ireland." The historical connection between Belfast and bicycles hinged on John Boyd Dunlop's invention of the pneumatic tire there in 1887, an invention which allowed cyclists literally to ride on air. "That's just a bit of folklore you know if you grow up there," Parker explained, "along with the fact that the *Titanic* was built there" (Berkvist 5). Moreover, he observed in 1985, "it is an aspect of social history which runs (I can put it no other way) in tandem with the political history of the Unionist/Nationalist ideological divide, in an uncanny and provocative fashion." The period from Dunlop's innovation to the early 1970s "encompasses the end of Parnellism, Randolph Churchill and the Orange Card, the Home Rule Bills, the Great War, Partition, and so on, right up to Bloody Sunday and Bloody Friday" (Parker, "Signposts" 28).

It is what Parker called the bicycle "conceit" (Berkvist 5) that made *Spokesong* so startlingly original in 1975 and what keeps it fresh even today. The play is set in a bicycle shop founded by Francis Stock in 1895 and now run by his grandson Frank. This family business is under siege from both republican and loyalist bombers, who will either blow it up or demand money to "protect" it, as well as the planners who want to tear it down as part of a scheme to build motorways through the center of the city. Parker's first stage direction explains that "the action takes place in Belfast, Northern Ireland, during the early 1970's and the eighty years preceding them" (Parker, *Spokesong* 8). Scenes alternate between the past, in which Francis (an "Empire Loyalist") woos and wins his beloved Kitty (a "Maud-Gonne–style Nationalist" and radical feminist), and the present, in which the starry-eyed Frank courts a practical schoolteacher named Daisy Bell (Parker, "Signposts" 28). An ambiguous character called the Trick Cyclist mediates between past and present — presiding over the action on stage, taking a number of parts, and singing most of the songs. In dress and deportment he recalls the variety act, a popular form of working-class entertainment in late Victorian and early twentieth-century Belfast, and Parker said he conceived of the Trick Cyclist as a chorus figure who embodies "the spirit of Belfast" (Berkvist 5). This "spirit" is often repressive, as is evidenced by a sampling of the roles the character assumes: the Reverend Peacock, who is scandalized by the sight of Kitty in "bifurcated garments" (16); Kitty's father, who disowns her for marrying a "bicycle tradesman" (36); the inspector chairing the inquiry into the motorway scheme, who, Frank says, is so determined not to make a fool of himself that he has "admitted his imagination into the morgue" as a precaution (33); and Daisy's father, "Tinker" Bell, head of the local Protestant paramilitary organization, who hits Frank up for contributions to the cause and "goes in every Friday to collect his dole money with an armed bodyguard" (53). On a more positive note, the Trick Cyclist represents antic playfulness, a delight in language for its own sake, which Parker also perceived in Belfast culture, and the songs that he sings, parodying the styles of distinct musical eras in turn, help to reinforce the illusion that the play takes place over a period of eighty years. Parker recalled ten years later that "I felt that I had at long last found a way of embracing the whole city, my city, in this play" (Parker, "Signposts" 28).

The year before *Spokesong* opened, Parker had contributed to a Schools series on "People at Work." The producer, Tony McAuley, had offered him the rare opportunity to write a fictional story about any occupation he chose and had been surprised and delighted when Parker decided to focus on the Corporation workers who were planting flowers around the center of Belfast, even as it was subject to constant bombing attacks (McAuley). Frank Stock is the "spokesman" for a similar naive optimism, daring to imagine a future in a city that seems consumed by past and present troubles. He runs the local Community Association, which is engaged in opposing the motorway scheme, and the play opens with him presenting an alternative plan to the panel assembled to hear reactions to the proposal. Frank advocates that free bicycles be distributed around the city center to minimize the reliance on cars. For him, the issue is people's control over their own lives. "So far as personal transport goes," he rhapsodizes, "the bicycle was the last advance in technology that everybody understands." In contrast, the fateful invention of the internal combustion engine put people "at the mercy of alien machines, mysteries for other people to solve" (19). As a reviewer for *Time* magazine summed it up, in Frank's view of the world, "the bicycle stands for sweet-souled individual freedom and the automobile for arrogant mass tyranny" (Kalem 58). This argument makes a strong appeal in a city in which the threat of car bombs is ever present. "Christ on a bicycle," Frank reflects: "You can see that. You can't see him driving a Jaguar. Or an Avenger. Or a Sting-ray. A car is just a hard shell of aggression, for the soft urban mollusc to secrete itself in. It's a form of disguise. All its parts are hidden. No wonder they're using them as bombs. It's a logical development. A bicycle hides nothing and threatens nothing. It is what it does, its form is its function. An automobile is a weapon of war" (42).

Ian Hill, a friend of Parker's from his university days, observed in a review of the Lyric's 1989 production of *Spokesong* that "to have known Parker is to see him in Frank: the wryness, the self mockery, the eclectic use of arcane and academic wordplay, the prevailing pervading love affair with a city of picture palaces and brown-shop-coated tradesmen, which was to fall as much to the fly-over planner as to the terrorist" (Ian Hill). While there is considerable truth to this claim, Parker was also aware of the limitations of his protagonist's point of view. Frank's nostalgic vision of the past is exemplified by the relationship between Francis and Kitty, who have nothing in common apart from their shared passion for bicycles, which, Parker noted, "is a form of love for humanity itself" (Parker, "Signposts" 28). This would seem to suggest that love can conquer all, that personal relationships can outweigh the bitterness of a divisive history and politics. It is important to remember, however, that these grandparents, idealized and lovable exponents of the Unionist and Irish Nationalist positions that took enduring shape at the end of the nineteenth century, appear to us only through Frank's romantic memory and imagination (Gillespie 7–9). His cynical adopted brother, Julian, who competes with him for Daisy's affections, protests that "they weren't in the smallest degree like that. . . . He was a vain and obsequious little Ulster tradesman, a crank and a bore, going over and over the same dog-eared tales of his youth and his war-experiences. . . . She was a spoiled daughter of the regiment, slumming it in the quaint backstreets and in her ridiculous lace-curtain nationalism" (60). Frank is a humanist who wants desperately to see the best in people, but in order to keep Daisy, he is forced to acknowledge some of the harder realities of Belfast life. The last major scene between Frank and the Trick Cyclist is an "exorcism" of Francis and Kitty, which entails, for Frank, the amputation of a part of his former identity and a modification of his philosophy. Life is not so simple as equating the bicycle with good and cars with bad; any technology is only as benign or destructive as the use to which it is put by humans (Gillespie 11–13). Jonathan Bardon records that even John Boyd Dunlop's invention had unforeseen consequences, for "though devised as an improvement for the bicycle, [it] was made just in time to ensure the success of the motor car" (Bardon, *Belfast* 135). Daisy, for her part, vacillates between Julian's witty nihilism and Frank's impractical idealism, finally deciding that no matter how bleak the present may be, the future will be worse if people stop appealing to the best qualities in each other. The play ends with Frank and Daisy pedaling off stage on a bicycle built for two; this final scene has the air of a *deus ex machina*. It is an upbeat and emotionally satisfying conclusion, rather desperately appended to an entertainment that has illustrated so well the intractable problem facing Frank and the other modern character — the problem of how to master the uncompleted history of Belfast.

Parker took a more uncompromising approach to the same problem in *Northern Star* (1984), which is set in "Ireland, the continuous past" (Parker, *Three Plays for Ireland* 13). In this play, it is the unfinished business of Irish republicanism that engrosses Parker. *Northern Star* focuses on the United Irishmen, instigators of the 1798 rebellion in Ireland and the original Irish republicans — that is, the first modern revolutionaries to envision a future for Ireland as an entity independent of Great Britain. The United Irishmen inspired, among others, the Young Irelanders (cultural nationalists of the 1840s led by Thomas Davis), the Fenians (physical-force nationalists of the mid-nineteenth century), the Irish Revolutionary Brotherhood (organizers of the 1916 Easter Rising), the IRA, and the Provisionals. In the elegant formulation of historian Kevin Whelan, the 1798 rebellion "never passed into history, because it never passed out of politics" (Whelan 133). One consequence of this is that historical interpretations of the formative 1790s in Ireland have always themselves been deeply political. In the immediate aftermath of 1798 and throughout the nineteenth century, for example, conservative Protestants, Whig liberals, repentant United Irishmen, Catholic leaders such as Daniel O'Connell, and later the Catholic Church itself — all for reasons of their own — contributed to a view of the rebellion as a spontaneous Catholic uprising against persecution by the Orange Order and the government of the day. This construction focused on County Wexford (where, in the event, the largest battles had taken place) and on warrior priests such as Father Murphy. It fit well with popular nineteenth-century Irish cultural nationalism, which had come to identify the "nation" with Irish Catholicism, but it distorted the actual character of the ill-fated revolution as a culmination of years of political activism on the part of the United Irishmen (Whelan 133–175). Now, another hundred years later, a new historical consensus has emerged that recognizes the 1798 rebellion as the mass-based, ideologically driven, and largely Protestant-led affair that it was. Stewart Parker, who started researching the United Irishmen in the late 1960s and who wrote *Northern Star* in the early 1980s, did not have the benefit of this most recent scholarship. Nevertheless, his intentions were not unlike those of the historians who have worked to recover the secular, egalitarian political ideals of the United Irishmen from the ash heap of the past.

Specifically, Parker wanted to restore the Belfast dimension of the 1798 rebellion to popular memory. This locus of revolutionary thinking and activity had been eclipsed by long focus on Wexford and Dublin, especially in the Republic of Ireland, but in point of fact, many of the most radical leaders of the United Irishmen — men such as Samuel Neilson, Thomas Russell, James Hope, and Henry Joy McCracken — were Belfast-based. Theobald Wolfe Tone, the most celebrated of the United Irishmen, came from Dublin but was closely affiliated with this Belfast wing of the move-ment and spent time in the North. Incredibly, given the political context of Parker's own lifetime (when working-class Protestants were likely to be the staunchest of Unionists), these founders of Irish republicanism were also, in the main, Presbyterians. In putting them at the heart of his drama, Parker was sending a direct message to his fellow Northern Protestants that, deny it though they might, they had a republican heritage. By placing the likes of McCracken at center stage, Parker was also signaling his dissatisfaction with the version of Irish history that had written Protestants out of the story of the nation. Lynne Parker, the playwright's niece, who directed the Rough Magic Theatre Company in a 1996 production of *Northern Star*, noted the disorienting effect that this re-centering had on Dublin audi-ences, members of which were far less familiar with the Belfast radicals than with the Dublin-based leaders of the rebellion (L. Parker).

McCracken is the protagonist of *Northern Star*, and Parker clearly felt a special affinity with him. Apart from being a gifted mimic (a detail Parker cherished), McCracken was a model of disinterested leadership, who stuck by the cause when most others had deserted it, taking command of the entire Army of the North after the arrest or resignation of more senior leaders a mere three days before the rising was due to begin. With few men and little support, he performed creditably on the field of battle until, ironically, his reinforcements were routed by an enemy retreat, causing his own troops to flee in panic. He was apparently without sectarian preju-dice, and, perhaps most important to Parker, despite his middle-class back-ground, he understood and sympathized with the problems of ordinary working people. All of this helped to make McCracken an ideal filter for Parker's own perspective on the United Irishmen, which was colored by his secular and socialist politics.

In Parker's opinion, the truly radical contribution of the United Irish-men was a new response to the question "What does it mean to be Irish?" Parker's McCracken answers the question thus:

> It meant to be dispossessed, to live on ground that isn't ours, Protestant, Catholic, Dissenter, the whole motley crew of us, planted together in this soil to which we've no proper title. . . . Look at me. My great-grandfather

> Joy was a French Huguenot, my great-grandfather McCracken was a
> Scottish Covenanter, persecuted, the pair of them, driven here from the
> shores of home, their home but not my home, because I'm Henry Joy
> McCracken and here to stay, a natural son of Belfast, as Irish a bastard as
> all the other incomers, blown into this port by the storm of history, Gaelic
> or Danish or Anglo-Norman, without distinction, it makes no odds, every
> mother's son of us children of nature on this sodden glorious patch of
> earth, unpossessed of deed or inheritance, without distinction. (Parker,
> *Three Plays for Ireland* 16–17)

Before the United Irishmen movement, members of the essentially Angli-
can Protestant Ascendancy had defined themselves as the Irish nation in a
fashion that excluded both Catholics and Dissenters from the full privileges
of citizenship. After the failure of the rebellion, and largely through the
agency of O'Connell's massive campaigns for Catholic emancipation and
the repeal of the Act of Union, Irish nationalism became almost indis-
tinguishable from Catholic nationalism (Whelan 152–153). The United
Irishmen succeeded for a short time in de-coupling a sense of the Irish
nation from sectarian allegiance. Looking back on them from the vantage
point of late twentieth-century Belfast, this did seem an extraordinary
achievement to Parker.

Nevertheless, the tone of *Northern Star* is not wholly celebratory, and
Parker's attitude toward the United men was far from reverential. Although
he was sympathetic to their original goal of "a cordial union among *all the
people of Ireland*" (Bardon, *Belfast* 220), Parker believed that their ultimate
decision to pursue political ends by military means was a mistake that would
inevitably, as one of his characters says, "spread the very disease it was
meant to cure" (Parker, *Three Plays for Ireland* 53). The United Irishmen, he
suggests, were responsible not only for the ideal of republicanism but also
for its tradition of violence. Whatever their intentions, the leaders of the
rebellion were not always able to control the forces they helped to set in
motion. In particular, well-publicized massacres at Scullabogue and Wexford Bridge cooled the ardor of liberal Protestants for Catholic emancipation and contributed to a reaction against the idea of an Irish nation that
could contain all the separate strands of Irish society. In Parker's view, a
man of McCracken's generous spirit could not have failed to see that the
legacy of the United Irishmen might not be entirely positive. The action of
Northern Star takes place during one of McCracken's last nights as a free
man, before his capture, trial, and execution. Looking back on the entire
United movement with the benefit of hindsight, Parker's McCracken worries that "all we've done . . . is to reinforce the locks, cram the cells fuller
than ever of mangled bodies crawling round in their own shite and lunacy,
and the cycle just goes on, playing out the same demented comedy of
terrors from generation to generation, trapped in the same malignant leg-

end, condemned to re-endure it as if the Anti-Christ who dreamed it up was driven astray in the wits by it and the entire pattern of depravity just goes spinning on out of control, on and on, round and round, till the day the world itself is burst asunder, that's the handsome birthright that we're handing on" (65).

Parker's interpretation of the 1790s in Ireland was obviously shaped by his experience of the 1970s, and the script of *Northern Star* is replete with parallels to the contemporary Troubles. An ironic mention of "O'Neill, the great moderate reformer" (43), for example, refers ostensibly to Lord O'Neill, "once the darling of the Presbyterian freeholders now in combat against him" (Bardon, *Belfast* 233), but this reference inescapably stirs up echoes of Captain Terence O'Neill, the prime minister of Northern Ireland in the late 1960s, whose attempts to liberalize the province were too little, too late. Toward the end of the play, a scene depicting McCracken and some of his fellow conspirators in prison utilizes imagery that is deliberately reminiscent of the dirty protest and hunger strikes of contemporary republican prisoners, while a graphic interrogation scene depicts, anachronistically, the government's use of bright lights and white noise on detainees. The implication, by extension, is that the doubts expressed by McCracken about the efficacy of violence might apply equally to the more self-scrutinizing of modern insurgents. Parker's message in 1984 was that support for civil rights, social justice, and a more equitable society in Ireland need not, indeed should not, translate into support for absolutely anything done by those who claim to act in the name of republicanism.

The structure of *Northern Star* is integral to its meaning. Parker alternates "confessional" scenes between McCracken and his lover Mary Bodle with "rhetorical" flashback scenes of the events leading up to the rising. In the latter, Parker imitates in turn the styles of great Irish playwrights—Sheridan, Boucicault, Wilde, Shaw, Synge, O'Casey, Behan, and Beckett—with nods to others thrown in for good measure. This multiplicity of voices underlines Parker's pluralistic vision of Irish identity while simultaneously commenting on the fact that the past and present in Ireland continue to shape each other. As Parker remarked in 1985, "You start speaking about an event that happened in Derry last week and immediately voices of 1641 are clamouring to be heard." The technique of pastiche, he explained, "allowed me to march the play throughout the decades towards the present day and say to the audience, forget about historical veracity, forget about realism, I'm going to tell you a story about the origins of Republicanism and I'm going to offer you a point of view on what's gone wrong with it and why it's become corrupt and why it's now serving the opposite ends to what it set out to serve, and I'm going to demonstrate this like a ventriloquist, using a variety of voices" (Carty). For Fintan O'Toole, the form of *Northern Star* reminds us that "the events of 1798 are still being, literally, played out": "An extraordinary tension is created by the way the styles of writing and performance move forward in time from the 18th century to the 20th. In terms of content, we are looking back on Henry Joy's tragic dilemmas. In terms of style, they are rushing forward to meet us" (O'Toole, "Second Opinion").

The line "Citizens of Belfast," which is repeated like a refrain throughout *Northern Star*, plays on this double valence of the unfolding action. It is aimed both at McCracken's imaginary audience, as he rehearses his "famous last words" (Parker, *Three Plays for Ireland* 15), and at the real-life citizens of Belfast, who Parker hoped would be in the theatre audience. In McCracken's last long speech, love and longing mingle with apprehension regarding the future:

> Why would one place break your heart, more than another? A place the like of that? Brain-damaged and dangerous, continuously violating itself, a place of perpetual breakdown, incompatible voices, screeching obscenely away through the smoky dark wet. Burnt out and still burning. Nerve-damaged, pitiable. Frightening. As maddening and tiresome as any other pain-obsessed cripple. And yet what would this poor fool not give to be able to walk freely again from Stranmillis down to Ann Street . . . cut through Pottinger's Entry and across the road for a drink in Peggy's . . . to dander on down Waring Street and examine the shipping along the river, and back on up to our old house . . . we can't love it for what it is, only for what it might have been, if we'd got it right, if we'd made it whole. If. It's a ghost town now and always will be, angry and implacable ghosts. Me condemned to be one of their number. We never made a nation. Our brainchild. Stillborn. Our own fault. We botched the birth. So what if the English do bequeath us to one another some day? What then? When there's nobody else to blame except ourselves? (75)

The ending of the play holds out only as much hope as audience members can find in themselves and each other. McCracken mounts the platform one last time and places a noose around his neck. "Citizens of Belfast . . . ," he begins, but gets no further before the beating of a lambeg drum (symbol of twentieth-century Unionist triumphalism) drowns out his words and the lights fade to black. In contrast to *Spokesong*, Parker refuses the neat resolution of any ending, let alone a happy one. What he offers instead is a bleak but bracing challenge to the audience to arrest the cycle of retribution.

Parker's stage play *Pentecost* (1987) must be seen as a counterbalance to *Northern Star*. Together they form part of a common enterprise for the playwright, what he describes as a "triptych" of plays set in Ireland in the eighteenth, nineteenth, and twentieth centuries, respectively (Parker, *Three Plays for Ireland* 9). *Northern Star* and *Pentecost* have more in common with each other than with the middle play in the series — *Heavenly Bodies* (1986), an exploration of the life and times of the Victorian melodramatist Dion Boucicault — by virtue of the fact that they both center on Belfast. In addition, both *Northern Star* and *Pentecost* place particular emphasis on aspects of Northern Protestant consciousness and mentality. The imagery evoked by McCracken's valediction to the audience in *Northern Star* is reiterated and expanded in *Pentecost*, as are McCracken's hopes and fears for the future. Both plays encourage Northern Protestants and Catholics to start seeing what they share instead of only the characteristics that divide them, but both remain crucially unresolved by the final blackout. Despite these affinities, audiences and readers are initially likely to find the differences between the two plays more striking. In contrast to *Northern Star*'s virtuoso theatricality, *Pentecost* is the most naturalistic stage play that Parker ever wrote — McCracken refers metaphorically to dead babies and angry ghosts; in *Pentecost* these tropes take literal form. *Northern Star* concerns itself with the public and political to an extent unusual in Parker's work, while *Pentecost* portrays the private anguish of its characters against a background of civil crisis. *Northern Star* is dominated by male characters; *Pentecost* is anchored by its women. Perhaps most important, in *Pentecost* the despair expressed by McCracken yields finally to a tentative optimism.

Parker regarded both of these works as "history plays," but whereas in *Northern Star* the challenge had been to find a way to make a rebellion that took place nearly 200 years previous seem relevant to modern audiences, in *Pentecost* Parker was attempting to treat historically events that he himself had lived through. He decided that a style of "heightened realism" was "most appropriate for my own generation, finally making its own scruffy way onto the stage of history and from thence into the future tense" (10). The play is set in Belfast at a time when violence and intimidation won out over what looked to many people to be a promising political settlement (one not unlike the Good Friday Agreement of 1998, in fact). During the Ulster Workers' Council (UWC) Strike of 1974, militant Protestant workers managed to topple the power-sharing executive intended to replace direct rule from London with local authority divided between Protestants and Catholics. Hard-line loyalists objected both to power-sharing and to the so-called Irish dimension of the agreement. Their strike began with the closing of factories and the shutting off of the power supply and proceeded to threats to the water and sewage systems before the Unionist members of the executive resigned, thus ending the experiment in self-government. The action of *Pentecost* takes place before, during, and immediately after the UWC Strike, which Parker remembered as "one of the most hopeless moments" of the recent Irish past (Clines).

The first stage direction of *Northern Star* describes the setting as a "half-built and half-derelict" cottage on the slopes of the Cavehill (13), a visual reminder of the uncompleted and discredited project of the United Irishmen. *Pentecost* also takes place in a typical working-class dwelling, in the "downstairs back part of a respectable . . . 'parlour' house" in Belfast. This house is the home of the recently deceased Lily Matthews, whose life story is archetypal of the working-class Protestant experience in that city

during the twentieth century. She moved into the house as a bride of eigh-
teen the same week that her husband Alfie returned from the First World
War (alive but impotent), was burned out of it during the sectarian disturbances of 1921, and returned to endure the Depression, the Blitz, and the
tormenting memory of her infidelity to Alfie during the year that he spent
looking for work in England. Stage directions make it clear that the house
has absorbed the personality of its long-time occupant:

> The rooms are narrow, but the walls climb up and disappear into the
> shadows above the stage. The kitchen in particular is cluttered, almost
> suffocated, with the furnishings and bric-a-brac of the first half of the
> century, all the original fixtures and fittings still being in place. But in spite
> of now being shabby, musty, threadbare, it has all clearly been the object
> of a desperate, lifelong struggle for cleanliness, tidiness, orderliness—
> godliness. (147)

This parlor house is the only one left inhabited on the whole street, stranded
in the middle of what amounts to a war zone between Protestant and
Catholic ghettos. As if that were not bad enough, one of the characters
remarks, "the very road itself is scheduled to vanish off the map" since it is
"the middle of a redevelopment zone" (154). Besieged by the resurgence of
past animosities and an uncertain future as well, the house is a physical
embodiment of the working-class loyalism that is responsible for the turmoil in the streets outside it.

The current occupants of the house—of which two are male, two
female; two Protestant, two Catholic; all in their late twenties or early
thirties—are forced in the course of the play to come to terms with the
cultural and political legacy of the kind of Northern Protestantism represented by Lily Matthews and the UWC Strike, respectively. Lenny Harrigan, a shiftless musician from a middle-class Catholic background, inher-
ited the house from his aunt, but it has only just come into his possession
after the death of Lily, the sitting tenant. He agrees to sell the house and all
of its contents to his estranged wife, Marian, in exchange for a divorce. She
immediately takes up residence, but soon he is staying there, too, much to
her displeasure, after a burglary at his flat. Ruth, a Protestant friend of
Marian's (from their days on the Northern Ireland youth swimming team)
who is in flight from her abusive policeman husband, and Peter, a friend of
Lenny's (from university) and the son of a Methodist minister, have also
taken refuge in the house by the end of the first act. Through the characters' interactions with each other, Parker illustrates a range of possible
responses to the pressures of the Troubles.

Peter serves as the mouthpiece for many of Parker's own sentiments
from the time of *Pentecost*'s setting, though the reactions of the others to
Peter register the playwright's ironic distance from his younger self by the
time he came to write the play. *Pentecost* is self-consciously a period piece,

filled not only with references to the tense political situation and the sounds of distant explosions, Orange bands, and military helicopters but also with allusions to the counter-culture of the late 1960s and early 1970s. Peter's stories about the student unrest he witnessed at an American university and the plan that he and Lenny hatched to end the Northern crisis by dumping LSD into the Silent Valley Reservoir (thus "turn[ing] on the population, comprehensively") (184–185), his "1974 casual chic" clothing and anglicized accent (200–201), and the heavy sack of muesli that he lugs with him from his new home in Birmingham (169) all mark him out as the most cosmopolitan of the characters. Peter confesses that he suffers from a disease he calls exilephilia, "whatever the direct opposite of homesickness is . . . [t]he desperate nagging pain of longing to be far, far away" (186), but he has been drawn back by the spectacle of "[h]istoric days in Lilliput" and a nostalgia for the "authentic Lilliputian wit" (170–171). When Lenny asks him whether he intends to call Northern Ireland "Lilliput" for the duration of his unanticipated visit, Peter responds with a tirade: "What, this teeny weeny wee province of ours and its little people, all the angry munchkins, with their midget brains, this festering pimple on the vast white flabby bum of western Europe, what would *you* call it?" "I call it home," Lenny answers dryly (171–172). Later, as Peter continues to taunt Lenny with his seeming inability to make "the great escape" from Belfast, Lenny flares up at him: "I'll live whatever life I choose, and I'll live it here, what's it to you, you think you're any further on? You seriously think I'd want what you have?" (173, 206). Ruth, whose own Unionism has been reinforced by her experience of several years of violence, accuses Peter of not knowing his "own" people any more: "You have no notion how they feel, you opted out. You lost touch. You see it all like the English now, 'a plague on both their houses' . . . easy to say when it isn't your own house that's in mortal danger" (185). Despite his abrasiveness and, at times, silliness (Marian refers to him as "that trend-worshipping narcissist"), Peter's view of the loyalist strike is essentially clear-headed. He sees it as "a lingering tribal suicide" (191) and believes that the past five years' worth of destruction could have been avoided if the Unionists who had "held all the cards" had only been "marginally generous" (184). The loyalist victory, when it comes, though, causes him finally to break down and admit that he, too, is implicated in what happens in Belfast, that part of himself will always be missing anywhere else.

Though each of the four characters experiences a similar moment of truth (Ruth resolves to leave her husband for good this time, Lenny realizes that his wife was as devastated as he was by the end of their marriage), it is Marian who is the pivotal character in *Pentecost*, the one who changes most profoundly in the course of the play. She comes across at first as a brusque and bitter woman, so preoccupied with her own personal crisis as to be oblivious to the political trauma. Five years earlier, in August 1969 (a "vintage month," as Peter points out), she and Lenny lost their infant child to cot death. This was the beginning of the end of their marriage, and at the start of Act I they have been separated for close to two years. Marian has suddenly decided to sell her antique business and her flat, and she buys the house from Lenny as a retreat from everyone and everything that has constituted her life up to that point. What she is really trying to escape, though, is herself. Through the action of the play, she becomes a person open to the possibility of positive transformation.

Marian is an individual woman captured by Parker at a moment of radical transition, but she is also representative of the first generation of Northern Catholics, who were coming into their own in a province that had been organized for the express purpose of excluding them. Her function on this level is underlined by the fact that she is the only one of the younger characters to communicate with the dead Lily Matthews. Lily, of whom a reviewer for the *Belfast Newsletter* said "could be anyone's Gran from east Belfast," appears as a character in the play, though Parker does not specify whether she should be regarded as a ghost or as a personification of Marian's inner voice. Lily objects vehemently to having an "idolater" living in her house, and she spends the first half of the play, without success, trying to scare Marian into leaving. In *Northern Star* it was the Protestant Henry Joy McCracken who announced that he was "here to stay"; in *Pentecost*, Marian tells Lily, "You think you're haunting me, don't you. But you see it's me that's actually haunting you. I'm not going to go away. There's no curse or hymn that can exorcise me. So you might as well just give me your blessing and make your peace with me" (180). Lily never does accept Marian's right to be there, but in their successive scenes, she gradually opens up to the younger woman until the secret that deformed her own life is at last laid bare. In Alfie's absence, Lily gave birth alone to an illegitimate child, the result of her brief affair with their lodger, and abandoned the baby on the porch of a Baptist church. For over forty years, she had been "condemned to life" in that house, her judgmental rectitude a facade erected to conceal her own deep sense of depravity (202). She was, she says,

> all consumed by my own wickedness, on the inside, nothing left but the shell of me, for appearance's sake . . . still and all. At least I never let myself down—never cracked. Never surrendered. Not one inch. I went to my grave a respectable woman, Mrs Alfred George Matthews, I never betrayed him. That was the way I atoned, you see. I done him proud. He never knew any reason to be ashamed of me, or doubt my loyalty. (196)

Parker suggests that self-loathing, projected as hatred of other people, resides at the root of any human conflict, including the Northern crisis. At the beginning of the play, Marian is herself in danger of turning out like Lily. When the latter asks her to stay away from where she is not welcome, Marian explains that she has a problem complying with the request, "seeing as the place where I'm least welcome of all is the inside of my own skull . . .

so there's something we can agree on at least, Lily. I don't like me either" (157). Marian has come to the house in the first place to avoid human contact, and she reacts unsympathetically to the misfortunes that bring Lenny and Ruth to her door. Marian even starts to sound like Lily, complaining to Lenny about the "filth and mess and noise and bickering, in every last corner." When he worries aloud that she may not be fit to be left alone, she rounds on him with the words, "It wouldn't maybe have occurred to you, it wouldn't maybe have penetrated even that dim featherweight brain — that being on my own is the one thing I am fit for?" (191).

After provoking Lily into admitting her soul-destroying secret, however, Marian starts to turn around. When she asks Lily's forgiveness at the end of their last scene, she finally begins to forgive herself. Marian's growing empathy for the dead Lily, accompanied by the realization that many of the Protestant woman's wounds were self-inflicted, issues in Marian not only a resolve to keep from becoming Lily, but a desire to free the older woman from the burden of her past. Midway through the play, Marian had conceived the idea of offering the house and its contents, the artifacts of Lily's life, to the National Trust as a representative example of Belfast working-class culture. By the end, Marian has decided that that was "a wrong impulse" that would only have had the effect of "condemning [Lily] to life indefinitely." Instead, she wants to live in the house — clearing it out, giving it the light and air it needs (202). Rather than turning into Lily, Marian will carry her with her into the future, along with the memory of her own dead son, Christopher. The play ends in a kind of secular pentecost, as Marian speaks of rebirth and renewal in a manner that transcends the discord and division dramatized in the last two scenes of the play. "Personally," she declares,

> I want to live now. I want this house to live. We have committed sacrilege enough on life, in this place, in these times. We don't just owe it to ourselves, we owe it to our dead too . . . our innocent dead. They're not our masters, they're only our creditors, for the life they never knew. We owe them at least that — the fullest life for which they could ever have hoped, we carry those ghosts within us, to betray those hopes is the real sin against the Christ, and I for one cannot commit it one day longer. (208)

The lights gradually fade on a moment of hesitant communion among the four characters on stage, as Lenny and Peter improvise a version of "Just a Closer Walk with Thee," on trombone and banjo, in response to Marian's words, and Ruth finds a Christian equivalent in the Acts of the Apostles: "Therefore did my heart rejoice, and my tongue was glad; moreover also my flesh shall rest in hope . . . Thou hast made known to me the ways of life" (208). In the final moments of the play, Ruth reaches across to open the window, symbolizing the new openness of the characters to each other and to the future.

Throughout *Pentecost*, Parker carefully preserves the possibility that there is a rational explanation for Lily's presence on stage. To explain how Marian comes to know the most intimate details of the dead woman's life, he has Marian find an old diary of Lily's under the cellar stairs. At first glance this may seem to be the most transparent of plot devices, but on another level, the fact that Marian learns to see the humanity in Lily through reading her reflections is a poignant allusion to the power of the written word to lift us out of ourselves, to alter perception and to foster understanding. In fact, Parker's entire career, by means of which he deliberately wed himself to his native place through an imaginative engagement with its history, was a declaration of faith in people's capacity to be educated into tolerance and appreciation of each other. In *Dramatis Personae*, a lecture delivered in 1986, Parker reaffirmed his belief in the value of drama and offered his vision of what a playwright could do for Belfast:

> [I]f ever a time and place cried out for the solace and rigour and passionate rejoinder of great drama, it is here and now. There is a whole culture to be achieved. The politicians, visionless almost to a man, are withdrawing into their sectarian stockades. It falls to the artists to construct a working model of wholeness by means of which this society can begin to hold up its head in the world. (Parker, *Dramatis Personae* 19)

Pentecost was Parker's most determined attempt to construct such a model. Tragically, it also turned out to be his last.

—17—

Frank McGuinness and the Ruins of Irish History

JAMES HURT

Frank McGuinness's career as a playwright has reached the end of its second decade, the last decade of the century following William Butler Yeats's and Augusta Gregory's challenge to Irish playwrights to "build up a Celtic and Irish school of dramatic literature [. . .] to bring upon the stage the deeper thoughts and emotions of Ireland." Few playwrights have taken up the challenge to address the matter of Ireland more originally and unexpectedly than McGuinness. From *The Factory Girls* (1980), which memorializes the female working-class culture of Donegal in the 1950s, to *Mutabilitie* (1997), set in 1598 in the midst of Hugh O'Neill's rising, McGuinness has dramatized again and again conflicted pressure points in Irish history. Even the plays not set in Ireland—*Innocence* (1986), set in Renaissance Rome, and *Someone Who'll Watch over Me* (1992), set in Beirut—are easily read as metaphoric treatments of Irish themes. Over and over, as Mic Moroney has commented, "McGuinness has lashed himself to the mast of Irish history" (16). Using the historiographic writings of Walter Benjamin, I will survey McGuinness's principal treatments of Irish history—*The Factory Girls, Observe the Sons of Ulster Marching towards the Somme, Innocence, Carthaginians, Someone Who'll Watch over Me*, and *Mutabilitie*—and try to generalize from these plays to arrive at descriptions of both McGuinness's view of Irish history and his practice as a writer of history plays.

McGuinness, insofar as he is a historian, writes the history of moments: an episode in the labor history of Donegal, the Battle of the Somme, Bloody Sunday, the Beirut hostage crisis. In this he resembles the historical materialist of Walter Benjamin's "Theses on the Philosophy of History":

Universal history has no theoretical armature. Its method is additive; it
musters a mass of data to fill the homogeneous, empty time. Materialistic
historiography, on the other hand, is based on a constructive principle.
Thinking involves not only the flow of thoughts, but their arrest as well.
Where thinking suddenly stops in a configuration pregnant with tensions,
it gives that configuration a shock, by which it crystallizes into a monad. . . .
[The historical materialist] takes cognizance of it in order to blast a specific
era out of the homogeneous course of history — blasting a specific life out
of the era or a specific work out of the lifework. (262–263)

To identify a "configuration pregnant with tensions," to give that configuration a "shock," and thereby to "blast" it out of the homogeneous course
of history — Benjamin's words describe quite precisely McGuinness's practice. *The Factory Girls* sets the pattern. McGuinness was inspired, he writes,
by the desire "to write a play that celebrated the working class culture of
women in the part of Donegal I grew up in"; the play is set in the Donegal
shirt factory where McGuinness's mother, aunts, and grandmother all
worked (*Plays 1* ix). His childhood memory, however, is placed quite precisely against the background of Ireland's economic stagnation in the years
after World War II. The shirt factory is in danger of closing, a victim of
economic depression and the flooding of the clothing market with cheap
goods from Asia. As a result, the factory girls face redundancies, a reduced
workweek, and heightened quotas.

The factory is the victim of mismanagement both nationally and locally. Eamon de Valera's government pursues an isolationist economic policy that has left the Irish economy stagnant, and the trade unions are too
weak and indifferent to offer any help. As Ellen, the girls' leader, says:
"Something happens in this factory. We ring Andy Bonner at the Union.
He thanks us for ringing and he rings Dublin. Dublin says, "Where? Donegal? Donegal?" Dublin gets a map of Ireland, looks for Donegal, Jesus that's
it, the jiggeldy-piggeldy bit at the top of the country . . ." (23). Locally, the
longtime managers of the factory, the Buchanans, have left, and the factory
is in the hands of the incompetent Rohan, a graduate of a business school
(he is in his twenties) whose only response to the factory's decline is to raise
the girls' quota from a dozen shirts in sixteen minutes to a dozen in thirteen
minutes. The Buchanans were Protestant and Rohan is a Catholic, but
economic considerations override sectarian ones. As Una says, "Sweetieball
Rohan doesn't own this factory, whoever might. He may be the first Catholic we've had over us but he's worse than all the Buchanans rolled into one.
I'd rather work for a Protestant than not know who exactly you're working
for, no matter who they put over you" (90). A shirt factory in Donegal in
the 1950s thus becomes "a configuration pregnant with tensions" which
McGuinness blasts out of the homogeneous course of history. He "arrests"
the configuration, "shocks" it, and "crystallizes" it into a monad, out of
which he blasts a specific life from the era, in this case, Ellen's.

The effect of McGuinness's shocks, by which he isolates single moments in Irish history and then explores the determinants of those moments, is a kind of Brechtian estrangement or alienation. McGuinness strips away the traditional associations of universal, homogeneous history and creates an estranged history, one that is presented freshly and concretely. The sources of shock (McGuinness's blasting caps, as it were) are the characteristic features of his dramatic style: his tough, witty protagonists, often homosexual, who seem to have emerged on the far side of great suffering; his unconventional liminal, marginal settings, which are often situated on the edge of impending disaster; the constant presence of death; and the recurring moments of spiritual transcendence, by which his characters are briefly relieved of their sufferings.

For help in understanding these features of McGuinness's dramatic vision, we can turn to another Benjamin text, *The Origin of German Tragic Drama*. This difficult but fascinating book (written but rejected as a doctoral dissertation in 1925) is directly a study of the baroque tragedies of seventeenth-century Germany, plays by such forgotten figures as Andreas Gryphius, Daniel Caspar von Lohenstein, and Jakob Bidermann, but more broadly and interestingly, it is a study of allegory and of the ways in which history can be staged. The recurring subject of these obscure plays was the fall of a king, either tyrant or martyr, as a result of the machinations of court intriguers, and Benjamin argues that the plays' tone is not tragic but rather melancholic. The proper term for the plays is not *Tragödie* but *Trauerspiel:* each represents a "play of mourning" or a "play of sorrow." The German mourning plays also differ from classical tragedy in their orientation toward time. Greek tragedy is set in mythic time; the mourning plays are set in historical time (62). They construct a dramatic world that is like a claustrophobic trap, as human history is assimilated to natural history, offering no escape from the cycle of death. Moreover, they offer no metaphysical consolation; their characters are pervasively melancholic and inspire their audiences to a sort of universal mourning. Benjamin finds the origins of this despair and melancholy in the conflicted theology of seventeenth-century Germany, which retained the medieval view of life as a series of trials but which had lost the medieval hope of salvation:

> Whereas the middle ages present the futility of world events and the transience of the creature as stations on the road to salvation, the German *Trauerspiel* is taken up entirely with the hopelessness of the earthly condition. Such redemption as it knows resides in the depths of this destiny itself rather than in the fulfillment of a divine plan of salvation. (81)

The German baroque tragedies are, then, history plays rather than true tragedies. Their treatment of history, however, is not literal or even symbolic but rather allegorical, and Benjamin devotes the long final chapter of his book to "Allegory and *Trauerspiel*."

For Benjamin, the principal distinction between allegory and symbol is not, as much modern criticism has it, that allegory presents reductive, one-to-one correspondences between ideas and signs while symbolism presents resonant, suggestive, multivalent ones. Benjaminian allegory is not merely a literary style but is also a kind of experience, as Bainard Cowan explains:

> [A]llegory arises from an apprehension of the world as no longer perma-nent, as passing out of being: a sense of its transitoriness, an intimation of mortality, or a conviction, as in Dickinson, that "this world is not conclu-sion." Allegory would then be the expression of this sudden intuition. But allegory is more than an outward form of expression; it is also the intu-ition, the inner experience itself. The form such an experience of the world takes is fragmentary and enigmatic; in it the world ceases to be purely physical and becomes an aggregation of signs. (110)

Symbol and allegory, like tragedy and *Trauerspiel*, have different orien-tations to time: the symbol expresses the momentary and the mystical, while allegory presents the sequential and the historical:

> The decisive category of time, the introduction of which into this field of semiotics was the great romantic achievement of these thinkers, permits the incisive, formal definition of the relationship between symbol and allegory. Whereas in the symbol destruction is idealized and the trans-figured face of nature is fleetingly revealed in the light of redemption, in allegory the observer is confronted with the *facies hippocratica* of history as a petrified, primordial landscape. (166)

Allegory presents history, then, as a "Hippocratic face," a skull or death's head. And, appropriately, the landscape of history is a ruined one:

> The allegorical physiognomy of the nature-history, which is put on stage in the *Trauerspiel*, is present in reality in the form of the ruin. In the ruin history has physically merged into the setting. And in this guise history does not assume the form of the process of an eternal life so much as that of irresistible decay. Allegory thereby declares itself to be beyond beauty. Allegories are, in the realm of thoughts, what ruins are in the realm of things. (177–178)[1]

In form and spirit, McGuinness's plays are certainly very far removed from the extravagant dramas of Gryphius, Lohenstein, and Bidermann, of which Benjamin writes, but Benjamin's repositioning of the concept of allegory as a tool for defining his dramatists' relation to history is quite suggestive in reference to McGuinness. McGuinness's dangerous, liminal landscapes — the trench, the graveyard, the cell — are contemporary con-cretizations of the "petrified, primordial" landscapes that Benjamin found in the baroque drama, and the corpses that litter McGuinness's plays — the dead of the Somme or of Bloody Sunday — display Benjamin's *facies hippo-cratica*, the death's-head of history.[2] But the coincidence of such emblems is less important than Benjamin's suggestion of the form that the relationship between history and the dramatic text may take, not direct and literal but rather indirect, oblique, and allegorical.

In the remainder of this essay, I want to survey McGuinness's principal plays for the recurrence in them of the elements of his allegories of Irish history. In particular, McGuinness sees Ireland as a country haunted by what Benjamin calls "melancholy," which Patrick McGee suggests might better be called "alienation" (152). Ireland, or at least the Ireland of which McGuinness chooses to write, is a country in which centuries of colonialism and its aftermath have created "a culture for which the real world has become meaningless, devoid of intrinsic value, fragmented yet mysterious" (McGee 151).

McGuinness "blasts" (as Benjamin says the materialist historian does) specific lives out of the troubled continuity of Irish history. The recurring McGuinness protagonist is an eloquent talker haunted by the past. (McGuinness's talkers might be compared to Brian Friel's talkers, from Private Gar of *Philadelphia, Here I Come!* on, and to the broader tradition of talkers in Irish drama, a significant feature of Irish theatrical self-construction. They might be contrasted with the stammering, inarticulate characters of much American drama.) The bravura verbal arias of McGuinness's later protagonists are anticipated in the earthy eloquence of *The Factory Girls*'s Ellen, who not only keeps the girls she supervises in line with her tongue, but also intimidates the management as well. In scene 3, she confronts the novice manager Rohan:

> *Ellen.* A dozen in thirteen minutes. Listen, Rohan, show me a shirt. Here, take a look at this. (*She throws a shirt.*) What do you see when you look at that, what do you see?
>
> *Rohan.* A simple piece of coloured cloth, stitched together. A unit of production that I need to go out this factory quicker and in greater numbers if against all the odds I'm to make this hole of a place survive.
>
> *Ellen.* Let me tell you what I see. I see a collar. Two cuffs. Eight buttons. Eight buttonholes. Bands. A back. Two sides. A lower line. When I look closer, do you know what else I see? A couple of thousand stitches. Why do I see it? I've been trained to see it. I've trained other people to see it. That's my job, Rohan, and I know my job cannot be done in the way and in the time you want it done, and I won't do it that way. (36–37)

Later in the play, we learn about the experiences Ellen has endured and that have forged her courage and eloquence. Vera, her temper frayed by the stress of the girls' sit-in strike at the factory and by worry over her children, accuses Ellen of being a bully: "You can batter down anybody you want to because you're only a bully. But you won't bully me. I can face up to you. I can — FUCK IT." She almost immediately apologizes, but Ellen replies,

What did you say? What did you say but what you thought? Weans, weans. Fuck them. They're not worth it. Three buried in a year. What loss. Believe me, behind all the handshaking and tears, people were saying a lot worse than you could, Vera. When I went near a woman that had a wean with her, you could see her panicking in case I touched it. The very look of me might affect them. I began to think I was a walking carrier. If it hadn't been for Una, I'd have been in a mental home. I spent the day cleaning everything. Going off my head cleaning. If I cleaned everything, I thought nobody else would have to go through it. Can you believe how knocked stupid I was? (69–71)

Ellen, like many McGuinness protagonists after her, has endured catastrophic loss and has emerged from the crucible tempered and with an eloquence that both masks her pain and indirectly expresses it. Such figures are, in a sense, twice-born; they have died symbolic deaths and are living in a second half-life.

In *Observe the Sons of Ulster*, Kenneth Pyper's emotional experiences are similar, for all his differences from Ellen. The death of his mysterious Paris lover has left him both tormented by obsessive self-loathing and graced by verbal dexterity that he uses both to tease and baffle his companions and to reveal himself freely to his lover David Craig. In the frame story, the deaths of his seven comrades in the Battle of Somme haunt him as well. In *Innocence*, part of Caravaggio, too, has died, along with his sister Caterina and her newborn son, victims of a crude cesarean operation. The death of the baby here, like the deaths of Ellen's children, is a *Kindermord*, the resonant motif of child-death that runs through dramatic literature from Euripides' *Medea* to Ibsen's *Little Eyolf*, and McGuinness uses this motif with its full implications of the death of the self. The motif reappears in *Baglady*, in the drowning of the Baglady's baby, and in *Carthaginians*, in the death of Maela's daughter (from cancer) on Bloody Sunday. McGuinness's protagonists have been marginalized by their grief, their Benjaminian melancholy. They have passed through the Valley of Death and emerged as holy outcasts who can say, like Prufrock, "I am Lazarus come from the dead, Come back to tell you all."

Many of them are also set apart from their societies by their homosexuality: Pyper, in *Observe the Sons of Ulster*; Caravaggio, in *Innocence*; Dido, in *Carthaginians*; and William, in *Mutabilitie*: all are explicitly gay, and homoerotic themes appear elsewhere as well, as in *Someone Who'll Watch over Me*. The homosexual thread in McGuinness's plays deserves separate, extended treatment, but the starting point for such a treatment might well be McGuinness's own comment, in a 1997 interview with Mic Moroney in the *Irish Times*:

If there is to be a new relationship between the islands — and the metaphor we've usually looked at is between man and woman — maybe we should be

looking at different images of peace and communication, and this is a
perfectly valid way of presenting imagery of a new way forward. [. . .] I
think there has been a tentativeness with showing a gay relationship on the
stage, and I'd like to think in the history of the Irish theatre, I had some
little influence in that. Particularly in — my God! — *Innocence*, when there
was roaring in the theatre. It was quite scary at the time. Even in *Observe
the Sons*, the first time, around twelve years ago, people weren't comfortable with this possibility between brave men — it shows you what they
know about soldiers. (16)

Even in this brief comment, McGuinness invites a metaphoric reading of
the homosexual themes as revisionary treatments of the marriage metaphor
in nineteenth century — and sometimes twentieth century — British ratio-
nalizations of Irish colonization. The myth of England as man and Ireland
as woman continues to flourish especially vigorously (as many myths do) in
the Unionist population of Northern Ireland; to cast as homosexual the
major spokesperson for Unionist ideology in *Observe the Sons of Ulster*, a
figure who is led through homosexual and homosocial experience to chant
"Ulster! Ulster! Ulster!" at the end of the play, is especially provocative. To
make Dido a homosexual in *Carthaginians*, with its evocations of Dido and
Aeneas, is equally suggestive metaphorically. This, of course, is not to say
that such characters as Pyper, Dido, and Caravaggio are not credible as
realistic characters. McGuinness's representation of homosexual desire,
like his representation of other topics, operates realistically while at the
same time taking on the contours of allegory.

McGuinness's protagonists, despite their characteristic wit and eloquence, are not *raisonneurs*, mouthpieces for McGuinness's readings of the
episodes he has arrested in the general flow of Irish history. Rather, they
have a special perspective on the events of which they are a part by virtue of
their temperaments, their confrontations with grief and mortality, and, in
many cases, their marginalized sexuality. But they do not explain history;
they embody it. For the most part, they are tough, ironic characters whose
wisdom is expressed less oracularly than humorously, often in cracks and
one-liners — all sons and daughters of Ellen from *The Factory Girls*, who
sums up her credo in this way: "A wasted life. Heartbreaking isn't it? Another martyr for old fucking Ireland. Well here's one martyr that's going to
be carried to her grave squealing" (87). The younger Pyper in *Observe the
Sons of Ulster*, Caravaggio in *Innocence*, Dido in *Carthaginians*, Edward in
Someone Who'll Watch over Me, and even, in her own way, the speaker in
Baglady all use language, and most characteristically the language of black
comedy, both to express and to defend against their survivors' wisdom.
They are all, in their own ways, martyrs for old fucking Ireland, even the
Renaissance Italian Caravaggio, but they are all going to be carried to their
graves squealing.

McGuinness's settings are similarly placed at oblique angles to Irish historical events, and they similarly embody, in arresting stage images, their historical content. The plays are set in desperate, dangerous times and places in Irish history: in and around Edmund Spenser's Kilcolman Castle in County Cork in 1598, during Hugh O'Neill's rising; in Northern Ireland and France in the months leading up to the Battle of the Somme; in Derry in 1972, in the aftermath of Bloody Sunday, when British paratroopers killed thirteen unarmed civil rights marchers; in Beirut in the 1980s, when Islamic guerillas took Western hostages, among them an Irishman.

These general times and places are concretized in vivid, unconventional stage settings. McGuinness has a strong visual imagination, and his settings have an emblematic quality. Part 3 of *Observe the Sons of Ulster*, "Bonding," distributes the eight soldiers among four spot sets, to which our attention is directed by lighting — they are lit either individually or in various combinations. Craig and Pyper are on "Boa Island, Lough Erne," Roulston and Crawford are in "a Protestant church," Millen and Moore are near "a suspended rope bridge," and McIlwaine and Anderson are in "the Field." They are, in other words, in locations that are rich with resonances of Northern Irish identity. Lower Lough Erne, in far-western Northern Ireland, is the location of a number of Iron Age statues of Irish gods. Boa Island is the site of a seventh-century pillar statue of two gods, who are standing back to back; its reproduction in the play suggests, perhaps, the bonding of Craig and Pyper. Roulston's and Crawford's Protestant church is a generalized setting, but Millen and Moore's suspended rope bridge is, again, a specific and readily identifiable locale: the rope bridge at Carrick-a-rede, just east of the Giant's Causeway at the northern tip of Northern Ireland, a sixty-foot–long rope bridge suspended eighty feet above the ocean between the mainland and a small island. "The Field" in which the drunken McIlwaine and Anderson sit with their lambeg drum is Finnahy Field, the staging area for the Belfast Twelfth of July marches — the "Holiest spot in Ulster," McIlwaine calls it (145).

The island, the church, the bridge, and the field are, in other words, spatial metonyms for the dead hands of Pyper's Protestant ancestors, which have controlled his art and his life. As he tells Craig, "I couldn't look at my life's work, for when I saw my hands working they were not mine but the hands of my ancestors, interfering, and I could not be rid of that interference. I could not create. I could only preserve" (163). The British trench at the Battle of the Somme, which is the setting for the last section of *Observe the Sons of Ulster*, "Bonding," is the logical extension of the quadruple settings of "Pairing" and is equally emblematic. As drenched in Loyalist myth and nostalgia as the battlefield of the Boyne, it emblematizes the final formation of the Loyalist ethos that propels the men, except for Pyper, over the top and to their deaths. As Craig foretells, Pyper is doomed to survive as an outsider, even in this universal bloodbath: "You're not of us, man. You're a leader. You got what you wanted. You always have, you always will. You'll come through today because you learned to want it" (192). In calling the settings of *Observe the Sons of Ulster* — the four settings of "Pairing" and the stark trench setting of "Bonding" — emblematic, I am drawing on the various terms that Benjamin employed to characterize the emblem: "hieroglyphic" (that is, existing between the verbal and the visual), analogous to the ruin, palimpsestic, constructed of fragments, and subject to simultaneous "dispersal" and "collectedness" (Bloomer 21). The settings are not merely appropriate to the action but they also carry independent meanings of their own, sometimes reinforcing the stage action, sometimes existing in oblique or ironic relation to it. The Irish gods who silently preside over the Craig and Pyper segments of "Pairing," for example, are often in tension with the characters' discussions of individual aspirations and freedom.

McGuinness's most characteristic settings are, like the settings of *Observe the Sons of Ulster*, Benjaminian ruins, sites presided over by the death's-head of history. The squalid hovel that shows the underside of Renaissance Rome in *Innocence*, the Derry cemetery of *Carthaginians*, the Beirut hostage cell of *Someone Who'll Watch over Me*, the desperate landscape of *Mutabilitie* — ravaged by "the late wars of Munster": all are versions of what Benjamin calls the "petrified, primordial landscapes" of history.

It is appropriate that the central emblem in these emblematic landscapes — always implied but never shown, the emblem within the emblem, as it were — is the corpse. Benjamin notes the phenomenon of a central figure in an emblem, approvingly quoting Johann Joachim Winckelmann: "The best and most perfect allegory of one or of several concepts is comprised of one single figure, or should be thought of as such" (*The Origin of German Tragic Drama* 186). He also identifies the corpse as central in baroque German drama: "In the *Trauerspiel* of the seventeenth century the corpse becomes quite simply the pre-eminent emblematic property" (218). One might add that the corpse plays an important part in the iconographies of Greek and Shakespearean tragedy as well. The point is not that the emblem carries the same meaning in Greek, Shakespearean, and German baroque drama that it does in McGuinness, but rather that it is a dramatic emblem ready to carry the meanings appropriate to the history of its time.

The bodies that haunt McGuinness's grieving protagonists are scattered throughout the plays, beginning with *The Factory Girls*, in which Ellen's three children, dead within a single year, haunt the action, and continuing, as we have seen, through *Observe the Sons of Ulster*, in which the bodies of his dead Paris lover and seven World War I comrades impel Pyper to speak; the bodies are present in *Innocence*, in which Caravaggio uses his art to commemorate his dead sister and her newborn baby as well as his models, glimpsed after death in his proleptic act 2 dream; and in *Carthaginians*, in which the private loss of Maela's daughter and the public loss of the Bloody Sunday dead drive the action of the watchers in the cemetery.

These deaths shape the perceptions of McGuinness's characters; that the silent presence of the bodies of the dead also functions emblematically in the plays becomes almost explicit in *Innocence*, where Caravaggio carries an actual skull in the initial dumb show as well as intermittently throughout the play. In this play, where many of the stage pictures parallel Caravaggio's painting, the most striking stage picture is the *pieta* arrangement of act 2, in which Caravaggio lies with his head in Lena's lap, evoking Caravaggio's 1609 painting *The Resurrection of Lazarus*. In this painting, set in Lazarus's dark catacomb, a shaft of light streams from the left, illuminating Lazarus's naked body, which is supported by an attendant. Christ stands at the left, his right arm pointing toward Lazarus. Lazarus's arms are themselves out-stretched, his right arm toward the light, the left downward toward a skull. Lazarus's body thus forms a cross, as Alfred Moir explains:

> The cross may refer to that on the habit of the Padri Crociferi [the order for which *The Resurrection of Lazarus* was painted]. But it also raises the possibility of another meaning: the still-limp left hand over the skull as representing the death of the soul wrought by sin, and the right hand reaching toward the light as suggesting man's hope for the achievement of eternal life, made possible through the sacrifice and resurrection of Christ. Lazarus's obedience to Christ then may imply both the conflict between good and evil and the possibility of human choice. (124)

McGuinness apparently adopted a secularized version of this reading of the emblematics of the painting. In Caravaggio's dream, the first figure to appear is his beloved sister, Caterina Merisi, whose life was sacrificed in a futile attempt to save her unborn child and who died cursing "all children and all fathers" and even God, "for creating woman" (272). She tells Cara-vaggio that he must give up painting before it kills him, but Caravaggio protests and calls up his subjects to justify his art: first his patron Cardinal and then his models, the Whore and the male prostitutes Lucio and An-tonio. This section of Caravaggio's dream is prophetic, foretelling the fu-ture of the subjects. The Cardinal has become a mad, homeless derelict, attended by a servant who hates him; the Whore has drowned herself in the river; Antonio has died of syphilis; and Lucio has starved to death. Caravag-gio is at first shattered by the bleak vision of the future of his models: "Let me die, Caterina. Let me die" (277). But in a striking, magical scene, he reasserts the validity of his art and its power to draw its subjects from darkness into light. He "*raises his hands. Light rises from his raised hands, drawing Whore, Antonio, and Lucio from the darkness*" (279). The hope of eternal life made possible by Christ in Caravaggio's painting becomes the power of Caravaggio's own art in McGuinness's treatment of it.

The emblematics of this scene resonate through McGuinness's other plays. If one hand, figuratively speaking, points downward toward the corpse, the other points upward toward transcendence, in moments that recall what Benjamin calls "*the ponderacion misteriosa*, the intervention of

God in the work of art": "Subjectivity, like an angel falling into the depths, is brought back by allegories, and is held fast in heaven, in God, by *pondera-cion misteriosa*" (*The Origin of German Tragic Drama* 235). In the bleak spiritual landscapes of Benjamin's baroque tragedies, when life retained its medieval character as a series of trials, but without the medieval hope of salvation, the direct, arbitrary intervention of God offers the only hope. In McGuinness's dramatic Ireland, similarly arbitrary moments of blessed-ness, enabled either by art or by individual human compassion, offer a similar hope. Such a moment occurs at the end of *The Factory Girls:*

> *Rebecca.* I saw a woman sleeping. In her sleep she dreamt Life stood before her and held in each hand a gift — in the one Love, in the other Free-dom. And she said to the woman, Choose. And the woman waited long and she said, Freedom. I heard the woman laugh in her sleep. Yes, I heard the woman laugh in her sleep. (*She closes her eyes.*)
>
> *Rosemary.* Come on, Rebecca, waken.
>
> *Rebecca opens her eyes.*
>
> *Rebecca.* I have, woman, I've wakened. (89)

Observe the Sons of Ulster rises to a problematic kind of transcendence in Pyper's chant, "Observe the sons of Ulster marching towards the Somme. I love their lives. I love my own life. I love my home. I love my Ulster. Ulster. Ulster. Ulster. Ulster. Ulster. Ulster. Ulster. Ulster. Ulster" (196). *Carthaginians* ends with a similar ritual, as Dido blesses his sleeping friends: "Watch yourself, Hark and Sarah. Watch yourself, Seph. Watch yourself, Paul. Watch yourself, Greta. Watch yourself, Maela. Remember me. Watch yourself, Dido. Watch yourself, Derry. Watch yourself. Watch yourself. Watch yourself" (379).

McGuinness has been praised for his imaginative range as a playwright, and he certainly does have this range. In terms of their subject matter, his plays sweep from the life of Caravaggio to the Beirut hostage crisis, and in form they sweep from the fairly straightforward realism of *The Factory Girls* to the lyrical freedom of *Mutabilitie.* But this range, this capacity to sur-prise, is built on the bedrock of a remarkably consistent vision. The essence of this vision is grief. McGuinness's protagonists live in a kind of afterlife, scarred by traumatic encounters with the death of friends, family, or loved ones. Their experiences, though, have not left them numbed or defeated but rather have given them the gift of tongues. Remarkable talkers, they rewrite their worlds in bravura feats of storytelling and dramatic improvisa-tion. The little plays they make up, from the Mock Battle of Scarva in the last scene of *Observe the Sons of Ulster* to Dido's play to end all Irish plays, Fionnuala McGonigle's "The Burning Balaclava," in *Carthaginians*, are plays within plays that mirror, often parodically, the plays in which they are embedded, in that they act to displace grief into art.[3] These witty, seasoned protagonists move through desperate landscapes of loss and danger, em-blems of Irish history, focused around the images of corpses, seldom shown but always present. The face of history in these plays is Benjamin's *facies hippocratica*, a death's-head. In such worlds, redemption can enter only arbitrarily and unexpectedly, like the unearned gift of God's grace. In McGuinness's world, though, the redemption is not divine but human, moments of blessedness achieved through art and human connection, pairing, and bonding.

In this discussion I have deliberately neglected *Someone Who'll Watch over Me*, McGuinness's brilliant 1992 play about the Lebanese hostages, and I would argue that despite its ostensible subject matter, this play functions as McGuinness's definitive allegory of Irish history. The only connection between Ireland and the hostages of the mid-1980s was the presence among them of the Irish Brian Keenan, whose memoir *An Evil Cradling* is the principal source of McGuinness's play. But by imagining in the hostage cell Edward Sheridan, an Irish journalist, and Michael Watters, an English academic, McGuinness manages to bring onstage in capsule form the long history of Irish–English conflict, as mediated and complicated by an American prisoner, Adam Canning.

The Beckettian minimalism of *Someone Who'll Watch Over Me* — a dark, bare cell with three characters chained to the wall — seems at first a startling reversal of McGuinness's open, fluid use of the stage in such plays as *Observe the Sons of Ulster* and *Innocence*. But looked at another way, the cell may be seen as the logical culmination of McGuinness's earlier settings, which, no matter how apparently open, always seem to carry a sign: "No Way Out" — the trench at the Battle of the Somme, for example, or the cemetery in *Carthaginians*. The end of history, the play suggests, is three people in a cell, totally at the mercy of unseen, unknown forces, the hostage-takers. Again, McGuinness has chosen "a configuration pregnant with tensions" and "blasted" it out of the homogeneous continuum of universal history.

He has also blasted out a single life, that of the Englishman Michael Watters. The three voices of the hostages are as beautifully balanced as the instruments in a string trio, but the lead voice is that of Michael, the character who is most changed by the hostage ordeal. He enters the play as an Irish stereotype of an Englishman: prissy, timid, suffocatingly genteel, and completely humorless. His first line when he awakes after his imprisonment is "I'm terribly sorry, but where am I?" (9). The circumstances of his capture are comically suggestive of genteel English life: "I was on my way to the market and I was looking for fruit, for pears, for I had invited a few people from the university for dinner and for dessert I wanted to make a pear flan. I was walking to the market" (10). Adam, the American, and especially Edward, the Irishman, cannot help teasing him mercilessly over such trivial issues as British turns of speech:

> *Michael.* I imagine being an actor is quite a boring life.
> *Edward.* Yea.
> *Adam.* Yea.

(*Silence.*)
Edward. Aye, boring.
Adam. Yea.
Michael. Yes.
Edward. No.
Michael. No.
Edward. What do you mean, "no"? You've just said yes.
Michael. I was agreeing with you. I thought you were agreeing with me. So
     I said no.
Edward. You say no when you're agreeing with someone?
Michael. If they've said no, yes.
Edward. Yes or no, what is it?
Michael. What?
Edward. Shut up. (14)

As the play goes on, the teasing occasionally darkens into open hostility, especially when Michael is indiscreet enough to refer to Irish English as a "dialect":

> *Edward.* Listen, times have changed, you English mouth, and I mean mouth. One time when you and your breed ruled the roost, you ruled the world, because it was your language. Not any more. We've taken it from you. We've made it our own. And now, we've bettered you at it. You thought you had our tongues cut out, sitting crying a corner, lamenting. Listen. The lament's over. We took you and your language on, and we won. Not bad for a race that endured eight hundred years of oppression, pal, and I speak as a man who is one generation removed from the dispossessed. (30)

Michael as stereotyped Englishman is humanized in the course of the play, as Edward, Adam, and the audience discover that behind his prim humorlessness lies a deep mourning for his dead wife. Adam asks him, "How did your wife die?" and Michael replies,

> Nita? An accident. Life was different without her.
> (*Silence.*)
> But Nita certainly would not have wanted me to turn into a weeping willow, so, one got on with sweet life as if, well, nothing happened. Something had happened. Professionally, I changed. Before her death I was full of ideas for publications. Nothing terribly exciting. Mostly on English dialects. Anyway, after the accident, I simply read the Old English elegies and the medieval romances, and I taught as best I could. I published nothing. I'd lost my wife and my ambition. My lack of publications didn't help at the time of the rationalization. Well, these things happen. (22)

Michael, in other words, takes his place among earlier McGuinness characters as one who has endured bereavement and survived into a kind of half-life. When Adam is taken away and presumably shot by the hostage-takers, and thus joins Michael's wife among the corpses, the memory of which haunts the cell, Michael becomes Edward's instructor in grieving:

> *Edward.* He is not —
> *Michael.* (*Roars*). Dead, he is, and you know it.
> *Edward.* You know nothing.
> *Michael.* I know about grief. About mourning. How it can destroy you. I
>   know.
> (*Silence.*)
> You know he's dead, don't you?
> (*Silence.*)
> Say it, he is dead.
> (*Silence.*)
> *Edward.* He died. I needed him. Jesus, I needed him. (40)

We even learn that Michael's absurd pear flan, which led to his capture, was inspired by his dead wife. He tells Adam and Edward that when he considered suicide, he had an imaginary conversation with her and instead did as she advised: "Make my pear flan. She adored my pear flan" (29).

The miniature Anglo-Irish Peace Process enacted by Michael and Edward in their Beirut cell is enabled by the wisdom and compassion that comes from mourning, mourning by Michael for his dead wife, and by both Michael and Edward, for their friend Adam. It is also enabled by art, by the work of healing narrative. *Someone Who'll Watch over Me* is a web of narratives: imaginary movies, jokes, tall tales, songs, and recitations. Like Didi and Gogo's endless game-playing in Beckett's *Waiting for Godot*, the hostages' narratives "pass the time," but they do more as well: they create bonds both among the hostages themselves and within the long span of human history.

The first serious clash between Michael and his two cellmates is healed when the characters imagine a self-referential movie in which each acknowledges the fear that underlies his irritation with the other:

> *Adam.* Shoot the movie.
> *Edward.* There were three bollocks in a cell in Lebanon. An Englishman,
>   an Irishman, and an American. Why they were in that cell was any-
>   body's guess, and why they were in Lebanon was their own guess.
> *Adam.* The American was the first to be caught. While he was on his own,
>   he was frightened of going mad.
> *Edward.* The Irishman was second to be caught. He would have went mad
>   without the American. They were joined, these two bolloxes, by a
>   third bollocks, an Englishman.
> *Michael.* The Englishman did not know if being in the cell in Lebanon had
>   driven the other two mad. What has happened to him in being kid-

napped strikes him as being madness, so he has attempted not to lose
his head in the face of severe provocation —

Edward. In not being afraid of them he's convinced them they have not
gone mad.

Adam. And in their way, in so far as is possible, they thank him for that
conviction.

(*Silence.*)

Michael. You both scare the shit out of me. (17)

Through the rest of the play, the three — and after Adam's death, the
two — find comfort and solidarity in songs (ranging from "Amazing Grace"
to "Chitty-Chitty Bang-Bang"), in imagined movies (*Gandhi, The Great
Escape*), in improvised fantasies (drinking parties, flights over the world),
and in Michael's summaries of medieval literature ("The Wanderer," *Sir
Orfeo*).

Significantly, the final moment of the play, when the freed Edward
parts from Michael, leaving him alone in the cell, is based upon a narrative
that Michael has learned from his father, who had himself been a prisoner
in the Second World War. His father told him,

> Don't be afraid of pain. Don't be afraid of controlling it. You have been
> raised by a strong woman. The bravest men sometimes behave like women.
> Before the Spartans went into battle, they combed each other's hair. The
> enemy laughed at them for being effeminate. But the Spartans won the
> battle. (59)

As Edward parts from Michael, he takes out a comb and combs Michael's
hair. He then gives the comb to Michael, who combs Edward's hair: "Right."
"Good luck." "Good luck."

In the "petrified, primordial landscape" of Irish history, here shrunk to the
dimensions of a dark prison cell, presided over by the ghosts of the dead,
there is a moment of redemption achieved through the art of narrative,
standing in the same relationship to Edward and Michael as *Someone Who'll
Watch Over Me* stands in relation to its audience, living as we do among the
ruins of history.

NOTES

1. Azade Seyhan sees Benjamin's theory of allegory as prefiguring postmodernism: "Benjamin's allegory is a palimpsest of past and present codes. The modernist
project in architecture and literature tended to highlight the representational orig-
inality or to showcase its 'nowness' and 'newness.' The postmodernist encounter
with tradition, on the other hand, incorporates the past and a sense of 'second-
handedness' into the present" (237).

2. Both Riana O'Dwyer and Eamonn Jordan have commented on McGuinness's highly charged settings: "The locus of the plays is usually Ireland, on the fringes of the national consciousness, exploring violence, sexuality, dislocation from affection, inadequate gender roles, the fear of aging, and of dying. It is the struggle with threat, by means of unconscious fantasy, which is voiced in these plays" (O'Dwyer, "Dancing in the Borderlands" 100). "Throughout the plays McGuinness finds dramatic spaces and events which previous Irish writers have been somewhat hesitant to appropriate; spaces that are as much unique, imaginative and repressed as they are real. The dramatic space gives on the one hand an openness and on another a sense of claustrophobia, as it is infringed by history, memory, fear, absence or loss" (Jordan vii).

3. Joan Fitzpatrick Dean insightfully analyzes the "self-dramatization" of McGuinness's characters, their tendency toward "game playing, nomination (the act of renaming people and things), the reenactment of historical and personal events, role playing and plays-within-plays — as well as such intertextual devices as storytelling, recitation, song, and the retelling of dreams" (98).

—18—

The End of History:
The Millennial Urge in the
Plays of Sebastian Barry

Scott T. Cummings

The 25 March 1997 edition of *The Irish Times* includes a review, by Fintan
O'Toole, of Donal O'Kelly's *Catalpa*, a one-man tour de force in which the
playwright–performer acts out the story of a New England whaling ship
and its 1876 voyage to rescue a group of Fenian prisoners from an Australian prison camp. O'Toole begins with the following observation:

> Considering how much popular interest there is in Irish history, it is
> remarkable there are so few history plays in our theatre. In most European
> countries, and especially in England, there is a substantial body of drama
> in which the past is recapitulated, recovered and redefined. Here — per-
> haps because history still has a present tense — there isn't. What we have
> are not history plays but plays about history: how it is made and why.
> (O'Toole, "Exploding the Story to Meld Many Worlds into One Tale" 12)

Before proceeding to discuss *Catalpa*, O'Toole cites Brian Friel's *Making
History*, Sebastian Barry's *The Steward of Christendom*, and Tom Mac Intyre's
Good Evening, Mr. Collins as other contemporary Irish dramas in which "the
border between the past and the present has ceased to exist."

O'Toole's distinction between the English history play and the Irish
historiographical play raises provocative questions about how contemporary Irish theatre participates in the understanding (and revision) of the
Irish past.[1] His sense of history's present tense also suggests some of the
dramaturgical challenges that Irish playwrights face today. If "the border
between the past and the present has ceased to exist," to what extent must
history be seen to operate in contemporary Irish drama as a providential or

deterministic force? What room does it leave for individual human agency? Can a character in a play change anything or make something happen, or is he a puppet on a historical string, constrained to act out or recapitulate an already established sequence of events? Is the domain of drama, the proverbial "here-and-now," the impotent mouthpiece of a hegemonic past? In short, to borrow a recent idiom, does history rule? With these questions in mind, this essay examines several plays by Sebastian Barry, plays which reflect the historiographical preoccupation mentioned by O'Toole, and attempts to define my sense of Barry's "millennial urge," a persistent trope in his dramas of transcendence and hope.

Sebastian Barry was already a respected young poet and novelist when he began writing for the stage in the late 1980s. In the span of just over a decade, he wrote a series of six plays — *Boss Grady's Boys* (1988), *The Prayers of Sherkin* (1990), *White Woman Street* (1992), *The Only True History of Lizzie Finn* (1995), *The Steward of Christendom* (1995), and *Our Lady of Sligo* (1998) — which established him as one of Ireland's leading contemporary playwrights. Thanks in large measure to the definitive performance of the late Donal McCann, *The Steward of Christendom* brought Barry international recognition. Following its award-winning world premiere in London, the Royal Court/Joint Stock co-production toured successfully in Ireland, Australia, and the United States. Barry's reputation was fortified by *Our Lady of Sligo*, starring Sinead Cusack and also directed by Max Stafford-Clark, this time in a Royal National Theatre/Joint Stock co-production. Subsequently edged out of the international limelight by the meteoric rise of Martin McDonagh and the emergence of Conor McPherson, Barry remains a contemporary figure of major importance whose work resonates with much of the tradition of modern Irish drama.

Barry's plays are steeped in Irish history — particularly the three decades preceding and following the establishment of the Irish Free State in 1922 — but they are not so overtly historical as Friel's *Making History* or Mac Intyre's *Good Evening, Mr. Collins*. That is to say, they do not depict significant events in national history or the lives of celebrated national figures. From Hugh O'Neill to Michael Collins, major figures of Irish history are kept at arm's length, offstage, just as much on the theatrical periphery as his chosen characters exist on the historical periphery. Like Sean O'Casey, for example, Barry populates his stage with characters drawn from history's rank and file. Their social class and background may vary — a former Dublin police superintendent, the alcoholic wife of a civil engineer, a music-hall dancer who marries an Irish veteran of the Boer War, a mercenary soldier turned outlaw in an American Wild West oddly situated in Ohio, a pair of aging hardscrabble farmers in Kerry — but they are all ordinary, everyday citizens who have been overlooked or pushed aside by the turbulent rush of events that has shaped modern Ireland.

Historian Roy Foster has described Sebastian Barry's project as "one of recovery—stitching back into the torn fabric of Irish history the anomalous figures from an extended Irish family" ("Lost Futures" 23).[2] But in appending their stories to the received historical record as an imaginative and subtly revisionist addendum, the plays suggest some ambivalence about that record and an animus toward history itself as an omnipresent force in present Irish life. History is Barry's Godot and his characters' ambiguous antagonist. If, in Beckett, Godot is a mysterious and unknown future that never arrives, in Barry, "History" is an intransigent and all-too-well-known past that will not go away. The omnipresence of the past, in the forms of history on a national level and memory on a personal level, makes the drama's self-perpetuating and continuous present tense—usually the moment of making decisions, executing plans, and causing events—a fragile and suspect proposition. Barry's characters exist in a present that is relatively free of immediate conflict and, to that degree, void of the possibility of change. Like Didi and Gogo, Barry's characters are constrained to a condition of waiting, and, while waiting, they go about their daily routines or look back (not altogether willingly) over a life marked by brief moments of glory followed by prolonged periods of frustration and disappointment.

The enactment of memory is particularly dominant in two recent Barry plays: *The Steward of Christendom* and *Our Lady of Sligo*. Indeed, these plays are so conspicuously similar in form that, from a cynical point of view, the latter seems like a formulaic attempt to repeat the success of the former. That formula goes something like this: Take a demented and dying figure whose hopes for a happy and prosperous life in independent Ireland have been eclipsed by disappointment and despair. Confine him or her to a hospital bed and bring in a stream of visitors, some living characters in the present, others ghost-like presences from the past. Compose a series of compelling and dizzyingly lyrical monologues which evince the hero's stubborn fortitude even as they recount his or her failures and humiliation. Then cast in the starring role a charismatic Irish actor—Donal McCann, Sinead Cusack—capable of a heart-wrenching depth of feeling. Get Max Stafford-Clark to direct. Produce in London.

Set in 1932, *The Steward of Christendom* tells the story of seventy-five–year-old Thomas Dunne, a bitter and demented man living out his days in a county home in Wicklow. In his heyday, he was a chief superintendent in the Dublin Metropolitan Police (DMP), the unarmed force that kept peace in the streets before Irish independence from the United Kingdom. For decades he served crown and country with a fierce patriotic pride, becoming the highest ranking Catholic officer in the Protestant-dominated DMP. He was there—in full dress uniform, with mixed emotions—on the day in 1922 when Michael Collins received the keys to Dublin Castle. Now, in his dotage, in an Ireland that has thrown off the colonial yoke, he is a traitor in hindsight and a man without a country.

Set in 1953, *Our Lady of Sligo* concerns fifty-three–year-old Mai Kirwin O'Hara, who lies dying of liver cancer in a Dublin hospital. The daughter of a successful insurance broker in Sligo, she grew up a member of an emerging Catholic bourgeoisie ready to inherit an independent Ireland based on Home Rule. Known in her youth as "the wild girl of Galway," she was a champion athlete, a talented musician, a promising businesswoman, and a stylish beauty who became notorious as the first woman ever to wear trousers in Sligo. Like Thomas Dunne, Mai's husband Jack rose in the world by serving the imperial cause — in the British Merchant Navy, the British Colonial Service in Africa, and the British Army during World War II — only to end up back in Ireland, laying sewage systems for holiday cottages on the Irish Sea north of Dublin.

As Roy Foster puts it, Mai and Jack, like Thomas Dunne, "feel the future was robbed from them. Immobilized in the terrible present, they try to make sense of their past, disabled by forever rehearsing unfulfilled expectations" ("Lost Futures" 23). In the face of such disillusionment, all three have chosen what can be seen as a form of internal exile. Thomas retired to his native Wicklow and gradually retreated into a madness that led to his institutionalization. First Jack and then Mai succumbed to a destructive alcoholism which has wreaked havoc on their family life, engendered a bitter hatred between them, and which has now brought Mai to the brink of death. It is from these outposts of defeat at the end of life that the retrospective actions of these memory plays take place.

That action takes several forms: dialogues with hospital staff or visiting family members; rambling monologues while the characters are alone or oblivious to others; and dramatic scenes which amount either to flashbacks, hallucinations induced by morphine or madness, or actual appearances by apparitions whose spirits occupy the present as truly as do the living. In *The Steward of Christendom*, this apparition is Thomas's son Willie, who was killed in the trenches of France during the First World War. Although dressed in his khaki wool uniform, he appears to Thomas as a thirteen-year-old boy whose pubescent voice has not yet broken. In *Our Lady of Sligo*, the ghost in question — Barry refers to him as a "presence" — is Mai's dead father, who appears "all seemingly in silver, a dust of silver on him like a man that has been brushed by a thousand moths, a larger silver fob-watch" (20).[3]

For the theatregoer, who has only the fleeting impressions of a once-through performance out of which to construct the reality of the play, past and present bleed and blend into each other in a way that makes them at moments indifferentiable. And for Thomas Dunne and Mai O'Hara, as they lay dying, isolated and alone and futureless, the past is so suffocatingly *there* in the room with them that the present tense itself must be seen as otherwise weak and attenuated, just as enfeebled as their failing health. There is, to echo Beckett, nothing to be done. As we come to know their life stories, the tone of each play becomes increasingly elegiacal, eventually conferring upon the sufferer the quasi-holy status of "the steward of Christendom" or "our lady of Sligo." For this reason, what starts off as a memory play can be seen to join the long tradition of plays concerned with the art of dying (*Ars Moriendi*).[4] From the medieval *Everyman* to Hofmannsthal's *Death and the Fool* to Beckett's *Endgame*, these plays feature an isolated, and often immobile, central character who faces the approach of death and who, in that extended moment, seeks to understand or redeem a life somehow wasted or misspent.

In Hofmannsthal's short, symbolist verse drama of 1893, Death comes for the aesthete Claudio and helps him to recognize that "Never have I on all these loving lips/Tasted the true draught of life" (47). After successive visits from the ghosts of his mother, his spurned lover, and his best friend, Claudio embraces death as his one last chance truly to live: "Since my life was Death, then, Death, be my life!" (65). The eschatology here is personal and individual compared to the universal end-time depicted in *Everyman* and *Endgame*. In those plays, all of human existence is at stake, and the millennium (or absence of it) is at hand. Given the doctrinal function of the morality play and Everyman's allegorical identity, Death for Everyman signals the Apocalypse, the onset of the biblical millennium, and the Last Judgment. The Messenger states the moral plainly in the play's prologue: "Man, in the beginning/Look well, and take good heed to the ending, Be you never so gay!" (207). The post-apocalyptic world of Beckett's *Endgame* is just as absolute, although it promises no return to paradise on earth if and when life in Hamm's shelter ever reaches its impossible end. "Finished, it's finished, nearly finished, it must be nearly finished," says Clov at the beginning, signaling the play's unending effort to come to the end (1).

The manner in which Barry presents the approaching deaths of Thomas Dunne and Mai O'Hara suggests a similar millennial momentum or urge, both a biblical wish for deliverance and a Beckett-like will to get to the end. Clearly, Barry is not writing on so vast a scale as Beckett or the author of *Everyman*, but neither are Thomas and Mai isolated individuals like Hofmannsthal's Claudio. To the extent that they are identified as creatures of independent Ireland, death represents not only an end to earthly suffering but also a release from national history and, conceivably, the dawn of a new era. The plays insinuate a national eschatology, not the end of the Irish state but the end of the beginning of the Irish state — that is, the period encompassing the birth of the nation and a subsequent, insistent nationalism which takes precedence over less patriotic concerns.

Partition, sectarianism, and other historical realities have made recent history a long and intermittently violent period in Ireland, one that is nearly coincident with the twentieth century. *The Steward of Christendom* and *Our Lady of Sligo* span the twentieth century as well: they are written in the 1990s, set around mid-century (1932 and 1953), and feature characters whose memories stretch as far back as the nineteenth century. This parallel helps Barry's work to reflect the intensifying urge in 1990s Ireland to bring this period of internecine conflict to an end, to find a lasting solution to its nearly intransigent problems, and to relegate the past to the past once and for all. Along these lines, Jochen Achilles sees Barry as one of a number of contemporary playwrights whose use of "a common language of transcendence" (444) both signals and promotes a paradigm shift in current Irish identity from the national to the cultural. "A specifically Irish identity," he writes, "is no longer viewed as a primordial and unitary given but as a distinct element among others which is tied to a multifaceted culture by communicative processes" (436).[5]

For Thomas Dunne and Mai O'Hara, this shift from national to cultural identity has not taken place, nor could it have. They are products of an earlier (nationalist) era, one which has failed to reward their unstinting service to it. Their imminent deaths, images of the national paradigm's obsolescence, do not directly forecast the shift to the cultural paradigm so much as they enact an individual myth of eternal return which transcends history. In memory and in delirium, their consciousness increasingly preoccupied with thoughts of childhood, Thomas and Mai each demonstrate a psychic regression over the course of the play, a regression which takes its ultimate form, in each play's closing moments, in an epiphanic reunion with a merciful, loving father.

At the end of *Our Lady of Sligo*, as Mai lies in her bed nearly comatose, her husband, daughter, and nurse at her side, the silvery spirit of her father appears one last time, accompanied for the first time by a little girl in a blue coat; this child could be Mai's sister Cissie (who died at age seven), or Mai herself when she was a girl, or even an angel of death come to rescue her from a life of pain. "There you are, there you are," she says at the sight of the little girl, and then in unison with the child, Mai intones the sad and soothing word "blue" twice in a row. Holding her father's hand, the little girl repeats, "Blue, blue." "Good girl, Mai-Mai, good girl," says her "Dada," as if coaxing her across the threshold of death as the color bleaches out of the light, bringing the play to an end (63).

At the end of *The Steward of Christendom*, Thomas's son Willie, as a boy of thirteen dressed in uniform, appears to him one last time within his cell-like room. Willie helps Thomas up off the floor and into bed as Thomas begins a long story about the day, when he was a boy, that his dog Shep ran away. As it turns out, the dog ate one of his father's sheep. When the young Thomas finally finds his pet, he hesitates to return home, knowing his hard-hearted father will kill the animal and punish him almost as severely. Thomas is surprised then, when he finally does return home, to find himself clutched tight in an embrace by his father. By this time in the play's present, Thomas and his son Willie lie there together on the bed, on the verge of a double sleep, holding each other, as Thomas utters the last words of the play: "And the dog's crime was never spoken of, but that he lived till he died. And I would call that the mercy of fathers, when the love that lies in them deeply like the glittering face of a well is betrayed by an emergency, and the child sees at last that he is loved, loved and needed and not to be lived without, and greatly" (301). Barry orchestrates these powerfully sad endings in a way that imbues them with a touch of the sublime. For both Thomas and Mai, "the mercy of fathers" represents a redemption from history, one which they have achieved in their delirium by working their way back to a time of innocence and to a self undifferentiated from the protective arms of the father, a time also before the history of independent Ireland took over. In that prelapsarian moment they are thrice redeemed, first from whatever guilt they feel for the suffering of others, second from their lot in the new Irish nation, and third from the pain of consciousness itself.

A similar prelapsarian impulse manifests itself in two earlier Barry plays, *Prayers of Sherkin* and *The Only True History of Lizzie Finn*, both of which take place before "the fall" into history marked by the Easter Rising of 1916 or the signing of the Anglo-Irish Treaty in 1921. Compared to *The Steward of Christendom* and *Our Lady of Sligo*, each has a fin-de-siècle feel to it, a sense of historical antiquity that makes it feel pristine, otherworldly, fabulous. The action of each hinges on an interdenominational romance which defies sectarian difference and resists parental authority; nevertheless, an air of serenity, harmony, and civility governs each play. Without much overt struggle, a young couple united in love emerges from a dwindling, isolated community and sets off into a wider Irish nation that is on the verge of sweeping social, political, and cultural change. To the extent that their departure hastens the demise of that dying community and initiates a new era of hope and vitality, the plays reflect the same subtle millennial urge as the later Barry plays.

Prayers of Sherkin takes place in the 1890s on a small island off the southwest coast of Ireland near Cork, home to a small Quaker-like religious sect which arrived there a century before to await the promised millennium and the New Jerusalem. Now, three generations later, their numbers have dwindled to the point of extinction, as they wait for a suitable husband to be sent to marry young Fanny Hawke, the only healthy woman of childbearing age. Difficulties arise when Fanny falls in love with Patrick Kirwin, a poor lithographer from the mainland and the son of an Irish Catholic and a Portuguese Jew. Out of devotion to her father, her clan, and her faith, Fanny denies her heart and rejects Patrick's suit until, one day in winter, when Fanny is walking alone on the beach, the founder of the sect appears to her in a vision and sets her free to go "into that Catholic darkness, into a century of unlucky stars" (106). And so, at the end of the play, she stands at the end of the island pier and awaits the boatman who will ferry her across to the mainland and her husband-to-be, effectively guaranteeing the end of the Sherkin Island group.

The Only True History of Lizzie Finn centers on a more spirited, carefree heroine, Lizzie Finn, who was raised in a Presbyterian orphanage and grew up to become a successful music-hall dancer in England. She falls in love with and marries Robert Gibson, who is just home from the Boer War and the only surviving heir of a Protestant Ascendancy family. Difficulties arise when the newlyweds return to his family's large estate on Dingle Bay in County Kerry. Here, Lizzie Finn weathers the disapproval of Robert's mother and the opprobrium of the local gentry, until one day Robert's mother, seeming to capitulate to the tide of history, simply walks out into the sea and drowns. Her death frees Lizzie and Robert to sell the Big House and to break up the demesne, signaling the end of Protestant hegemony, at least in one small corner of Kerry. Like Fanny Hawke and Patrick Kirwin, Robert and Lizzie head off for the bright lights of Cork City, the music hall, and what Jack O'Hara in *Our Lady of Sligo* calls "that new world of Ireland" (22).

Both *Prayers of Sherkin* and *The Only True History of Lizzie Finn* end on a note of bittersweet hopefulness and millennial expectation, which must be seen with some irony in the retrospective light of *The Steward of Christendom* and *Our Lady of Sligo*. That is, the fates of Thomas Dunne and Mai and Jack O'Hara suggest what awaits Lizzie Finn/Robert Gibson and Fanny Hawke/Patrick Kirwin in "that new world of Ireland." If the past is characterized as a broken promise in the two plays set *after* 1922, then the future can be seen as a promise waiting to be broken in the two plays set *before* 1922. Proleptically and retrospectively, the foundational moment of the modern Irish state, the period from the Easter Rising through the War of Independence and the Civil War to the ascension of "King De Valera" (as one character refers to him in *The Steward of Christendom*), looms over the lives of Barry's characters like a dark cloud. It is a history, or a history yet to be, which is so ever-present as to engender a millennial urge for deliverance.

But it is only an urge. Barry's plays do not present a direct image of apocalypse, as do recent works by two of his American peers, contemporaries Tony Kushner and José Rivera. In contrast to the prevailing air of serenity in *Prayers of Sherkin* and *The Only True History of Lizzie Finn*, Kushner's *Angels in America* (1991) and Rivera's *Marisol* (1992) present highly theatrical visions of a world on the eve of destruction. If Kushner's famous epic is "a gay fantasia on national themes," Rivera's surrealistic drama might be seen as "a single woman's nightmare on urban violence and decay." In *Marisol*, a middle-class Puerto Rican woman from the Bronx (named Marisol Perez) is abandoned by her guardian angel, a young black woman with silver wings and a black leather jacket who takes up an Uzi and sets off to join the ongoing War in Heaven. This leaves Marisol to fend for herself in a disintegrating world in which coffee and apples are extinct, the state of Ohio is on fire, the moon has strayed from its orbit, and credit-card holders who exceed their spending limits are sent to a house of detention in

Brooklyn. In a phantasmagoric series of violent encounters, she meets a variety of urban misfits, most of them men, whose manic aggression is rooted in poverty, homelessness, and other social ills. The play ends as Marisol, a random murder victim, envisions the victory of the rebel angels, aided by the innocent of the earth, and the blinding dawn of the new millennium: "New ideas rip the Heavens. New powers are created. New miracles are signed into Law. It's the first day of the new history. Oh God. What light. What possibilities. What hope" (45).

Like José Rivera, Tony Kushner projects his bizarre, baroque vision of apocalypse on the urban canvas of New York City, but in doing so, he invokes a broader, more overtly national image of the entire United States of America and a purposefully historical perspective, which *Marisol* lacks. Kushner's angel is the theatrical embodiment of Walter Benjamin's Angel of History, as introduced in his "Theses on the Philosophy of History," who crashes through the ceiling of Prior Walter's apartment to enlist him as the prophet of a curious apocalypse.[6] Kushner invokes a grab bag of social, historical, and geophysical catastrophes — including the AIDS epidemic and homophobia, McCarthyism and Reaganomics, the San Francisco earthquake and Chernobyl, the hole in the ozone and the Holocaust — to create an image of an American cosmos in which, as the character of Ethel Rosenberg says, "History is about to crack wide open. Millennium approaches" (112).

But it is an ambivalent millennium, as Stanton B. Garner, Jr. makes clear in his essay "*Angels in America:* The Millennium and Postmodern Memory":

> On the one hand, the play evokes the closure essential to apocalypticism, its vision of cataclysm and its dual prospects of annihilation and utopian transformation. [. . .] At the same time, the play is characterized by a subtle undermining of the narrative of rupture and ultimacy and the biblical imagery that accompanies it. (177)

That is, Kushner approaches the millennial moment, and then, deploying postmodern "principles of supplementarity and deferral," he sidesteps or leaps over it, generating a false or postponed apocalypse and a discontinuous continuity for history itself. As opposed to Kushner's theatrically self-conscious "two-part epic that keeps outlasting itself" (182), Rivera's *Marisol* explodes in an eternal instant in which "galaxies spring from a single drop of angels' sweat while hundreds of armies fight and die on the fingertips of children in the Bronx" (45).

Compared to the immediate, flamboyant millennialism of Kushner and Rivera, the millennial urge in Barry's plays might seem to be restrained and remote. They lack all the crash and bang of the American ones, the sensational violence, the grandiose emotionalism, the insistent angels, the apocalyptic flair. In Barry, even the most severe events and feelings have an aura of being twice removed from a present reality, first by their historical status and then again by the lyricism with which Barry imbues them. Composed as if they were poems for the stage, both *Prayers of Sherkin* and *The Only True History of Lizzie Finn* follow a gentle, uneventful rhythm that makes them idylls of what Christopher Murray has called "a spiritual elsewhere" ("Such a Sense of Home" 247); each seems to meander through the seasons of its action, a dramatic leaf adrift on the river of time. *The Steward of Christendom* and *Our Lady of Sligo* are, in essence, interior monologues rendered as plays; each one's forward momentum obeys the flow of thought of a character who floats in and out of consciousness, seemingly at random. All of Barry's characters speak a rich, lyrical language that renders their experience with poignancy and grace. This is precisely what makes the millennial urge in Barry's work so palpable, as if the form of the play itself was fomenting the peace that the characters yearn for, if not now then in a world to come.

On two occasions, Barry himself has articulated a desire for a different peace in the editorial pages of *The New York Times*. Like anyone of his generation in Ireland, his entire adult life has been clouded by "the Troubles" in the north and elsewhere, a factor which contributed to his spending several years abroad in the early 1980s. Although his plays do not explicitly portray life in contemporary Ireland, political or otherwise, their millennial urge to break free of the past would seem to stem in part from his response to the turbulent times in which he lives. At the start of the negotiations presided over by former U.S. Senator George Mitchell in the fall of 1997, Barry expressed his earnest and naked hope that the talks would prove to be "the start of a fresh history, as if Ireland, not just Northern Ireland, has been re-invented on this the 15th of September." And then, to advance that hope and to coax that new history along, he offered a parable of sorts:

> Once upon a time the island of Ireland was in two halves, one at either side of the proto-Atlantic. An older American continent closed with an older Europe, and as the seas again parted to make the present Atlantic, the tiny island was set adrift in the Southern Hemisphere. Then through millennia it drifted north across the equator and docked where she lies now. It is an old place and half of it might be said to belong to America, certainly half to Europe.
>
> Certainly we must listen to the meaning of this enormous geological story, we must listen to the meaning of everything, down to the last whistle of the wind. That everything in truth is temporary, certainly mere land itself, and all we have of eternity is human love, human peace. (Barry, "Irish History Remade" A23)

The trope here is telling. Just as in the plays, Barry goes back to a time before Ireland was Ireland, as though the best or only way to end an intractable era of violence and discord is to return to a point of origin, to get back to the Garden. The strategy, dramaturgically as well as rhetorically, is mythic in nature, millennial in tone, and perhaps naive — willfully so, I would say — but it is not nostalgic. It manifests a fervent, if paradoxical, impulse to return to the past in order to move beyond it once and for all.

N O T E S

This essay is dedicated to Michael Bigelow Dixon of the Actors Theatre of Louisville for his tireless support of new plays and young playwrights.

1. This concern has been a dominant one in Irish drama scholarship in recent years. See, for example, "The History Play Today," a mid-1980s survey of the genre, in which Christopher Murray argues that "the collapse of the history play . . . reflects the contemporary paralysis of history itself in Ireland as a whole" (269), and "Historical Obsession in Recent Irish Drama," in which Gerald Fitzgibbon examines works by Friel, Murphy, McGuinness, and Leonard for the ways in which they manifest "the obsession with the past as the formative force determining the configuration of the present" (42).

2. Some of these "anomalous figures" — for example, Thomas Dunne in *The Steward of Christendom*, Fanny Hawke in *Prayers of Sherkin*, and Mai O'Hara in *Our Lady of Sligo* — are based on Barry's own forebears, but the plays are not biographical in any documentary sense. Barry uses an imagined family history to reinforce and validate his concern with national history.

3. All quotations from *Our Lady of Sligo* are taken from the edition of the text published by Methuen in conjunction with the play's 1998 premiere at the Royal National Theatre. All quotations from *The Steward of Christendom* are taken from the 1997 Methuen anthology, *Plays: 1*.

4. This affinity with the *Ars Moriendi* drama was initially suggested to me by casual remarks made by Al Wertheim during the seminar on "Nationalism and a National Theatre: One Hundred Years of Irish Drama," held 26–29 May 1999 at Indiana University.

5. See Jochen Achilles, " 'Homesick for Abroad': The Transition from National to Cultural Identity in Contemporary Irish Drama," *Modern Drama* 38 (winter 1995): 435–449. Achilles analyzes Friel's *Making History* and Barry's *Prayers of Sherkin* as exemplary instances of this shift, which he describes in general as follows:

> In colonial times a uniform national identity was habitually and for obvious reasons associated with progress in the Irish context. In the postcolonial period, such self-sufficiency is increasingly viewed as hampering progress, as indicative of the perpetuation of an outdated impasse. Cosmopolitanism and multiculturalism, formerly considered as detracting from the national cause, are more and more viewed as the only direction in which cultural progress may be sought. The culturalist paradigm — that is, a new perspective of progress which calls for a mediation between the familiar and the unfamiliar and a reconciliation of the particular and the general — is beginning to replace the nationalist paradigm. (435)

6. For a delineation of the Benjamin connection, see David Savran, "Ambivalence, Utopia, and A Queer Sort of Materialism: How *Angels in America* Reconstructs the Nation" (16–19). Benjamin's famous description of the angel of history, inspired by a Paul Klee painting, is as follows:

His face is turned toward the past. Where we perceive a chain of events, he sees one single catastrophe which keeps piling wreckage upon wreckage and hurls it in front of his feet. The angel would like to stay, awaken the dead, and make whole what has been smashed. But a storm is blowing from Paradise; it has got caught in his wings with such violence that the angel can no longer close them. This storm irresistibly propels him into the future to which his back is turned, while the pile of debris before him grows skyward. This storm is what we call progress. (258)

WORKS CITED

Abbey Company United States Tour, 1911–1912, Part 2 (bound scrapbook). National Library of Ireland, MS 25,499.

Acheson, James. *Samuel Beckett's Artistic Theory and Practice*. London: Macmillan, 1997.

Achilles, Jochen. " 'Homesick for Abroad': The Transition from National to Cultural Identity in Contemporary Irish Drama." *Modern Drama* 38 (1995): 435–449.

Ahmad, Aijaz. *In Theory: Classes, Nations, Literatures*. London: Verso, 1992.

Allen, Robert. "Stewart Parker: Playwright from a Lost Tribe." *The Irish Times*, 31 January 1997, 9.

Alter, Peter. "Symbols of Irish Nationalism." In *Reactions to Irish Nationalism*, ed. Alan O'Day, 1–20. London: Hambledon Press, 1987.

Amiran, Eyal. *Wandering and Home: Beckett's Metaphysical Narrative*. University Park: Pennsylvania State University Press, 1993.

Anderson, Benedict. *Imagined Communities: Reflections on the Origin and Spread of Nationalism*. London: Verso Editions, NLB, 1983.

Aretxaga, Begoña. *Shattering Silence: Women, Nationalism, and Political Subjectivity in Northern Ireland*. Princeton: Princeton University Press, 1997.

Armstrong, Alison. "Introduction." In *The Herne's Egg: Manuscript Materials*, xiii–xvi. Ithaca, N.Y.: Cornell University Press, 1993.

Armstrong, W. A. "The Sources and Themes of *The Plough and the Stars*." *Modern Drama* 4, no. 3 (December 1961): 234–242.

Ayling, Ronald. "Sean O'Casey's Dublin Trilogy." In *Sean O'Casey: A Collection of Critical Essays*, ed. Thomas Kilroy, 77–89. Englewood Cliffs, N.J.: Prentice-Hall, 1975.

Baden-Powell, George. *The Saving of Ireland: Industrial, Financial, Political*. Edinburgh: William Blackwood and Sons, 1898.

Bair, Deirdre. *Samuel Beckett: A Biography*. New York: Summit Books, 1978.

Bardon, Jonathan. *Belfast: An Illustrated History*. Belfast: Blackstaff, 1982.

———. *A History of Ulster*. Belfast: Blackstaff, 1992.

Barry, Sebastian. "Irish History, Remade." *New York Times*, 15 September 1997, A23.

———. *Our Lady of Sligo*. London: Methuen, 1998.

———. *Plays: 1. (Boss Grady's Boys, Prayers of Sherkin, White Woman Street, The Only True History of Lizzie Finn*, and *The Steward of Christendom.)* London: Methuen, 1997.

Bataille, Georges. *Erotism: Death and Sensuality*. 1957. Trans. Mary Dalwood. San Francisco: City Lights, 1982.

Battersby, Eileen. "The Image Maker." *The Irish Times*, 12 June 1997. http://www.irish-times.com/irish-times/paper/1997/0612/fea1.htm

Beckett, Samuel. *Act Without Words II*. In *The Collected Shorter Plays*, 47–51. New York: Grove Press, 1984.

———. *Endgame*. New York: Grove Press, 1958.

———. *Krapp's Last Tape*. In *The Collected Shorter Plays*, 53–63. New York: Grove Press, 1984.

――――. *Murphy.* London: Routledge, 1938.

――――. *Rockaby.* In *The Collected Shorter Plays,* 271–282. New York: Grove Press, 1984.

――――. *That Time.* In *The Collected Shorter Plays,* 225–235. New York: Grove Press, 1984.

Behan, Brendan. *The Complete Plays.* Ed. Alan Simpson. New York: Grove Press, 1978.

――――. *Confessions of an Irish Rebel.* London: Hutchinson, 1965.

――――. *The Hostage.* 1958 Theatre Workshop Version. New York: Grove Press, 1958.

Bell, Geoffrey. *The Protestants of Ulster.* London: Pluto Press, 1987.

Bell, Sam Hanna. *The Theatre in Ulster.* Dublin: Gill and Macmillan, 1972.

Beltaine: An Occasional Publication. No. 1 (May 1899). Reprint, London: Frank Cass & Co., 1970.

Beltaine: The Organ of the Irish Literary Theatre. No. 2 (February 1900). Reprint, London: Frank Cass & Co., 1970.

Benjamin, Walter. *The Origin of German Tragic Drama.* Trans. John Osborne. New York: Verso, 1998.

――――. "Theses on the Philosophy of History." In *Illuminations,* ed., with an introduction, by Hannah Arendt, trans. Harry Zohn, 253–264. New York: Schocken, 1968.

Bentley, Eric. *In Search of Theater.* New York: Vintage, 1953.

Berger, Peter L., and Thomas Luckmann. *The Social Construction of Reality.* Harmondsworth: Penguin, 1971.

Berkvist, Robert. "A Freewheeling Play about Irish History." *New York Times,* 11 March 1979, D5+.

Berrow, Hilary. "Eight Nights in the Abbey." In *J. M. Synge Centenary Papers 1971,* ed. Maurice Harmon, 75–87. Dublin: Dolmen Press, 1972.

Bertens, Hans. "The Postmodern *Weltanschauung* and Its Relation with Modernism: An Introductory Survey." In *Approaching Postmodernism,* ed. Douwe Fokkema and Hans Bertens, 9–51. Amsterdam: John Benjamins, 1986.

Billington, Michael. "Excessive Talent for Plundering Irish Past." *Manchester Guardian Weekly,* 10 August 1997, 26.

Blake, Ann. "The Fame of Sean O'Casey: A Reconsideration of the Dublin Plays." *Sydney Studies in English* 12 (1986–1987): 64–77.

Bloomer, Jennifer. *Architecture and the Text: (S)crypts of Joyce and Piranesi.* New Haven, Conn.: Yale University Press, 1993.

Blythe, Ernest. *The Abbey Theatre.* Dublin: National Theatre Society, n.d.

Boland, John. "Back to Broad Strokes." *Hibernia* 45, no. 10 (6 March 1980): 21.

Boucicault, Dion. "Shaughraun." *New York Herald,* 7 March 1875, 5.

Boyce, D. George. *Nationalism in Ireland.* Baltimore: Johns Hopkins University Press, 1982.

――――. "Past and Present: Revisionism and the Northern Ireland Troubles." In *The Making of Modern Irish History: Revisionism and the Revisionist Controversy,* ed. D. George Boyce and Alan O'Day, 216–238. London: Routledge, 1996.

Bradley, Anthony, and Maryann Gialanella Valiulis, eds. *Gender and Sexuality in Modern Ireland.* Amherst: University of Massachusetts Press, 1997.

Bradshaw, Brendan. "Nationalism and Historical Scholarship in Modern Ireland." *Irish Historical Studies* 26, no. 104 (1989): 329–351.

Brater, Enoch, ed. *Feminine Focus: The New Women Playwrights.* Ann Arbor: University of Michigan Press, 1989.

Brecht, Bertolt. *Brecht on Theatre.* Ed. and trans. John Willett. New York: Hill and Wang, 1964.

Bretherton, George. "A Carnival Christy and a Playboy for All Ages." In *Critical Essays on John Millington Synge*, ed. Daniel J. Casey, 126–136. New York: G. K. Hall, 1994.

Brogan, Patricia Burke. *Eclipsed.* Galway: Salmon Publishing, 1994.

Brown, Terence. *Ireland: A Social and Cultural History, 1922–Present.* Ithaca, N.Y.: Cornell University Press, 1985.

Browne, Noël. *Against the Tide.* Dublin: Gill and Macmillan, 1986.

de Búrca, Séamus. *Brendan Behan.* Newark, Del.: Proscenium Press, 1971.

Butler, Judith. *Gender Trouble: Feminism and the Subversion of Identity.* New York: Routledge, 1990.

Callaghan, Dympna. "Interview with Seamus Deane." *Social Text* 38 (1994): 39–50.

Campbell, Flann. *The Dissenting Voice: Protestant Democracy.* Belfast: Blackstaff, 1991.

Campbell, Kerry. "Cuppas and Corpses: Kerry Campbell Talks to Chris Reid." *Belfast Review*, October 1983, 24–25.

Carney, Jim. "A Conversation on Tom Murphy's Homecoming." *The Herald*, 7 December 1985, 3.

Carr, Marina. *Low in the Dark.* In *The Crack in the Emerald: New Irish Plays*, ed. David Grant, 63–140. London: Nick Hern Books, 1990.

———. *The Mai.* Loughcrew: Gallery Press, 1995.

———. *Portia Coughlan.* In *The Dazzling Dark: New Irish Plays*, ed. Frank McGuinness, 235–309. New York: Faber and Faber, 1996.

Carroll, Paul Vincent. "Can the Abbey Be Restored?" In *The Abbey Theatre: Interviews and Recollections*, ed. E. H. Mikhail, 188–192. London: Macmillan, 1988.

Carson, Douglas. Interview by author. Belfast, Northern Ireland, 21 November 1998.

Carty, Ciaran. "Northern Star Rising on the Tide." *Sunday Tribune*, 29 September 1985.

Case, Sue-Ellen. "From Split Subject to Split Britches." In *Feminine Focus: The New Women Playwrights*, ed. Enoch Brater, 126–146. Ann Arbor: University of Michigan Press, 1989.

Casey, Daniel J., ed. *Critical Essays on John Millington Synge.* New York: G. K. Hall, 1994.

Cathcart, Rex. *The Most Contrary Region: The BBC in Northern Ireland 1924–1984.* Belfast: Blackstaff, 1984.

Chesser, Eustace. *Live and Let Live: The Moral of the Wolfenden Report.* New York: Philosophical Library, 1958.

Clarke, Austin. "The Riotous Are Bold." *The Irish Times*, 15 and 16 April 1949, 6.

Clines, Francis X. "Theater Crosses Borders in Ireland, Fueled by the Troubles and a Love of Language." *New York Times*, 27 September 1987.

"Clinton Praises Nation's Veterans." *Ann Arbor News*, 1 June 1999.

Cohn, Ruby. *Just Play: Beckett's Theater.* Princeton: Princeton University Press, 1980.

———. *Samuel Beckett: The Comic Gamut.* New Brunswick, N.J.: Rutgers University Press, 1962.

Committee on Homosexual Offences and Prostitution, Sir John Wolfenden, Chair. *Report of the Committee on Homosexual Offences and Prostitution.* London: Home Office, 1957.

Condren, Mary. *The Serpent and the Goddess: Women, Religion, and Power in Celtic Ireland.* San Francisco: Harper and Row, 1989.

Connla. "Literature and Politics." *Ulad* 1 (1904): 17–18.

———. "The Theatre and the People." *Ulad* 3 (1905): 13.

Connolly, Sean. "Translating History: Brian Friel and the Irish Past." In *The*

Achievement of Brian Friel, ed. Alan J. Peacock, 149–163. Gerrards Cross: Colin Smythe, 1993.

Connor, Steven. "Between Theatre and Theory: *Long Observation of the Ray.*" In *The Ideal Core of the Onion,* ed. John Pilling and Mary Bryden, 79–98. Bristol: Beckett International Foundation, 1992.

———. *Samuel Beckett: Repetition, Theory and Text.* London: Basil Blackwell, 1988.

Cooney, John. "McQuaid's Shadow." *The Irish Times,* 4 April 1998, Weekend, 1–2.

Corkery, Daniel. *The Hidden Ireland: A Study of Gaelic Munster in the Eighteenth Century.* Dublin: Gill, 1925.

Courtney, Sister Marie-Therese. *Edward Martyn and the Irish Theatre.* New York: Vantage, 1956.

Cowan, Bainard. "Walter Benjamin's Theory of Allegory." *New German Critique* 22–25 (1981–1982): 109–122.

Cowell, John. *No Profit but the Name: The Longfords and the Gate Theatre.* Dublin: O'Brien Press, 1988.

Cronin, Sean. *Irish Nationalism: A History of Its Roots and Ideology.* Dublin: Academy Press, 1980.

Cullingford, Elizabeth. "British Romans and Irish Carthaginians: Anticolonial Metaphor in Heaney, Friel, and McGuinness." *PMLA* 111, no. 2 (1996): 222–239.

Cunningham, Francine. "A Man's Passion for a People's Theatre." *The Irish Times,* 25 April 1990, 8.

Daly, Mary E. " 'Oh, Kathleen Ni Houlihan, Your Way's a Thorny Way!': The Condition of Women in Twentieth-Century Ireland." In *Gender and Sexuality in Modern Ireland,* ed. Anthony Bradley and Maryann Gialanella Valiulis, 102–126. Amherst: University of Massachusetts Press, 1997.

———. "Women in the Irish Free State 1922–39: The Interaction between Economics and Ideology." *Journal of Women's History* 6/7, no. 4/1 (1995): 99–116.

Dantanus, Ulf. *Brian Friel: The Growth of an Irish Dramatist.* Gothenburg, Sweden: Gothenburg Studies in English 59, 1985.

Dawe, Gerald. "Drama." Review of *Bailegangaire* and *Conversations on a Homecoming. Linen Hall Review* 4, no. 2 (1987): 26.

"Deadly Tram Rides." *Dublin Evening Mail,* 12 January 1907, 2.

Dean, Joan Fitzpatrick. "Self-Dramatization in the Plays of Frank McGuinness." *New Hibernia Review* 3, no. 1 (Spring 1999): 97–110.

Deane, Seamus. *Celtic Revivals: Essays in Modern Irish Literature, 1880–1980.* London: Faber, 1985.

———. "Irish Theatre: A Secular Space?" *Irish University Review* 28, no. 1 (1998): 163–174.

Deeny, James. *To Cure and to Care: Memoirs of a Chief Medical Officer.* Dun Laoghaire, County Dublin: Glendale Press, 1989.

Deevy, Teresa. *Three Plays: "Katie Roche," "The King of Spain's Daughter" and "The Wild Goose."* London: Macmillan, 1939.

Deleuze, Gilles. "Coldness and Cruelty." In *Masochism: Coldness and Cruelty by Gilles Deleuze and Venus in Furs by Leopold von Sacher-Masoch,* 15–138. New York: Zone Books, 1989.

Dening, Penelope. "The Wordsmith of Camberwell." *The Irish Times,* 8 July 1997. http://www.irish-times.com/irish-times/paper/1997/0708/fea7.htm

Derrida, Jacques. *Limited Inc.* Evanston, Ill.: Northwestern University Press, 1988.

Diamond, Elin. *Unmaking Mimesis: Essays on Feminism and Theatre.* New York: Routledge, 1997.

Dickerson, Glenda, and Breena Clarke. *Re/Membering Aunt Jemima: A Travelling Menstrual Show.* In *Contemporary Plays by Women of Color: An Anthology,* ed. Kathy A. Perkins and Roberta Uno, 32–45. New York: Routledge, 1996.

Dizon, Louella. *Till Voices Wake Us.* In *Contemporary Plays by Women of Color: An Anthology*, ed. Kathy A. Perkins and Roberta Uno, 127–157. New York: Routledge, 1996.

Donleavy, J. P. "What They Did in Dublin with *The Ginger Man.*" In *The Plays of J.P. Donleavy.* Harmondsworth: Penguin, 1974.

Doyle, Roddy. *Brownbread* and *War!* New York: Penguin, 1992.

———. "Introduction." In *Brownbread* and *War!*, Roddy Doyle, 1–2. New York: Penguin, 1992.

"Dr. Butler's Tonic Digestive Pills." Advertisement. *Dublin Evening Mail*, 29 January 1907, 2.

Ellmann, Richard. *Four Dubliners.* New York: George Braziller, 1987.

Esslin, Martin. *Mediations: Essays on Brecht, Beckett and the Media.* New York: Grove Press, 1982.

———. *The Theatre of the Absurd.* Revised ed. New York: Doubleday, 1969.

Everyman and Medieval Miracle Plays. Ed. A. C. Cawley. London: Dent, 1956.

Fairweather, Eileen, Roisin McDonough, and Melanie McFadyean. *Only the Rivers Run Free: Northern Ireland, the Woman's War.* London: Pluto Press, 1984.

Fallon, Brian. *An Age of Innocence: Irish Culture 1930–1960.* Dublin: Gill and Macmillan, 1998.

Farrell, Michael. *Northern Ireland: The Orange State.* London: Pluto Press, 1980.

Fay, Frank. F. Fay's *The Laying of the Foundations.* Prompt book, 1902. Frank Fay Papers, MS 10950, National Library of Ireland.

Fay, Frank J. *Towards a National Theatre: Dramatic Criticism.* Ed. Robert Hogan. Dublin: Dolmen Press, 1971.

Fay, Gerald. *The Abbey Theatre: Cradle of Genius.* New York: Macmillan, 1958.

Fay, W. E. "A Note on National Games." *Sinn Féin*, 12 January 1907, 4.

Feeney, Joseph. "Martin McDonagh: Dramatist of the West." *Studies* 87, no. 345 (1998): 24–32.

Feeney, William J. *Drama in Hardwicke Street.* Cranbury, N.J.: Associated University Press, 1984.

———. "Introduction." *George Spelvin's Theatre Book*, ed. William J. Feeney (Fall 1979).

Fitzgibbon, Gerald. "Historical Obsession in Recent Irish Drama." In *The Crows behind the Plough: History and Violence in Anglo-Irish Poetry and Drama*, ed. Geert Lernout, 41–59. Amsterdam: Rodopi, 1991.

Fitzpatrick, David. "De Valera in 1917: The Undoing of the Easter Rising." In *De Valera and His Times*, ed. John P. O'Carroll and John A. Murphy, 101–112. Cork: Cork University Press, 1983.

Fitz-Simon, Christopher. *The Irish Theatre.* London: Thames and Hudson, 1983.

Foran, Charles. "The Troubles of Roddy Doyle." *Saturday Night*, April 1996, 58–64.

Foster, R. F. "Lost Futures: Sebastian Barry's *Our Lady of Sligo.*" *The Irish Review* 22 (1998): 23–27.

———. *Modern Ireland, 1600–1972.* New York: Penguin Books, 1988.

———. *W. B. Yeats: A Life. I: The Apprentice Mage 1865–1914* . New York: Oxford University Press, 1997.

Frampton, Kenneth. "Towards a Critical Regionalism: Six Points for an Architecture of Resistance." In *The Anti-Aesthetic: Essays on Postmodern Culture*, ed. Hal Foster, 16–30. Seattle, Wash.: Bay, 1983.

Frazier, Adrian. *Behind the Scenes: Yeats, Horniman, and the Struggle for the Abbey Theatre.* Berkeley: University of California Press, 1990.

Friel, Brian. *Dancing at Lughnasa.* London: Faber, 1990.

———. "Exiles." Program note for *The Blue Macushla*, Abbey Theatre, 6 March 1980.

————. *Making History.* London: Faber and Faber, 1989.

————. *Selected Plays.* Ed. Seamus Deane. Washington, D.C.: Catholic University Press, 1980.

Friel, Judy. "Rehearsing *Katie Roche.*" *Irish University Review, Jubilee Issue: Teresa Deevy and Irish Women Playwrights* 25, no. 1 (1995): 117–125.

Gardner, Raymond. "Too Many People Have Writing in the Head. . . ." *Guardian,* 6 December 1976, 8.

Garner, Stanton B., Jr. "*Angels in America:* The Millennium and Postmodern Memory." In *Approaching the Millennium: Essays on Angels in America,* ed. Deborah R. Geis and Steven F. Kruger, 173–184. Ann Arbor: University of Michigan Press, 1997.

Garvin, Tom. *The Evolution of Irish Nationalist Politics.* New York: Holmes and Meier, 1981.

————. "The Rising and Irish Democracy." In *Revising the Rising,* ed. Máirín Ní Dhonnchadha and Theo Dorgan, 21–28. Derry: Field Day, 1991.

Genet, Jean. *Le Balcon.* London: Methuen, 1982.

————. *The Balcony.* Rev. ed. New York: Grove Press, 1958.

————. *The Blacks: A Clown Show.* Trans. Bernard Frechtman. New York: Grove Press, 1960.

————. "Comment Jouer *Le Balcon.*" In *Le Balcon,* Jean Genet, 139–142. London: Methuen, 1982.

————. *The Maids* and *Deathwatch.* Trans. Bernard Frechtman. New York: Grove Press, 1954.

————. *Miracle of the Rose.* 1951. Trans. Bernard Frechtman. New York: Castle, 1966.

————. *Oeuvres Complètes.* 5 vols. Paris: Gallimard, 1951–1962.

Gibbons, Luke. "Technologies of Desire: Media, Modernity, and Sexuality in Recent Irish Cinema." University of Virginia's Center for Media and Culture Conference, "Irish Film: A Mirror Up to Culture," Charlottesville, Va., 10 May 1999.

————. *Transformations in Irish Culture.* Cork: Cork University Press, 1996.

Gillespie, Robert. "The Play's Director, Talking to the Editors." In *Spokesong; or, the Common Wheel* (Dutch edition ed. Jop Spiekerman and Nora Schadee). The Netherlands: Wiker, 1977.

Goldring, Maurice. *Pleasant the Scholar's Life: Irish Intellectuals and the Construction of the Nation State.* London: Serif, 1993.

Gómez-Peña, Guillermo. *The New World Border: Prophecies, Poems and Loqueras for the End of the Century.* San Francisco: City Lights, 1996.

Grant, David, ed. *The Crack in the Emerald.* London: Nick Hern Books, 1990.

Gray, John. "Field Day Five Years On." *Linen Hall Review,* Summer 1985, 4–10.

Greaves, C. Desmond. *Sean O'Casey: Politics and Art.* London: Lawrence and Wishart, 1979.

Greene, David H. "J. M. Synge: A Reappraisal." In *Critical Essays on John Millington Synge,* ed. Daniel J. Casey, 15–27. New York: G. K. Hall, 1994.

Greene, David H., and Edward M. Stephens. *J. M. Synge, 1871–1909.* New York: New York University Press, 1989.

Gregory, Lady Augusta. *Our Irish Theatre.* New York: Oxford University Press, 1972.

Grene, Nicholas. "Distancing Drama: Sean O'Casey to Brian Friel." In *Irish Writers and the Theatre,* ed. Masaru Sekine, 47–70. Gerrards Cross: Colin Smythe, 1986.

————. *Synge: A Critical Study of the Plays.* Totowa, N.J.: Rowman and Littlefield, 1975.

Griffith, Arthur. "The Abbey Theatre." *Sinn Féin*, 2 February 1907, 2.
———."All Ireland." *The United Irishman*, 17 October 1903, 1.
———. "The Immorality of the British Army." *Sinn Féin*, 9 February 1907, 2.
Harmon, Maurice. "Definitions of Irishness in Modern Irish Literature." In *Irishness in a Changing Society*, ed. The Princess Grace Irish Library, 45–63. Totowa. N.J.: Barnes and Noble, 1989.
Harrington, John P. *The Irish Play on the New York Stage, 1874–1966*. Lexington: University Press of Kentucky, 1997.
Harris, Claudia. *Inventing Women's Work: The Legacy of Charabanc Theatre Company*. Gerrards Cross: Colin Smythe, forthcoming.
Harris, José. *Private Lives, Public Spirit: A Social History of Britain, 1870–1914*. Oxford: Oxford University Press, 1993.
Herr, Cheryl. *Critical Regionalism and Cultural Studies: From Ireland to the American Midwest*. Gainesville: University of Florida Press, 1996.
———. *For the Land They Loved*. Syracuse, N.Y.: Syracuse University Press, 1991.
Hickey, Des. "Local Hero." *The Sunday Independent*, 21 September 1990.
Hickey, Des, and Gus Smith, eds. *A Paler Shade of Green*. London: Leslie Frewin, 1972. As *Flight from the Celtic Twilight*. Indianapolis: Bobbs-Merrill, 1973.
Hill, Ian. "Spokesong." *Guardian*, 9 September 1989.
Hill, Leslie. " 'Fuck Life': *Rockaby*, Sex, and the Body." In *Beckett On and On*, ed. Lois Oppenheim and Marius Buning, 19–26. Madison, N.J.: Fairleigh Dickinson University Press, 1996.
Hirsch, Edward. "The Imaginary Peasant." *PMLA* 106 (1991): 1116–1133.
Hobson, Bulmer. *Ireland, Yesterday and Tomorrow*. Tralee: Anvil, 1968.
Hofmannsthal, Hugo von. *Three Plays: Death and the Fool, Electra, The Tower*. Trans. Alfred Schwarz. Detroit: Wayne State University Press, 1966.
Hogan, Robert. *After the Irish Renaissance: A Critical History of the Irish Drama since "The Plough and the Stars."* Minneapolis: University of Minnesota Press, 1967.
———. *The Experiments of Sean O'Casey*. New York: St. Martin's Press, 1960.
Hogan, Robert, Richard Burnham, and Daniel Poteet, eds. *The Abbey Theatre: The Rise of the Realists, 1910–1915*. Dublin: Dolmen Press, 1979.
Hogan, Robert, and James Kilroy. *The Irish Literary Theatre 1899–1901*. Dublin: Dolmen Press, 1975.
Holloway, Joseph. *Joseph Holloway's Abbey Theatre: A Selection from His Unpublished Journal, Impressions of a Dublin Playgoer*. Edited by Robert Hogan and Michael J. O'Neill. Carbondale: Southern Illinois University Press, 1967.
Hopkins, Eric. *Childhood Transformed: Working-Class Children in Nineteenth-Century England*. Manchester: Manchester University Press, 1994.
H.S.D. "A Dramatic Freak." *Dublin Evening Mail*, 28 January 1907, 2.
Hughes, Eamonn. " 'To Define Your Dissent': The Plays and Polemics of the Field Day Theatre Company." *Theatre Research International* 15, no. 1 (1990): 67–77.
Hunt, Hugh. *The Abbey: Ireland's National Theatre, 1904–1979*. London: Gill and Macmillan, 1979.
Hunter, A. S. "Health and Nationality." *Sinn Féin*, 5 January 1907, 1.
"I Don't Care a Rap: Mr. Synge's Defense." *Dublin Evening Mail*, 29 January 1907, 1.
Ionesco, Eugène. *Notes and Counternotes: Writings on the Theatre*. Trans. Donald Watson. New York: Grove Press, 1964.
"Irish Studies at Boston College." Boston College Office of Publications and Print Marketing and the Irish Studies Program, October 1998.
Jarman, Neil. *Material Conflicts: Parades and Visual Displays in Northern Ireland*. New York: Berg, 1997.
Jeffares, A. Norman, ed. *Yeats: Selected Criticism*. London: Macmillan, 1970.
Johnston, John. *The Lord Chamberlain's Blue Pencil*. London: Hodder, 1990.

Jordan, Eamonn. *The Feast of Famine: The Plays of Frank McGuinness*. Bern, Switzerland: Peter Lang, 1997.

Joyce, James. "The Day of the Rabblement." In *The Critical Writings of James Joyce*, ed. Ellsworth Mason and Richard Ellmann, 68–72. New York: Viking Press, 1959.

———. *Dubliners*. New York: Penguin, 1988.

———. *A Portrait of the Artist as a Young Man*. New York: Penguin, 1964.

K. "Theatre of Ireland." *Sinn Féin*, 8 May 1909, 1.

Kalem, T. E. "Wheelborne." *Time*, 27 February 1978, 58.

Kavanagh, Peter. *The Story of the Abbey Theatre: From Its Origins in 1899 to the Present*. New York: Devin-Adair, 1950.

Kearney, Richard. "Language Play: Brian Friel and Ireland's Verbal Theatre." In *Brian Friel: A Casebook*, ed. William Kerwin, 77–116. New York: Garland, 1997.

———. *The Wake of Imagination: Toward a Postmodern Culture*. Minneapolis: University of Minnesota Press, 1988.

Keenan, Brian. *An Evil Cradling*. London: Hutchinson, 1992.

Kellaway, Kate. "Through a Glass, Darkly." *The Observer*, 12 January 1992, 44.

Kenneally, Michael. *Portraying the Self: Sean O'Casey and the Art of Autobiography*. Gerrards Cross: Colin Smythe, 1988.

Kennedy, Dennis. *Granville Barker and the Dream of Theatre*. Cambridge: Cambridge University Press, 1985.

Kenny, P. D. "That Dreadful Play." *The Irish Times*, 30 January 1907, 9.

Keogh, Dermot. *Twentieth-Century Ireland: Nation and State*. Dublin: Gill and Macmillan, 1994.

Kerr, Colin. "The Quality of Mercier." *The Evening Herald*, 3 November 1988, 26–27.

Kiberd, Declan. "The Elephant of Revolutionary Forgetfulness." In *Revising the Rising*, ed. Máirín Ní Dhonnchadha and Theo Dorgan, 1–20. Derry: Field Day, 1991.

———. *Inventing Ireland*. London: Jonathan Cape, 1995.

———. "Irish Literature and Irish History." In *Oxford Illustrated History of Ireland*, ed. R. F. Foster, 275–338. Oxford: Oxford University Press, 1989.

———. *Synge and the Irish Language*. London: Macmillan, 1979.

Kiely, David M. *John Millington Synge: A Biography*. Dublin: Gill and Macmillan, 1979.

Kilroy, James F. "The Playboy as Poet." In *Critical Essays on John Millington Synge*, ed. Daniel J. Casey, 119–125. New York: G. K. Hall & Co., 1994.

Kilroy, Thomas. "A Generation of Playwrights." *Irish University Review* 22, no. 1 (1992): 135–141.

Kosok, Heinz. *O'Casey the Dramatist*. Trans. Heinz Kosok and Joseph T. Swann. Gerrards Cross: Colin Smythe, 1985.

Kott, Jan. *The Theater of Essence*. Evanston, Ill.: Northwestern University Press, 1984.

Krause, David. "The Paradox of Ideological Formalism." *Massachusetts Review* 28, no. 3 (Autumn 1987): 516–524.

———. *Sean O'Casey: The Man and His Work*. Enlarged ed. New York: Macmillan, 1975.

———. "Sean O'Casey and the Higher Nationalism: The Desecration of Ireland's Household Gods." In *Theatre and Nationalism in Twentieth-Century Ireland*, ed. Robert O'Driscoll, 114–133. Toronto: University of Toronto Press, 1971.

Kushner, Tony. *Angels in America: A Gay Fantasia on National Themes. Part One: Millennium Approaches*. New York: Theatre Communications Group, 1993.

Laffan, Michael. "Insular Attitudes: The Revisionists and Their Critics." In *Revising the Rising*, ed. Máirín Ní Dhonnchadha and Theo Dorgan, 106–121. Derry: Field Day, 1991.

Laurence, Dan H., and Nicholas Grene, eds. *Shaw, Lady Gregory and the Abbey: A Correspondence and a Record*. Gerrards Cross: Colin Smythe, 1993.

Lee, J. J. "In Search of Patrick Pearse." In *Revising the Rising*, ed. Máirín Ní Dhonnchadha and Theo Dorgan, 122–138. Derry: Field Day, 1991.

———. *Ireland: 1912–1985*. Cambridge: Cambridge University Press, 1989.

Leeney, Cathy. "Themes of Ritual and Myth in Three Plays by Teresa Deevy." *Irish University Review, Jubilee Issue: Teresa Deevy and Irish Women Playwrights* 25, no. 1 (1995): 88–116.

Lemass, Seán. "An Tóstal." In *An Tóstal Official Souvenir Handbook*. Dublin: Tourist Board, 1953.

Leonard, Hugh. *Stephen D*. New York: Evans, 1965.

Libera, Antoni. "Structure and Pattern in That Time." Trans. Aniela Korzeniowska. *Journal of Beckett Studies* 6 (1980): 81–89.

Loftus, Belinda. *Mirrors: William III and Mother Ireland*. Dundrum Co. Down, Northern Ireland: Picture, 1990.

Longley, Edna. "From Cathleen to Anorexia: The Breakdown of Irelands." In *A Dozen Lips*, 162–187. Dublin: Attic Press, 1994.

Loomba, Ania. *Colonialism/Postcolonialism*. London: Routledge, 1998.

Lowery, Robert G. "Sean O'Casey: A Chronology." In *Sean O'Casey: Centenary Essays*, ed. David Krause and Robert G. Lowery, 1–12. Gerrards Cross: Colin Smythe, 1980.

Lukàcs, Georg. "The Sociology of Modern Drama." Trans. Lee Baxandall. In *The Theory of the Modern Stage*, ed. Eric Bentley, 425–450. Harmondsworth: Penguin, 1968.

Luke, Peter, ed. *Enter Certain Players: Edwards, Mac Liammóir and the Gate, 1928–1978*. Dublin: Dolmen Press, 1978.

Lyons, F. S .L. *Culture and Anarchy in Ireland, 1890–1939*. Oxford: Clarendon Press, 1979.

———. "The Shadow of the Past." *The Irish Times*, 11 September 1972, 12.

Lyons, Laura Elizabeth. "Writing in Trouble: Protest, Literature and the Cultural Politics of Irish Nationalism." Ph.D. dissertation, University of Texas at Austin, 1993.

MacAnna, Tomás. "Ernest Blythe and the Abbey." In *The Abbey Theatre: Interviews and Recollections*, ed. E. H. Mikhail, 167–172. London: Macmillan, 1988.

———. "Nationalism from the Abbey Stage." In *Theatre and Nationalism in Twentieth-Century Ireland*, ed. Robert O'Driscoll, 89–101. Toronto: University of Toronto Press, 1971.

MacDonagh, Thomas. "Pagans." In *George Spelvin's Theatre Book*, ed. William J. Feeney (Fall 1979): 30–53.

Macken, Walter. *Recall the Years*. Dir. Tomás MacAnna, with Frank Dermody and Edward Golden. Abbey Theatre, Dublin, 18 July 1966.

Macleod, Roy. "On Visiting the 'Moving Metropolis': Reflections on the Architecture of Imperial Science." In *Scientific Colonialism: A Cross-Cultural Comparison*, ed. N. Reingold and M. Rothenberg, 217–249. Washington, D.C.: Smithsonian Institution Press, 1987.

MacLiammóir, Mícheál. *The Importance of Being Oscar*. Dublin: Dolmen Press, 1963.

MacNamara, Brinsley. "The Abbey Theatre: Is It on the Decline?" In *The Abbey Theatre: Interviews and Recollections*, ed. E. H. Mikhail, 117–121. London: Macmillan, 1988.

MacNamara, Gerald. *The Mist That Does Be on the Bog*. TS. Linenhall Library, Belfast.

———. *No Surrender!* TS. Linenhall Library, Belfast.

———. *Thompson in Tir na nOg*. Dublin: Talbot, 1913.

Mahony, Christina Hunt. "Barry, McPherson and McDonagh in the States — Cops, Critics, and Cripples." *Irish Literary Supplement* 17, no. 2 (1998): 6–8.

Making History. Theatre program. Field Day Theatre Company, 1988.

Marcus, Phillip L. "The Celtic Revival." In *The Irish World: The Art and Culture of the Irish People,* ed. Brian De Breffney, 200–234. New York: Harry N. Abrams, 1977.

Martin, F. X. "The Evolution of a Myth: The Easter Rising, Dublin 1916." In *Nationalism: The Nature and Evolution of an Idea,* ed. Eugene Kamenka, 56–80. Canberra: Australian National University Press, 1973.

Martyn, Edward. "A Comparison between Irish and English Audiences." *Beltaine* 2 (1900): 12–13.

Maslin, Janet. "Janet Maslin on *Pulp Fiction.*" http://www.voyagerco.com/catalog/pulp/indepth/ liners.html

Maxwell, D. E. S. Introduction. "Irish Drama 1899–1929: The Abbey Theatre." In *The Field Day Anthology of Irish Writing,* 3 vols., ed. Seamus Deane, 2: 562–568. Derry: Field Day, 1991.

———. "Northern Ireland's Political Drama." *Modern Drama* 33, no. 1 (1990): 1–14.

Mayne, Rutherford. *The Troth.* Dublin: Mausel, 1909.

———. *The Turn in the Road.* Dublin: Mausel, 1909.

Mazumdar, Pauline M. H. *Eugenics, Human Genetics, and Human Failings: The Eugenics Society, Its Sources and Its Critics in Britain.* London: Routledge, 1992.

McAuley, Tony. Interview by author. Belfast, Northern Ireland, 14 November 1998.

McCourt, Frank. *Angela's Ashes: A Memoir.* New York: Scribner, 1996.

McDiarmid, Lucy. "Augusta Gregory, Bernard Shaw, and the Shewing-Up of Dublin Castle." *PMLA* 109, no. 1 (January 1994): 26–44.

McDonagh, Donagh. "The Death-Watch Beetle." In *The Abbey Theatre: Interviews and Recollections,* ed. E. H. Mikhail, 184–188. London: Macmillan, 1988.

McDonagh, Martin. *The Beauty Queen of Leenane.* London: Methuen, 1996.

———. *The Cripple of Inishmaan.* London: Methuen, 1997.

———. *The Lonesome West.* London: Methuen, 1997.

———. *A Skull in Connemara.* London: Methuen, 1997.

McDonald, Frank. Editorial. *The Irish Times,* 12 February 1997. Reprinted in the program to *The Dublin Trilogy.* 1998 Dublin Theatre Festival, Tivoli Theatre, 13–18 October 1998.

McGee, Patrick. *Telling the Other: The Question of Value in Modern and Postcolonial Writing.* Ithaca, N.Y.: Cornell University Press, 1992.

McGuinness, Frank. "Introduction." In *The Dazzling Dark: New Irish Plays,* ed. Frank McGuinness, ix–xii. London: Faber and Faber, 1996.

———. *Mutabilitie.* London: Faber and Faber, 1997.

———. *Plays I.* London: Faber and Faber, 1996. (Contains *The Factory Girls, Observe the Sons of Ulster Marching towards the Somme, Innocence, Cathaginians,* and *Bag Lady.*)

———. *Someone Who'll Watch over Me.* London: Faber and Faber, 1992.

McHenry, Margaret. "The Ulster Theatre in Ireland." Ph.D. dissertation, University of Pennsylvania, 1931.

McLoughlin, T. O. "Violence, Disintegration, and the New Vision in O'Casey's Plays." *Studies* 71 (1982): 344–359.

McNulty, Edward. *The Lord Mayor.* Dublin: Talbot Press, 1915(?).

McQuaid, Archbishop John Charles. "Public Affairs: An Tóstal 1953–1960." McQuaid Papers, Dublin Diocesan Archive.

Mengel, Hagal. *Sam Thompson and the Modern Drama in Ulster.* New York: Peter Lang, 1986.

Mercier, Paul. *Buddleia*. Dublin: Passion Machine, 1995 (Working draft).

"Microbes and Their Doings: The Curious Tricks They Play." *Dublin Evening Mail*, 3 October 1903.

Mikhail, E. H. *The Abbey Theatre: Interviews and Recollections*. London: Macmillan, 1988.

———, ed. *Lady Gregory: Interviews and Recollections*. London: Macmillan, 1977.

Minute Book of the Irish American Club, Philadelphia. McGarrity Papers, NLI 17,501.

Mise. "*The Shuiler's Child*." *Sinn Féin*, 8 May 1909, 1.

Mitchell, Jack. "Inner Structure and Artistic Unity." In *Sean O'Casey: Centenary Essays*, ed. David Krause and Robert G. Lowery, 99–111. Gerrards Cross: Colin Smythe, 1980.

Mitchell, Susan L. "Dramatic Rivalry." *Sinn Féin*, 8 May 1909, 1.

Moir, Alfred. *Caravaggio*. New York: Abrams, 1989.

Moody, T. W. "Irish History and Irish Mythology." In *Interpreting Irish History: The Debate on Historical Revisionism*, ed. Ciaran Brady, 71–86. Dublin: Irish Academy Press, 1994.

Moore, George. "Is the Theatre a Place of Amusement?" *Beltaine* 2 (1900): 7–9.

Moroney, Mic. "Coming Home." *The Irish Times*, 29 November 1997, section 3, 16.

"Mr. Synge's Secret." *Dublin Evening Mail*, 5 February 1907, 2.

Mulhern, Francis. "A Nation, Yet Again: The Field Day Anthology." *Radical Philosophy* 65 (Autumn 1993): 23–29.

Mulkerns, Helena. "McDonagh Play Gets Mixed Reaction." *The Irish Times*, 9 April 1998.
    http://www.irish-times.com/irish-times/paper/1998/0409/hom19.htm

Murphy, Thomas. *Bailegangaire*. In *After Tragedy: Three Irish Plays*, 41–77. London: Methuen, 1988.

———. *Conversations on a Homecoming*. In *After Tragedy: Three Irish Plays*, 79–115. London: Methuen, 1988.

———. *The Gigli Concert*. In *After Tragedy: Three Irish Plays*, 1–39. London: Methuen, 1988.

———. *The Morning after Optimism*. Dublin: Mercier, 1973.

———. *The Sanctuary Lamp*. Rev. ed. Dublin: Gallery, 1984.

Murphy, Una. "UDA Mobilises CuChulainn." *The Irish Times*, 19 January 1993, 4.

Murray, Christopher. "Brian Friel's *Making History* and the Problem of Historical Accuracy." In *The Crow behind the Plough: History and Violence in Anglo-Irish Poetry and Drama*, ed. Geert Lernout, 61–77. Amsterdam: Rodopi, 1991.

———. "The History Play Today." In *Cultural Contexts and Literary Idioms in Contemporary Irish Literature*, ed. Michael Kenneally, 269–280. Totowa, N.J.: Barnes and Noble, 1988.

———. "Introduction: The Stifled Voice." *Irish University Review, Jubilee Issue: Teresa Deevy and Irish Women Playwrights* 25, no. 1 (1995): 1–10.

———. " 'Such a Sense of Home': The Poetic Drama of Sebastian Barry." *Colby Quarterly* 37 (1991): 242–248.

———. "Thomas Murphy." In *Contemporary Dramatists*, ed. D. L. Kirkpatrick, 391–392. Chicago: St. James Press, 1988.

———. *Twentieth-Century Irish Drama: Mirror Up to Nation*. Manchester: Manchester University Press, 1997.

Mustafa, Shakir. "Damning Uphill and Down Dale: Demythologizing Ireland." *The Canadian Journal of Irish Studies* 23, no. 2 (December 1997): 1–22.

———. "Nationalism, Revisionism, and Modern Irish Literature." Ph.D. dissertation, Indiana University, 1999.

Myler, Thomas. "Drowning with Passion." *The Evening Herald*, 9 April 1991.

Ní Dhonnchadha, Máirín, and Theo Dorgan, eds. *Revising the Rising*. Derry: Field Day, 1991.

Ni Fhloinn, Bairbre. "Urban Legends." Program to *The Dublin Trilogy.* 1998 Dublin Theatre Festival, Tivoli Theatre, 13–18 October 1998.

Nic Shiubhlaigh, Máire. *The Splendid Years: Recollections of Máire Nic Shiubhlaigh, as Told to Edward Kenny, with Appendices and Lists of Irish Theatre Plays, 1899–1916.* Dublin: J. Duffy, 1955.

Nora, Pierre. "Between Memory and History: Les Lieux de Mémoire." *Representations* 26 (spring 1989): 7–25.

Norstedt, Johann A. *Thomas MacDonagh: A Critical Biography.* Charlottesville: University of Virginia Press, 1980.

Nowlan, David. "'Morning after Optimism' at the Abbey." *The Irish Times,* 16 March 1971, 10.

O'Brien, Conor Cruise. *Ancestral Voices: Religion and Nationalism in Ireland.* Dublin: Poolbeg, 1994.

O'Casey, Seán. *Autobiographies.* 2 vols. London: Macmillan, 1981.

———. "Censorship." *The Bell* 9, no. 5 (February 1945): 401–407.

———. *Complete Plays.* 5 vols. London: Macmillan, 1984.

———. *The Drums of Father Ned.* London: Macmillan, 1960.

———. *The Letters of Sean O'Casey.* 4 vols. Edited by David Krause. New York: Macmillan, 1975–1997.

———. *Three Plays.* New York: St Martin's Press, 1968.

O'Connor, Garry. *Sean O'Casey: A Life.* New York: Atheneum, 1988.

O'Conor, Pat. *Emerging Voices: Women in Contemporary Irish Society.* Dublin: Institute of Public Administration, 1998.

O'Doherty, Martina Ann. "Deevy: A Bibliography." *Irish University Review, Jubilee Issue: Teresa Deevy and Irish Women Playwrights* 25, no. 1 (1995): 163–170.

O'Dwyer, Riana. "Dancing in the Borderlands: The Plays of Frank McGuinness." In *The Crows behind the Plough: History and Violence in Anglo-Irish Poetry and Drama,* ed. Geert Lernout, 99–115. Amsterdam: Rodopi, 1991.

———. "Play-Acting and Myth-Making: The Western Plays of Thomas Murphy." *Irish University Review* 17, no. 1 (1987): 31–40.

O'Faoláin, Sean. *The Great O'Neill: A Biography of Hugh O'Neill, Earl of Tyrone, 1550–1616.* New York: Duell, Sloan and Pearce, 1942.

———. *An Irish Journey.* London: Longman, Green, 1941.

Ó hAodha, Micheál. *Theatre in Ireland.* Totowa, N.J.: Rowman and Littlefield, 1974.

O hUaithne, F. "Health, Nationality, and Vaccination." *Sinn Féin,* 12 January 1907, 3.

O'Kelly, Seumas. *The Shuiler's Child.* Chicago: De Paul University, 1971.

O'Loughlin, John F. Letter to "Friend John D." Pittsburgh, 22 January 1912. McGarrity Papers, National Library of Ireland, MS 17,501.

Ong, Walter. *Orality and Literacy: The Technologizing of the Word.* New York: Methuen, 1982.

———. *The Presence of the Word: Some Prolegomena for Cultural and Religious History.* New Haven, Conn.: Yale University Press, 1967.

O'Neill, Michael J. *The Abbey at the Queen's: The Interregnum Years 1951–1966.* Nepean, Canada: Borealis Press, 1999.

O'Riordan, John. *A Guide to O'Casey's Plays, from the Plough to the Stars.* New York: St. Martin's Press, 1984.

O'Sullivan, Michael. *Brendan Behan: A Life.* Dublin: Blackwater Press, 1997.

O'Toole, Fintan. "A Brilliant Début." *The Irish Times,* 24 December 1996. http://www.irish-times.com/cgi-in/highli . . . th=/irish-times/paper/1996/1224/fea1.htm

———. "Exploding the Story to Meld Many Worlds into One Tale." *The Irish Times,* 25 March 1997.

———. "Lives of Noisy Desperation." *The Sunday Tribune,* 1 December 1985.

———. "Murderous Laughter." *The Irish Times*, 24 June 1997. http://www.irish-times.com/irish-times/paper/1997/0624/fea2.htm

———. "Nowhere Man." *The Irish Times*, 26 April 1997. http://www.irish-times.com/irish-times/paper/1997/0426/fea1.htm

———. "Recent Theatre." *Ireland of the Welcomes*, September/October 1996, 20–23.

———. "Second Opinion." *The Irish Times*, 12 October 1996.

———. "Shadows over Ireland." *American Theatre*, July/August 1998, 16–19.

———. " 'Studs' Scores Again in the Replay." *The Irish Times*, April 1990.

———. "Today: Contemporary Irish Theatre — The Illusion of Tradition." *Ireland and the Arts*, Special Issue of *Literary Review*, ed. Tim Pat Coogan, 132–137. London: Namara Press, 1983.

———. "Tribune Portrait: Tom Murphy." *Sunday Tribune*, 1 May 1983, 5.

"Paints the Playboy in Glowing Colors." *The Gaelic American*, 21 October 1911, 1.

Parker, Lynne. Interview by author. Dublin, Ireland, 18 July 1997.

Parker, Stewart. *Catchpenny Twist*. New York: Samuel French, 1984.

———. *Dramatis Personae*. Belfast: John Malone Memorial Committee, 1986.

———. "The Iceberg." Typescript, 1974.

———. "Signposts." *Theatre Ireland* 11 (1985): 27–29.

———. *Spokesong*. New York: Samuel French, 1980.

———. *Three Plays for Ireland*. Birmingham: Oberon, 1989.

Paulin, Tom. "A New Look at the Language Question." In *Ireland's Field Day*, ed. Field Day. London: Routledge, 1985.

"Pennsylvania Air Bad for 'Playboy.' " *The Gaelic American*, 27 January 1912, 1, 3.

Peter, John. "Three of a Kind." *Sunday Times*, 3 August 1997. http://www.sunday-times.co.uk/cgi-bin/BackIssue?1617608

"Philadelphia Spanks 'The Playboy.' " *The Gaelic American*, 20 January 1912, 1, 7.

Pilkington, Lionel. "Violence and Identity in Northern Ireland: Graham Reid's *The Death of Humpty Dumpty*." *Modern Drama* 33, no. 1 (1990): 15–29.

Pine, Richard. *Brian Friel and Ireland's Drama*. London: Routledge, 1990.

P.M.E.K. "A Plea for the Playboy." *Sinn Féin*, 9 February 1907, 3.

Purcell, Lewis. "The Enthusiast." *Ulad* 3 (1905): 29–35.

Quinn, Antoinette. "Cathleen ni Houlihan Writes Back: Maud Gonne and the Irish Nationalist Theater." In *Gender and Sexuality in Modern Ireland*, ed. Anthony Bradley and Maryann Gialanella Valiulis, 39–59. Amherst: University of Massachusetts Press, 1997.

Radner, Joan, ed. *Feminist Messages: Coding in Women's Folk Culture*. Chicago: University of Illinois Press, 1993.

Read, Alan. *Theatre and Everyday Life: An Ethics of Performance*. New York: Routledge, 1993.

"Real Comedy Off the Stage." *The Gaelic American*, 27 January 1912, 4.

Reid, Christina. *The Belle of the Belfast City*. In *Christina Reid: Plays One*, 177–250. London: Methuen, 1997.

———. *Tea in a China Cup*. In *Christina Reid: Plays One*, 1–65. London: Methuen, 1997.

Reid, Forest. "Pan's Pupil." *Ulad* 3 (1905): 17–19.

Reid, J. Graham. *The Death of Humpty Dumpty*. Dublin: Co-op Books, 1980.

Reynolds, W. B. Editorial. *Ulad* 1 (1904): 1–2.

———. Editorial. *Ulad* 2 (1905): 1.

———. Editorial. *Ulad* 3 (1905): 2.

———. Editorial. *Ulad* 4 (1905): 2.

Richards, Shaun. " 'A Question of Location': Theatrical Space and Political Choice in *The Plough and the Stars*." *Theatre Research International* 15, no. 1 (1990): 28–41.

Richtarik, Marilynn. *Acting between the Lines: The Field Day Theatre Company, 1980–1984.* Oxford: Clarendon Press, 1995.

"Riot in Theater." *New York World,* 28 November 1911, 2.

Rivera, José. *Marisol. American Theatre* 10, no. 7/8 (1993): 30–45.

Robinson, Lennox. *Patriots: Selected Plays of Lennox Robinson.* Ed. Christopher Murray. Gerrards Cross: Colin Smythe, 1982.

Roche, Anthony. "Against Nostalgia: The Year in Irish Theatre, 1989." *Éire-Ireland* 24, no. 4 (Winter 1989): 114–120.

———. *"Bailegangaire:* Storytelling into Drama." *Irish University Review* 17, no. 1 (1987): 114–128.

———. *Contemporary Irish Drama: From Beckett to McGuinness.* Dublin: Gill and Macmillan, 1994.

———. "Ireland's Antigones: Tragedy North and South." In *Cultural Contexts and Literary Idioms in Contemporary Irish Literature,* ed. Michael Kenneally, 246–255. Totowa, N.J.: Barnes and Noble, 1988.

———. "Woman on the Threshold: J. M. Synge's *In the Shadow of the Glen,* Teresa Deevy's *Katie Roche* and Marina Carr's *The Mai."* *Irish University Review* 25, no. 1 (1995): 143–162.

Roll-Hansen, Diderik. "Dramatic Strategy in Christina Reid's *Tea in a China Cup."* *Modern Drama* 30 (1987): 389–395.

Rolston, Bill. "Culture as a Battlefield: Political Identity and the State in the North of Ireland." *Race and Class* 39 (1998): 23–35.

———. *Drawing Support 2.* Belfast: Beyond the Pale, 1996.

———. " 'When You Are Fighting a War You Gotta Take Setbacks': Murals and Propaganda in the North of Ireland." *Polygraph* 5 (1992): 120–125.

Ryan, Frederick. *The Laying of the Foundations.* In *Lost Plays of the Irish Renaissance,* eds. Robert Hogan and James Kilroy, 23–38. Newark, Del.: Proscenium Press, 1970.

Ryan, Joseph. "Nationalism and Irish Music." In *Irish Musical Studies 3: Music and Irish Cultural History,* ed. Gerard Fillen and Harry White. Dublin: Irish Academic Press, 1995.

Sacks, Leeny. *"The Survivor and the Translator."* In *Out from Under: Texts by Women Performance Artists,* ed. Lenora Champagne, 119–152. New York: Theatre Communications Group, 1990.

Sartre, Jean-Paul. *Saint Genet: Actor and Martyr.* Trans. Bernard Frechtman. London: Heinemann, 1963.

Saul, George Brandon. "Introduction." In *The Shuiler's Child.* Chicago: De Paul University, 1971.

Savran, David. "Ambivalence, Utopia, and a Queer Sort of Materialism: How *Angels in America* Reconstructs the Nation." In *Approaching the Millennium: Essays on Angels in America,* ed. Deborah R. Geis and Steven F. Kruger, 13–39. Ann Arbor: University of Michigan Press, 1997.

Schrank, Bernice. "Anatomizing an Insurrection: Sean O'Casey's *The Plough and the Stars."* *Modern Drama* 29, no. 2 (1986): 216–228.

———. "Dressing Up in *The Plough and the Stars." Canadian Journal of Irish Studies* 7, no. 2 (1981): 5–20.

———. *Sean O'Casey: A Research and Production Handbook.* Westport, Conn.: Greenwood Press, 1996.

———. " 'You Needn't Say No More': Language and the Problems of Communication in *The Shadow of a Gunman."* In *O'Casey: The Dublin Trilogy: A Casebook,* ed. Ronald Ayling, 67–80. Houndmills: Macmillan, 1985.

Seumar. "Irish Drama at the Antient Concert Rooms: *The Laying of the Foundations."* *The United Irishman,* 8 November 1902, 1.

Seyhan, Azade. "Allegories of History: The Politics of Representation in Walter Benjamin." In *Image and Ideology in Modern/Postmodern Discourse*, ed. David B. Downing and Susan Bazargan, 231–248. Albany, N.Y.: SUNY Press, 1991.

Shannon, Catherine B. "The Changing Face of Cathleen ni Houlihan: Women and Politics in Ireland, 1960–1966." In *Gender and Sexuality in Modern Ireland*, ed. Anthony Bradley and Maryann Gialanella Valiulis, 257–274. Amherst: University of Massachusetts Press, 1997.

Shannon, Elizabeth. *I Am of Ireland: Women of the North Speak Out*. Amherst: University of Massachusetts Press, 1997.

Shaw, Bernard. *Collected Letters 1898–1910*. Ed. Dan H. Laurence. New York: Dodd, 1972.

———. *The Great Composers: Reviews and Bombardments by Bernard Shaw*. Ed. Louis Crompton. Berkeley: University of California Press, 1978.

———. *The Shewing-Up of Blanco Posnet: Complete Plays with Prefaces*. Vol. 5, 169–276. New York: Dodd, 1962.

Simpson, Alan. *Beckett and Behan and a Theatre in Dublin*. London: Routledge, 1962.

Smith, B. L. *O'Casey's Satiric Vision*. Kent, Ohio: Kent State University Press, 1978.

Smith, Gus. "Tom Murphy Rocks 'Cradle of Genius.' " *Sunday Independent*, 12 October 1975, 16.

Smyth, Gerry. *Decolonisation and Criticism: The Construction of Irish Literature*. London: Pluto Press, 1998.

———. *The Novel and the Nation: Studies in the New Irish Fiction*. London: Pluto Press, 1997.

Soloway, R. A. *Demography and Degeneration: Eugenics and the Declining Birthrate in Twentieth-Century Britain*. Chapel Hill: University of North Carolina Press, 1990.

Spivak, Gayatri. "Can the Subaltern Speak?" In *Marxism and the Interpretation of Culture*, ed. Cary Nelson and Lawrence Grossberg, 271–316. Urbana: University of Illinois Press, 1988.

"Stamp out the Atrocious Libel." *The Gaelic American*, 14 October 1911, 4.

Stephens, James. "Hunger." In *The Field Day Anthology of Irish Writing*, vol. 2, ed. Seamus Deane, 1106–1112. Derry: Field Day, 1992.

"The Study of Cancer. Treatment and Remedy." *Dublin Evening Mail*, 2 January 1907.

Swift, Carolyn. *Stage by Stage*. Dublin: Poolbeg Press, 1985.

Swift, Jonathan. "A Modest Proposal." In *The Field Day Anthology of Irish Writing*, vol. 1, ed. Seamus Deane, 389–391. Derry: Field Day, 1992.

Synge, John M. *The Aran Islands*. Boston: John W. Luce & Co., 1928.

———. "Historical or Peasant Drama." In *The Playboy of the Western World and Other Plays*, 149. New York: Oxford University Press, 1995.

———. *In The Shadow of the Glen*. In *Samhain* 1904: 34–44.

———. *J. M. Synge: Plays*. Ed. Ann Saddlemyer. Oxford: Oxford University Press, 1969.

———. Letter to the editor. *Irish Times*, 31 January 1907, 5.

———. *The Plays and Poems of J. M. Synge*. London: Methuen, 1963.

Thompson, William Irwin. *The Imagination of an Insurrection, Dublin, Easter 1916: A Study of an Ideological Movement*. New York: Oxford University Press, 1967.

Thornton, Weldon. *J. M. Synge and the Western Mind*. Gerrards Cross: Colin Smythe, 1979.

Tifft, Stephen. "The Parricidal Phantasm: Irish Nationalism and the Playboy Riots." In *Nationalisms and Sexualities*, ed. Andrew Parker, et al., 313–332. New York: Routledge, 1992.

de Tocqueville, Alexis. "Some Observations on the Drama amongst Democratic

Nations." Trans. Henry Reeve. In *The Theory of the Modern Stage: An Introduction to Modern Theatre and Drama*, ed. Eric Bentley, 479–484. New York: Penguin, 1968.

Toibín, Colm. "Dublin's Epiphany." *The New Yorker*, 3 April 1995, 45–53.

———. "Mercier's Fierce Realism." *The Sunday Independent*, Arts and Books section, 9 November 1986, 1.

———. "Thomas Murphy's Volcanic Ireland." *Irish University Review* 17, no. 1 (1987): 24–30.

Tymoczko, Maria. "A Theatre of Complicity." *Irish Literary Supplement* 16, no. 2 (1997): 16.

Valiulis, Maryann Gialanella. "Power, Gender and Identity in the Irish Free State." *Journal of Women's History* 6/7, no. 4/1 (1995): 117–136.

Valiulis, Maryann Gialanella, and Mary O'Dowd, eds. *Women and Irish History: Essays in Honour of Margaret MacCurtain*. Dublin: Wolfhound Press, 1997.

Van Gennep, Arnold. *The Rites of Passage*. Chicago: University of Chicago Press, 1960.

Van Sloten, Johanneke. "Beckett's Irish Rhythm Embodied in His Polyphony." In *Beckett On and On*, ed. Lois Oppenheim and Marius Buning, 44–60. Madison, N.J.: Fairleigh Dickinson University Press, 1996.

"Veno's Seaweed Tonic." Advertisement. *Dublin Evening Mail*, 26 January 1905, 5.

"A Voice for the Lost Generation." *The Sunday Tribune*, November 1986, 19.

Wade, Alan, ed. *The Letters of W. B. Yeats*. New York: Macmillan Co., 1955.

Ward, Margaret. *Unmanageable Revolutionaries: Women and Irish Nationalism*. London: Pluto Press, 1983.

———. "The Women's Movement in the North of Ireland: Twenty Years On." In *Ireland's Histories: Aspects of State, Society and Ideology*, ed. Seán Hutton and Paul Stewart, 149–163. London: Routledge, 1991.

Watson, G. J. *Irish Identity and the Literary Revival: Synge, Yeats, Joyce and O'Casey*. 2nd ed. Washington, D.C.: Catholic University of America Press, 1994.

Watt, Stephen. *Joyce, O'Casey, and the Irish Popular Theater*. Syracuse, N.Y.: Syracuse University Press, 1991.

Weintraub, Stanley. "Shaw's Other Keegan: O'Casey and G. B. S." In *Sean O'Casey: Centenary Essays*, ed. David Krause and Robert G. Lowery, 212–226. Gerrards Cross: Colin Smythe, 1980.

Welch, Robert. "'Isn't This Your Job? — To Translate': Brian Friel's Languages." In *The Achievement of Brian Friel*, ed. Alan J. Peacock, 134–148. Gerrards Cross: Colin Smythe, 1993.

Welch, Robert, ed. *The Oxford Companion to Irish Literature*. Oxford: Clarendon Press, 1996.

Whelan, Kevin. *The Tree of Liberty: Radicalism, Catholicism and the Construction of Irish Identity 1760–1830*. Notre Dame, Ind.: University of Notre Dame Press, 1996.

White, Harry. *The Keeper's Recital: Music and Cultural History in Ireland, 1770–1970*. Notre Dame, Ind.: University of Notre Dame Press, 1998.

———. "*The Sanctuary Lamp*: An Assessment." *Irish University Review* 17, no. 1 (1987): 71–81.

White, Hayden. *The Content of the Form: Narrative Discourse and Historical Representation*. Baltimore: Johns Hopkins University Press, 1987.

Whyte, J. H. *Church and State in Modern Ireland 1923–1979*. 2nd ed. Dublin: Gill and Macmillan, 1980.

Williams, Caroline. "This Is One for the Sisters." *Theatre Ireland*, Winter 1993.

Williams, Raymond. "The Endless Fantasy of Irish Talk." In *Sean O'Casey*, ed., with an introduction, by Harold Bloom, 13–20. New York: Chelsea, 1987.

Wilmer, Steve. "Women's Theater in Ireland." *New Theatre Quarterly* 7 (1991): 353–360.

Worthen, W. B. "Homeless Words: Field Day and the Politics of Translation." *Modern Drama* 38 (1995): 22–41.

Yeats, Lily. Two Letters to John Butler Yeats, 21 and 26 August 1909. NLI 031.112 (2).

Yeats, Michael B. *Cast a Cold Eye.* Dublin: Folens Press, 1999.

Yeats, W. B. *The Collected Letters of W. B. Yeats: Volume III, 1901–1904.* Ed. John Kelly. Oxford: Oxford University Press, 1994.

———. *The Death of Synge. Autobiographies.* London: Macmillan, 1991.

———. *Essays and Introductions.* New York: Collier Books, 1961.

———. *Explorations.* Selected by Mrs. W. B. Yeats. New York: Collier Books, 1962.

———. "The Irish Dramatic Movement." In *Dramatis Personae*, W. B. Yeats, 186–200. New York: Macmillan, 1936.

———. *Memoirs.* Ed. Denis Donoghue. New York: Macmillan, 1972.

———. "Mr. Yeats' New Play." *The United Irishman*, 5 April 1902, 5.

———. "A People's Theatre: A Letter to Lady Gregory." In *The Theory of the Modern Stage: An Introduction to Modern Theatre and Drama*, ed. Eric Bentley, 327–338. New York: Penguin, 1968.

"Zam-Buk Skin Rub." Advertisement. *Dublin Evening Mail*, 4 January 1907, 5.

CONTRIBUTORS

NELSON O'CEALLAIGH RITSCHEL holds a Ph.D. from Brown University and presently teaches at Stonehill College. His "James Connolly's *Under Which Flag, 1916*" appeared in the *New Hibernia Review* (Winter 1998), and his essay "Arthur Griffith's Debate on Synge" was featured in *Lit: Literature, Interpretation, Theory*'s special issue "Ireland: The Presence of the Past, Part II" (Summer 1999). His critical history of the Irish Theatre movement is with a university press.

SCOTT T. CUMMINGS teaches and directs plays in the Theater Department of Boston College. His theater criticism and scholarship have appeared in a variety of publications, from *Modern Drama* and *Theatre Journal* to *American Theatre* and the *Boston Phoenix*.

CHRISTIE L. FOX is currently a Ph.D. candidate in Folklore at Indiana University. Her research interests include theatre, parades, Irish studies, folk drama, performance theory, and ethnography. Her dissertation will focus on parades as a genre of performance. Previous publications include work on gender and ethnography.

JOHN P. HARRINGTON is Dean of Humanities and Social Sciences at The Cooper Union in New York City. He is the author of *The Irish Beckett* and *The Irish Play on the New York Stage*. Harrington is editor of W. W. Norton's anthology *Modern Irish Drama* and co-editor, with Elizabeth J. Mitchell, of the collection of essays *Politics and Performance in Contemporary Northern Ireland*.

SUSAN CANNON HARRIS is Assistant Professor in the Keough Institute for Irish Studies at the University of Notre Dame. She has published articles on Yeats and Joyce in *Modern Drama, Éire-Ireland,* and *The James Joyce Quarterly*. Her essay for this volume is adapted from a book she has recently completed on gender and sacrifice in modern Irish drama.

KATHLEEN HOHENLEITNER teaches literature and composition at the University of Central Florida. She wrote her dissertation, " 'The Disquiet between Two Aesthetics': Brian Friel and the Field Day Theatre Company," at the University of Notre Dame.

JAMES HURT is Professor of English and co-director of the Irish Studies Program at the University of Illinois, Urbana-Champaign. His books include *Catiline's Dream: An Essay on Ibsen's Plays; Film and Theatre;* and *Writing Illinois.* A number of his plays have been produced, including *Angel Band* and *Abraham Lincoln Walks at Midnight.*

JOSÉ LANTERS is Associate Professor of English at the University of Wisconsin-Milwaukee, and formerly Associate Professor of Classics and Letters at the University of Oklahoma. She has published numerous articles on Irish fiction and drama. Her new book on Irish Menippean satire, entitled *Unauthorized Versions,* is forthcoming.

LAURA E. LYONS is Associate Professor of English at the University of Hawai'i. Her work on the intersection of feminism and nationalism appears in journals such as *boundary 2* and *Genders.* She has co-authored work on Indian and Irish nationalism. She is currently working on a manuscript addressing the role of protest and ephemera in contemporary Irish Republicanism.

LUCY MCDIARMID is Past President of the American Conference for Irish Studies, Professor of English at Villanova University, and a former Guggenheim Fellow. She is the author and editor of several books; her book *The Posthumous Life of Roger Casement and Other Modern Irish Controversies* is forthcoming in 2001.

CARLA J. MCDONOUGH is Associate Professor of English at Eastern Illinois University, where she teaches courses in drama and writing. She is the author of *Staging Masculinity: Male Identity in Contemporary American Drama* (1997), and has published articles about Sam Shepard, David Mamet, Christina Reid, David Henry Hwang, and Adrienne Kennedy. Currently she is working on a book-length study of Kennedy's theater.

EILEEN MORGAN is Assistant Professor of English at the State University of New York at Oneonta. She completed a dissertation at Indiana University on twentieth-century Irish fiction and film in 1998, and her essay on Neil Jordan's film *Michael Collins* appeared recently in *New Hibernia Review.* She is currently working on Sean O'Faoláin's biographies of De Valera and on Edna O'Brien's 1990s trilogy, and is preparing a book-length study on the influence of radio in Ireland.

CHRISTOPHER MURRAY teaches dramatic literature at University College, Dublin. He has published widely on Irish drama and theatre, most recently *Twentieth-Century Irish Drama: Mirror Up to Nation* (1997). He is, at present, working on a book on Sean O'Casey.

SHAKIR MUSTAFA teaches in the department of Modern Languages and Literatures at Boston University. He recently completed a dissertation on Irish revisionism and modernist Irish literature. His work has appeared in such journals as *New Hibernia Review* and *The Canadian Journal of Irish Studies*, and he is currently working on a translation of Arabic short stories into English.

LAUREN ONKEY is Associate Professor of English at Ball State University in Muncie, Indiana, where she teaches twentieth-century Irish, British, and postcolonial literature. Her recent publications include "'A Melee and Curtain': Black-Irish Relations in Ned Harrigan's *The Mulligan Guard Ball*," in *Jouvert: an online journal of postcolonial studies* (Fall 1999), and "Not Quite White? Black 47's Funky Ceili," in *New Hibernia Review* (Spring 1999).

MARILYNN RICHTARIK is Assistant Professor of English at Georgia State University in Atlanta. She is the author of *Acting between the Lines: The Field Day Theatre Company and Irish Cultural Politics, 1980–1984* (1995) and is currently working on a critical biography of Belfast playwright Stewart Parker.

JUDITH ROOF is Professor of English at Michigan State University. She is author of *Reproductions of Reproduction: Imaging Symbolic Change; Come As You Are: Sexuality and Narrative;* and *A Lure of Knowledge: Lesbian Sexuality and Theory,* and co-editor of *Staging the Rage: The Web of Misogyny in Modern Drama.*

MARY TROTTER is Assistant Professor of English at Indiana University–Purdue University at Indianapolis. She has published several articles and chapters on political theatre in Ireland, and her book on the diversity of nationalist theatre and performance practices during the Irish literary renaissance is forthcoming.

STEPHEN WATT is Professor of English and Cultural Studies at Indiana University-Bloomington, and the author of *Postmodern/Drama: Reading the Contemporary Stage* (1998) and *Joyce, O'Casey, and the Irish Popular Theater* (1991). In addition to publishing essays on Irish and Irish-American Culture, he has written extensively on higher education, most recently *Academic Keywords: A Devil's Dictionary for Higher Education* (1999), co-authored with Cary Nelson. At present, he and Nelson are completing a sequel to *Acadmic Keywords,* and he is working on a book on bohemian subcultures in the 1950s.

INDEX